2008 Vol. 64, No. 4

Young People's Perspectives on the Rights of the Child: Implications for Theory, Research and Practice
Issue Editors: Martin D. Ruck and Stacey S. Horn

Journal of Social Issues, Vol. 64, No. 4, 2008, pp. 685–699

Charting the Landscape of Children's Rights

Martin D. Ruck[*]

City University of New York

Stacey S. Horn

University of Illinois

This issue of the Journal of Social Issues *presents current theory, research, and methodological considerations pertaining to "Young People's Perspectives on the Rights of the Child." The following brief introduction charts the landscape of children's rights by outlining the purpose and goals of the issue, provides a short historical overview on the topic, sets the context for the individual articles, and highlights the recurring themes making up this issue of JSI. The authors of the articles in this issue extend current knowledge and thinking on the topic of children rights and also set the foundation for future empirical work, practice, and policy pertaining to children's rights and rights-focused research.*

Over the past several decades, there has been a substantial increase in social and political commitment to the rights of children as well as an increased tendency to grant to children some of the rights typically accorded only to adults. Accompanying this increased commitment has been a noticeable change in orientation from issues dealing with children's protection or nurturance rights to those dealing with children's self-determination or self-expression rights. This shift in orientation regarding children's rights is notable in that children are now more frequently seen as having a right to participate in decisions about their own lives as opposed to the view that children's rights only involve the need to be taken care of or protected. The commitment to young people's rights to both nurturance and self-determination is evident within the legal, medical, and mental health professions, as well as institutions that serve children and adolescents such as social service agencies, hospitals, health clinics, and schools.

---

[*]Correspondence concerning this article should be addressed to Martin D. Ruck, Graduate Center, City University of New York, 365 Fifth Avenue, New York, NY 10016 [e-mail: mruck@gc.cuny.edu].

Increased international awareness of children's rights is reflected in the United Nations Convention on the Rights of the Child (CRC, U.N. General Assembly, 1989). This document, which outlines children's political, civil, social, and economic rights, has been ratified by every member country of the United Nations with the exception of Somalia and the United States. Somalia is unable to move toward ratification of the Convention, as it currently has no recognized government. The United States has signed the Convention, but ratification remains a highly contentious issue.[1]

As the most rapidly and universally ratified treaty in history, the CRC has already had a remarkable impact on how children and youth are viewed and treated around the world (Hart, 1997). In keeping with the increased commitment to children's rights concerning both nurturance and self-determination the CRC attempts to achieve a balance between children's protection and participation rights. This balance is reflected in two fundamental tenets that underpin the CRC, "the best interest of the child" and "the evolving capacities of the child." The Convention also includes articles outlining young people's right to the adequate provision of services and resources to enable children to develop their abilities to the fullest. Therefore it is not surprising that children's rights within the CRC are often described in terms of the 3 P's: protection, provision, and participation rights (Troope, 1996).

In this issue of the *Journal of Social Issues*, we define "children" as individuals under the age of 18 years who have not yet reached the age of maturity as determined by either state, provincial, federal legislation, or national law. In addition, we focus on the importance of considering the nurturance and self-determination distinction, which predates the CRC and the protection, provision, and participation framework. We are well aware, however, of the importance of children's rights pertaining to provision (see Ruck, Abramovitch, & Keating, 1998); hence, our conceptualization of children's nurturance rights includes considerations of both protection and provision issues (see Cherney & Shing, 2008; Peterson-Badali & Ruck, 2008). Finally, given our interest in young people's perspectives on children's rights, in this issue we focus on the perspectives of middle school age children and adolescents rather than younger children. Our rationale here is threefold. First, older children are better able to provide their thoughts and perspectives as they pertain to social issues, such as children's rights. Second, and not unrelated to the first, this age period represents a time when developmental changes result in more abstract, relativistic, and future-oriented thinking (Keating, 1990), which has direct implications for young people's thinking and attitudes about rights. Third, this is an age period where young people see both types of rights as increasingly important in their daily lives (Helwig, 1995; Ruck et al., 1998;

---

[1]For discussion of the United States reluctance to ratify the Convention see Kilbourne (1996); Limber and Wilcox (1996); Walker et al. (1999).

Ruck, Peterson-Badali, & Day, 2002). For example, during this period, issues pertaining to care and protection remain salient while at the same time the desire for self-determination and autonomy is at its peek (Steinberg, 2001; Steinberg & Silverberg, 1986). Thus in this issue, while the majority of contributions focus on middle school age children and/or adolescents, we are nevertheless keenly aware that issues surrounding children's perspectives on rights may also be of pertinence to even younger children who may be more likely to have their basic rights violated due to their limited capacity and dependent status.

A major concern in extending additional rights to children and youth is whether they understand their rights in a reasonable and meaningful way. This is a central question given that how individuals think about rights may impact the effectiveness with which those rights serve their intended functions of either protection or self-determination. In addition, how young people think about and understand their protection and participation rights has important implications for advocacy, young people's legal and political socialization, education, as well as social and public policy.

Purpose and Goals of This Issue

In 1978 a little over a decade before the U.N. adopted the CRC (U.N. General Assembly, 1989) the *JSI* published an issue edited by Norma Deitch Feshback and Seymour Feshback (1978) titled "The Changing Status of Children: Rights, Roles and Responsibilities." One of the aims of the issue was to highlight the complexity, breadth, and range of topics pertaining to children's rights as a social issue. The majority of the articles in the volume offered either historical or theoretical perspectives on children's rights. Only two papers provided empirical elaboration on the topic, one in terms of an examination of public opinion toward children's rights (Rogers & Wrightsman, 1978) and the other looking at the roles and responsibilities of parents and children in alternative family structures (Eiduson & Alexander, 1978). In addition, most of the papers took what might be considered an adult-centered approach in terms of how they conceptualized children's rights. Only two papers addressed the balance or tension between children's nurturance and self-determination rights (see Baumrind, 1978; Rogers & Wrightsman, 1978) and only the Rogers and Wrightsman (1978) article actually assessed the views of young people about their nurturance and self-determination rights by including them as participants in their survey. Nevertheless, the articles in that issue played a central role in bringing the topic of children's rights to the foreground as important not only for child advocates and policymakers but also for social and behavioral scientists.

It has been three decades since that thematic issue on children's rights and almost 20 years since the adoption of the CRC. Not surprisingly during this time social scientists have become more vocal about the need for research and advocacy on children's rights. This is evidenced by the number of special journal issues focusing on children's rights, (e.g., Hart, 1982; Hart & Pavlovic, 1991; Murphy-Berman & Weisz, 1996; Wilcox & Naimark, 1991) as well as reports on the issue from major psychological organizations such as the Society for Research on Child Development (Limber & Flekkoy, 1995) and the International Society for the Study of Behavioural Development (Verma, Chen, & Miller, 2001). The importance of children's rights for social scientists is also evident in the Society for the Psychological Study of Social Issues endorsement of the CRC. Further, the American Psychological Association has adopted the principles of the Convention to guide psychological research, education, practice, and advocacy (Melton, 2001). Despite the increasing interest and considerable pubic and political concern with children's rights, however, social scientist have only recently begun to investigate the growth and development of young people's thinking about their rights and the importance of these rights in their own lives, as well as the implications that young peoples' understanding of their rights has for their well-being and participation (Helwig & Turiel, 2002).

As mentioned above there has been limited empirical attention to children's and adolescents' perspectives on their rights and a lack of available research on the implications of young people exercising their participation rights in social contexts (Ruck & Verbeek, 2002). Given that the CRC focuses attention on the child's experience and perspective one of the aims of this issue of *JSI* is to provide relevant theory and empirical research addressing the ways in which children and youth conceptualize their need for and entitlement to protection and participation in contexts such as the family, school, community, and greater society. Additionally, in this issue, we address the implications that this research has for policy and practice centered around the rights of children and youth in these varying social contexts.

A Brief History of Children's Rights

The notion of children as individuals possessing specific rights is considered to be of relatively recent origin (for historical reviews see Hart & Pavloic, 1991; Takanishi, 1978). Historically, children have been viewed as "nothing more than smaller, weaker, less intelligent versions of adults... [and] were not viewed as being qualitatively different from [adults] or having any special needs, or as making any significant contribution to their own development" (Paplia & Olds, 1989, p. 11). It is believed that prior to the 16th century there was no conception of childhood as a unique or distinct period of life, except that parents, more commonly fathers, were given unlimited power and control over children.

Even up to the first quarter of the 19th century children were, for the most part still viewed as the personal property or extensions of their parents with little or no legal rights whatsoever (Stier, 1978). Such a view was consistent with both the social organization and economic structure of the period. However, as a direct result of the technological and socioeconomic changes of the early 20th century, and a change in the conceptualization of childhood as a unique and important period of life, various social movements developed in attempts to offer some form of protection to children. As issues relating to children became the focal point of social reform, society was required to "articulate its obligations to children." These obligations, which eventually were conceived as children's protection rights, initially included the "preservation of life and health, freedom from premature toil, education of children, and care of dependent children" (Takanishi, 1978, p. 13).

Regardless of the aims of the various fledgling children's rights movements, it would not be until the 1960s that the constitutional standing of children would be affirmed in the United States. In a landmark decision for children (In re Gault, 1967) the U.S. Supreme Court noted that, "neither the Fourteenth Amendment nor the Bill of Rights is for adults alone" (p. 13). Two years later the court noted that "children are 'persons' under the Constitution (Tinker v. des Moines Independent Community School District, 1969). And almost a decade later, the Supreme Court stated, "Constitutional rights do not mature and come into being magically only when one attains the state defined age of majority" (Planned Parenthood v. Danforth, 1976, p. 5204). Thus the last half of the 20th century has seen the emergence of children, not as property of their parents but as persons entitled to many of the same self-determination rights as their adult counterparts.

Nevertheless, the various rights and limited freedoms given to children did not exactly correspond to the myriad of rights given to their adult counterparts (Hart, 1991). This opinion is also echoed by legal scholars Wilson and Tomlinson (1986) who wrote:

> The laws in North American society are unabashedly discriminatory in that they limit or withhold from persons under a particular age... those fundamental rights and freedoms, which are integral to every person over that age living in a "free and democratic society."
> (p. 2)

Historically, children's rights have been typically predicated on the assumption that the interests of the child are best determined by the parent, or whoever has the legal custody of the child.

In contrast, the current children's rights movement focuses on the balance between two widely distinct orientations concerning the extension of children's rights (Rogers & Wrightsman, 1978). The nurturance orientation entails the provision and protection by society of rights that are beneficial to children (e.g., right to education). In contrast, the self-determination orientation focuses on children's right to have some measure of control over their own lives (e.g., the right to choose one's own religion). While the nurturance orientation is based on the paternalistic assumption that society or the state ascertains what is in the best interest of the child; the self-determination orientation is based on the child's decision of what is or is not in the child's own best interest or within their own personal prerogative (Rogers & Wrightsman, 1978; Walker, Brooks, & Wrightsman, 1999).

It is in the U.N. CRC (1989) where we most clearly see the emphasis on balancing children's need for nurturance and their right to self-determination. A critical and important aspect of the CRC is its emphasis on children's and adolescents' right to actively participate in society. In addition, the Convention is an important document in three significant ways (Melton, 1991, 1996). First, it recognizes that children are indeed persons entitled to legally enforceable protections as well as respect. Second, it includes structures for the implementation and monitoring of children's rights. Third, through the Convention's overriding theme of respect for the dignity of the child, the wide range of contexts pertaining to children's rights are brought together under one unifying theme. By promoting respect for the dignity of children as persons with their own rights and freedoms the Convention challenges traditional notions of the dependent status of children.

Finally, it has been suggested that coming up with a developmentally appropriate balance between children's self-determination and nurturance rights can only be made on the basis of empirical evidence regarding young people's ability to understand and exercise such rights in a reasonable and meaningful manner (Hart & Pavlovic, 1991). To that end, we next turn to the various developmental models and theory that have served to inform current research and knowledge on the developmental trajectory of children's and adolescents' perspectives on the rights of the child.

Developmental Research on Young People's Perspectives on Children's Rights

Initial work on young people's conceptions of rights originated in the 1970s and 1980s through research on moral reasoning (Kohlberg, 1969; Piaget, 1960) and political socialization (Tapp & Kohlberg, 1971; Tapp & Levine, 1974). According to these approaches, the development of children's thinking was best described in terms of a stage model where one global orientation characterized the child's thinking across all contexts or situations. Researchers utilizing this framework to investigate how children think about rights (self-determination rights or civil liberties) have suggested that the developmental trajectory of children's thinking in this area follows a similar global progression from egocentric thinking characteristic of young children to abstract modes of thought not seen before early adolescence (Gallatin & Adelson, 1970; Melton, 1980, 1983; Melton & Limber, 1992).

However, in contrast to global stage models of development, recent and emerging work in the area of children's social-cognitive development has been informed by employing a contextual or domain-specific model or approach (Turiel, 1983, 1998). According to this perspective children use different forms of reasoning to assess a wide range of social issues or domains of development. Therefore, in the area of rights, a domain model would indicate that children and adolescents use different forms of reasoning depending on the type of right (nurturance or self-determination) and the context in which the right is embedded (Helwig, 1995, 1997; Ruck et al., 2002). For example, research employing a domain-specific approach indicates that children's and adolescents' thinking about nurturance rights is related to their understanding of familial roles and relationships, whereas their understanding about self-determination rights corresponds to how they think about moral rules and to their growing sociolegal knowledge (Ruck & Peterson-Badali, 2006).

Given the increased international interest in children's rights, developmentalists have also recently begun to consider the influence of cultural values on young people's conceptions of rights and the tensions that arise between individuals' rights and prerogatives and cultural traditions, norms, and practices. Contrary to arguments suggesting that the notion of children's right to self-determination (e.g., autonomy, personal freedom) is a particularly individualistic concept and therefore more likely to be important to children from Western (individualistic) cultures, this recent work suggests that children from diverse cultures endorse both types of rights (nurturance vs. self-determination) rather than giving primacy to one type over the other. That is, concepts of autonomy and personal freedom are also central for youth in traditional or collectivistic societies (Helwig, 2006; Neff & Helwig, 2002). Furthermore, much of this recent work suggests that across different cultures individuals consider various features of the "rights situation" when required to make decisions and evaluative judgments about rights, rather than simply working from broad ideological templates. In some cases individuals even reject existing cultural practices, particularly when those practices differentially impact certain segments or groups within the population (e.g., women; Neff & Helwig, 2002).

The articles in this issue draw on sociohistorical and sociopolitical analyses of children's rights, as well as global and domain-specific developmental frameworks pertaining to the issue of children's rights. The work presented here contributes to the growing knowledge based on the development of children's understanding of rights in three important and interrelated ways: first, by exploring children's and adolescents' knowledge and understanding of their rights in different social and cultural contexts; second, by examining significant tensions and challenges in affording rights to youth (e.g., when they conflict with prevailing norms); and finally, by considering the implications of children's and adolescent's evolving capacities and understanding regarding their rights for both policy and practice.

Some Current Tensions in Affording Children Rights

It often seems to be the case that one cannot consider the issue of children's rights in the absence of concerns regarding "taking the idea of children's rights too far" (see Melton, 1996 and Murphy-Berman & Weisz, 1996 for a discussion of this issue). The notion of "taking children's rights too far" is usually with reference to extending young people's self-expression or participation rights at the expense of their nurturance (protection and provision) rights. To that end, we suggest that few social scientists or researchers would advocate for a full "kiddie-libbers" perspective on children's rights or argue for children having the full range of rights held by their adult counterparts. Indeed, even children and adolescents when questioned about the rights young people should have do not advocate for the full range of adult rights, but rather their claims are more likely to focus on age-appropriate nurturance and self-determination rights (e.g., see Ruck et al., 1998). As has been suggested above and elsewhere (see Ruck et al., 1998; Ruck et al., 2002; Ruck & Peterson-Badali, 2006), the tension between what rights children have and what rights children should have can best be made on the basis of a developmentally appropriate balance between children's nurturance and self-determination rights and that fundamentally pays attention to both the "developing capacities" and "inherent dignity" of the child. The articles in this issue begin to address this tension in that the majority of contributions utilize developmental frameworks for investigating children's rights. The articles also inform this tension in that they provide perspectives from young people themselves regarding the balance between nurturance and self-determination.

Another issue and challenge in affording rights to children and youth—one not unrelated to the notion of taking children's rights too far—centers on the tension between the rights of children and the right of parents. Critics and opponents of children's rights and the CRC often raise the argument that promoting the rights of children infringes on the rights of parents (e.g., giving children the right to disregard parental authority or sue their parents—see Melton, 1996, for a discussion of this debate). Such arguments, however, are flawed, as the CRC is by design compatible with both parental rights and family rights. Specifically, the CRC recognizes the primacy of parents and families in the care and protection of children. To that end, almost a quarter of the articles making up the CRC either explicitly (see e.g., Articles 5, 7, 9, 10, 16, 18, and 27) or implicitly (see e.g., Articles 16, 18, 22, 24, and 26) serve to promote and protect the child's right to a family environment. As Melton (1996) has pointed out, by recognizing the importance of the family environment to children's well-being parental rights and authority are therefore promoted and protected by the state in the CRC rather than being undermined. While this may be a flawed criticism of the CRC itself, this tension is, no doubt real for individuals working within the children's rights arena. In this volume, we have included articles (e.g., Horn, Szalacha, & Drill, 2008) that begin to explore this tension by examining the ways in which affordance of rights to young people comes into conflict with social and cultural norms.

Finally, the relationship between children's rights and children's responsibil- ities also needs to be addressed. Critics of the CRC have argued that the current emphasis on *rights* privileges children's rights over children's responsibilities. For instance, according to Phillips (1993, cited in Limber & Wilcox, 1996) U.S. ratification of the CRC would lead to "a state-guaranteed license for children to rebel." In reality, the CRC clearly recognizes the importance of the responsibilities of children and respect for the rights others. For example, Article 15 recognizes children's right to meet together and join groups or associations, unless exercising those rights violates the rights of others. Similarly, Article 29, which deals with the aims of education, promotes children's respect for their parents, their own cultural identity, and for other cultures and the natural environment. In addition, available empirical evidence, although limited, suggests that during early adolescence young people come to see rights as serving to teach them responsibilities, values, and respect for the rights of individuals (Ruck, Keating, Abramovitch, & Koegl, 1998). As others have recently noted, rights and responsibilities are clearly reciprocal constructs and that the former loses its meaning without consideration of the latter (Baurmind & Thompson, 2002; Ruck et al., 2002).

The articles in this issue of *JSI* address these current challenges and tensions and also provide theoretically and empirically based knowledge that will help social scientists, children's right's advocates, and policymakers negotiate these tensions.

Organization of the Issue

We have organized the issue into three sections in order to provide a coherent framework for the individual articles. The first section presents articles focusing on theoretical, conceptual, and methodological issues pertaining to young people's perspectives on the rights of the child. Second, empirical papers addressing children's perceptions of protection and participation rights in differing social contexts are presented. The third section presents articles focusing on cultural and cross-cultural perspectives on young people's views concerning their rights. Finally, we end with an integrative commentary, which highlights the overarching themes of the issue and provides insights and directions for future research and policy.

Theoretical, Conceptual, and Methodological Considerations

The articles in this section present new theoretical and conceptual perspectives on the topic of children's rights. In the opening contribution, Daiute (2008) sets the foundation for understanding the various assumptions about child development and social–political systems inherent in the U.N. CRC (U.N. General Assembly, 1989). Employing discourse theory, sociohistorical theory and geo-political theory she analyzes how the CRC defines the child, the child's agents, developmental considerations, and exceptions to the CRC. The article also carefully addresses the tensions inherent in advocating for the rights of the child such as tension between children's rights and nation's rights. Daiute also argues for the importance of examining the impact of everyday settings on children's lives in order to fully appreciate their understanding of themselves and others in relation to children's rights.

Included among the numerous participation or self-determination articles in the CRC are articles outlining the young person's right or freedom to information (e.g., Articles13 and 17). In the second article in this section, Levesque (2008) considers whether children actually have a right to controversial ideas and infor-mation. He illustrates how U.S. policy and law function to restrict young people's right to seek, receive, and impart information. An important consideration in his contribution is the focus on adolescent jurisprudence as an approach to law that considers the realities of adolescence and ways to develop laws appropriate with those realities. His analysis also raises critical questions about the importance of adolescents' right to information from both a human rights and a developmental perspective.

In the final article of this section, Peterson-Badali and Ruck (2008) review the methodological issues associated with examining young people's understand-ing, knowledge, and attitudes associated with children's self-determination and nurturance rights. The authors critique the strengths and weaknesses of vary-ing methods, such as pencil-and-paper attitude scales, semistructured interviews, and open-ended questions, and discuss the ways in which the approaches differ in terms of how researchers have defined children's rights and the distinction between children's participation and protection. In their article, they raise the important question of whether or not these approaches accurately capture young people's views and perspectives about their rights. Based on their comprehensive review they are able to provide a strong argument for a new approach to the study of children's understanding of rights and propose borrowing methods from the moral reasoning field that allow for the assessment of children's and adolescents' "real-life" knowledge and judgments about the rights of young people. The authors describe how they have used this approach in their own program of research with various populations of young people including maltreated children and youth.

Young People's Views of Protection and Participation in Everyday Contexts

The articles in the second section provide empirical accounts of young peo-ple's views of their rights in various social contexts. In the first article, Sher-rod (2008) examined young people's views of the rights and responsibilities of citizenship. He argues that how young people think about citizenship not only has implications for their political behavior but also the degree to which they may be willing and able to exercise their protection and participation rights outlined in the U.N. CRC. Sherrod's analysis reveals that adolescents' views of rights relate to the components of nurturance and self-determination as outlined in the CRC while views of responsibility consist of both civic-oriented and polity-oriented forms of responsibilities. The findings of Sherrod's study have important implications in terms of the promotion of citizenship and rights for young people and how they come to understand their rights outlined in the CRC.

The U.N. CRC makes a strong case for students' rights to a safe and emotionally healthy school environment (Nairn & Smith, 2003). This is an important issue for lesbian, gay, bisexual, or transgender (LGBT) youth who are frequently the victims of violence or discrimination perpetrated not only by their peers, but in some cases teachers, administrators, and counselors. In the second article in this section, Horn et al. (2008) examined heterosexual adolescents' beliefs and attitudes about homosexuality, as well as adolescents' knowledge and attitudes about LGBT students' rights to safety at school. The article addresses critical tensions regarding the obligations of schools to protect LGBT students from harm when those practices may be viewed as endorsing homosexuality as acceptable and, therefore, impinging on the rights of others within the school community (parents, students, and teachers) to their belief systems. This work has important implications for schools and communities working to provide a safe and supportive environment for all students, regardless of their sexual orientation or gender identity.

Finally, in the last article in this section, Flanagan, Stout, and Gallay (2008) presented findings from a 3-year longitudinal investigation of early, middle, and late adolescents' understanding of an individual's right to engage in risky behaviors and public health beliefs. Their contribution raises important questions about the development of adolescents' beliefs about individual rights and social responsibility concerning the public right to intervene in potentially health compromising situations. The findings are considered in terms of developmental differences in young people's views as well as with regard to endorsements of social responsibility and implications for public health.

Cultural and Cross-Cultural Perspectives on Children's Rights

The articles included in this section all highlight the impact of possible cultural differences on young people's knowledge and understanding of children's rights and rights-related issues. In the first article, Cherney and Shing (2008) examined cross-cultural differences in children's perceptions of nurturance and self-determination rights. Previous work on this topic suggests that cultural differences between individualistic and collectivistic orientations have direct implications for children's thinking about their rights. Cultures that value individualism should place a higher value on self-determination rights, while cultures encouraging collectivism would place greater emphasis on nurturance rights (Cherney & Perry, 1996). Importantly, in their article, Cherney and Shing not only attempt to replicate earlier cross-cultural findings pertaining to children's attitudes toward their rights, but they also directly examine children's perceptions of those rights that are found in the U.N. CRC. Their research provides evidence both for differences and similarities across cultures (Malaysia, Europe, and the United States) in terms of young people's endorsement of children's rights.

In the next article in this section, Torney-Purta, Wilkenfeld, and Barber (2008) present findings from a large-scale 27 country survey of adolescents' understanding of international human rights. Drawing on data from the IEA Civic Education Study the authors examine adolescents' knowledge of human rights compared to other forms of civic knowledge, attitudes about the rights of ethnic minorities and immigrants, and beliefs regarding self-determination rights. Additionally, the authors investigate individual and country-level predictors of adolescents' human rights knowledge, attitudes, and participation. They conclude their article with an exploration of the significance of their findings for research-based policy.

Finally, in the last article making up this section Khoury-Kassabri and Ben-Arieh (2008) presented the results of a comparative investigation of attitudes toward and understanding of rights and rights violations in a sample of 12- to 14-year-old Jewish, Arab-Christian, and Arab-Muslim adolescents living in Jerusalem. The results indicate that nationality plays an important role in how these adolescents view children's rights (e.g., Jewish adolescents held more favorable views regarding children's rights than Arab adolescents). However, questions remain as to the role religion and religiosity play in influencing young people's beliefs about children's rights.

In the concluding commentary, Gary Melton (2008) addressed the central themes of this volume and offers a more philosophically grounded perspective with respect to children's rights. He argues that we seriously consider moving beyond the focus on *balancing* (e.g., balancing children's and parents' rights, balancing self-determination and nurturance, balancing rights and responsibilities) and work on strategies, which will allow children to participate meaningfully in community life and society. Finally, Melton provides an example of child advocacy employing such an approach.

The articles in this issue of *JSI* bring together a variety of theoretical perspectives, North American and international work on the topic, as well as consider the relevance of the principles of the CRC (e.g., "best interests of the child," "the evolving capacities of the child," and "dignity of the child") through the lenses of social scientists, policymakers, and young people. As such this issue will be of interest to all those whose work pertains to bettering the lives children and youth. It is our hope that it will stimulate further research on this topic, as well as improved policy and practice regarding the rights and needs of young people for protection and participation across a range of contexts.

References

Baumrind, D. (1978). Reciprocal rights and responsibilities in parent-child relations. *Journal of Social Issues, 34*, 179–196.

Baumrind, D., & Thompson, R. (2002). The ethics of parenting. In M. Bornstein (Ed.), *The handbook of parenting: Vol. 5. Practical issues in parenting* (2nd ed., pp. 3–34). Hillsdale, NJ: Erlbaum.

Cherney, I., & Perry, N. (1996). Children's attitudes toward their rights: An international perspective. In E. Verhellen (Ed.), *Monitoring children's rights* (pp. 241–250). Dordrecht, The Netherlands: Martinus Nijhoff.

Cherney, I. D., & Shing, Y. L. (2008). Children's nurturance and self-determination rights: A cross-cultural perspective. *Journal of Social Issues, 64*, 835–856.

Daiute, C. (2008). The rights of children, the rights of nations. *Journal of Social Issues, 64*, 701–723.

Eiduson, B. T., & Alexander, J. W. (1978). The role of children in alternative family styles. *Journal of Social Issues, 34*, 149–167.

Feshback, N. D., & Feshback, S. (1978). Toward an historical, social, and developmental perspective on children's rights. *Journal of Social Issues, 34*, 1–7.

Flanagan, C. A., Stout, M., & Gallay, L. (2008). It's my body and none of your business: Developmental differences in adolescents' perceptions of health. *Journal of Social Issues, 64*, 815–834.

Gallatin, J., & Adelson, J. (1970). Individual rights and the public good: A cross-national study of adolescents. *Comparative Political Studies, 2*, 226–244.

Hart, R. A. (1997). *Children's participation: The theory and practice of including young citizens in community development and environmental care.* New York: UNICEF.

Hart, S. N. (1982). The history of children's psychological rights. *Viewpoints in Teaching and Learning, 58*, 1–15.

Hart, S. N. (1991). From property to person status: Historical perspectives on children's rights. *American Psychologist, 46*, 53–59.

Hart, S. N., & Pavloic, Z. (1991). Children's rights in education: An historical perspective. *School Psychology Review, 20*, 345–358.

Helwig, C. (1995). Adolescents' and young adults' conceptions of civil liberties: Freedom of speech and religion. *Child Development, 66*, 152–166.

Helwig, C. (1997). The role of agent and social context in judgments of speech and Religion. *Child Development, 68*, 484–495.

Helwig, C. (2006). The development of personal autonomy throughout cultures. *Cognitive Development, 21*, 458–473.

Helwig, C. C., & Turiel, E. (2002). Rights, autonomy, and democracy: Children's perspectives. *International Journal of Law and Psychiatry, 25*, 253–270.

Horn, S., Szalacha, L. A., & Dill, K. (2008). Schooling, sexuality, and rights: An investigation of heterosexual students' social cognition regarding sexual orientation and the rights of gay and lesbian peers in school. *Journal of Social Issues, 64*, 791–813.

In re Gault, 387 U.S. (1967).

Keating, D. P. (1990). Adolescent thinking. In S. Feldman & G. Elliott (Eds.), *At the threshold: Theory, research, and social issues* (pp. 54–89). Cambridge, MA: Harvard University Press.

Khoury-Kassabri, M., & Ben-Arieh, A. (2008). Adolescents' approach toward rights: Comparison between Christian, Jewish, and Muslim children in Jerusalem. *Journal of Social Issues, 64*, 881–901.

Kilbourne, S. (1996). U.S. failure to ratify the Convention on the rights of the child: Playing politics with children's rights. *Transnational Law & Contemporary Problems, 6*, 437–461.

Kohlberg, L. (1969). Stage and sequence: The cognitive-developmental approach to socialization. In D. Goslin (Ed.), *Handbook of socialization theory and research* (pp. 347–480). Chicago: Rand Mcnally.

Levesque, R. J. R. (2008). Regardless of frontiers: Adolescents and the human right to information. *Journal of Social Issues, 64*, 724–747.

Limber, S. P., & Flekkoy, M. G. (1995). The U. N. Convention on the Rights of the Child: Its relevance for social scientists. *Social Policy Report, 9*(2), 1–15.

Limber, S. P., & Wilcox, B. L. (1996). Application of the U. N. Convention on the Rights of the Child to the United States. *American Psychologist, 51*, 1246–1250.

Melton, G. B. (1980). Children's concepts of their rights. *Journal of Clinical Child Psychology, 9*, 186–190.

Melton, G. B. (1983). *Child advocacy: Psychological issues and interventions.* New York: Plenum Press.

Melton, G. B. (1991). Socialization in the global community: Respect for the dignity of children. *American Psychologist, 46,* 66–77.

Melton, G. B. (1996). The child's right to a new family environment: Why children's rights and family values are compatible. *American Psychologist, 51,* 1234–1238.

Melton, G. B. (2001). Making the Convention on the Rights of the Child "real law." *International Society for the Study of Behavioral Development Newsletter, 38*(2), 16–18.

Melton, G. B., & Limber, S. P. (1992). What rights mean to children: Children's own views. In M. Freeman & P. Veerman (Eds.), *Ideologies of children's rights* (pp. 167–187). Dordrecht, The Netherlands: Martinus Nijhoff.

Melton, G. B. (2008). Beyond balancing: Toward an integrative approach to children's rights. *Journal of Social Issues, 64,* 903–920.

Murphy-Berman, V., & Weisz, V. (1996). U. N. Convention on the Rights of the Child: Current challenges. *American Psychologist, 51,* 1231–1233.

Nairn, K., & Smith, A. B. (2003). Taking students seriously: Their rights to be safe at school. *Gender and Education, 15*(2), 133–149.

Neff, K., & Helwig, C. C. (2002). A constructivist approach to understanding the development of reasoning about rights and authority within cultural contexts. *Cognitive Development, 17*(3–4), 1429–1450.

Paplia, D. E., & Olds, S. W. (1989). *Human development* (5th ed.). New York: McGraw-Hill.

Peterson-Badali, M., & Ruck, M. D. (2008). Studying children's perspectives on self-determination and nurturance rights: Issues and challenges. *Journal of Social Issues, 64,* 749–769.

Piaget, J. (1960). *The moral judgment of the child.* New York: Free Press.

Planned Parenthood v. Danforth, 44 U. S. L. W., 5197, July 1, 1976

Ruck, M. D., Abramovitch, R., & Keating, D. (1998). Children's and adolescents' Understanding of rights: Balancing nurturance and self-determination. *Child Development, 64,* 404–417.

Ruck, M. D., Keating, D. P., Abramovitch, R., & Koegl, C. J. (1998). Adolescents' and children's knowledge about rights: Some evidence for how young people view rights in their own lives. *Journal of Adolescence, 21,* 275–289.

Ruck, M. D., & Peterson-Badali, M. (2006). Youths' perceptions of rights. In L. R. Sherrod, C. Flanagan, & R. Kassimir (Eds.), *Youth activism: An international encyclopedia.* New Haven, CT: Greenwood Publishing.

Ruck, M. D., Peterson-Badali, M., & Day, D. (2002). Adolescents' and mothers' understanding of children's rights in the home. *Journal of Research on Adolescence, 12*(3), 373–398.

Ruck, M. D., & Verbeek, P. (2002). Young people's participation rights: Research, application and theory. Unpublished manuscript.

Rogers, C. M., & Wrightsman, L. S. (1978). Attitudes towards children's rights: Nurturance or self-determination? *Journal of Social Issues, 34,* 59–68.

Sherrod, L. (2008). Adolescents' perceptions of rights as reflected in their views of citizenship. *Journal of Social Issues, 64,* 771–790.

Steinberg, L. (2001). We know some things: Adolescent-parent relationships in retrospect and prospect. *Journal of Research on Adolescence, 11,* 1–20.

Steinberg, L., & Sliverberg, S. B. (1986). The vicissitudes of autonomy in early adolescence. *Child Development, 57,* 841–851.

Steir, S. (1978). Children's rights and society's duties. *Journal of Social Issues, 34,* 46–58.

Takanishi, R. (1978). Childhood as a social issue: Historical roots of contemporary child advocacy movements. *Journal of Social Issues, 34,* 8–28.

Tapp, J., & Kohlberg, L. (1971). Developing senses of law and legal justice. *Journal of Social Issues, 27*(2), 65–91.

Tapp, J., & Levine, F. (1974). Legal socialization: Strategies for an ethical legality. *Stanford Law Review, 27,* 1–72.

Tinker v. des Moines Independent Community School District, 393 U. S. 503. (1969).

Torney-Purta, J., Wilkenfeld, B., & Barber, C. (2008). How adolescents in 27 countries understand, support, and practice human rights. *Journal of Social Issues, 64,* 857–880.

Troope, S. (1996). The Convention of the Right of the Child; implications for Canada. In M. Freeman (Ed.), *Children's rights.* Aldershot, UK: Dartmouth Publishing Company.

Turiel, E. (1983). *The development of social knowledge: morality and convention.* Cambridge: Cambridge University Press.

Turiel, E. (1998). The development of morality. In W. Damon (Series Ed.) & N. Eisenberg (Vol. Ed.), *Handbook of child psychology: Vol 3, Social, emotional, and personality development* (5th ed., pp. 863–932). New York: Wiley.

United Nations General Assembly. (1989, November 17). *Adoption of a Convention on the rights of the child.* New York: Author.

Verma, S., Chen, X., & Miller, J. G. (2001). Child rights and well-being: Psychological, behavioral and policy concerns. *International Society for the Study of Behavioral Development Newsletter, 38*(2), 2.

Walker, N. E., Brooks, C. M., & Wrightsman, L. S. (1999). *Children's rights in the United States: In search of a national policy.* Thousand Oaks, CA: Sage.

Wilcox, B. L., & Naimark, H. (1991). The rights of the child: Progress toward human dignity. *American Psychologist, 46*(1), 49.

Wilson, J., & Tomlinson, M. (1986). *Wilson: On children and the law.* Toronto, Canada: Butterworth.

MARTIN D. RUCK is an Associate Professor of Urban Education and Developmental Psychology at the Graduate Center of the City University of New York. His work examines the overall process of cognitive socialization—at the intersection of race, ethnicity and class—in terms of children's and adolescents' thinking about human rights, educational opportunity, and social justice. Currently, he is investigating how children's perceptions of social exclusion and discrimination are influenced by their social experiences and interpretations of rights and justice. His research on the topic of children's understanding of rights has appeared in *Child Development, Journal of Adolescence, Journal of Applied Social Psychology, Journal of Early Adolescence*, and *Journal of Research on Adolescence*. He has recently extended his work on young people's perceptions of their rights to the U.K. and South Africa.

STACEY S. HORN is an Associate Professor of Educational and Developmental Psychology in the Department of Educational Psychology at University of Illinois at Chicago. She received her PhD from the University of Maryland at College Park in Human Development. Dr. Horn is interested in the development of moral and social reasoning, peer groups and intergroup relations; stereotypes, prejudice, and discrimination related to sexual orientation and gender identity. Her applied work investigates the relationships among institutional structures and adolescents' social and moral reasoning, specifically related to peer interactions. Stacey is on the Editorial Board for the *Journal of Youth and Adolescence*, the *Journal of Gay and Lesbian Youth,* serves on the governing board of the Jean Piaget Society and is Chair of the Governing Board for the Illinois Safe Schools Alliance. Her research has been published in journals such as *Developmental Psychology, the International Journal of Behavior and Development, Cognitive Development*, and the *Journal of Youth and Adolescence*.

Journal of Social Issues, Vol. 64, No. 4, 2008, pp. 701–723

The Rights of Children, the Rights of Nations: Developmental Theory and the Politics of Children's Rights

Colette Daiute*

City University of New York

The Convention on the Rights of the Child (CRC), U.N. General Assembly (1989) is a major breakthrough in defining children as fully human and working to ensure them the attendant benefits worldwide. While children's rights as equal human beings may seem obvious in the 21st century, the politics of establishing and ensuring such rights are contentious. The CRC is a brilliant negotiation of conceptions of the child and international relations, yet certain tensions in the children's rights process lead to a lack of clarity in a global situation that continues to leave millions of children at risk. Analyzing the CRC and related practices from a developmental perspective can help identify obstacles to the advancement of children's rights, especially those related to opportunities for rights-based thinking and the exercise of self-determination and societal-determination rights.

In this article, I offer a qualitative analysis of children's rights in the context of what I refer to as the CRC activity-meaning system. I present a theoretical framework for considering this system of policy and practice as enacted in the CRC treaty and related monitoring, reporting, qualifying, and implementing documents. A discourse analysis of conceptions of the child and those responsible for ensuring their rights in seven representative documents (including the CRC Treaty, a report by the U.N. Committee on the Rights of the Child, minutes of a U.N. Security Council meeting, reports by a State-Party, and a report by a civil society group in that country) reveals tensions inherent in the CRC activity-meaning system.[1] Emerging from this analysis is a tension between children's rights and nation's rights. Created in part via explicit and implicit assumptions about child development in the CRC as these posit responsibilities across actors in the broader

---

*Correspondence concerning this article should be addressed to Colette Daiute, The Graduate Center, City University of New York, 365 5th Ave., New York, NY 10016 [e-mail: cdaiute@gc.cuny.edu].

[1]Documents for this analysis were selected to represent the major actors in the CRC system and to provide a case study following a sequence of required and alternative reports related to activities by one State-Party (Colombia) over a period of several years.

CRC system, this tension challenges the implementation of children's rights and the development of children's rights-based understandings. I use this analysis to explain why future research and practice should address the development of children's rights-based understanding not only in terms of maturation or socialization but also as integral to salient conflicts in their every day lives.

The Convention on the Rights of the Child (CRC, U.N. General Assembly, 1989) is an international treaty adopted by the 159 Members of the United Nations General Assembly in 1989 and subsequently ratified by all but two U.N. member nations (the U.S.[2] and Somalia). The CRC consists of a Preamble and 54 Articles stating the rights of "the child" and the responsibilities of "States Parties" in ensuring those rights. The Convention outlines social, economic, cultural, civil, and political rights assured via binding processes of implementing and monitoring by ratifying states. The United Nations Committee on the Rights of the Child (the CRC Committee) is central in orchestrating this process designed "to provide an international mechanism for monitoring progress on implementation" of the Convention "working with other Treaty Bodies, United Nations agencies, and other organizations to promote the Convention and the realization of the rights of the Child." This CRC system is, moreover, the first human rights treaty that involves nongovernmental organizations with an official role in reporting on its implementation (www.crin.org). The CRC also advocates that children have a say in matters that affect them, but, as I will show, their perspectives enter into the dialogue mostly via alternative reports and research.

Most scholarly discussion about the CRC focuses on the treaty document itself, but it is in this broader CRC system of activities that we can identify issues related to ensuring or limiting children's rights. A potential contribution of developmental psychology is to analyze the conception of the child, how this conception fits with the politics of international relations required for ensuring rights, and any tensions resulting from such interdisciplinary endeavors. Identifying these tensions is important for understanding challenges to implementing the CRC and for designing research on children's rights-based understanding and participation. Toward these ends, this article presents an analysis of the broader CRC system, including the treaty and documents enacting related monitoring, reporting, and qualifying activities.

After a brief description of the CRC, I discuss the analytic design in terms of a sociocultural activity theory of human development, present the discourse

---

[2]There has been little written about the reasons for the United States' failure to ratify the CRC. In personal communication, Roger Hart, who has been involved in the CRC development and implementation reports legal and political reasons. The United States has claimed that individual states must approve all treaty signatures, which not all states have done. In addition, Hart reports political pressures, in particular, from powerful southern states that did not want to ratify the CRC because of the apparently expansive nature of children's rights to make decisions about issues like birth control independently of their parents.

analysis methodology derived from this theory, and review results of the analysis. Based on these results, I explain how notions of child development implicit in the CRC document leave children's rights vulnerable to the politics of treaty-making. Results of the analysis also suggest the need to make sociopolitical aspects of child development more explicit, especially in relation to children's rights-based understandings and opportunities for children's self-determination.

Questions guiding the inquiry include: What is the nature of children's rights discourse across the CRC activity-meaning system? What tensions emerge from an analysis of the broader CRC activity-meaning system? How could these tensions affect opportunities for children's development of rights-based understandings and practices of self-determination rights? What developmental theory might allow for critical and creative analyses of children's rights-based understandings and actions? Based on the analysis, I will explain that focusing on developmental theory and the politics of treaty-making suggests the need for a developmental approach that considers children as social beings who interact with the material and symbolic circumstances in their environments, including the political processes like rights, which are essential to their lives.

The CRC

The following excerpts illustrate the CRC discourse.

From the *Preamble*
    ... the Universal Declaration of Human Rights, the United Nations has proclaimed that childhood is entitled to special care and assistance...

From *Article 12*
    States Parties shall assure to the child who is capable of forming his or her own views the right to express those views freely in all matters affecting the child, the views of the child being given due weight in accordance with the age and maturity of the child.

From *Article 14*
    States Parties shall respect the right of the child to freedom of thought, conscience, and religion ... [and] shall respect the rights and duties of the parents and, when applicable, legal guardians, to provide direction to the child in the exercise of his or her right in a manner consistent with the evolving capacities of the child.

From *Article 38*
    States Parties shall refrain from recruiting any person who has not attained the age of fifteen years into their armed forces.

Scholars argue that participation by 193 nations suggests that the Convention is an advance of modern civilization, because children's status as complex persons with rights worth international and local protection was first mentioned in Declaration of the Rights of the Child in 1924 (Hart, S.N., 1982, 1991; Hart, R.A., 1999). On the other hand, there is also evidence of the limits of the treaty and its implementation. Scholars have offered numerous critiques of the CRC, stating that "philosophical, legal, political, constitutional, methodological, and cross cultural" aspects of the CRC may serve to "facilitate or constrain" its effectiveness (Murphy-Berman & Weisz, 1996, p. 1231). Critics have noted, in particular, the predominantly Western perspective (Wilcox & Naimark, 1991) and the latent imperialism embedded in the moral and utopian assumptions guiding such human rights treaties (Dahbour, 2003; Koshy, 1999). Activists have, however, used the strong wording of the CRC to advocate for children's rights and to pressure governments to create programs for children's participation (Hart, 1999).

Intrigued with the relationship between nurturance and self-determination rights, developmental psychologists have examined children's and adults' understandings of different categories of rights and responsibilities of ensuring those rights (Ruck, Abramovitch, & Keating, 1998). Although the CRC and related activities rely on certain definitions of the child, relatively little discussion of child development theory explicitly guides the CRC or interactions between any theoretical assumptions and the politics of implementing the CRC. A treaty based on conceptions like "evolving capacities of the child" could, for example, usefully identify those capacities and the nature of their development, especially because such definitions differ across developmental theories. While leaving open the specific nature of "evolving capacities" may allow for diverse interpretations across cultures (Landsdown, 2005), it also potentially allows cultural and political powers to override children's rights. When focusing in this way on the figure of the child and the nature of development, we ask, for example, what kinds of capacities within and across contexts constitutes maturity to participate in war at age 15, while still requiring that the child adhere to religious and political practices defined by the family and the State.

Toward a Developmental Reading of Children's Rights Discourse

Developmental psychology has an important role to play in analyzing the CRC. Theories of child development, presumably, provide at least some of the foundation for the rights and responsibilities it advocates. Developmental theory is implied in the major definitions, principles, and myriad efforts to implement practices toward improving children's rights (Hart, 1999). Nevertheless, the document offers no explicit discussion about the foundational theory of child development. Furthermore, although theory and research on human development remain implicit, political processes, like State sovereignty are explicit. This contrast is perhaps not surprising given the power of State Parties for making the Convention a reality.

If the treaty endows rights based on "evolving capacities" but does not define these capacities nor the circumstances and course of their development, the nature of the protections remains open to question. While one theory posits that children are not capable of critical reflection before the age of 12 (Piaget, 1968), for example another theory posits that critical reflection depends on the nature of challenges children face in their lives (Burton, Obeidallah, & Allison, 1996). Children growing up in the context of war or inequality would, on this view, be able to reason critically about precisely those issues (Daiute, 2006). Although the purpose of the CRC is not to define developmental theory, the basis of developmental concepts could affect its interpretation and implementation. We should, thus, address questions about the theory of child development embedded in the CRC system, the representation of children as psychosocial actors, and interactions of those representations with the politics of international treaty-making. Ultimately, being able to support children's rights-based understandings and action depends on such clarity.

A complete review of theories of child development is not possible in this article, but previous reviews have highlighted several diverse emphases (Damon & Lerner, 2006). Most developmentalists today recognize the integrated biosociobehavioral nature of child development in that the maturation of the child's body and brain relates to experiencing and understanding the social and physical world. Nevertheless, major theories differ in whether they emphasize biological or social processes (Damon & Lerner, 2006). Versions of the two most popular theories guiding contemporary research are cognitive developmental theories, which have made great contributions by explaining the increasingly complex cognitive organization of the child's mind (Piaget, 1968) and social theories, which have offered explanations of how mind is shaped through symbolic interaction in cultural systems (Bronfenbrenner & Morris, 1998; Vygotsky, 1978).

Because there is no explicit discussion of the foundational principles of child development in or attached to the CRC, I drew on sociocultural theory (Leont'ev, 1978; Vygotsky, 1978) focusing on the development of higher order processes, like those required for rights-based understanding and self-determination, as they occur in the symbolic activity of discourse (Harre & van Langenhove, 1999; Wertsch, 1991). I generated questions, a design, and analysis of child development theory within the CRC and related activities from the perspective that development is an interaction of individual and society.

Following the proposal that "Every function in the child's cultural development appears twice: first, on the social level, and later, on the individual level; first *between* people (*interpsychological*) and then *inside* the child (*intrapsychological*)" (Vygotsky, 1978, p. 57), the social–political context with which children interact from birth not only affects them but defines them. For this reason, developmental analysis of children's rights—whether and how children are treated as members of sociopolitical life—must consider how children interact in society, not only in terms of abstract cognitive processes but also in terms of what is going on in their environments. For example, children being recruited to fight on behalf of their country or to cope with inferior educational systems may perceive that public institutions are limiting their rights to life, learning, and play, but it is in precisely such situations where their reflection and any potentially critical results of such reflection are undermined by the State's need for child soldiers or its inability to provide education.

The sociocultural perspective posits that social institutions shape individuals and that individuals can transform social institutions (Engestrom & Miettinen, 1999). Consistent with this theory, children must have opportunities for critical and creative engagement in salient activities, which include exposure to important relations in society as well as to interpersonal interactions in the peer domain. On this view, development occurs within actual social processes including conflicts, and developmental trajectories are defined in terms of social struggles, which may be debilitating or transcendent. As we see later on, this could mean involving children in such activities as discussions of war, social exclusion, or education budgets rather than protecting them from such discussions. Ideally, civic activities are positive, like those involving youth as apprentices in social organizations devoted to improving society, but, in societies at war or with great economic inequalities, civic activities can be extremely negative. In such contexts, understanding children's rights as a developmental process becomes especially important.

Analyzing Children's Rights Discourses

This inquiry involves applying sociocultural activity theory to design and implement a discourse analysis of children's rights policy related to the CRC. The theory-based design draws on two concepts of sociocultural theory. As with other legal and policy practices, documents are reference points for a broader range of activities by institutional actors. Given this way of thinking about children's rights policy, I drew on the sociocultural concepts of activity-meaning system and dialogic relations to generate the research questions, design, and analysis process. Activity systems are those symbolically linked interactions of individuals in meaningful contexts and institutions (Engestrom & Miettinen, 1999). The developmental idea is that as children grow, they act and interact in relevant culturally mediated systems, which determine the values, concepts, and practices in their lives. These values, concepts, and practices are created in discourse and, thus, build in relation to the specifics of every day life. Children's rights policy, like other policies, is embedded within such a system of institutions, activities, and relationships. With the following theoretical formulations, we focus on interactions across seven different kinds of documents in the CRC system.

Documents, like everyday oral discourse and nonverbal symbol systems, are created in the midst of activity-meaning systems. Because each document in the

CRC activity-meaning system occurs within a series of meetings, it is a response to previous interactions and directed toward future ones (Bakhtin, 1986). Documents, thus, express dialogic relations in several ways (Bakhtin, 1986). Because they enact values, policy documents are discursive practices (Harre & van Langenhove, 1999) available for analysis of the principles, concepts, and tensions involved in society, which, in our study, is focused on the children's rights process. The documents in the CRC system are also dialogic because they are directed explicitly and implicitly to specific and general audiences of participants in the children's rights process. Analyzing language in context, for example, by linking the statements and values in one document to others in our theory-based system is one among several techniques mentioned here that makes this a discourse analysis (as compared to a content analysis that relies only on explicit statements, usually in nouns and verbs contained in texts). Another element of discourse analysis is paying attention to the small words, such as "the" in phrases like "the child," implying a universal form (citations on the increasing use and systematic nature of discourse analysis include Bakhtin, 1986; Bamberg, 2006; Engestrom & Miettienen, 1999; Harre & Van Langenhove, 1999).

Drawing on practices such as requirements for follow-up to receipt of a document also captures this notion of discourse activity system. Periodic reports by States that ratify the CRC, for example, are responses to a treaty requirement. Agenda items by the CRC Committee are, in turn, responses to periodic reports, which may be accepted or discussed for violations at a CRC Committee meeting. Through such ongoing interactions, participants in the CRC system negotiate the meaning of children's rights. Consistent with this view that culture is mediation in meaningful discourse, we define children's rights as embedded in a cultural–political system.[3]

The first phase of the present inquiry was to apply sociocultural theory to design an analysis of the children's rights activity-meaning system. This involved identifying the range of documents that address one another and selecting exemplars of each major phase of the interaction. With the CRC system design established, I conducted discourse analyses for information about the nature and relationships among these documents. The discourse analysis focused on identifying the implicit developmental theory in the CRC itself, including definitions of the "child" as stated and as implied in the description of rights and responsibilities and the determination of agents acting on the child's behalf. The next phase of the discourse analysis involved identifying activities enacted in the CRC documents, which include qualifying, monitoring, reporting, and implementing. I then discuss implications of the analysis for allowing children to express and develop their rights-based understandings.

---

[3]This definition of culture as socially mediated activity differs from definitions of culture as a set of beliefs and rituals belonging to a specific national, ethnic, gender, class, or other group.

The CRC Activity-Meaning System

The CRC activity-meaning system is enacted in the CRC treaty and related documents, as listed in Table 1. As shown in Table 1, this collection includes the CRC (Preamble and 54 Articles), "Declarations and Reservations" (Kuper, 1997; U.N. Treaty Collection, 2001), the U.N. General Assembly Security Council Item no. 63 on the Promotion and Protection of the Rights of the Child, 61st Session, the CRC Committee Consideration of Reports Submitted by States Parties under Article 44 of the Convention, Concluding Observation: Colombia, 42nd Session, a State Party Report: "Third Periodic Report of Colombia, and the Alternative Report to the Report of the Government of Colombia on the Situation of the Rights of the Child." I selected these documents because they represent the major actors involved in stating, ensuring, and monitoring children's rights and follow a sequence of reporting and monitoring for Colombia, a State Party figuring prominently in the process.

The CRC, like other international treaty practices, involves a system of interactions, like reporting and monitoring by key participants. As shown in the column labeled "Activity-Meaning" on Table 1, these documents constitute a system of activities including policy making, qualifying, monitoring, and reporting. This theory-based design provides a way of considering the broader CRC process relevant to children's sociopolitical understandings.

Implicit Developmental Theory in the CRC

Reading the CRC document, we ask "Who is the child? Who are the child's agents? What do these representations imply about the child's reasoning and development as a social–political agent? How do these explicit and implied definitions of the child occur in relation to the representations of political actors mentioned in the CRC?" The discourse analysis to address these questions involved identifying all references to the "child," those individuals, roles, and institutions defined as acting on behalf of the child, the nature of relationships among these actors, stated and implied developmental processes, and qualifications of these relationships and processes for different categories of rights. After compiling these identifications, I compared them to those stated in the major contemporary explanations of development: maturational, socialization, and sociocultural.

The general model of human development embedded in the CRC—although not explicitly discussed—is one of a gradually maturing organism—expressed in terms like "evolving capacities of the child" and "will be given weight in accordance with age and maturity." Characteristic of the CRC discourse is its reference to "the child," implying that "child" is a universal category. The related discourse of maturation suggests that this universality is biological. At the same time, there's a process of socialization implied, via expressions about the prominent role of

Table 1. Documents in the CRC Activity-Meaning System for Discourse Analysis

Actor/Document	Activity-Meaning
International	
1) *United Nations CRC*	Policy-making treaty
2) *Office of the U.N. High Commissioner on Human Rights (OHCHR)*	Qualifying activity
Declarations and reservations to the CRC	(State-Parties take issue with CRC)
3) *U.N. General Assembly, Security Council Agenda Item no. 63*	Monitoring activity
On Promotion & Protection of the Rights of the Child	(for State-Party violations & concerns)
61st Session, 26 October 2006	
4) *Committee on the Rights of the Child, consideration of*	Monitoring Activity
reports submitted by States Parties under Article 44	(Summary of State Report)
Of the Convention, concluding observations: Colombia,	
42nd Session, 2 June 2006 (Re: Colombia's 3rd per.report)	
5) *Committee on the Rights of the Child, Implementation of the*	Monitoring activity
Convention on the Rights of the Child, Colombia	(Request for additional report)
National actors	
6) *Third periodic report of Colombia (CRC/C/129/Add.6) (8/05)*	Reporting activity
7) *Alternative report to the report of the government of*	Reporting-monitoring
Colombia on the situation of the Rights of the Child	
Local actors	
Citations of child and youth perspectives in local programs	Reporting child/youth views

"States Parties" and families to make decisions on the child's behalf, qualifications like "taking into account the rights and duties of the child's parents," and exceptions such as accommodations to State Parties recruiting children into armed conflict at age 15 when necessary, although childhood is otherwise protected up to age 18.

Who is the Child?

As stated in Article 1 of the Convention, *"a child means every human being below the age of eighteen years unless under the law applicable to the child, majority is attained earlier."*

The child's status as an individual person, like all other humans, is the basis for rights in the CRC. Results of the analysis reveal explicit and implicit representations of the child, as an individual person deserving of human rights, yet vulnerable, emergent, dependent, and determined by the broader social structures of the family and the state. Because the child described in the CRC matures only gradually, he or she is deemed in need of protection until the age of 18, except in the case of armed conflict, when this age can be lowered to 15.

For the most part, "the child" is represented as in need of protection and, thus, vulnerable in the face of myriad threats. Most of the rights are based on the child's physical or cognitive immaturity and attendant needs for shelter, sustenance, protection from abuse, protection from coercion, exploitation, and harmful activities like unhealthy labor and armed conflict. The details of the Articles also represent the child as singular, passive, and generic. The child's status as an individual is underscored in rights to "privacy, respect, reputation, honor, dignity." Although vulnerable, the child is eventually able to exercise rights, although the nature of transition to increased ability is not stated.

As stated in one quarter of the 54 articles (Hart, 1999), the child is endowed with some rights to participation such as the right to express views in matters that affect him or her and to assemble peacefully. Although included, participation rights are always qualified to be consistent with the interests of the State. Moreover, rights to freedom from discrimination based on culture, race, creed, and other unique qualities are granted the child through the family and the State, thus limiting the child's self- and societal-determination.

An implication of a developmental trajectory comes from statements like "the child should be prepared to live an individual life in society, consistent with the spirit and ideals of the United Nations – spirit of peace, dignity, tolerance, freedom, equality, and solidarity." The CRC does not mention milestones or qualitative shifts in the child's understanding or behavior across the years from birth to 18, which leaves discretion about different levels of maturity to the family and the State. In the absence of a description of developmental processes, the default model is one of socialization to local values and practices that the child would presumably internalize by age 18.

Who are the Child's Agents?

The CRC represents two primary agents on the child's behalf: the family environment and State Parties. The child's relationships are, thus, hierarchical—in terms of membership in a family that protects and socializes the child and membership in the State that protects and socializes the family. Analyses reveal a range of family responsibilities and rights, including the family's role in providing a home for the child and the family's role in social reproduction (such as in their responsibility to provide the child with a name and language). As stated in the Preamble, parties to the Convention declare they are "Convinced that the family as the fundamental group of society and the natural environment for the growth and well-being of all its members and particularly children, should be afforded the necessary protection and assistance so that it can fully assume its responsibilities within the community." As the primary agent for the child, the family is defined in Article 5: "parents or, where applicable, the members of the extended family or community as provided for by local custom, legal guardians or other persons legally responsible for the child."

The family provides continuity for social reproduction, by providing identity in a name, heritage language, and "harmonious development of his or her personality." The designation of the family environment may seem obvious as the child's primary domain of nurturance, especially to those of us in Western industrial and postindustrial societies, but the family is also a mediator for divisive issues, like culture, religion, and politics. The nesting of the child's rights within the institution of the family is, for example, a way that the CRC allows for the protection of traditional values, practices, and ideologies. What this designation misses, however, is the child's participation in society—as a means of development and as a potentially transformative force of social change should children, for example, disagree with family practices or participate in new activities auguring trajectories that differ from tradition. Children in countries of the former Soviet bloc participate in activities to promote democratic citizenship, for example which their families might find to be quite foreign or untenable.

The CRC States Parties are the primary agents mediating for the child's rights, sometimes through the family, as discussed in the previous section, but mostly through their direct involvement in the CRC and in domestic laws. Ratifying States promise to "recognize the rights of the child," "promote," "take all appropriate measures to secure" and "protect" the child's rights, to "treat [the child] without discrimination," to "ensure" the child's best interests, to "develop," "establish," and "preserve" the child's identity (such as to provide a birth certificate). Ratifying States promise a range of protections (such as to take appropriate legislative and administrative measures to ensure children's rights). The State also promises to respect, to take appropriate legislative and administrative measures, to promote values (such as spirit of international cooperation), to teach "preventive health care guidance for parents," to prepare the child for responsible life, to refrain from recruiting and abusing the child, and to make principles and provisions of the Convention widely known. State Parties are also afforded a wide range of exceptions, such as the right to recruit young people to fight their wars even before the age of maturity if necessary.

Limitations on Children's Rights

Across the wide range of rights in the Convention, national values and laws are sovereign and qualifying each right in some way. Most of the articles, in short, allow States Parties to limit a child's right "in conformity with the law" and "in the interests of national security or public safety, public order, the protection of public health or morals or protection of the rights and freedoms of others" (p. 15). The child's right to his or her family, expressed as the right not to be separated from the family, limits the primary buffer between the child and the State: "Where such separation results from any action initiated by a State Party, such as the detention, imprisonment, exile, deportation or death (including death arising from any cause while the person is in the custody of the State) of one or both parents or the child."

The CRC establishes children's rights as universal but posits limits in terms of their developmental capacities to act on their own behalf. Noticeably missing in the Convention is representation of the child as a social being or social agent. None of the articles highlights equal relationships—such as with peers, siblings, or other social institutions where the child might have responsibilities or an effect on others. The absence of any mention of social relational reasoning and interaction skills underscores the underrepresentation of capacities and, more importantly, underrepresentation of children's social–political participation. What then is the meaning of self-determination? How does it differ from societal-determination? How do these capacities develop? More critical questions could ask about whether and how children apply perceptual and analytic skills (such as perspective-taking) to local material and symbolic circumstances, such as those related to debates about gender equity and religious practices.

In summary, extremes of both maturation and socialization theories are implicit in the CRC. As noted in Articles 12 and 14 above, children's rights, such as those to freedom of expression and conscience are defined in terms of "evolving capacities" and "in accordance with age and maturity," thereby expressing a maturational view of development. These same rights are also limited by the "rights and duties of the parents and, when applicable, legal guardians to provide direction to the child" and to determine "the best interests of the child." These parental roles suggest a socialization model of development, by implying that the child's view would ultimately echo the parents' view and, moreover that parents would not limit their children's rights according to the CRC. Assumptions about how children's capacities develop in relation to circumstances and injustices in their daily lives remain unexamined. Although maturation and socialization views may both assume that children eventually can reason critically about their own lives, theory-based analyses of the development of children's sociopolitical reasoning seems crucial to the appropriate balancing of nurturance and self-determination rights. If, for example, States and parents limit deliberation of precisely those contentious issues in society where children's rights may be most challenged, how would children develop, express, and exercise these rights?

Negotiating Rights across the CRC System

In this section, I discuss how an analysis of dialogic relations across the CRC activity-meaning system offers insights about the dilemmatic nature of defining children's rights. The analysis of the broader CRC system illustrates how State Parties qualify their compliance with the treaty, thereby limiting children's role in expressing and developing their rights-based understandings.

Qualifying Rights

Children's rights are qualified not only within the CRC document, as mentioned above, but also in the broader CRC system. As indicated in Table 1, the children's rights system allows for qualifying activity, as demonstrated in the formal process of *Declarations and Reservations*. A few examples of "Declarations and Reservations" illustrate CRC respect for cultural and religious Conventions, such as Djibouti's declaration that it "shall not consider itself bound by any provisions or articles that are incompatible with its religion and traditional values" (U.N. Treaty Collection, 2001, p. 8) and the Holy See's reservation that "Family planning and education services in Article 24.2, [will] mean only those methods of family planning which it considers morally acceptable that is the natural methods of family planning" (U.N. Treaty Collection, 2001; p. 11). In more political vein, Cuba asserts that "under the domestic legislation in force, majority is not attained at 18 years of age for purposes of the full exercise of civic rights" (p. 7). Because declarations and reservations clarify or claim exemptions to specific CRC articles, they are involved in an ongoing negotiation of the Treaty.

An analysis of the nature of declarations and reservations offered insights about how State Parties tailor the CRC to their circumstances and goals. This analysis involved identifying the frequency of CRC Articles cited in qualifications by State Parties in "Declarations and Reservations to the Convention on the Rights of the Child."

Table 2. CRC Article Mentions in "Declarations and Reservations to the Convention on the Rights of the Child"

Article	Focal Issue of Article	Frequency of Mention
21	Child protection in adoption	17
14	Child right to freedom of thought, conscience, religion	14
7	Child right to birth registration, name, & nationality	12
37	Child protection from punishment	12
38	Protection of children affected by armed conflict	12
2	Child protection from discrimination	8
9	Protection from separation from parents	8
40	Protection in the administration of juvenile justice	8
10	Child right to entering/leaving country for family unification	7
13	Child right to freedom of expression	7
15	Child right to freely associate & peaceful assembly	7
16	Child right to privacy	7

Note. There were no mentions for Articles 27, 33–36, 42–50, 52–54.
For the remainder of Articles, there were 6–1 mentions.

As shown in Table 2, several Articles emerge as particularly contentious by the relative frequency of mentions, while others were mentioned infrequently or not at all. The analysis revealed that the most frequently qualified Articles are Article 21 on child protection in adoption (17 State Party mentions), Article 14 on the child's right to freedom of thought, conscience, and religion (14 State Party mentions), Article 7 on the child's right to birth registration, name, and nationality (12 State Party mentions), Article 37 on child protections against punishment (12 mentions), and Article 38 related to treatment and participation in armed conflict, in particular assurances to not be recruited before the age of 15 (12 mentions). While those 12 Articles received the majority of mentions, another 17 articles received between 1 and 6 mentions, and 25 Articles were not mentioned at all. Another way to summarize these data is that 5 Articles were cited in 46% of the State Party declarations and reservations, while the remaining 44% were spread across 11 Articles.

Interestingly, 10 of the 12 Articles mentioned most frequently are focused on rights emphasizing children's self-determination. For example, children's rights to freedom of thought (Article 14), freedom of expression (Article 13), right to freely associate (Article 14), and right to privacy (Article 16) are explicitly related to self-determination. Others, in contrast, are more implicitly related to self-determination, such as Article 37 that claims protection from punishment and Article 10 that claims the child's right to enter/leave the country for family unification. While these are based in part on nurturance principles, qualifying children's rights to protection from punishment could also be qualifying their right to speak out against laws or practices they find unjust. Because relatively few articles overall focus on children's self-determination (approximately 25% as cited above), it is important to note that qualifications focus disproportionately on those self-determination rights. Articles that no State Party questioned had to do with protecting children against various kinds of abuse and exploitation (sexual abuse, exposure to substance abuse, abduction, and other exploitation), the State Party implementation and monitoring of CRC procedures, and language.

With this analysis extended beyond the CRC treaty to the Declarations and Reservations, we observe, for example, how children's rights occur within and are limited by the rights of State Parties. We see, moreover, in the declarations that children's rights are qualified in terms of political and cultural priorities of the State Party. The analysis, thus, revealed that ensuring children's self-determination is viewed as more problematic for State Parties than protecting children from certain ills. In addition to noting this tension between children's rights and State Party rights, the analysis foregrounds the relative lack of an explanation for children's sociopolitical development and rights-based understandings, beliefs, and actions.

Based on the qualifying activity examined in the declarations and reservations, we can raise questions about the definition and possibility of children's self-determination rights. If children's rights to freedom of thought, self-expression, free association, etc. can be limited by State Party and family rights, what is the implied explanation of children's development of capacities related to these abilities? How does such limiting of children's rights exploit the lack of explicitness in particular about the nature of children's sociopolitical development and rights-based understandings in the CRC system? Does the implicit maturational model allow the rights of families and states to override the rights of the immature child? Do assumptions about socialization compromise children's rights by implying that their views will inevitably mirror those of their elders?

There are several directions to pursue in addressing these questions. Embedding children's rights in nation's rights is necessary for negotiating a children's rights treaty. Qualifications also allow for cultural diversity, but equating children's rights to cultural-political rights of their elders limits the possibility that they would contest the status quo. If that is the case, we ask "What is the nature of children's self-determination defined in the CRC system?" What mechanisms are there in the CRC system to address how children's perspectives might differ from those of their parents and national institutions?

Monitoring and Reporting

The next section further foregrounds the tensions between children's rights and nation's rights inherent in the CRC activity-meaning system. While qualifying activity privileges the State Party perspective, monitoring and reporting open the field of debate to the international and local areas. Monitoring occurs by the international organizations of the United Nations Security Council and the U.N. Committee on the Rights of the Child. State Parties and nongovernmental organizations are involved in reporting to those international organizations, which creates an implicit monitoring by the nonstate actors. Table 1 lists a sequence of monitoring and reporting documents by international, State, and nonstate actors to illustrate the CRC activity-meaning system. In addition to gathering these documents as illustrations of the broader CRC activity-meaning system, I analyzed the dialogical nature of interactions across actors in the system.

The sequence of documents listed in Table 1 extends the CRC negotiation process beyond the statement of the treaty (no. 1 on Table 1) and the privilege of State Parties to qualify their ratifications (no. 2 on Table 1) to a process of monitoring and reporting (United Nations Treaty Collection, 9 October, 2001). This iterative sequence of interactions includes monitoring by the international organizations, included here with the U.N. General Assembly Security Council Agenda Item no. 63 noting violations of CRC articles by certain State Parties (no. 3 on Table 1), and the CRC Committee monitoring activity focused on Colombia, which had been previously noted for violations (no. 4 and no. 5 on Table 1). Each State-Party must periodically present reports on their efforts to ensure children's rights, 2 years after ratifying the CRC and then in 5- year intervals. They are also required to respond to violations and concerns noted by the international committees.

Interactions across this sequence of documents are quite explicit. For example, the U.N. Security Council cited Colombia, along with several other countries, for violations and concerns about allowing children to fight in that country's internal conflict. In its 3rd periodic report, Colombia then acknowledged that "The most critical aspect of the Colombian reality today is the internal armed conflict" (Colombian Government, 2004). A subsequent CRC Committee monitoring document referred to the issue of displaced children: "The Committee takes note of the State party's [Colombia's] intention to increase resources to internally displaced children, however expresses grave concern of the very high number of children who continue to be displaced in Colombia, the 3rd largest number of displaced persons in the world" (www.unhcr.org).

The CRC Committee then directed Colombia to address a "List of issues . . . in connection with the consideration of the third periodic report of Colombia," stating further that "Under this section the State party is requested to submit in written form additional and updated information, if possible, before 5 April 2006." The State-Party report then replied to "the list of issues raised," again acknowledged that "the most critical problem in Colombia today is the internal armed conflict," and offered assurances that it has implemented "programs relating to children that have been developed by responsible institutions."

Another voice in this CRC system is the civil society sector, represented by The NGO Group of nongovernmental organizations. The NGO Group Liason Unit "supports participation of the NGOs, particularly national coalitions, in the reporting process to the Committee on the Rights of the Child . . . to ensure the implementation of the Convention," especially through their production of

"Alternative Reports" (http://www.crin.org/NGOGroupforCRC/index.asp). An example of such a report is the "Alternative report to the report of the government of Colombia on the situation of rights of the child in Colombia (2005)." This report acknowledges that the Colombian government had assumed certain responsibilities for children's rights, yet this document also criticizes the government's lack of effectiveness in improving the situation of Colombian children, especially children of the poor, whom the report states as an overwhelming majority of the population.

The Alternative Report quotes the government, for example, as proposing "to incorporate in the military program of 'peasant soldiers' approximately 100,000 youth" (Alternative Report, p. 13). Also taken up in this report is the government's negotiation and amnesty of paramilitary groups who prey upon children: "Amongst the main concerns [are] that the negotiations have denied the root causes of serious human rights abuses committed by the paramilitaries; . . . that negotiations have been carried out in spite of [the fact that] these groups continue to commit crimes; that there have not been taken the necessary measures to dismantle and disarticulate their ties with members of the official armed forces or to guarantee the rights of victims and the society to truth" (Alternative Report, p. 13). Such claims of the government failure to protect youth from participation in armed conflict include quotes by children: "I was promised a job and that they were going to pay me one million [Colombian pesos] for each guerilla leader that I killed. I am expert in explosives and then I can work planning mines and other explosives" (Alternative Report, p. 79). Like the reports by the Colombian government, such reports are directed explicitly to the Committee of the CRC, but there is also implicit dialogue among the actors within Colombia.

As we have seen, monitoring and reporting activities expand the CRC activity-meaning system by increasing the dialogue among local participants and by including children's perspectives, especially by introducing "Alternative Reports," which check state power and often include children directly in the CRC process. Nevertheless, across the CRC systems, the child continues to be represented as the object of children's rights discourse, rather than as an agent in the process of interpreting rights and violations of rights. The analysis above reveals the dilemma of rights system that protects children by embedding them as family and state possessions rather than as collectively empowered agents in society. Although there may be no obvious way out of the dilemma within the state of the art of international diplomacy at the present time, we can advance inquiry about children's rights by continuing to pose questions about how children develop and how they understand precisely those rights-based issues their governments and families challenge. Toward this end, it behooves us to find ways to include young people's perspectives more explicitly and systematically in research on the CRC system.

Research inspired by sociocultural theory positing that children's development interacts with the specific circumstances of their every day lives, such as conflicts and injustices they face, offers insights about the context-dependent nature of children's reasoning about sociopolitical issues relevant to rights-based discourse. Several examples follow to illustrate how eliciting children's perspectives about contentious sociopolitical issues belie assumptions about maturation and socialization. These examples suggest the need for increasingly systematic research to assess whether children's experiences with rights violations lead to understandings that occur earlier than maturational theories would posit and how those experiences might lead to understandings that differ from those of their elders.

Integrating Children's Perspectives in the CRC Activity-Meaning System

Because children's rights are embedded in the rights of nations, primarily in the guise of protection of the "evolving capacities" of the gradually maturing child, research can make a major contribution by considering the sociopolitical nature of development. Given the theoretical and practical ambiguity of the CRC activity-meaning system in establishing the basis of children's rights-based reasoning, we draw on research that elicits children's understandings about conflict and diversity, two rights-related issues that State Parties qualify.

To integrate young people's explicit participation in the broader CRC system, it is important that their voices come in as more than anecdotal quotes. Systematic research with young people reflecting on issues where their rights have been compromised suggests that they reason in complex ways at relatively younger ages than we would expect from a maturational or socialization perspective. Three studies eliciting children's perspectives in relation to local crises suggest the complexity of children's reasoning about issues related to rights and the fact that this reasoning does not necessarily echo that of the elders entrusted to advocate on their behalf.

In her recent ethnographic study with children involved in armed conflict, Sta. Maria (2006) described a situation in the Philippines where children as young as 11 are recruited into civil struggles in spite of the State's ratification of the CRC and laws against recruiting minors. Explaining the pathways of Filipino children's participation in armed conflict, Sta. Maria explains that armed insurgency groups such as the New People's Army (NPA) and the Moro Islamic Liberation Front (MILF) provide orphaned and impoverished children with nurturance and a community in exchange for their participation in conflict-related tasks.

Based on interviews with children in the Philippines, Sta. Maria reports that children's experiences with violence become the basis for their development. Sandra, for example, explained that she had joined the NPA to escape poverty and an abusive family situation as a child. In addition to finding protection and opportunity in the NPA activities, Sandra also learned that when she left home, her "stepfather stopped beating her mother." Expressing her problem-solving further, Sandra explained, "If I have the chance, I want to go to college and study something related to what I did as a medic in the NPA – I was good at what I did, I even used to operate on those who were shot... Mama asked me why I wanted to stay with the NPA. I told her that I wanted to experience life as an NPA... Back then, I wasn't afraid of dying... At least I had a chance to tell my Mama the reasons why I was going. It was the first time I told her about how I felt," (Sta. Maria, 2006, p. 35). Examining such thinking to identify how young people like Sandra define nurturance and self-determination rights in relation to specific challenges and opportunities in their environments seems a productive step toward establishing context-sensitive methods and definitions of children's rights-based reasoning.

Another study asked young people to reflect on their experiences and needs at the end of the 1990s war in the Balkans. In that context, where the state and adult generation had been silencing talk of war to protect children from the horrors they had experienced, children spoke clearly about their rights to learn about their history, including the recent wars. Based on interviews with children and their parents in two areas of the Balkans, researchers report that both Serb and Croatian children said they wanted to know more about the war and explained why this knowledge is important (Freedman & Abazovic, 2006). The tension between parents' view of protection and the children's need for participation shouts out in these typically conflicting quotes: "We should learn about the causes of the war and how disputes should be resolved in order to avoid wars. . . . I believe we should talk about it," while the following is typical of the parents interviewed: "We have been trying not to burden them [the children]. We don't talk about politics at home so we are trying to protect them as much as we can." Children are, moreover, aware of the suppression, as one boy said, "They avoid the subject at home" (Freedman & Abazovic, 2006, p. 23). The issue in this situation is the right to knowledge, which becomes salient in the Balkans because of the ongoing tensions that children observe daily in spite of the silence denying those tensions. Children's thirst for a particular kind of knowledge thus emerges in a specific contentious context.

In the United States, there is also evidence that young people exposed to conflict in urban contexts reason in critical ways. In one study, for example, although the curriculum and teachers in a violence prevention program emphasized resolving conflicts by employing a range of interpersonal communication strategies, 7- through 10-year-old children identifying with African-American, Latino, and immigrant backgrounds noticed that discriminatory practices can make conflict resolution difficult if not impossible. These 7- to 9-year-old children, like the children in the Balkans, spontaneously focused on tensions reflecting broader issues in the society, perhaps those discussed in the privacy of their homes or among trusted peers. The following quote, for example, is the beginning of a longer conversation by two children who were recent immigrants to the U.S.: "What a bad country America is... It has a lot of pollution. I mean look at the manners they have... the bad language... and you can't even get used to them" (Daiute, Stern,

& Lelutiu-Weinberger, 2003, p. 97). Children who feel marginalized in a society may become particularly attuned to such critical details and the fact that it is okay to express such critique among peers but not in larger class discussions, one among many instances of higher order thinking that occurred in this study (Daiute et al., 2003). In the absence of such opportunities to discuss contentious issues, it may seem that children are unable to reflect on them or must be protected from the realities of social marginalization.

The significance of these brief accounts is that they suggest the promise of research on children's rights-based understandings in the context of contentious issues in their every day lives. As they notice and respond to the issues in their environments, children's sociocognitive capacities may emerge differently, suggesting the need for context-sensitive research and practice. Sandra, for example, linked past and future action when pressured to explain her involvement in the guerilla movement; the young Balkans expressed discomfort about something society was trying to protect them from; and the young children in the United States distanced themselves from the powerful mainstream context when they had the protection of like-minded peer support. Across these examples, we hear children using higher order thinking skills, such as Sandra's transformation of a debate with her mother about participation in the NPA into a statement of self-discovery and potential pathway to a productive future and the Balkan children's apparent knowledge of issues that their parents had tried to hide from them.

Future research could usefully explore in more detail whether and how such context-sensitive discourse has an impact on children's rights-based reasoning and action. This approach would build on theory that is specific in terms of the interdependence between individual and societal development, thereby extending beyond maturational and socialization models implicit in the CRC system.

This approach is consistent with other scholars' examination of the influence of context on children's rights-based understandings (Horn, this issue; Peterson-Badali & Ruck, this issue; Sherrod, this issue). Working from theory positing that rights-based reasoning develops in relation to children's experiences, rather than any absolute age-based capacities, recent research has identified differences in children's thinking about rights, citizenship, and sociomoral issues across positions in society. Experiences of maltreatment, ethnicity, socioeconomic status, and their local sociopolitical ideologies affect how they think about the nature and assignment of rights (Peterson-Badali & Ruck, this issue; Sherrod, this issue; Turiel, 2002). Research has also begun to consider interactions of children's thinking about relationships between rights, civic responsibilities (such as acting on behalf of others, including or excluding others, etc.) as functions of children's positions in society (Horn, this issue; Sherrod, this issue). Consistent with this context-sensitive research, a sociocultural activity approach suggests the value of examining children's rights-based reasoning in relation to the specific issues that are contentious in the society, like those qualified across the CRC activity-meaning system and located in monitoring and reporting documents typically at the margins of the system.

Given the sociocultural hypothesis that it is specific situations where critical thinking emerges, such ongoing research would also require methods that allow children to express their rights-based understandings in a range of ways over contexts and time. For this reason, future research could beneficially elicit narratives from children living in situations where their self-determination rights, in particular, might be in conflict with those of the state and other institutions. As we saw in the analysis above, moreover, issues of conflict and intergroup relations tend to be those that State Parties qualified and exempted from their agreement to comply with the CRC. These qualified issues are, thus, contentious, and, I would argue, those issues that are broadly discussed in the society or exposed by uncomfortable silences. From the perspective that children's development is interdependent with the activities in their society, we could expect that conflicts and silences would be highly salient to children in such contexts.

Implications

In summary, this analysis of the representations of the major actors in the CRC activity-meaning system reveals conceptual issues and power relations that limit children's rights. Although the relatively reduced vision of the child addresses the political problem of acquiring ratifications in the short run, the emphasis on nurturance rights at the expense of participation rights limits the potential value of the CRC. By analyzing child development as a social–cultural–political process, rather than as a maturational or socialization processes, we may be better able to identify challenges and define human development in relation to circumstances where children are growing up, including the complex situations that challenge their rights. Consistent with the analysis presented here, I suggest that the issues that the State Party wants to control further in terms of children's rights are contentious ones in the society, such as girls' education or birth control. Based on previous research on interactions among children and youth (Daiute et al., 2003; Giroux, 2001), I posit that it is precisely such contentious issues that are being discussed privately if not publicly among young people. By broadening the unit of analysis to the CRC activity-meaning system, we see how the discourse of children's rights can address contentious issues within state parties and from the perspective of young people. These issues of salience in everyday discourse would, thus, be ones provoking children's critical reflection and perhaps the basis for expression about "matters that affect them," those matters promised and limited in the broader CRC system. I point out these tensions to suggest a theoretical basis and direction for future research, interventions, and ongoing policy-related inquiry. In particular, identifying these tensions suggests the need for research focusing on how children understand the issues that are contentious in a society, such as taboos against discussions or activities, like those related to war, and the transformation of cultural practices related to social, political, or economic change.

Koshy, a human rights scholar, makes another point we can apply to developmental theory: "while the very meaning of utopia seems to impel us toward an exhaustive possibility, an absolute manifestation, or an end-point, . . .We are only always getting there and the horizon keeps moving as we proceed" (1999, p. 27). The many threats to claims for children's rights in the CRC suggest we are far from utopia. If our research could account for detours that occur when children struggle with a range of less-than-ideal circumstances, we may be able to create models that provide new insights about young people's thinking and agency within these situations of social ills that ensnare them.

References

Alternative Report to the Report of the Government of Reporting-monitoring Colombia on the Situation of the Rights of the Child. (www.crin.org)

Bakhtin, M. M. (1986). The problem of speech genres. In C. Emerson & M. Holquist (Eds.), *Speech genres and other late essays* (Trans. Vern W. McGee, pp. 60–102) Austin: University of Texas Press.

Bamberg, M. (2006). Stories: Big or small. Why do we care? *Narrative Inquiry, 16*(1), 139–147.

Bronfenbrenner, U., & Morris, P. (1998). The ecology of developmental processes. In W. Damon (Gen. Ed) & R. M. Lerner (Vol. Ed), *Handbook of child psychology: Theoretical models of human development* (Vol. 1, pp. 993–1028). New York: Wiley. *Children's Rights International Network*. (www.crin.org).

Burton, L., Obeidallah, D., & Allison, K. (1996). Ethnographic insights on social context and adolescent development. In R. Jessor, A. Colby, & R. Schweder (Eds.), *Ethnography and human development*. Chicago: University of Chicago Press.

Colombian Government. (2004). *Third report of the Colombian State before the Committee of the Rights of the Child*. Bogota. (www.icbf.gov.co).

CRC, U.N. General Assembly. (1989). *Adoption of a convention on the rights of the child*. New York: United Nations.

Dahbour, O. (2003). Human rights and human needs. *Paper presented at the 2nd International Conference of Human Rights*, Mofid University, Iran.

Daiute, C. (2006). The problem of society in youth conflict. In C. Daiute, Z. Beykont, C. Higson-Smith, & L. Nucci (Eds.), *International perspectives on youth conflict and development* (pp. 3–20). New York: Oxford University Press.

Daiute, C., Stern, R., & Lelutiu-Weinberger, C. (2003). Negotiating violence prevention. *Journal of Social Issues, 59*, 83–101.

Damon, W., & Lerner, R. M. (Eds.). (2006). *Handbook of child psychology, volume 1, theoretical models of human development* (6th ed). New York: Wiley.

Engestrom, Y., & Miettinen, R. (1999). Introduction. In Y. Engestrom, R. Miettinen, & R-L. Punamaki, R-L. (Eds.), *Perspectives on activity theory* (pp. 1–18). New York: Cambridge University Press.

Freedman, S. W., & Abazovic, D. (2006). Growing up during the Balkan wars of the 1990's. In C. Daiute, Z. Beykont, C. Higson-Smith, & L. Nucci (Eds.), *International perspectives on youth conflict and development* (pp. 57–72). New York: Oxford University Press.

Giroux, H. A. (2001). *Theory and resistance: Towards a pedagogy for the opposition*. Westport, CT: Bergin & Garvey.

Harre, R., & Van Langenhove, L. (1999). *Positioning theory: Moral contexts of intentional action*. Malden, MA: Blackwell Publishers

Hart, R. A. (1999). *Children's participation: The theory and practice of including young citizens in community development and environmental care*. New York: UNICEF.

Hart, S. N. (1982). The history of children's psychological rights. *Viewpoints in Teaching and Learning, 58*, 1–15.

Hart, S. N. (1991). From property to person status: Historical perspectives on children's rights. *American Psychologist, 46*, 53–59.

Koshy, S. (1999). From cold war to trade war: Neocolonialism & human rights. *Social Text, 58*(1), 1–32.

Kuper, J. (1997). Reservations, declarations, and objections to the 1989 Convention on the Rights of the Child. In J. P. Gardner (Ed.), *Human rights as general norms and a state's rights to opt out: Reservations and objections to human rights conventions* (pp. 104–113). London, UK: The British Institute of International and Comparative Law.

Landsdown, G. (2005). *The evolving capacities of the child.* Florence, Italy: UNICEF Innocenti Research Center.

Leont'ev, A. N. (1978). *Activity, consciousness, and personality.* Englewood Cliffs, NJ: Prentice-Hall.

Murphy-Berman, V., & Weisz, V. (1996). U.N. Convention on the Rights of the Child: Current challenges. *American Psychologist, 51*, 1231–1233.

Piaget, J. (1968). *Six psychological studies.* New York: W.W. Norton.

Ruck, M. D., Abramovitch, R., & Keating, D. P. (1998). Children's and adolescents' understanding of rights: Balancing nurturance and self-determination. *Child Development, 64*(2), 404–417.

Sta. Maria, M. A. (2006). Paths to Filipino youth involvement in violent conflict. In C. Daiute, Z. Beykont, C. Higson-Smith, & L. Nucci (Eds.), *International perspectives on youth conflict and development* (pp. 29–42). New York: Oxford University Press.

Turiel, E. (2002). *The culture of morality.* New York: Cambridge University Press.

United Nations Treaty Collection (9 October, 2001). Declarations and Reservations. From http://www.unhchr.ch/html/menu3/b/treaty15/_asp.htm.

Vygotsky, L. S. (1978). *Mind in society.* Cambridge, MA: Harvard University Press.

Wertsch, J. (1991). *Voices in the mind.* Cambridge, MA: Harvard University Press.

Wilcox, B. L., & Naimark, H. (1991). The rights of the child: Progress toward human dignity. *American Psychologist, 46*, 1–19.

COLETTE DAIUTE is Professor of Psychology at the Graduate Center, City University of New York. Dr. Daiute does research on social development as an interactive process of individuals and societies. Toward this end, she is doing several case studies to consider diversity within and among young people growing up in the context of political crises and transitions across countries of the former Yugoslavia and in Colombia South America, including migrants to the United States from both regions. Colette Daiute's recent publications include *International perspectives on youth conflict and development* (Oxford University Press, 2006), *Narrative analysis: Studying the development of individuals in society* (Sage Publications, 2004), and "Critical narrating by adolescents in troubled times" (In K. McLean & M. Pasupathi, Eds., *Narrative development in adolescence.* New York: Springer) and "Young people and armed conflict" (A. Furlong, Ed., *Handbook of youth and young adulthood.* UK: Routledge).

Journal of Social Issues, Vol. 64, No. 4, 2008, pp. 725–747

Regardless of Frontiers: Adolescents and the Human Right to Information

Roger J.R. Levesque*

Indiana University

Legal systems struggle to keep pace with rapid technological advances and chang- ing social conditions that provide adolescents with much wanted and unwanted information. We examine this struggle as we note prevailing tensions guiding the development of adolescents' rights. We find that the United States typically adopts an inculcative approach, an approach that generally treats adolescents as in need of control and indoctrination into the values of prior generations. We also find an emerging human rights approach that adopts a more liberative view, one that seeks to bestow adolescents with greater control over their own rights and aims to shape informational environments that allow adolescents to prepare for their own futures. The divergence leads us to explore why adolescent jurisprudence—an approach to law that begins with adolescents' realities and charts ways to develop laws consistent with those realities—would benefit from taking human rights ori- entations more seriously. We end by highlighting how liberative approaches are consistent with our understanding of adolescents' realities and how such ap- proaches appropriately urge us to revisit our society's fundamental commitments to justice.

Tensions Shaping Adolescents' Informational Rights

The First Amendment's Free Speech jurisprudence, which controls our ex- change of information, can be understood as operating within two extremes: one that centers on the control of ideas and inculcation of values and another that fosters freedom to engage in a robust marketplace of ideas (see Redish & Finnerty, 2002). The "inculcation of values" approach views individuals as in need of indoctrina- tion into the established values of prior generations. This approach permits adults

---

*Correspondence concerning this article should be addressed to Roger J.R. Levesque, 302 Sycamore Hall, Indiana University, Bloomington, IN 47405 [e-mail: rlevesqu@indiana.edu].

as well as the majority of professionals working at various levels of government to decide which values are ours and which values are most important for us. The rival, "marketplace of ideas" approach roots in efforts to protect individual liberty, including the freedom of speech. This liberative approach views the essence of our legal system as deriving from the collective wisdom of a multiplicity of un-coerced individual choices that represent a wide variety of ideas of what is good, true, and right. This competing perspective finds suspicious the indoctrination of values through a government-operated control of ideas; it views such inculcation as a hallmark of totalitarianism rather than democratic freedom consistent with the foundational elements of modern human rights law. These two opposing ori-entations have played key roles in modern Free Speech jurisprudence, from the earliest cases (West Virginia State Board of Education v. Barnette, 1943) to the latest (Morse v. Frederick, 2007); and they certainly play a central role in contem-porary legal battles involving speech codes, media access, hateful expressions, and a variety of other efforts to regulate speech and temper its potential destructiveness (see, e.g., Virginia v. Black, 2003; United States v. American Library Association, 2003).

Not surprisingly, the tension caused by the two orientations figures promi-nently in efforts to envision adolescents' informational rights. Each approach em-braces a very different view of adolescent development and adolescents' proper place in society. The inculcation model generally grants parents and other care-takers the right, coupled with the high duty, to prepare adolescents for their appropriate societal role. The approach generally leaves determinations of what constitutes "appropriate" roles in the hands of those who control adolescents' rights. Importantly, the model does not deny that adolescents have rights; the model simply views adults and state actors as best suited to control the nature and exercise of those rights. Conversely, the marketplace approach more readily questions the power adults wield over the information adolescents may receive and impart. Although this view is much less suspicious of parents than it is of governments, it seeks to bestow upon adolescents themselves, as much as prac-ticable, the capacity to control their own informational rights. Under this view, adolescents would control even their right to information and ideas that could con-tradict their parents and other caretakers' views of what would constitute suitable and necessary information for proper adolescent development. Taken to its logical conclusion, this approach obviously can lead to quite radical results—adolescents, which for our purposes include only adolescents under the age of 18, actually no longer would be "minors" in the traditional sense of the term. At bottom, the two rather different approaches create a tension that urges us to approach the right to information by focusing on either of two questions: Should adolescents be treated as young children, as a protected class shielded from ideas, messages, and views? Or, should adolescents be treated as developing individuals who are in the process of becoming adults and, as such, should be exposed to free speech for what it is?

These both are quite fundamental questions, and properly envisioning adolescents' rights requires that we address them both. Both orientations allow us to recognize adolescents' peculiar place in society and law; and, because of that, they allow us to confront better the realities of adolescents' experiences as well as the demands of our rapidly changing civil society.

This article examines adolescents' right to information, both what it is and what it could be. We begin with an examination of what has been touted as the most expansive and liberative view of rights ever imagined: modern international human rights law. Given the complexity and sheer volume of this area of law, we focus directly on Free Speech, especially children's informational rights because international law now has demarked a special place for adolescents in its United Nations Convention on the Rights of the Child ("Children's Convention" or "CRC") (1989). The analysis reveals an expansive view of the right to information, one that goes beyond the typical right to access media and that encompasses, for example, the right to receive and impart information and the creation of environments conducive to the development of skills permitting individuals to engage those environments effectively. We then detail how U.S. law typically approaches adolescents' informational rights as we highlight important differences between U.S. and human rights law. That analysis essentially reveals two competing visions of adolescents' rights, with the human rights framework generally embracing the market of ideas approach and the U.S. approach pervasively espousing the inculcative model. The divergence leads us to explore why adolescent jurisprudence—an approach to law that begins with adolescents' realities and charts ways to develop laws consistent with those realities—would benefit from taking human rights orientations more seriously. Our discussion necessarily moves beyond narrow views of adolescents' access to media and toward a broader conceptualization that recognizes the need to consider more fully the totality of adolescents' private and public informational environments, including, for example, those in families, schools, clinics, justice systems, peer relationships as well as those in formal and informal communities. It is this more expansive view, as we will see, which appropriately captures the pervasively ignored (and undefined) human rights mandate that information rights must be recognized "regardless of frontiers."

The Nature of Adolescents' Human Right to Information

International human rights law arguably provides the strongest statements recognizing adolescents' right to seek, receive, and impart information and ideas. Human rights law boldly recognizes that adolescents possess that human right through any media and regardless of frontiers. The right appears so expansive that human rights law generally does not even make distinctions between the informational rights of adults and those of minors. Human rights law generally tolerates limitations on adolescents' informational rights to the extent that such limits also apply to adults, such as restrictions to protect the public's health, safety, and morals. In addition and even quite radically, human rights law requires governments to take it upon themselves to foster the development of various media to ensure access to information and ideas to the fullest extent possible. Framed in generalities, informational rights under human rights law clearly reveal an expansive right, one that embraces the marketplace orientation and seeks to recognize the need for adolescents to control their own futures. A close look at actual human rights mandates, however, reveals important nuances and restrictions, and those nuances may matter greatly to any effort to recognize and develop adolescents' right to information. These nuances may temper the overall liberative message of the human rights approach, which may leave open whether the more expansive or restrictive approach best serves adolescents' best interests and those of their families and society.

The Children's Convention provides an illustrative and appropriate starting point. The convention directly applies to adolescents, as it defines a child as "every human being below the age of eighteen years unless under the law applicable to the child, majority is attained earlier" (Id., Art. 1). Although one would think that minors would have few informational rights, the convention forthrightly addresses their right to information and defines it quite expansively. The most relevant article, Article 13, reads as follows:

1. The child shall have the right to freedom of expression; this right shall include freedom to seek, receive, and impart information and ideas of all kinds, regardless of frontiers, either orally, in writing or in print, in the form of art, or through any other media of the child's choice.
2. The exercise of this right may be subject to certain restrictions, but these shall only be such as are provided by law and are necessary:
   (a) For respect of the rights or reputations of others; or
   (b) For the protection of national security or of public order (order public), or of public health or morals.

Although the article's first section seems to recognize a radically expansive right, its second section may severely limit the freedom. For example, public order, health, and morals certainly may be interpreted in narrow ways that limit speech. These modifiers at least raise the issue of whether a legal system would construe expressive freedoms as necessarily involving adolescents' morals and in need of control and whether those morals must be treated differently than adults' morals. These are important considerations given the U.S.'s historical and current use of moral justifications for limiting adolescents' rights more than those of adults (Levesque, 2000). In addition, the need to respect the rights of others may prove quite limiting, because, as we will see, U.S. law typically grants parents the right to control their children's rights. This raises the central issue of whether the rights of others include parental rights or the statement simply sets the same limit it does for adults. Reasonable arguments can be made for both sides of these important issues. Clearly, Article 13 has not necessarily resolved the fundamental inculcative and marketplace tensions involved in shaping adolescents' rights. Article 13, however, does not stand alone. Its expansive focus on the marketplace, as well as its limitations harkening the inculcative approach, must be interpreted in light of the convention's other mandates.

The Children's Convention supplements Article 13 with other articles that can expand the right even further and, in some instances, limit it. Most notably, the convention requires States Parties (countries that formally commit themselves to abiding by the treaty) to assure the child who is capable of forming his or her own views the right to express those views freely in all matters affecting the child; it further requires that the views of the child be given due weight in accordance with the child's age and maturity (Id., Art. 12). The convention also requires governments to "respect the right of the child to freedom of thought, conscience and religion (Id., Art. 14, § 1), a requirement that respects rights of parents or legal guardians to direct the exercise of this freedom in a manner consistent with the evolving capacities of the child" (Id., Art. 14, § 2). As with the right to information, the freedom to manifest one's religion or beliefs may be subject only to such limitations as are prescribed by law and are necessary to protect public safety, order, health or morals, or the fundamental rights and freedoms of others (Id., § 3). Informational rights also are furthered by the recognition that governments also "shall ensure that the child has access to information and material from a diversity of national and international sources, especially those aimed at the promotion of his or her social, spiritual and moral well-being and physical and mental health" (Id., Art. 17). The right to information also finds protection in the freedoms of association and peaceful assembly (Id., Art. 15), where the convention again rejects all restrictions on the exercise of these rights other than those imposed in conformity with the law and which are necessary in a democratic society in the interests of national security or public safety, public order, the protection of public health or morals, or the protection of the rights and freedoms of others. Again, however, the concern for public health and morals also limits opportunities for expression as the convention urges the protection of children from sexual exploitation by forbidding, for example, the exploitative use of children in pornographic performances and materials (Id., Art. 34). Yet another potential limitation comes in the manner the convention also seeks to respect the rights, responsibilities and duties of parents, and others acting as parents to protect the rights of children; but the convention limits the control others have on adolescents to the extent that it requires those controlling adolescents to provide, in a manner consistent with the evolving capacities of the child, appropriate direction and guidance in the child's exercise of recognized rights (Id., Art. 5). Equally significant, the convention requires public or private social welfare institutions, courts of law, administrative authorities, and legislative bodies to adopt the best interests of the child as the primary consideration in all actions involving children (Id., Art. 3). Very importantly for jurisdictions that place a high priority on privacy, the convention pointedly states that "No child shall be subjected to arbitrary or unlawful interference with his or her privacy" (Id., Art. 16), and makes no mention of permissible restrictions on that right to privacy. Last, the convention requires all States Parties to ensure the implementation of recognized rights in their countries (Id., Art. 4). Together, these are rather expansive rights that push existing boundaries, such as through the need to consider "evolving capacities"—an open invitation to recognizing the period of adolescence and granting adolescents greater control over their rights. But boundaries still exist, such as the need to respect the rights of parents and others who have control over adolescents; and how those rights will figure in the eventual development of adolescents' rights remains to be seen. The convention may not mandate the weight granted to specific rights, but the recognition that adolescents can increasingly control their own rights certainly means a reduction in the weight typically granted to those of others.

Although the Children's Convention's recognition of children's rights has its important limits, the rights it enshrines clearly rival the human rights movement's recognition of adults' rights. This recognition of children's human rights law leads many to view the convention as a radical departure from human rights law (e.g., because of its apparent movement away from parental rights and its embracing private enforcement of rights, Levesque, 1996). Yet a close look at human rights law reveals that the convention actually was not, in many ways, that imaginative and groundbreaking in its recognition of the human right to information. The convention's drafters essentially lifted the materials from two prior human rights treaties, the Universal Declaration of Human Rights ("Universal Declaration") (1948) and the International Covenant on Civil and Political Rights (1966). These treaties essentially provided the template that recognizes, for example, that "*Everyone* has the right to . . . seek, receive and impart information and ideas through any media and regardless of frontiers" (Universal Declaration, Art. 19 [emphasis added]). These, and other treaties like them, provide a substantial foundation: they do not make age-based distinctions and, equally importantly, the United States has ratified and committed itself to enforcing some of them through its own laws. Together, these quite striking protections reveal the remarkable extent to which governments, including the United States, recognize the need to take informational rights seriously. Equally impressive is the very limited extent to which the legal instruments take it upon themselves to limit the rights of adolescents.

Human Rights Law's Departure from U.S. Laws Addressing Adolescents' Informational Rights

We already have seen that the international enumeration of rights that include adolescents' rights to information does not necessarily resolve the fundamental tension involving whether we should give power to adults and state officials to control adolescents' rights or grant adolescents' increasing power to control their own marketplace of ideas. Most notably, the important limitations based on public order, health, and morals, as well as the rights of others, clearly allow for important restrictions on adolescents' informational rights. Yet, taken as a whole, international enumerations of adolescents' rights tend to move toward granting adolescents greater rights, both in the form of actual control of those rights and in the form of fostering environments that would provide greater opportunities for adolescents to develop abilities to exercise those rights. The potential to increase recognition and respect for adolescents' rights leads us to examine the extent to which such an approach would differ from U.S. laws. A proper examination of adolescents' informational rights places those rights within a general orientation to adolescents' place in the law. As suggested earlier, we will find a striking divergence between the approach espoused by the United States and that of human rights law. That divergence suggests that, if taken seriously, human rights approaches should dramatically transform our vision of adolescents' informational rights.

Arguably the most remarkable feature of human rights law involves the manner it actually provides a statement about rights that directly includes adolescents. By default, the Children's Convention covers all children up to the age of 18. American jurisprudence only haphazardly addresses adolescents' informational rights. Despite the United States' vigorous commitment to the First Amendment freedom of speech, this lack of clear rules is not surprising. Even First Amendment law as applied to adults leaves much unsettled and actually leaves open many possible ways to either limit or allow expression (see, e.g., Virginia v. Black, 2003), including the right to information (see, e.g., United States v. American Library Association, 2003). Adolescents' First Amendment rights must meet challenges similar to those adults face. In addition to those challenges, adolescents' rights are further unsettled because of adolescents' peculiar status. As a result, the extent to which adolescents gain free speech protections fluctuates within different contexts and with different adolescents.

The major reason for fluctuations in U.S. law's approach to adolescents' informational rights rests on the extent to which the legal system allows governments to limit the rights of individuals deemed as incapable of exercising their own rights. This constitutes yet another important divergence from human rights law. The U.S. legal system generally bestows adolescents' rights on adults who care for adolescents, rather than on the adolescents themselves. Parents retain the fundamental right to raise their children as they see fit. This general rule pervades adolescent jurisprudence and finds unshakable precedent in U.S. law. The now classic, illustrative case, *Wisconsin v. Yoder* (1972), considered whether parents could remove their adolescent children from public schools. The parents' central claim involved their fear that "high school tends to emphasize intellectual and scientific accomplishments, self-distinction, competitiveness, worldly success, and social life with other students," all of which the parents had found incompatible with their Amish values (Id., p. 211). The Court ruled in favor of the parents and did not even consider the rights of the adolescents to express their own views on the matter. Even more strikingly, the Court expressly ruled in favor of the parents because their children had reached adolescence and were susceptible to mainstream ideas and culture. *Yoder* thus stands for the general rule that parents have the right to limit their adolescents' access to ideas, even ideas for which society has developed vast systems to inculcate and otherwise has deemed as instrumental for proper individual and civic development. By default and by state support, constitutional jurisprudence ensures that parents enjoy the plenary right to dictate the informational environments that will influence their children's lives. If there were any disagreements before, *Wisconsin v. Yoder* (1972) clearly put them to rest as it roundly defeated efforts to challenge the role of parents in controlling their adolescents' marketplace of ideas.

The human rights approach also substantially differs from U.S. law in that it explicitly requires legal systems to consider the "evolving capacities" of minors when considering the extent to which they should control their rights. The United States actually has developed a similar mechanism, but its use has yet to apply broadly to adolescents' rights given that parents tend to be deemed as in control of those rights. The leading Supreme Court case in this area, *Bellotti v. Baird* (1979), involved the right to privacy in the context of making decisions about obtaining abortions. The Court held that a state may require a pregnant minor to obtain parental consent for an abortion (which involves the right to privacy), unless she can convince a judge either that she is mature enough to make the decision independently or that the abortion is in her best interests. Yet, in that case, the Court also emphasized that states could limit adolescents' freedom because, among other reasons, "during the formative years of childhood and adolescence, minors often lack the experience, perspective, and judgment to recognize and avoid choices that could be detrimental to them" (Id., p. 635). The Court offered three factors that traditionally have been used to justify distinguishing the rights of minors from those of adults: (a) the "peculiar vulnerability" of children; (b) their presumed "inability to make critical decisions in an informed, mature manner"; and (c) the significance of the "parental role in child rearing" (Id., p. 634). Importantly, however, the use of what has become known as the "mature minor" rule is far from expansive. Especially in the context of information and ideas, courts tend to focus on the particular vulnerabilities of minors, as we will see below, and presumptively assume that adolescents need not have a voice in these matters, let alone recognize adolescents as being capable of exercising their rights and as not needing to involve their parents when seeking, imparting, or using certain types of information.

The human rights approach also diverges considerably from the U.S. approach to the right to receive information. A small number of cases now directly addresses the extent to which adolescents may gain access to information the government controls. The law, in this regard, clearly allows for governmental restriction of access, even access to information critical to adolescents' healthy development. The leading case in this area, *Bowen v. Kendrick* (1988), let stand the public funding of abstinence-based-only sexuality education programs and pro-adoption-only reproductive services provided by religious institutions that may not necessarily provide the type of comprehensive services secular institutions could otherwise provide adolescents. As a result, the Supreme Court let stand the service provision even though the resulting bias most likely will not be known to adolescent clients and adolescent clients may actually be in vulnerable positions that make it unlikely that they will be able to exercise their own convictions without knowing other options available to them (Levesque, 2002a). Another important case, *Board of Education v. Pico* (1982, p. 867), would actually recognize students' "right to receive ideas" in the context of school officials' removal of books from libraries. But that recognition still granted schools considerable freedom to decide which books it would place in their libraries; and it also accorded schools, in designing their curricula, substantial discretion to control minors' access to ideas. The Court would later revisit the right of the government to censor ideas in the context of public libraries; and it would use the opportunity to provide full support for the state's broad power to limit patrons' access to information as a condition attached to the library's receipt of federal funds (United States v. American Library Association, 2003).

The U.S. law also very much limits the human right to impart ideas through the media of one's choice, a limitation that contradicts the spirit of the human right to express ideas in any media. Two leading cases in this area reveal the remarkable restrictions placed on adolescents' rights in the contexts in which they are most likely to want to express themselves and reach their peers. In *Hazelwood School District v. Kuhlmeier* (1988) the Court permitted school officials to censor the content of an official high school newspaper. The Court allowed school officials to delete two articles, one dealing with teen pregnancy and another with teen experiences with parental divorce, because they were deemed too sensitive and unsuitable for their peers. A few years earlier, the Court had allowed school officials to censor political speech during school assemblies. The Court did so in *Bethel School District No. 403 v. Fraser* (1986) and on the grounds that the school officials had the power to direct the type of speech it wanted to inculcate in its students (in this instance, the speech had sexual innuendos) and control its educational message. Both cases have been interpreted as granting schools sweeping authority to control school activities (Levesque, 2002b). Indeed, under the *Hazelwood* standard, if student expression interferes with the school's power "to assure that participants learn whatever lessons the activity is designed to teach," school officials may restrict it (Hazelwood School District v. Kuhlmeier, 1988, p. 271). Although controversial, the standard was recently upheld by a recent case that supported a public school's authority to prohibit speech advocating illegal activities, even when the speech was made off school grounds but still at a school sponsored event. That case, *Morse v. Frederick* (2007), involved a principal's confiscation of a student's banner briefly displayed to those who were waiting for the Olympic Torch Relay to pass through Juneau, Alaska. The Court supported the principal's conduct, including her decision to suspend the student for several days, based on the finding that the banner's message, "BONG HiTS 4 JESUS," reasonably could be interpreted as encouraging illegal drug use, which violated established school policy. Together, these are quite important cases because they limit severely the prior cases that had given adolescents, at least in school contexts, the right to exercise political rights (Tinker v. Des Moines Independent Community School District, 1969) as well as the right not to take part in exercises that would require them to express ideas they did not believe (West Virginia State Board of Education v. Barnette, 1943).

In contexts that human rights law permits restrictions, the U.S. approach has been less than consistent. For example, human rights mandates potentially allow restrictions on adolescents' rights due to public morals, order or health. The United States does permit states to restrict minors' right to receive or express information deemed morally problematic for adolescents and their healthy development, and it permits those restrictions even when laws protect adults' rights to the same materials. The most obvious restriction takes the form of "variable obscenity" in which materials that are obscene for one group (adolescents) may not be obscene for another (adults), which allows for restricting the target group's access to the materials. The leading case in this area, *Ginsberg v. New York* (1968), involved the conviction of a magazine vendor for selling an adult magazine to a 16-year-old boy. The Court upheld the conviction as it explained that, although the magazine clearly was not obscene for adults, the state had acted within First Amendment bounds in adopting a distinct, broader definition of obscenity for minors. Because obscene speech enjoys no First Amendment protection, states under *Ginsberg* may completely bar minors from receiving materials deemed obscene for them but not for adults. Importantly, the protections are not entirely protective because parents may do what the states cannot. Parents remain free to provide indecent (but not obscene as to adults) materials to their children; indeed, a major rationale for upholding the statute at issue in *Ginsberg* was that it helped parents control the upbringing of their children, including their access to information. In addition to this broad rule, adolescents clearly may not be obscene or even express what would be indecent (and thus permissible) if they were adults. Another leading case in this area, *New York v. Ferber* (1982), allowed states to prohibit the distribution of pornographic materials involving adolescents. Given that the case actually involved two teenage boys engaged in apparently noncoercive sexual acts, the case also incidentally involved the rights of minors to express their sexuality. *Ferber* had held not only that society may limit materials harmful to minors but also that society must be able to limit materials derived from minors. Indeed, it was the involvement of minors in the production of the materials that provided the Court with its strongest rationale for limiting the expression. The Court would embrace the approach when dealing with broadcast media. In *FCC v. Pacifica Foundation* (1978, pp. 749–750), the Supreme Court restricted the broadcast of speech that was merely "indecent," not "obscene as to minors" under *Ginsberg*, largely because minors might hear the indecent speech. And, as with *Ginsberg*, parents remained free to expose their children to restricted materials. In both *Ginsberg* and *Pacifica*, the goal was to limit the general exposure of problematic materials to youth.

Important cases after *Ginsberg*, *Ferber*, and *Pacifica* revealed the extent to which the rationales for protecting adolescents from harm actually are not necessarily taken that seriously and may not be particularly persuasive. The Court actually has placed important limits on this line of cases; and those limits render suspect the validity of the rationales in these contexts. For example, the Court declined to extend *Pacifica* to other media. The Court has not extended the rationale to telephone communications (Sable Communications of California, Inc. v. FCC, 1989). In addition, and rather importantly, the Court has not extended the rationale to efforts that have aimed to regulate the Internet (see Reno v. American Civil Liberties Union, 1997). Both of these media allow more free expression, which permits adolescents to have greater access to them (both in terms of receiving and imparting information) and accessing the same types of materials other cases deemed problematic for adolescents. In addition, the Court has recognized limits on the *Ginsberg* principle. First, the Supreme Court has made clear that states may not simply ban minors' exposure to a full category of speech, such as nudity, when only a subset of that category can plausibly be deemed "obscene" for them. This was the rule that allowed the Court to strike down an ordinance prohibiting drive-in movie theaters from showing any movies containing nudity if visible from the street (Erznoznik v. City of Jacksonville, 1975) and to lift a federal ban on mailing unsolicited contraceptive advertisements (Bolger v. Youngs Drug Products Corporation, 1983). These cases, respectively, sought to protect the rights of the public and parents to access information, moreso than to protect the rights of adolescents themselves. Second, the Court recently has suggested that states must determine *Ginsberg*-type "obscenity" by reference to the entire population of minors—including the oldest minors, whose faculties are not as limited as *Ginsberg* presumes younger minors to be. Thus, in *Reno v. American Civil Liberties Union* (1997), the Court distinguished the statute at issue in *Ginsberg* from the Communications Decency Act on the ground that the *Ginsberg* "harmful to minors" law had not applied to 17-year-olds. The Court went on to stress "that the strength of the Government's interest in protecting minors is not equally strong throughout the [age] coverage of this broad statute" (Id., p. 878). But it would be a stretch to conclude that this concern provided the Court's strongest rationale rather than the concern for protecting the free exchange of ideas over the Internet (see, most recently, Ashcroft v. American Civil Liberties Union, 2004). These important cases reveal that the United States does exhibit some movement away from the inculcative approach to adolescents' informational rights, but the reason for doing so has less to do with the need to recognize the rights of adolescents than it does the need to protect the rights of parents and other adults to access and impart information.

When adolescents are not within the direct control of parents or an institution like a school, their rights typically mirror those of adults. This mirroring, however and again, typically has to do more with the need to protect adults' rights than it does with a particular concern about adolescents' rights. For example, the Court in *R.A.V. v. City of St. Paul* (1992) did not distinguish adolescents from adults when it ruled that individuals have the right to speak racist and hateful speech in public. Notably, that case involved a group of white adolescents who had fashioned a cross from broken chair legs and had burned it on the lawn of a black family. The Court unanimously agreed that the legal system must protect such expressions, even undoubtedly harmful expressions. In *R.A.V.*, however, the Court did not even consider the minority status of the adolescents; it seemed more concerned with establishing a rule protecting expression. As applied to adolescents, the rule makes considerable sense in light of another Court ruling holding that adolescents could be punished more severely for criminal actions if those actions resulted from hate. This was the ruling in *Wisconsin v. Mitchell* (1993), which upheld the state's penalty-enhancement statute for hate crimes, a result that stands for the state's freedom to regulate proscribed conduct and to impose higher sentences for crimes motivated by thoughts and beliefs. The distinction between the cases is important because the perpetrators of hate crimes cannot shield themselves with First Amendment speech protections when they commit crimes in order to express their hatred. The approach is rather significant—it allows individuals to express themselves and it assumes that they can determine their actions—regardless of whether they are adolescents. In the name of protecting society, then, the legal system allows for treating adolescents like adults, which results, in this regard, in infringing on their rights to act on ideas. The extent to which adolescents are given rights may well be debatable but this line of cases makes clear that, especially when broader societal concerns are at issue, adolescents typically are treated like everyone else and given reduced rights.

Moving beyond the right to receive and impart information into other rights that would help foster an environment conducive to a fuller exercise of those rights, we again see how the international movement would move U.S. law into important directions. Several examples again are illustrative when we compare U.S. law with those of the Children's Convention. The most obvious constitutional issues addressed by the Supreme Court that would need to be reconsidered in a more systematic manner include those directly involving the freedom to practice one's own religion and deep convictions (compare Article 30 with Prince v. Massachusetts, 1944), the right to privacy (compare Article 16 with Hodgson v. Minnesota, 1990), the right to education (compare Article 29 with San Antonio Independent School District v. Rodriguez, 1973), the right to be heard in proceedings directly affecting them (compare Article 12 with Parham v. J.R., 1979), protection from child abuse and neglect (compare Article 19 with DeShaney v. Winnebago County Dept. of Soc. Services, 1989; Suter v. Artist, M., 1992), freedom of association and the right to social development (compare Article 15 with Dallas v. Stanglin, 1989), right to medical care (compare Article 24 with Harris v. McRae, 1980), right to public assistance (compare Article 27 with Dandridge v. Williams, 1970), and right to control private associations (compare Article 8 with Troxel v Granville, 2000; Michael H. v. Gerald D., 1989). All of these constitutional issues were resolved by precedent-setting cases related to minor's access to information and relationships as well as the extent to which our society structures institutions so that adolescents can benefit from such information. These cases would be important to consider in that, unlike the international movement, these cases do not impose positive duties for government action; instead they reveal the ability to respect rights simply by government inaction. Unlike the U.S. approach, the human rights approach contains a vision of society in which the state actively supports adolescents and fosters environments conducive to fulfilling their basic human rights.

The Increasing Need for "Adolescent Jurisprudence" to Take Human Rights Orientations More Seriously

The potential differences in United States and human rights law necessarily lead us to consider the extent to which U.S. law would benefit from taking human rights law seriously. The human rights movement and U.S. law have yet to move toward a single vision of adolescents' proper place in law and society. Indeed, there actually is yet no such thing as a coherent "adolescent jurisprudence." As applied to adolescents' informational rights, the United States generally adopts an inculcative approach that grants parents and adults control over adolescents' rights whereas the human rights approach tends to press for a free market of ideas, one that bestows adolescents with greater control over their own rights. Although it would be unwise to champion extremes of either approach, it increasingly becomes clear that the U.S. approach would benefit from considering human rights mandates more seriously. Our current understanding of adolescent development and the situations in which adolescents find themselves favor revisioning the U.S. approach to adolescents' informational rights.

Adolescents could benefit from access to information necessary for them to exercise their recognized rights, act in their own best interests, live up to civic aspirations, and lead a more fulfilling life. Adolescents could benefit from access to medical and social service information to protect themselves from, for example, sexually transmitted diseases, relationship violence, unwanted pregnancy, and other harms associated with intimate relationships (Levesque, 2000, 2003). Adolescents further could benefit from information they are presumed to have. Many interactions between adolescents and law enforcement, for example, treat adolescents like adults and fail to account for adolescents' developing abilities, knowledge and skills (Levesque, 2006). Adolescents also could benefit from information that would contribute to society's democratic ideals. For example and generally unrecognized, adolescents could have a right to information that would foster their understanding of race, culture, and alternative worldviews—all of which could foster the type of democratic, multicultural society and civic responsibility envisioned by law (Levesque, 2002b). Adolescents also could benefit from access to information relating to their mental and spiritual health, such as access to information about mental health services (Levesque, 2002b) and different religions and spiritual beliefs (Levesque, 2002a). Adolescents clearly could benefit from the development of informational rights that would recognize adolescents' needs and further other recognized rights.

The need to reconsider adolescents' rights to information certainly deals more than with its potential role in furthering adolescents' rights; the need also stems from the law's necessity to reflect more forthrightly adolescents' realities. By far the most important informational challenge facing society and adolescents involves the rapid move toward informational independence. For adolescents, this informational independence means that adolescents now have more access to different media than ever before; and much of that media is individualized to pique their interest and consumed without much adult supervision and control (see Roberts & Foehr, 2004). This independence gains significance when it occurs in the absence of social-psychological foundations that would better ensure adolescents' opportunities to adjust responsibly to unparalleled technological advances and changing social conditions that foster that independence. Our society's response, especially its failed response, to popular media currently best illustrates the need to respond more effectively to adolescents' informational environments.

Informational independence continues even despite evidence that, whether wittingly or unwittingly, adolescents increasingly take seriously wanted and unwanted media information, ideas, and images. We know, for example, that certain types of media content, such as portrayals of violence (Huesmann, Moise, Podolski, & Eron, 2003), drug use (Thompson, 2005), and sexuality (Brown, 2002; Ward, 2003) as well as the media's push toward various forms of consumerism (Chaplin & John, 2005; Gunter, Oates, & Blades, 2005; Valkenburg, 2000), potentially play powerful roles in adolescents' identity development. Empirical evidence leaves no doubt that information emanating from various media influences adolescent's developing sense of self. The role of this new information independence has led media researchers to list mass media as equal in importance to most other socializing agents, including such traditional institutions as parents, schools, and churches (see Christenson & Roberts, 1998; Strasburger & Wilson, 2002).

The new place of information in adolescent development becomes most problematic to the extent that it subjects adolescents to the media's risks. For example, longitudinal studies now link even a modest diet of television watching (less than 2 hours a day) during childhood and adolescence to adverse health indicators that include obesity, poor fitness, smoking, and raised cholesterol levels (Hancox, Milne, & Poulton, 2004). Numerous studies also report negative relationships between various measures of adolescents' academic performance and exposure to television (Neuman, 1995), music media (Christenson & Roberts, 1998), and to video games and computer games (Leiberman, Chaffeee, & Roberts, 1988). Recent reviews also report distinct negative effects of various media on scholastic performance (see Shin, 2004). In addition and despite complaints about television's portrayal of irresponsible behaviors, portrayals of recklessness continue unabated and without consequences, as revealed by research that tracks violence, risky sex, and the use of drugs, alcohol, and tobacco (see, e.g., Will, Porter, Geller, & DePasquale, 2005). The effect of these portrayals goes beyond the obvious. A recent meta-analysis of studies examining adolescents' viewing of violent television found that such viewing had its greatest "antisocial" effect on nonviolent and nonaggressive activities, with the largest effect being on the reduction in family discussions, which had an effect size of 2.33, an extremely high effect, and less socializing (.75 effect) and contributed to role stereotyping (.90 effect), materialism (.40), and passivity (.36) (Mares & Woodard, 2005). These are strikingly high effects sizes, the metric now commonly used to denote the magnitudes of effects. There is no paucity of research linking the wide variety of media exposure to an even wider variety of negative effects.

We know, however, that the media does not act alone. We know that important social forces, such as parents, peers, and social institutions, influence the media's eventual impact on adolescents. How the legal system influences those social forces, and their responses to adolescents, ultimately will decide how adolescents respond to an increasingly free market of ideas. By far, the most dominant legal and social response to dealing with problematic (and good) media seeks to increase parental involvement in their adolescents' media exposure. Although such responses may work well for young children, they may not work so well with adolescents. The only study that has examined parents' efforts to mediate the television viewing of their adolescent children reveals that parental efforts to mediate the effects of televised violence and sex may well backfire. A survey of both parents and students indicated that restrictive mediation, a mode dominating the adolescent period, related to less positive attitudes toward parents, more positive attitudes toward the content, and more viewing of the content with friends (Nathanson, 2002). Perhaps even more distressing given popular pleas to have parents spend more time with their children's media, coviewing relates to both more positive attitudes toward and viewing of television violence and sex (Nathanson, 2002). Encouraging parents to take part in their adolescents' media remains far from an optimal solution.

Despite the complexity of media effects, both positive and negative, censorship remains the dominant response to shaping adolescents' media environment. This censorship provides the most compelling reason to revisit the failure to address adolescents' rights, for it reveals the current futility of regulations. Adolescents do have access to media the law deems inappropriate; and they do not seem to have access to ways to learn how to respond to that failure. We know, for example, that parents can no longer exert as much control over their adolescents' access to media messages. Important lines of research reveal other limitations that result from relying on parents' censorship. Studies show that parents may have rules in place that restrict certain television programs and media, but it is unclear whether parents provide the socially acceptable restrictions, or whether adolescents acknowledge the rules, or whether parents consistently enforce them. In addition, parents clearly have tools at their disposal that can limit their children's access to media; but only a very small percentage of parents install or activate the new devices, with fewer using blocking devices (Jordan, 2004; Mitchell, Finkelhor, & Wolak, 2005). Even greater use of new blocking devices, though, would not necessarily lead to dramatic reductions in adolescents' access to targeted materials. For example, the use of filtering and blocking software only leads to a modest reduction in unwanted exposure to what parents are most concerned about—sexual materials; and various other forms of parental supervision do not associate with any reduction in exposure (Mitchell, Finkelhor, & Wolak, 2003). Further, meta-analyses of experiments testing the effects of ratings document some effectiveness for younger children but also a prevalence of unanticipated "boomerang" effects for adolescents (see, e.g., Cantor & Wilson, 2003). Censorship efforts are far from foolproof and may actually foster antithetical effects.

Industry self-regulation, the other dominant response to media identified as potentially harmful (see Campbell, 1999), has yet to result in the effective curtailment of problematic media exposure to adolescents. The television industry has shown an inability to regulate itself. Sexual content and graphic violence and vulgar language are more prevalent than ever before (see Wilson et al., 1998). Most notably, the Federal Trade Commission's report, Marketing violent entertainment to children: A fourth follow-up review of industry practices in the motion picture, music recording & electronic game industries (2004), recently concluded that while the entertainment industry has taken steps to identify content that may be inappropriate for children, the companies in those industries still routinely target children under 17 in their marketing of products that their own ratings systems deem inappropriate or in need of parental caution.

Adolescents' encounters with media certainly do not only lead to negative outcomes. The new media, for example, fosters considerable hope among professionals committed to adolescents' healthy development. Most notably, adolescents typically experience difficulties accessing a wide panoply of traditional health services. E-health holds the promise to help fill gaps. The Internet combines positive features of traditional lay and professional, personal, and impersonal sources. Although it is unlikely to supplant the role of trusted peers and adults and may not lead to accessing information as easily as many may have hoped, the Internet already plays an important role in adolescents' repertory of health information sources (Gray, Klein, Noyce, Sesselberg, & Cantrill, 2005). Adolescents explore their own values and identities and struggle with issues that may not be easily discussed with parents and peers. Variations in adolescents' access to high quality information and privacy certainly will continue to impact the extent to which the Internet allows for offering mutual support, fostering social networks, and obtaining answers to specific health concerns (Skinner, Biscope, & Poland, 2003). But it does seem that the Internet can nurture interactions that contain the key ingredients of successful helping relationships—those that provide information and emotional support for healthy development in relatively safe and anonymous ways.

The potential harm accruing to adolescents who lack media access also reveals the remarkable extent to which adolescents can benefit from access to modern media. Some of the more pernicious effects of media may befall those who lack access. Leading commentators conclude that current uses of computer technology both at school and at home actually worsen the digital divide between relatively wealthy and poor families (Attewell, 2001). This is not surprising. Like adults, adolescents who lack resources to engage informational environments (Bucy & Newhagen, 2004), even if they have access to computers at school, run the risk of missing out on the kind of information necessary to function successfully in today's world. This divide certainly has important developmental consequences. Our information society evolves rapidly and inevitably sustains rapid social change that rests on two powerful forces—increased intercultural interaction and an economic system that treats knowledge as a commodity. Together, these transformations present major implications for adolescents' skills, learning strategies and developing sense of self. The explosion of knowledge means an inability to retain knowledge in fields and a focus on being able to obtain, organize, manage, and critically evaluate information. The expansive, global reach of media technology increasingly requires the ability to operate in a global society and that ability rests on the inner and social resources available to engage vast amounts of information. Adolescents clearly can benefit from tools that link them to information, but only if our society provides them with environments that can foster appropriate engagement.

Recent neuroscientific evidence relating to brain development may lead some to wonder whether adolescents actually have the capacity to evaluate and engage information responsibly. Some commentators suggest that adolescents must be protected from media influences so that such influences do not adversely affect their neurobiological development (Saunders, 2005). Research does indeed indicate that maturational brain processes continue well through adolescence (Keating, 2004). Although this line of research remains more speculative than popular commentaries suggest, our broader understanding of adolescent development does not necessarily support an aggressive turn to limiting adolescents' access to life experiences. Our understanding of development does not do so for the simple reason that adolescents are more like adults than children. Researchers have long found that more similarities than differences mark adolescents and adults' decisional capacities (Scott, Reppucci, & Woolard, 1995). Even adolescents' evaluations of risk also may not be as deficient as once thought (Millstein & Halpern-Felsher, 2002). Policy suggestions that focus on limitations run the risk of ignoring adolescents' abilities, especially their ability to make sound decisions and their need to learn how to make such decisions.

It would be disingenuous to propose that empirical evidence speaks with one voice. Our broader understanding of adolescent development, however, supports the human rights approach much more than is suggested by particular commentaries seeking to limit adolescents' access to information. Developmentally primed for engagement and interaction with others, adolescents are fundamentally open to engaging ideas, arguably even more so than most adults. Adolescents embrace, reject, and consider ideas to determine their current and possible sense of self. Leading frameworks for understanding identity formation emphasize the dynamic, progressive organization of the child's drives, abilities, beliefs, and individual history leading to the adolescent's development of an internal self structure capable of responding to the demands of contemporary civil society for both personal fulfillment and civic responsibility (see, e.g., Martin, 2007). As adolescents actively engage in the process of sorting out their identities, they look to others for ideas and consider a wide variety of sources. As they share personal thoughts and feelings and learn to become sensitive to the needs, desires, and thoughts of others, adolescents gain deeper understandings of themselves and others. This exploration provides a necessary precursor to successful identity development; healthy adolescents engage in identity exploration as they actively seek out information and test hypotheses about their theory of self (Dunkel & Lavoie, 2005). This active process of identity exploration and formation actually constitutes the central task of adolescence; and research increasingly links it to effective civic development and to positive mental health central to self-fulfillment (see Levesque, 2007 for a review). This more integrative view indicates how, as a period for reorganizing psychological, social, and neurobiological regulatory systems, adolescence constitutes a period fraught with both risks and needed opportunities for developing effective competencies. This more integrative view reinforces the proposition that our society, including our legal system, needs to structure adolescents' experiences in ways that foster engagement with ideas.

Conclusion

The American creed always has professed that those who hope to govern themselves must have access to information, even including the right to receive, produce, and express controversial and unpopular ideas. Yet, although few would challenge the significance of informational rights and the need for such rights in democratic living, many become quite hesitant to bestow adolescents with informational rights. As a result, our legal system has yet to respond effectively to adolescents' changing realities. Our legal system pervasively allows parents, teachers, counselors, social workers, doctors, police, attorneys, judges, strangers, and a host of government actors to control adolescents' informational rights. That approach varies considerably from the emerging human rights paradigm that seeks to include adolescents in decisions that affect them and, consistent with their evolving capacities, grant them greater control over their own rights. In so doing, the human rights approach attempts to shape informational environments so that adolescents could benefit from access to information necessary for them to exercise their recognized rights, act in their own best interests, live up to civic aspirations, and lead a more fulfilling life.

The need to turn toward the human rights approach, at least in terms of its general orientation, finds support from existing social science research and a close look at the potential deficiencies of our current legal regulation of adolescents' informational environments. Current U.S. efforts are notable for their focus on inculcating appropriate information, efforts that tend to censor adolescents' access to information. Typical responses to dealing with media portrayals, images and effects, for example, predominantly leave matters to parents, and, if not parents, then to the media itself. This essentially means that the legal system directly sets the limit to what should be available for adults (e.g., it would prohibit child pornography and other obscene materials from circulating) and then generally leaves it to parents, those acting as parents, and the media itself to determine adolescents' access to information available in the marketplace. These efforts increasingly fail on several fronts. They fail to inculcate the values that justified the censorship in the first instance, a failure made obvious by the pervasiveness of media in adolescents' lives and the remarkable extent to which adolescents actually have access to materials deemed problematic as to them. That failure is likely to increase given technological advances and renewed Free Speech commitments to protecting those advances. Censorship also fails to inculcate appropriate values to the extent that it fails to provide adolescents with ways to respond appropriately to potentially harmful materials that do reach them. Efforts also most obviously fail when they do not consider the many sources that influence adolescents' access and responses to information, ranging from parents, schools, peers, to community resources, and to adolescents' own dispositions. Efforts also fundamentally fail when our legal system allows for treating adolescents as adults, such as to punish them, when they wrongly use their available information. The reality of adolescents' everyday lives serves as a testament to the law's deep limitations.

Without doubt, how to direct adolescents' informational environments constitutes an important concern not just for individual adolescents but also for our system of free expression and civil society itself. Important consequences emerge from censorship efforts and efforts to inculcate appropriate ideas in the name of adolescents. These efforts contribute to the tacit assumption that the government's proclaimed interests are virtually immune from scrutiny once the state claims the need to protect parental rights and to shield minors from harm. They suggest that the boundaries of the speech from which adolescents can be protected are virtually limitless. As a result of an apparent lack of boundaries, our legal system can rely on mere generalized assertions to support broad regulations impinging on the right to information. This approach to adolescents' rights, especially the lack of attention to it, raises serious moral, ethical, medical, and legal concerns. To be sure, the human rights approach certainly has its own limits. But, one of its most fundamental contributions undoubtedly involves the extent to which it urges us to rethink current policies marked by contradictory visions about the proper role of adolescents' voices, parents' authority and obligations, the state's responsibilities, and our society's fundamental commitments to justice in matters concerning adolescents. That fundamental mandate is the most critical contribution human rights law offers those interested in ameliorating the place adolescents occupy in our society.

References

Ashcroft v. American Civil Liberties Union, 542 U.S. 656 (2004).

Attewell, P. (2001). The first and second digital divides. *Sociology of Education, 74*, 252–259.

Bellotti v. Baird, 443 U.S. 622 (1979).

Bethel School District No. 403 v. Fraser, 478 U.S. 675 (1986).

Board of Education v. Pico, 457 U.S. 853 (1982).

Bolger v. Youngs Drug Products Corporation, 463 U.S. 60 (1983).

Brown, J. D. (2002). Mass media influences on sexuality. *Journal of Sex Research, 39*, 42–45.

Bowen v. Kendrick, 487 U.S. 589 (1988).

Bucy, E. B., & Newhagen, J. E. (2004). *Media access: Social and psychological dimensions of new technology*. Mahwah, NJ: Lawrence Erlbaum Associates.

Campbell, A. J. (1999). Self-regulation and the media. *Federal Communications Law Journal, 51*, 711–772.

Cantor, J., & Wilson, B. (2003). Media and violence: Intervention strategies for reducing aggression. *Media Psychology, 5*, 363–403.

Chaplin, L. N., & John, D. R. (2005). The development of self–brand connections in children and adolescents. *Journal of Consumer Research, 32*, 119–129.

Christenson, P. G., & Roberts, D. F. (1998). *It's not only rock and roll: Popular music in the lives of adolescents*. Cresskill, NJ: Hampton Press.

Convention on the Rights of the Child, G.A. res. 44/25, annex, 44 U.N. GAOR Supp. (No. 49) at 167, U.N. Doc. A/44/49 (1989).

Dallas v. Stanglin, 490 U.S. 19 (1989).

Dandridge v. Williams, 397 U.S. 471 (1970).

DeShaney v. Winnebago County Dept. of Soc. Services, 489 U.S. 189 (1989).

Dunkel, C. S., & Lavoie, J. C. (2005). Ego-identity and the processing of self-relevant information. *Self & Identity, 4*, 349–359.

Erznoznik v. City of Jacksonville, 422 U.S. 205 (1975).

FCC v. Pacifica Foundation, 438 U.S. 726 (1978).

Federal Trade Commission (2004). *Marketing violent entertainment to children: A fourth follow-up review of industry practices in the motion picture, music recording & electronic game industries, a report to congress*. Available at http://www.ftc.gov/opa/2004/07/040708kidsviolencerpt.pdf (last visited January 9, 2006).

Ginsberg v. New York, 390 U.S. 629 (1968).

Gray, N. J., Klein, J. D., Noyce, P. R., Sesselberg, T. S., & Cantrill, J. A. (2005). Health information-seeking behavior in adolescence: The place of the Internet. *Social Science and Medicine, 60*, 1467–1478.

Gunter, B., Oates, C., & Blades, M. (2005). *Advertising to children on TV: Content, impact, and regulation*. Mahwah, NJ: Lawrence Erlbaum Associates.

Hancox, R. J., Milne, B. J., & Poulton, R. (2004). Association between child and adolescent television viewing and health: A longitudinal birth cohort study. *Lancet, 364*, 257–262.

Harris v. McRae, 448 U.S. 297 (1980).

Hazelwood School District v. Kuhlmeier, 484 U.S. 260 (1988).

Hodgson v. Minnesota, 497 U.S. 417. (1990).

Huesmann, R., Moise, J., Podolski, C., & Eron, L. (2003). Longitudinal relations between children's exposure to television violence and their later aggressive and violent behavior in young adulthood: 1977–1992. *Developmental Psychology, 39*, 201–221.

Ingraham v. Wright, 430 U.S. 651 (1977).

International Covenant on Civil and Political Rights, 999 U.N.T.S. 171 (1966).

Jordan, A. (2004). The role of media in children's development: An ecological perspective. *Journal of Developmental and Behavioral Pediatrics, 25*, 196–206.

Keating, D. P. (2004). Cognitive and brain development. In R. M. Lerner & L. D. Steinberg (Eds.), *Handbook of adolescent psychology* (2nd ed., pp. 45–84). New York: Wiley.

Leiberman, D. A., Chaffee, S. H., & Roberts, D. F. (1988). Computers, mass media, and schooling: Functional equivalence in uses of new media. *Social Science Computer Review, 6*, 224–241.

Levesque, R. J. R. (1996). International children's rights: Can they make a difference in American family policy? *American Psychologist, 51*, 1251–1256.

Levesque, R. J. R. (2000). *Adolescents, sex and the law: Preparing adolescents for responsible citizenship*. Washington, DC: American Psychological Association.

Levesque, R. J. R. (2002a). *Not by faith alone: Religion, law and adolescence*. New York: New York University Press.

Levesque, R. J. R. (2002b). *Dangerous adolescents, model adolescents: Shaping the role and promise of education*. New York: Kluwer Academic.

Levesque, R. J. R. (2003). *Sexuality education: What adolescents' rights require*. Hauppauge, NY: Nova Science Publishers.

Levesque, R. J. R. (2006). *The psychology and law of criminal justice processes*. Hauppauge, NY: Nova Science Publishers.

Levesque, R. J. R. (2007). *Adolescents, media, and the law: What developmental science reveals and free speech requires*. New York: Oxford University Press.

Mares, M.-L., & Woodard, E. (2005). Positive effects of television on children's social interactions: A meta-analysis. *Media Psychology, 7*, 301–322.

Martin, J. (2007). The selves of educational psychology: Conceptions, contexts, and critical considerations. *Educational Psychologist, 42*, 79–89.

Michael H. v. Gerald D., 491 U.S. 110 (1989).

Millstein, S. G., & Halpern-Felsher, B. L. (2002). Judgements about risk and perceived invulnerability in adolescents and young adults. *Journal of Research on Adolescence, 12*, 399–422.

Mitchell, K. J., Finkelhor, D., & Wolak, J. (2003). The exposure of youth to unwanted sexual material on the Internet: A national survey of risk, impact, and prevention. *Youth and Society, 34*, 330–358.

Mitchell, K. J., Finkelhor, D., & Wolak, J. D. (2005). Protecting youth online: Family use of filtering and blocking software. *Child Abuse and Neglect, 25,* 753–765.

Morse v. Frederick, 127 S. Ct. 2618 (2007).

Nathanson, A. I. (2002). The unintended effects of parental mediation of television on adolescents. *Media Psychology, 4,* 207–230.

Neuman, S. B. (1995). *Literacy in the television age* (2nd ed.). Norwood, NJ: Ablex.

New York v. Ferber, 458 U.S. 747 (1982).

Parham v. J.R., 442 U.S. 584 (1979).

Prince v. Massachusetts, 321 U.S. 158 (1944).

R.A.V. v. City of St. Paul, 505 U.S. 377 (1992).

Redish, M. H., & Finnerty, K. (2002). What did you learn in school today? Free speech, values inculcation, and the democratic-educational paradox. *Cornell Law Review, 88,* 62–118.

Reno v. American Civil Liberties Union, 521 U.S. 844 (1997).

Roberts, D. F., & Foehr, U. G. (2004). *Kids and media in America: Patterns of use at the millennium.* New York: Cambridge University Press.

Sable Communications of California, Inc., v. FCC, 492 U.S. 115 (1989).

San Antonio Independent School District v. Rodriguez, 411 U.S. 1 (1973).

Saunders, K. W. (2005). A disconnect between law and neuroscience: Modern brain science, media influences, and juvenile justice. *Utah Law Review, 2005,* 695–741.

Scott, E. S., Reppucci, N. D., & Woolard, J. L. (1995). Evaluation adolescent decision making in legal contexts. *Law and Human Behavior, 19,* 221–244.

Shin, N. (2004). Exploring pathways from television viewing to academic achievement in school age children. *Journal of Genetic Psychology, 165,* 367–381.

Skinner, H., Biscope, S., & Poland, B. (2003). Quality of internet access: Barrier behind Internet use statistics. *Social Science and Medicine, 57,* 875–880.

Strasburger, V. C., & Wilson, B. J. (2002). *Children, adolescents, & the media.* Thousand Oaks, CA: Sage.

Suter v. Artist, M., 503 US 347 (1992).

Thompson, K. M. (2005). Addicted media: Substances on screen. *Child and Adolescent Psychiatric Clinics of North America, 14,* 473–489.

Tinker v. Des Moines Independent Community School District, 393 U.S. 503 (1969).

Troxel v Granville, 530 U.S. 57 (2000).

Universal Declaration of Human Rights, U.N.G.A. Res. 217 (1948).

United States v. American Library Association, Inc., 539 U.S. 194 (2003).

United States v. Belmont, 301 U.S. 324 (1937).

Valkenburg, P. M. (2000). Media and youth consumerism. *Journal of Adolescent Health, 27,* 52–56.

Virginia v. Black, 538 U.S. 343 (2003).

Ward, L. M. (2003). Understanding the role of entertainment media in the sexual socialization of American youth: A review of empirical research. *Developmental Review, 23,* 347–388

West Virginia State Board of Education v. Barnette, 319 U.S. 624 (1943).

Will, K. E., Porter, B. E., Geller, E. S., & DePasquale, J. P. (2005). Is television a health and safety hazard? A cross-sectional analysis of at-risk behavior on primetime television. *Journal of Applied Social Psychology, 35,* 198–222.

Wilson, B. J., Kunkel, D., Linz, D., Potter, J., Donnerstein, E., Smith, S. L., Blumenthal, E., & Berry, M. (1998). Violence in television programming overall: University of California, Santa Barbara study. In M. Seawall (Ed.), *National television violence study* (Vol. 2, pp. 3–204). Thousand Oaks, CA: Sage Publications.

Wisconsin v. Mitchell, 508 U.S. 476 (1993).

Wisconsin v. Yoder, 406 U.S. 205 (1972).

ROGER J.R. LEVESQUE, JD (Columbia Law School), PhD (Psychology, the University of Chicago), is Professor of Criminal Justice at Indiana University and Editor-in-Chief of the *Journal of Youth and Adolescence*. He currently serves as Department Chair. He has written extensively in the area of adolescents' rights, human rights, and family policy. His books include *Rethinking Child Maltreatment Law* (Springer), *Adolescents, Media, and the Law* (Oxford), *Adolescents, Sex, and the Law* (American Psychological Association), *Not by Faith Alone: Religion, Adolescence, and the Law* (New York University Press), *Culture and Family Violence* (American Psychological Association), and *Child Sexual Maltreatment* (Indiana).

Journal of Social Issues, Vol. 64, No. 4, 2008, pp. 749–769

Studying Children's Perspectives on Self-Determination and Nurturance Rights: Issues and Challenges

Michele Peterson-Badali*

University of Toronto

Martin D. Ruck

City University of New York

Over the past three decades there has been a growing interest in children's and adolescents' rights and the tendency to grant young people many of the rights traditionally reserved for adult members of society. Increased awareness of children's rights is clearly reflected in the UN Convention on the Rights of the Child (CRC; United Nations, 1989), which recognizes children as worthy of citizenship and attempts to increase the commitment of nations worldwide to children's rights. If children's rights are to serve their intended function—to protect children from harm and promote their development and well-being—it is essential to examine how children understand and think about their rights. In this article we review the literature on children's and adults' thinking about children's rights and discuss conceptual and methodological considerations related to this body of research, including the importance of how we conceptualize the construct of children's rights, the types of questions researchers pose about young people's attitudes, knowledge and reasoning regarding children's rights, and the methods used to answer these questions. We address the implications of developmental research on young people's perspectives on children's rights.

Concern for the rights of children[1] has existed as a moral, social, political, and economic issue for over a century in Western society. The 19th century saw

---

*Correspondence concerning this article should be addressed to Michele Peterson-Badali, Department of Human Development and Applied Psychology, OISE/University of Toronto, 252 Bloor Street West, 9th floor, Toronto, Ontario, Canada, M5S 1V6 [e-mail: mpetersonbadali@oise.utoronto.ca].

[1]In this article the terms *child* and *children* will refer to individuals from birth to 18 years of age.

the emergence of a collective concern for nurturance rights—children's rights to the provision of basic care and to protection from harm and exploitation— that contributed to legislative change such as the establishment of universal free education and limitations on child labor. In the last half of the 20th century the focus shifted to rights of participation and self-determination, based on the assertion that children are not property of their parents or the state, but are legal persons who are entitled to many of the same rights as adults. Most recently there has been an emphasis on balancing the entitlements stemming from children's right to nurturance and their right to self-determination. This emphasis is seen most clearly in the UN Convention on the Rights of the Child (CRC; United Nations General Assembly, 1989), which brings international attention to the issue of children's nurturance and self-determination rights. This balance is evident in two fundamental tenets of the CRC, "the best interests of the child" and "the evolving capacities of the child." The Convention gives legal force to the claims made regarding children's rights in those countries that have ratified the document (see Daiute, this issue). To date the CRC has been ratified by all signatories with the exception of the United States and Somalia.[2]

The empirical study of issues related to children's rights is a more recent phenomenon but one that has grown considerably over the past three decades. However, with several notable exceptions, it is only recently that researchers have begun to examine children's *own* thinking about children's rights issues. Exploring children's perspectives regarding rights is important for a number of reasons (Melton & Limber, 1992). It signals respect for children as persons whose conceptions and views about rights matter, helps inform the design of age-appropriate structures and processes for implementing those rights, and facilitates children's legal and political socialization (Melton & Limber, 1992; Morrow, 1999). It has also been suggested that any attempt to achieve a balance between children's nurturance and self-determination rights be made on the basis of empirical evidence of children's ability to understand such rights as well as children's own views concerning rights (Hart & Pavolic, 1991; Ruck, 1994). Indeed, if rights are to serve their intended function—to protect children from harm and promote their development and wellbeing—it is critical to examine rights understanding in those who are making rights-related decisions (Peterson-Badali, Morine, Ruck, & Slonim, 2004).

Empirical interest in children's rights emerged in the late 1970s and early 1980s. With growing social, political, and legal advocacy for children's self-determination rights, new and at times radical views of the entitlements, duties, and capacities of children were thrust alongside the more traditional conceptions of children and childhood. In 1978 the *Journal of Social Issues* published what is

---

[2]However, it should be noted that a number of countries ratifying the CRC have entered declarations and reservations to various provisions or articles (see Daiute, this issue).

possibly the first scholarly compilation devoted entirely to the topic of children's rights. Issue editors Norma and Seymour Feshbach argued for the importance of (a) providing a clear conceptual framework for considering children's rights and (b) engaging in systematic empirical study "of the values and perceptions of the consumer—children and their families" (Feshbach & Feshbach, 1978, p. 2). We will begin this article with a brief overview of how children's rights have been defined or conceptualized in the scholarly and empirical literature. We then review the research on children's rights that has emerged over the last several decades, with a focus on the nature of the questions posed by researchers and the methods used to answer them. We end by addressing the implications of developmental research on children's perspectives regarding their rights for future research and practice.

Defining Children's Rights

The question of how to define the construct of children's rights was recognized by early scholars and researchers as an important, and potentially contentious, one. In the pre-CRC era, in particular, various authors defined the scope of issues to be considered "children's rights" quite differently. For example, legal scholars such as Serena Stier stressed that children's rights should be limited to those entitlements that can be subjected to judicial protection and argued that couching children's *needs* as rights dilutes the "concept of a right as it properly applies to constitutionally enunciated notions" (Stier, 1978, p. 55). Similarly, in his taxonomy of children's rights, Wald (1986) identified "rights against the world" (e.g., the right to adequate health care or a safe community) as protections due, rather than rights held by, children. Both Stier and Wald argued that these encompass moral and social goals that are not enforceable by court order but that should be pursued through legislative processes (which can then lead to legitimate legal claims). Others stated that defining children's rights in terms of legal rights overly narrows the scope of children's rights, which can also be derived from "moral, ethical, and 'natural' reasoning" (Flekkoy & Kaufman, 1997) and transcend the laws of any given nation. Rogers and Wrightsman (1978) discussed a continuum of rights, with already recognized legal rights at one extreme, rights that would likely be legally recognized if brought before a court in the middle, and statements of what the law *ought* to be at the other extreme. The United Nations CRC contains many rights that the legal scholars cited above would define as needs of, or protections due, children. Indeed, one of the notable strengths of the CRC is that it includes the full continuum of rights, ranging from those already legally enshrined in many of the signatory nations to those that are largely aspirational and still unrealized in many countries (e.g., accessibility of higher education based on children's capacity; right to an adequate standard of living for all children).

The foregoing discussion highlights a broad landscape of rights to which children may be entitled. The law and morality/ethics have been identified as frameworks for defining children's rights, and by extension for considering the issues and challenges associated with them, with the CRC embodying the latter—more inclusive—definition of children's rights. In addition to defining the breadth of the construct of children's rights, scholars have proposed typologies to capture the nature of the rights involved. The notion of development is intimately connected with how rights have been conceptualized in these typologies. For example, as articulated at the beginning of this article, one very basic distinction is made between children's rights to nurturance and self-determination (e.g., Rogers & Wrightsman, 1978; Wald, 1983). This is an important dichotomy in several respects. First, the two types of rights are often seen as conflicting with one another. For example, denying children the right to make their own decisions about particular issues (e.g., education, medical care) has often been framed in terms of their need for (or right to) protection and care. Second, children tend to be passive recipients of nurturance rights and such rights are often fulfilled by adults (such as parents) or the state. In contrast, rights to participation or self-determination, by definition, involve active engagement on the part of children. Consideration of age, or capacity, also manifests very differently with respect to nurturance and self-determination rights. Many participation rights are bestowed only after a certain age or if children demonstrate the competencies deemed necessary to exercise them. Prior to that time they are accessed by adult proxies (e.g., right to consent to treatment) or are simply unavailable (e.g., right to vote).

Not surprisingly, over the last three decades scholars have focused on human development as a critical framework within which to study children's rights and to address the complexities mentioned above. The relationships, as well as distinctions, between nurturance and self-determination rights are intimately connected to children's development, and there is a need for developmental research to assist in determining how best to achieve the delicate balance of these two seemingly contradictory sets of entitlements. Indeed, some scholars (Ochaita & Espinosa, 1997; Verhellen, 1994) argue that the dichotomy—and the tensions and conflicts that accompany it—may be unnecessary in that children's right to protection, or nurturance, is best achieved through the promotion of their "individual autonomy and active construction of their own development" (Ochaita & Espinosa, 1997, p. 280).

In the following paragraphs we provide an overview of the empirical literature on children's rights over the last three decades. As argued at the beginning of this article, the perspectives of children on their rights are of critical importance. However, the perspectives of adults are also important, as children's access to rights is generally facilitated or impeded by adults. Consistent with the literature, our review of children's and adults' thinking about children's rights has been divided into three sections: attitudes, reasoning, and knowledge. Each of these research foci is associated with different methodological approaches, and together their results can be used to advance our conceptual frameworks as well as to inform policy and practice with respect to children's rights.

A Review of the Literature

Attitudes toward Children's Rights

In response to growing advocacy for, and recognition of, children's legal personhood and access to self-determination rights in the 1960s and 1970s, early children's rights research focused on attitudes toward children's rights, primarily those of adults. The views of children and adolescents were incorporated into subsequent research and recent studies have compared children's and adults' views. In examining attitudes, most authors have taken a broad view of children's rights, and measures have included a range of "potential" rather than legally defined children's rights issues. Stimuli typically consist of statements of potential children's rights (e.g., children should have the right to wear whatever clothing they want regardless of the weather) or brief vignettes depicting conflicts regarding issues (usually between parents and children) to which participants respond using Likert-type scales measuring extent of agreement with, or dichotomous endorsement/rejection of, the right. Research goals have included describing overall levels of support for children's rights among respondents, comparing support for nurturance and self-determination rights, examining whether support for rights varies according to the age of the "target child" depicted, and exploring sociodemographic factors that predict attitudes toward children's rights.

Not surprisingly, most studies report variability in support for children's rights on the part of adults (e.g., Borhnstedt, Freeman, & Smith, 1981; Morton, Dubanoski, & Blaine, 1982; Peterson-Badali, Ruck, & Ridley, 2003; Rogers & Wrightsman, 1978) as well as children (e.g., Day, Peterson-Badali, & Ruck, 2006; Hart & Zeidner, 1993; Peterson-Badali et al., 2004; Rogers & Wrightsman, 1978; Ruck, Abramovitch, & Keating, 1998; Ruck, Tenebaum, & Sines, 2007), suggesting that this is a social issue that has not achieved consensus in terms of public opinion. However, a clearer picture emerges when rights to self-determination are compared to nurturance rights. While support for children's nurturance rights is quite high and fairly consistent across respondents, both children (Day et al., 2006; Hart & Zeidner, 1993; Peterson-Badali et al., 2004; Rogers & Wrightsman, 1978; Ruck, Abramovitch, et al., 1998) and adults (Peterson-Badali et al., 2003; Rogers and Wrightsman, 1978; Ruck, Peterson-Badali, & Day, 2002) show significantly less, as well as greater variability in, support for self-determination rights, although not all studies of youth show greater support for nurturance rights than self-determination (e.g., Ruck et al., 2002; Ruck et al., 2007).

In order to examine the heterogeneity in support for children's rights, researchers have explored demographic, cultural, and social factors thought to relate to children's rights attitudes and have noted the importance, once again, of distinguishing nurturance and self-determination rights in this respect (e.g., Peterson-Badali et al., 2004).

Respondent and target age. Variability in support for rights is related to the age of the child in question ("target child"). With both child and adult respondents, the evidence with respect to the relationship between age and nurturance is mixed, with some studies showing equally strong support for nurturance rights regardless of the age of the target child (e.g., Peterson-Badali et al., 2003; Ruck et al., 2002, with respect to child respondents) and others suggesting somewhat diminished (albeit still strong) support for nurturance for older as compared to younger adolescents (Ruck et al., 2002, with respect to adult respondents; Ruck, Abramovitch, et al., 1998).

There is consistent evidence that adults' support for children's self-determination rights increases with the age of the child (Borhnstedt et al., 1981; Helwig, 1997; Peterson-Badali et al., 2003; Ruck et al., 2002), and there are data to suggest that, consistent with legislation and case law, adults view extending self-determination rights as dependent on children's capacities to exercise rights in a mature fashion (Helwig, 1997; Peterson-Badali et al., 2003; Ruck et al., 2002). However, support for self-determination rights also appears to be related to the age of the respondent. In adults, there is some evidence that support for children's self-determination rights declines with participant age (Borhnstedt et al., 1981; Rogers & Wrightsman, 1978). In child samples, participant age may interact with the age of the target child. For example, the results of several studies suggest that children of all ages are not particularly supportive of self-determination rights for young children (i.e., those who have not yet reached adolescence; Ruck, Abramovitch, et al., 1998). However, beginning in early adolescence, children support self-determination rights when thinking about children close to their own age (e.g., Day et al., 2006; Peterson-Badali et al., 2004). Like adults, however, older adolescents are significantly less supportive of self-determination rights for younger adolescents (Day et al., 2006).

When children's and adults' views are compared, North American research has found that children favor self-determination rights to a greater extent and nurturance rights to a lesser extent than adults generally (Rogers & Wrightsman, 1978) and their parents (Day et al., 2006; Peterson-Badali et al., 2004; Ruck et al., 2002). However, there is evidence that older adolescents and mothers are more similar in their thinking about self-determination rights issues than are younger adolescents and mothers. For example, in Ruck et al.'s (2002) study of children's rights in the home, mothers of 6th and 8th graders were more likely than their children to support nurturance rights and less likely to support self-determination rights whereas mothers of 10th graders did not differ from their children in support for nurturance or autonomy rights. In their study of Jewish and Palestinian families, Ben-Arieh, Khoury-Hassabri, and Haj-Yahia (2006) reported an interesting interaction with culture. Similar to their young adolescent North American counterparts, Jewish Israeli adolescents were more supportive than their mothers of children's rights in general and civil rights in particular. In contrast, Palestinian adolescents' mothers were more supportive of children's rights in general, and political rights in particular, than were their adolescent children, with no differences in support for civil rights. The authors suggest that the sociopolitical context in which children's rights issues are situated interacts with developmental and cohort factors to shape children's and adults' attitudes in complex ways. The relationship between cultural variables and rights attitudes is discussed further below.

Respondent gender.   While the adult literature suggests that women are somewhat more supportive of children's nurturance rights than men (Peterson-Badali et al., 2003; Rogers & Wrightsman, 1978), sex differences in support for children's rights have been inconsistently reported in the child literature, with some studies indicating stronger support for nurturance rights in girls than boys (Covell & Howe, 1995; Day et al., 2006; Hart, Pavlovic, & Zeidner, 2001; Peterson-Badali et al., 2004; Rogers & Wrightsman, 1978) and others reporting no differences (Ruck, Abramovitch, et al., 1998; Ruck et al., 2002). In contrast, a recent study examining how British adolescents view the rights of asylum-seeker children found that while both girls and boys supported the asylum-seeker children's nurturance rights, girls were more likely than boys to support self-determination rights for asylum-seekers children (Ruck et al., 2007).

Socioeconomic status (SES).   The literature with respect to the relationship between SES and children's rights attitudes is also mixed. While Borhnstedt et al. (1981) reported that education was positively associated with adults' support for children's self-determination rights, other studies (e.g., Day et al., 2006; Zimmerman, Temple, Peterson-Badali, Ruck, & Day, 1999) have found no relationship. Similarly, there is some evidence that children's attitudes are positively related to SES (Hart et al., 2001; Melton, 1980), but such findings have not consistently emerged (e.g., Day et al., 2006; Zimmerman et al., 1999).

Ethnocultural variables.   Support for the existence of racial, ethnic, and religious differences in adults' attitudes toward children's rights is found in several studies (e.g., Borhnstedt et al., 1981; Morton et al., 1982). Other studies (e.g., Day et al., 2006; Peterson-Badali et al., 2003) have not found ethnocultural differences in adults' attitudes toward children's rights, though nationality differences have emerged (Peterson-Badali et al., 2003). Variations in adults' support for children's rights as a function of race/ethnicity, religious affiliation, and nationality have been interpreted as reflecting a broader attitudinal construct of liberalism–conservatism (Borhnstedt et al., 1981; Peterson-Badali et al., 2003) as well as the social organization and values of the cultural groups (Ben-Arieh et al., 2006; Morton et al., 1982). Ben-Arieh et al. (2006) suggested that while the concept of children's rights is "salient among diverse cultures...it may also be less compatible with non-Western cultures than with North American and Western European cultures" (p. 387). In this regard, it is interesting that studies of children have reported consistency in views about children's rights, even when cultures characterized by very different social orientations (e.g., individualism vs. collectivism) are compared (e.g., Cherney & Shing, 2003; Helwig, 2006). Indeed, in examining the development of autonomy across cultures Helwig (2006) provided evidence that notions of personal autonomy and rights are viewed as important by children and adolescents from a variety of cultural contexts. Cross-cultural discrepancies in children's endorsement of children's rights (e.g., Hart et al., 2001; Melton & Limber, 1992) may reflect differences in emphasis on nurturance and self-determination rights within a particular society rather than a fundamental disagreement regarding the importance of both types of rights.

Dynamic social variables.   In addition to studying static sociodemographic characteristics, researchers have begun to examine dynamic variables that may relate to children's and adults' (particularly parents') views about children's rights. These variables are of particular interest because they can offer possible clues about *how* attitudes develop and change. For example, there is evidence that children's and parents' support for children's rights is related to parents' attitudes toward broader familial and social issues (e.g., sociopolitical attitudes such as liberalism/conservatism, parenting style; Day et al., 2006; Peterson-Badali et al., 2004), as well as children's own experiences within the family, such as participation in family decision making (Peterson-Badali et al., 2004). This is not surprising given that parents are generally the primary socializing agents for children, and the home is a key context where children learn to understand and negotiate rights-related issues.

In summary, research on attitudes toward children's rights suggests that support for children's rights to nurturance in various domains of their lives is very strong across respondent groups. These attitudes are consistent with the initial "child-saving" focus of the children's rights movement and traditional views of children as dependent and in need of care and protection. Support for self-determination rights is weaker, though it is positively related to the age of the child under consideration. Paralleling both scholarly discourse (e.g., Baumrind, 1978; Baumrind & Thompson, 2002; Ochaita & Espinosa, 1997) and jurisprudence (e.g., youth criminal justice, mature minor, and consent to treatment statutes and case law), developmental considerations appear to play a role in both adults' and children's attitudes, including maturity as a prerequisite for the extension of self-determination rights and the duty of adults to provide nurturance to children who are not yet capable of fending for themselves (e.g., Neff & Helwig, 2002; Peterson-Badali et al, 2003; Ruck, Abramovitch, et al., 1998; Ruck et al., 2002). Finally, there is evidence (though some of it mixed) that rights attitudes are related to static sociodemographic variables such as age and sex. More interesting are the relationships with dynamic variables such as adults' and children's attitudes toward family relationships and children's *experience* with participation and autonomy within the family.

These findings give hints regarding the processes that may shape young people's developing attitudes regarding children's rights and that may account for important individual differences in children's thinking. However, research has been exclusively cross-sectional and thus has precluded examining causal linkages between variables. In addition, while a benefit of the typical approach to "attitudes research"—the use of scales with large numbers of items—is the ability to assess a broad range of issues in an efficient manner, this method does not allow for depth in exploring children's thinking about children's rights. The way they reason about children's rights—their rationales for their support or lack thereof—is as important to study as attitudes themselves. From a theoretical perspective, studying reasoning about rights issues sheds more light on the developmental processes that shape children's social understanding. From a practical perspective, rational reasoning is an important component of the legal definition of competence (e.g., to make medical treatment decisions) and thus is critical to examine when extending rights to children may have the potential for negative consequences, or harm. The next section of this article examines the literature on children's reasoning about rights issues.

Reasoning about Children's Rights

In addition to the study of attitudes toward children's rights, early research focused on the significance of broad cognitive-developmental changes for children's thinking about rights issues. Building on the global stage theories of Piaget (1970), Kohlberg (1969), and the work of Tapp and Levine (1974) on legal socialization, Melton (1980, 1983) argued that children's understanding of rights is characterized by qualitative shifts beginning with a concrete, authority-based perspective (e.g., adults give and take away rights) and culminating in a universal, principled view that is not achieved until late adolescence, if at all. The methods for studying children's reasoning about rights were also based on the social and moral reasoning research of Piaget and Kohlberg, and focused on analyses of children's justifications for their responses to vignettes depicting rights dilemmas.

In his seminal study of children's knowledge and reasoning about children's self-determination rights, Melton (1980) interviewed 1st-, 3rd-, 5th-, and 7th-grade students of varying socioeconomic backgrounds. As he predicted, the youngest children held the view that rights were privileges granted by authority, while the older children had developed some understanding of one's entitlement to rights. Several subsequent studies (e.g., Cherney & Perry, 1996; Melton & Limber, 1992) supported the notion that children's understanding of rights develops in accordance with these broad shifts in thinking.

In contrast, beginning in the mid-1990s a number of studies of children's reasoning about rights employed a social cognitive domain approach and reported results that were inconsistent with a global stage account (see Ruck & Horn, this issue). For example, Helwig (1995, 1997, 1998) found that, contrary to Melton's assertion that children fail to understand the inherent nature of rights until mid to late adolescence, even children as young as six appreciated that civil liberties (such as freedom of speech and religion) were universal rights rather than privileges given by those in authority. However, when asked to think about assertion of these rights in specific situations, children increasingly took contextual features into account, such as whether the rights conflict with other moral, social, or developmental concerns (e.g., Helwig, 1995, 1997), resulting in "more discriminative, nuanced, and context-sensitive" discussion of rights issues (Neff & Helwig, 2002, p. 1433). Consistent with this perspective, research by Ruck and colleagues (e.g., Ruck, Abramovitch, et al., 1998, Ruck et al., 2002) found that 8- to 16-year-old children reasoned differently about rights depending on the type of right in question (e.g., nurturance vs. self-determination) as well as the situations in which the rights issues were embedded. For self-determination situations, participants' justifications for asserting or withholding rights included an explicit focus on rights or rights-related concepts such as personal autonomy. In contrast, judgments about nurturance situations focused on the roles and duties—and not the rights—of the parties involved (e.g., parents and children). Researchers (e.g., Neff & Helwig, 2002; Ruck et al., 2002) have argued that the complexities of these results are consistent with a constructivist perspective on the development of children's social-cognitive understanding. Within this framework, children construct social and moral conceptions by interacting with different features of social situations (Neff & Helwig, 2002; Nucci, 2001; Turiel, 1998) and reason differently about social issues depending on factors specific to a particular situation or context.

As the preceding review illustrates, research in children's rights has been dominated by methodological approaches in which *researchers* define the parameters of the rights domain for participants through the content of the questionnaire items and vignettes that participants receive. We suggest that rights issues also need to be explored in terms of how they are constructed and understood by *individuals themselves*. Thus, it is critical to use methods that allow researchers access to children's thinking about rights in a manner that is less influenced by researchers' own constructions of rights issues than is the case with traditional attitude scales and vignettes. This is important from both a theoretical and practical standpoint.

Data on how children understand abstract social concepts such as rights have been used to address competing theories of cognitive development (see above). Equally important, researchers have argued that children's direct participation in societal or institutional processes that have implications for their rights and well-being should be tied to their understanding of the concept of a "right." For example, extending "waiveable" rights to children must depend on their having sufficient understanding of the central features of a right—an entitlement belonging to the child that cannot be exercised, or taken away by, someone else—as well as the meaning and implications of specific rights (e.g., the due process rights to silence and legal counsel; Grisso, 1981; Peterson-Badali & Abramovitch, 1992).

Knowledge of Children's Rights

One means of gathering data on how children think about rights without cueing or constraining their ideas based on adult notions involves the use of open-ended interview questions. Such declarative knowledge questions explore children's understanding of critical features of rights not tapped by attitude scales, for example, the concept of a right as an entitlement (rather than a privilege, need, or desire), the fact that as a class children possess rights (and which ones), and the principle of the universality and irrevocability of rights. Understanding what children know about these aspects of rights is important for determinations of legal competency, mentioned above, but also has broader implications for the likelihood that children will assert and advocate for rights in various contexts.

When asked to define a "right," data suggest that children's knowledge does indeed develop from very rudimentary, concrete understanding to a more principled, but also nuanced, conception.[3] For example, many young children (6– 8 years of age) either do not know or express misconceptions about what a right is (e.g., confuse a right with a privilege that is given and taken away by authority figures; Melton, 1980; Ruck, Keating, Abramovitch, & Koegl, 1998). In a study of American 1st to 7th graders, Melton (1980) reported that older children were less likely than younger children to express ignorance or misunderstanding of a right but that even by age 12, most young people defined rights as rules or laws "enacted by and potentially changed by people" (Melton, 1980, p. 187) rather than as universal principles that derive from moral entitlements and that transcend laws.

More recent research has examined older children's conceptions of rights. In a study of 15- to 16-year-old students from New Zealand who responded to

---

[3] It should be noted that although the language of "development" is used in the present discussion, all studies reviewed are cross-sectional and therefore reflect age differences rather than development. The authors are not aware of any longitudinal research in this area.

questionnaires surveying their knowledge of children's rights and the CRC, Taylor, Smith, and Nairn (2001) found that the most common definition of a right was an entitlement, given by 27% of their sample, followed by the more concrete responses, "something you are allowed to do" (19%) and "something you can have or do" (11%). A study of 11- to 15-year-old Canadian students (Peterson-Badali & Ruck, 2006) yielded similar results, with students commonly defining a right as "something you have/can do" (25%), followed by a privilege (18%). Age/grade differences were consistent, for the most part, with the argument that children's knowledge becomes more abstract and precise with age. For example, the oldest adolescents were more likely than younger children to define a right as an entitlement (29% vs. 5%, respectively) or a belief/principle (6% vs. 0%) and less likely than the 11-year-olds to confuse a right with a desire (0% vs. 10%). Similarly, in a study of Canadian 8- to 16-year-old children (Ruck, Keating et al., 1998), only by age 14 did students begin to define a right as an entitlement (15%), and 10- to 16-year-old children were less likely than the 8-year-old participants to indicate that they did not know what a right is.

Evidence from cross-national studies, as well as studies of specific populations of children, suggests that children's conceptions of rights reflects not only their developing cognitive and social competencies but their experiences, including the general experience of living within a particular sociocultural environment, as well as more specific experiences associated with particular life circumstances. For example, Melton and Limber (1992) noted the emphasis placed by Norwegian children on nurturance rights in comparison to American children, who "respond in terms of liberty—the ability to make choices" (p. 178), and attributed this discrepancy to sociopolitical differences between the countries. Melton (1980) also reported differences in young children's conceptions of rights as a function of SES, with low-SES young children lagging behind their more privileged age-mates. He argued that children's understanding of rights is facilitated by direct experiences of having rights fulfilled—with the experience of entitlement (Melton, 1980; Melton & Limber, 1992).

With this thesis in mind, Peterson-Badali, Ruck, and Bone (2008) examined rights conceptions in adolescents with histories of abuse and/or neglect living in child welfare care. Participants most commonly defined a right as an entitlement, and did so more frequently than in previous research with nonmaltreated children of similar age (Peterson-Badali & Ruck, 2006; Ruck, Keating, et al., 1998; Taylor et al., 2001). These youth also more frequently defined rights in terms of rules or laws (15%) than in previous studies by Taylor et al. (3%; 2001) and Peterson-Badali and Ruck (5%; 2006) but consistent with earlier research (13%; Ruck, Keating, et al., 1998). This may be a result of "rights education" children in care are mandated to receive from their workers on a regular basis. Such education typically involves informing youth about what rights they have as children in care, though it also includes mention of what rights are.

When rights conceptions are examined by asking children to give examples of rights belonging to children, studies have consistently shown that they generate a variety of nurturance (e.g., protection from abuse, access to basic needs, psychological needs, education, and medical care), and self-determination (including civil liberties and decision making) rights (Casas et al., 2006; Peterson-Badali & Ruck, 2006; Taylor et al., 2001). Nurturance and self-determination rights are mentioned by children of all ages and across diverse populations (e.g., from various countries and from diverse backgrounds within nations) but differences in emphasis, as well as specific examples of these broad categories, are also evident.

Age differences between children and adolescents are consistent with expectations based on children's cognitive and social (e.g., autonomy) development. For example, Ruck, Keating, et al. (1998) reported that younger children were more likely than older children and adolescents to express misconceptions or fail to generate examples of rights belonging to children. They were also more likely to mention play and recreation than older children, whereas older children were more likely than the youngest children to mention education, care and safety, and decision making. However, in two studies involving two distinct adolescent samples (nonmaltreated adolescents and maltreated adolescents), rights mentioned were remarkably similar across age (Peterson-Badali & Ruck, 2008; Peterson-Badali et al., 2008).

Differences are also evident according to children's nationality, culture, and social backgrounds. Melton and Limber's (1992) comparison of Norwegian and American children is discussed above. In addition, consistent with the notion that rights conceptions are shaped by one's particular experiences, maltreated adolescents (Peterson-Badali et al., 2006) identified freedom from abuse/right to safety more frequently than those in previous studies (Casas et al., 2006; Peterson-Badali & Ruck, 2008; Taylor et al., 2001). However, there is reason to believe that children's conceptions of rights do not emanate solely from what they have experienced in their own lives, as we will see in the following section.

"Self-Generated" Rights

In addition to asking open-ended questions, we have explored young people's conceptions of children's rights issues using a method that extends the traditional rights vignette design by having participants discuss *self*-generated dilemmas. This approach was initially developed within the moral reasoning field (e.g., Gilligan, 1982; Lyons, 1983; Wark & Krebs, 1996) in order to capture a more complete conception of the parameters of the morality domain than critics argued was elicited by the traditional Kohlbergian approach. As a result, new understandings about developmental and gender differences in moral reasoning (e.g., Pratt, Golding, Hunter, & Sampson, 1988; Wark & Krebs, 1996) evolved from research that has contrasted experimenter-generated moral dilemma vignettes with participants' self-generated moral dilemmas. Similarly, it is important to explore the rights that children and adults themselves generate, as these reflect their experience of what issues are salient in their lives.

Self-generated rights are explored by asking respondents to "tell me about a situation involving a children's rights issue. It does not have to be something that happened to you." Responses are followed up by asking participants to describe what right is involved in the situation they have described. Respondents are asked to generate rights situations in three contexts: home/ family, school, and the broader community. To date we have interviewed several samples of children from Toronto, Canada, ranging in age from 9 to 18, including students in public and independent schools (Peterson-Badali & Ruck, 2006; Peterson-Badali et al., 2004) and youth in child welfare care (Peterson-Badali et al., 2008).

Much of the data that has emerged using this methodology is consistent with findings regarding children's knowledge about their rights. Children identified rights situations involving a wide range of nurturance and self-determination issues including abuse and safety, basic needs (shelter, food), psychological needs (e.g., respect, to be listened to), education, medical care, civil liberties, and decision making about a variety of facets of their lives, including health issues, discretionary time, peers, finances, and family matters. However, the rights issues identified also varied depending on the context as well as on child factors (e.g., age, maltreatment). Child abuse/safety was the one issue that cut across all contexts, with 20–25% of children generating scenarios relating to this right. Psychological needs issues were also salient to many children and not surprisingly were mentioned more often in the home and school contexts (roughly 20% of scenarios) than in the broader community. A similar trend was evident for decision making. Issues involving civil liberties (e.g., protection of privacy, freedom of expression) were generated by many respondents, particularly in the school and broader community contexts where as much as 30–40% of youth described scenarios falling into this category. Some rights issues generated were unique to particular contexts. For example, not surprisingly, respondents generated scenarios describing children's right to education or to appropriate teaching in the school context. The right to medical care was mentioned by less than 10% of respondents, and only with reference to the broader community context. The right to access basic needs, such as food and clothing, was mentioned exclusively in the home context.

Thus far, age differences in the types of rights generated have been surprisingly few and vary somewhat according to the sample. For example, compared to younger (9- to 11-year-old) participants, decision making was highly salient to our 11- to 15-year-old respondents, which is consistent with the importance and development of autonomy during this period. In addition, compared to the younger student sample, civil liberties scenarios were generated more frequently in both the older student and maltreated adolescent samples, but only in the broader community context. In terms of the broad categories of nurturance and self-determination, there were no age differences, with children of all ages generating rights situations involving both types of rights.

The rights generated also varied in interesting ways between the maltreated and nonmaltreated children. Psychological needs and civil liberties were issues common to both the student and maltreated samples. However, compared to nonmaltreated children, for maltreated children, basic needs, education, and medical care were more salient and abuse/safety was actually *less* an issue for this group. In addition, decision making in home and school contexts was mentioned less frequently by youth in care, despite the samples' similar age range. In interpreting these findings, we suggest that young people generate rights situations dealing with issues that are salient to them in their current, rather than historical, circumstances—in the "here and now." It is interesting that, while the respondents in the maltreated sample all had significant histories of abuse and/or neglect, they did not appear to focus on abuse as a rights issue. Instead, compared to the nonmaltreated sample, they were more concerned with meeting basic needs in their daily lives, which may be a very salient and current concern for children living in state care. The fact that they focused less on decision making than nonmaltreated age-mates may be accounted for by this relatively greater focus on the entitlement to basic nurturance rights such as having appropriate clothing, enough to eat, or access to necessities for personal hygiene. It is also possible that these maltreated youth, who were all living in out of home care (in foster homes or group residences) actually experienced more opportunities for autonomous decision making than children living in more traditional family circumstances and were therefore less focused than nonmaltreated children on decision making as a salient entitlement.

Together, these findings also suggest that children tend to be concerned with rights relating to needs or goals that have not been fully realized for developmental reasons (e.g., age restrictions placed on behaviors by parents or society) or due to personal circumstances, and may focus less on entitlements that they *already* experience. This interpretation runs counter to Melton's (1980) suggestion that children's understanding about rights issues depends on the experience of having rights fulfilled. This contradiction may stem from the fact that to date we have not used the self-generated methodology to probe and examine *reasoning* to the extent that traditional vignette studies have. However, when understanding is assessed by analyzing children's declarative knowledge about children's rights, the data do not support the prediction that maltreated children, who have arguably had significantly less experience of having rights fulfilled than "typical" age-mates, show less sophisticated understanding.

It is clear from the preceding review that the use of different methods allows for a rich picture of children's thinking—including attitudes, reasoning, and knowledge—about children's rights. For example, results of studies using vignettes to examine children's reasoning about rights, as well as those using open-ended questions to elicit their declarative knowledge, reveal age-related changes that appear to be linked to developing cognitive abilities. Data from attitude questionnaires, as well as from the open-ended methods (declarative knowledge questions, self-generated rights vignettes), support the contention that children's thinking also emerges from their *experiences*—whether these are defined in terms of the broad social–political–cultural context in which they live or more immediate experiences of socioeconomic (dis)advantage, parenting and familial perspectives on rights-related issues, or personal histories, such as rights abuses. However, research also suggests that children do not have to directly experience having certain rights fulfilled in order to be able to identify and talk about those rights.

Implications for Research and Practice

The empirical work discussed in this article illustrates the importance and usefulness of considering the "evolving capacities" and "best interests of the child," not only as they relate to the exercise of rights but also in terms of understanding of rights. As scholars and practitioners work to develop frameworks for balancing children's protection and participation rights, it is essential that they take into account research on how young people understand children's rights in various settings and contexts. Despite the importance of examining children's own views of their rights, researchers have only recently begun to seriously consider young people's perspectives (Helwig & Turiel, 2002, 2001).

The research reviewed here illustrates the value of children being able to express their views in matters concerning them, which is an important component of citizenship (Earls & Carlson, 2002). Whether these views are taken seriously by adults is another question. Comparing children and adults revealed similarities in perspectives as well as in some of the variables that may underpin those attitudes. Research has also uncovered discrepancies between children and adults, particularly with respect to children's self-determination rights, which appear rooted in beliefs regarding developmental readiness to make decisions with significant long-term consequences for children's lives. As adults are powerful gatekeepers of children's access to rights, children's rights agendas are largely (and paradoxically) in the hands of those who often seek to limit the expression of their rights (see Levesque, this issue).

However, the fact that both children and adults show strong support for children's nurturance rights is an encouraging place to begin in terms of advocacy for children's rights. The more ambivalent stance toward children's rights to self-determination, expressed particularly in adult samples, though not surprising, may be related at least in part to the way that attitudes have been measured in most studies to date. The nurturance-self-determination distinction articulated by Rogers and Wrightsman (1978) predated the framing of rights in terms of the "3 P's" of the CRA—protection, provision and participation. Much of the existing attitudes research stems from the former typology and has utilized self-determination questions that imply *independent* decision making on the part of children, which tends to be viewed negatively by many adults and, to a lesser extent, by children and adolescents. In contrast, framing self-determination in terms of *participation* is important because it allows for children's and youth's voice without implying that they have full decision-making authority with respect to the issue in question. Measuring attitudes toward participation using models that articulate the full spectrum of participation (e.g., Hart, 1997; Shier, 2001) from the complete lack of children's presence at one extreme, through involvement (e.g., being heard), to autonomous authority over decisions at the other end of the continuum would allow for a more nuanced look at attitudes toward children's involvement in numerous aspects of their lives. These models also provide an important connection with the developmental considerations discussed earlier in that as children's cognitive and social abilities develop, their capacity to meaningfully engage in deeper and more autonomous levels of participation grows. Because the models focus not solely on decision making as the outcome of participation, they allow for types of involvement that are suitable for children whose capacities are not fully developed.

In addition, the majority of the available research examining children's perspectives on rights was quantitatively oriented and rooted in a Western perspective. Future work would benefit from more qualitative and participatory focused research (Kirby, 2002). For example, studies on young people's views of social injustice (see Daiute & Fine, 2003; Fine & Burns, 2003) have benefited from incorporating such approaches. Partnering with children as active coconstructors of the questions and methods of children's rights studies is not only consistent with respect for youth as citizens, but with the developmental benefit to children of participation.

Developmental research also needs to more closely consider beliefs about children's rights in non-Western cultural contexts. In addition, continued focus on children characterized by various forms of disadvantage is also critical, as it is for these children that rights have particularly crucial implications. There is also a pressing need for longitudinal research on the development of children's knowledge, attitudes, and reasoning about their rights; the connection between children's thinking about rights and actual *participation* with respect to rights-related decisions; as well as the conditions and/or contexts that promote or impede meaningful engagement in rights dialogue at the familial and societal levels.

In terms of policy and practice, the goal of expanded opportunities for children to actively participate in formal and informal structures and processes across the varied spheres of their lives—home and family, school, community, etc.—is consistent with the research reviewed in this article as well as advocated by the CRC. Furthermore, at least in the family context, there is a relationship between children's experience of participation and the expression of positive attitudes regarding children's rights. Equally important is the demonstrated link between children's participation in the family and *parents'* support for children's self-determination rights. While it is likely that parents who believe in children's rights to autonomy are more likely to permit and support their participation in family life, it may also be that seeing children participate may have a positive impact on parents' (and other adults') attitudes regarding children's rights as well as their views on children's abilities to contribute actively to their families, schools, and communities. Participation may also serve as an important vehicle for rights education and capacity building for children, although whether rights understanding improves as a function of participation is an empirical question that has received little study.

Alongside opportunities for participation, education regarding children's rights is a critical priority. While some basic knowledge of rights is demonstrated by even young children, many hold significant misconceptions about rights that may undermine the ability of rights to protect them, and although knowledge and ability to reason about rights improves with age, only a minority of adolescents understand some of the central features of rights. Not only is knowledge about children's rights likely to help children better protect themselves (Covell & Howe, 2001), it is also a key to promoting citizenship, as well as teaching children "respect for the rights of others, social responsibility, and to support justice and equality" (Howe & Covell, 2005, p. 6).

The issue of children's rights is a complex and at times potentially controversial one, both in terms of children's entitlement to care and protection and the right to participation and autonomous decision making. Understanding children's and adolescents' perspectives on their rights will enable those involved in research, policy and practice to better promote young people's well-being and development.

References

Baumrind, D. (1978). Parental disciplinary patterns and social competence. *Youth and Society, 9,* 239–276.

Baumrind, D., & Thompson, R. (2002). The ethics of parenting. In M. Bornstein (Ed.), *The handbook of parenting: Vol. 5. Practical issues in parenting* (2nd ed., pp. 3–34), Hillsdale, NJ: Erlbaum.

Ben-Arieh, A., Khoury-Kassabri, M., & Haj-Yahia, M. M. (2006). Generational, ethnic, and national differences in attitudes toward the rights of children in Israel and Palestine. *American Journal of Orthopsychiatry, 76,* 381–388.

Borhnstedt, G. W., Freeman, H. E., & Smith, T. (1981). Adult perspectives on children's autonomy. *Public Opinion Quarterly, 45,* 443–462.

Casas, F., Saporiti, A., Gonzalez, M., Figuer, C., Rostan, D., Sadurni, M., Alsinet, C., Guso, M., Grignoli, D., Mancini, A., Ferrucci, F., & Rago, M. (2006). Children's rights from the point of view of children, their parents and their teachers: A comparative study between Catalonia Spain and Il Molise Italy. *International Journal of Children's Rights, 14,* 1–75.

Cherney, I., & Perry, N. (1996). Children's attitudes toward their rights: An international perspective. In E. Verhellen (Ed.), *Monitoring children's rights* (pp. 241–250). Dordecht, The Netherlands: Martinus Nijhoff.

Cherney, I., & Shing, Y. L. (2003, April). *Children's attitudes toward their rights: A cross-cultural perspective.* Paper presented at the Biennial Meeting of the Society for Research on Child Development, Tampa, FL.

Covell, K., & Howe, R. B. (1995). Variations in support for children's rights among Canadian youth. *International Journal of Children's Rights, 3*, 189–196.

Covell, K., & Howe, R. B. (2001). *The challenge of children's rights for Canada.* Waterloo, ON: Wilfred Laurier University Press.

Daiute, C., & Fine, M. (2003). Youth perspectives on violence and injustice. *Journal of Social Issues, 59*, 1–14.

Earls, F., & Carlson, M. (2002). Adolescents as collaborators: In search of well-being. In M. Tienda & W. J. Wilson (Eds.), *Youth in cities: A cross-national perspective* (pp. 58–83). New York: Cambridge University Press.

Feshbach, N. D., & Feshbach, S. (1978). Toward an historical, social, and developmental perspective on children's rights. *Journal of Social Issues, 34*, 1–7.

Fine, M., & Burns, A. (2003). Class notes: Toward a critical psychology of class and schooling. *Journal of Social Issues, 59*, 841–860.

Flekkoy, M. R., & Kaufman, N. H. (1997). *The participation rights of the child: Rights and responsibilities in family and society.* Bristol, PA: Jessica Kingsley.

Gilligan, C. (1982). *In a different voice.* Cambridge, MA: Harvard University Press.

Grisso, T. (1981). *Juveniles' waiver of rights: Legal and psychological competence.* New York: Plenum.

Hart, R. (1997). *Children's participation: The theory and practice of involving young citizens in community development and environmental care.* New York: UNICEF.

Hart, S., & Pavolic, Z. (1991). Children's rights in education: An historical perspective. *School Psychology Review, 20*, 345–358.

Hart, S., Pavlovic, Z., & Zeidner, M. (2001). The ISPA cross-national children's rights research project. *School Psychology International, 22*(2), 99–129.

Hart, S., & Zeidner, M. (1993). Children's rights perspectives of youth and educators: Early findings of a cross national project. *International Journal of Children's Rights, 1*, 165–188.

Helwig, C. C. (1995). Adolescents and young adults' conceptions of civil liberties: Freedom of speech and religion. *Child Development, 66*, 152–166.

Helwig, C. C. (1997). The role of agent and social context in judgments of speech and religion. *Child Development, 68*, 484–495.

Helwig, C. C. (1998). Children's conceptions of fair government and freedom of speech. *Child Development, 69*, 518–531.

Helwig, C. C. (2006). The development of personal autonomy throughout cultures. *Cognitive Development, 21*, 458–473.

Helwig, C. C., & Turiel, E. (2001). Commentary: Children's rights and the conflict between autonomy and social hierarchy. *International Society for the Study of Behavioral Development Newsletter* (No. 2, Serial No. 38), 18–20.

Helwig, C. C., & Turiel, E. (2002). Rights, autonomy and, democracy: Children's perspectives. *International Journal of Law and Psychiatry, 25*, 253–270.

Howe, R. B., & Covell, K. (2005). *Empowering children: Children's rights education as a pathway to citizenship.* Toronto, Canada: University of Toronto Press.

Kirby, P. (2002). Involving young people in research. In B. Franklin (Ed.), *The new handbook of children's rights: Comparative policy and practice* (pp. 268–284). London: Routledge.

Kohlberg, L. (1969). Stage and sequence: The cognitive-developmental approach to socialization. In D. A. Goslin (Ed.), *Handbook of socialization theory and research* (pp. 347–480). Chicago: Rand McNally.

Lyons, N. P. (1983). Two perspectives: On self, relationships and morality. *Harvard Educational Review, 53*(2), 125–145.

Melton, G. (1980). Children's concepts of their rights. *Journal of Clinical Child Psychology, 9*, 186–190.

Melton, G. (1983). *Child advocacy: Psychological issues and interventions.* New York: Plenum.

Melton, G. B., & Limber, S. (1992). What children's rights mean to children: Children's own views. In M. Freeman & P. Veerman (Eds.), *Ideologies of children's rights* (pp. 167–187). Dordrecht, The Netherlands: Martinus Nijhoff.

Morrow, V. (1999). We are people too: Children and young people's perspectives on children's rights and decision-making in England. *International Journal of Children's Rights, 7*, 49–170.

Morton, T. L., Dubanoski, R. A., & Blaine, D. D. (1982). Cross-cultural perceptions of children's rights. In J. S. Henning (Ed.), *The rights of children: Legal and psychological perspectives* (pp. 141–160). Springfield, IL: Charles C Thomas.

Neff, K. D., & Helwig, C. C. (2002). A constructivist approach to understanding the development of reasoning about rights and authority within cultural contexts. *Cognitive Development, 17*, 1429–1450.

Nucci, L. (2001). *Education in the moral domain.* Cambridge, UK: Cambridge University Press.

Ochaita, E., & Espinosa, M. A. (1997). Children's participation in family and school life: A psychological and developmental approach. *International Journal of Children's Rights, 5*, 279–297.

Peterson-Badali, M., & Abramovitch, R. (1992). Children's knowledge of the legal system: Are they competent to instruct legal counsel? *Canadian Journal of Criminology, 34*, 139–160.

Peterson-Badali, M., Morine, S., Ruck, M. D., & Slonim, N. (2004). Predictors of maternal and child attitudes towards children's nurturance and self-determination rights. *Journal of Early Adolescence, 24*, 159–179.

Peterson-Badali, M., & Ruck, M. D. (2006). *Adolescents' knowledge of children's rights.* Unpublished manuscript.

Peterson-Badali, M., Ruck, M. D., & Bone, J. (2008). Rights conceptions of maltreated children living in state care. *International Journal of Children's Rights, 16*, 99–119.

Peterson-Badali, M., Ruck, M. D., & Ridley, E. (2003). College students' attitudes toward children's nurturance and self-determination rights. *Journal of Applied Social Psychology, 33*, 730–755.

Piaget, J. (1970). Piaget's theory. In P. Mussen (Ed.), *Carmichael's manual of child psychology* (pp. 703–732). New York: Wiley.

Pratt, M. W., Golding, G., Hunter, W., & Sampson, R. (1988). Sex differences in adult moral orientations. *Journal of Personality, 56*(2), 373–391.

Rogers, C. M., & Wrightsman, L. S. (1978). Attitudes towards children's rights: Nurturance or self determination? *Journal of Social Issues, 34*, 59–68.

Ruck, M. D. (1994). *Children's understanding of nurturance and self-determination rights.* Unpublished doctoral dissertation, University of Toronto, Toronto, ON.

Ruck, M. D., Abramovitch, R., & Keating, D. P. (1998). Children's and adolescents' understanding of rights: Balancing nurturance and self-determination. *Child Development, 64*, 404–417.

Ruck, M. D., Keating, D. P., Abramovitch, R., & Koegl, C. J. (1998). Adolescents' and children's knowledge about rights: Some evidence for how young people view rights in their own lives. *Journal of Adolescence, 21*, 275–289.

Ruck, M. D., Peterson-Badali, M., & Day, D. (2002). The relationship between adolescents' and parents' understanding of children's rights. *Journal of Research on Adolescence, 12*, 373–398.

Ruck, M. D., Tenebaum, H., & Sines, J. (2007). Brief report: British adolescents' views about the rights of asylum-seeker children. *Journal of Adolescence, 30*, 687–693.

Shier, H. (2001). Pathways to participation: Openings, opportunities and obligations. *Children and society, 10*, 107–117.

Stier, S. (1978). Children's rights and society's duties. *Journal of Social Issues, 34*, 46–58.

Tapp, J. L., & Levine, F. J. (1974). Legal socialization: Strategies for an ethical legality. *Stanford Law Review, 27*, 1–72.

Taylor, N., Smith, A. B., & Nairn, K. (2001). Rights important to young people: Secondary student and staff perspectives. *International Journal of Children's Rights, 9*, 137–156.

Turiel, E. (1998). The development of morality. In W. Damon (Ed.), *Handbook of child psychology, Socialization* (5th ed., Vol. 3, pp. 863–932). New York: Wiley.

United Nations Convention on the Rights of the Child. (1989). *UN General Assembly* (New York: UNICEF, 1989).

Verhellen, E. (Ed.). (1994). *Children's rights: Monitoring issues*. Gent, Belgium: Mys & Breesch.

Wald, M. S. (1986). Children's rights: A framework for analysis. In B. Landau (Ed.), *Children's rights in the practise of family law* (pp. 3–27). Toronto, Canada: Carswell.

Wark, G. R., & Krebs, D. C. (1996). Gender and dilemma differences in real life moral judgments. *Developmental Psychology, 32*, 220–230.

Zimmerman, S., Temple, M., Peterson-Badali, M., Ruck, M. D., & Day, D. (1999, April). *Maternal influences on children's and adolescents' thinking about rights*. Poster presented at the biennial conference of the Society for Research in Child Development, Albuquerque, NM.

MICHELE PETERSON-BADALI, is an Associate Professor in the department of Human Development and Applied Psychology at the University of Toronto, Canada. Her research interests include children's developing knowledge, reasoning, perceptions, and experiences of children's rights; young people's legal capacities; and youth justice policy. Current projects include studies of parental involvement in the youth justice process and young people's knowledge and attitudes regarding their due process rights and youth justice experiences (including relationships with parents and lawyers). Her research has been published in *Law and Human Behavior, Criminal Justice and Behavior, Journal of Adolescence, Journal of Applied Social Psychology, Journal of Early Adolescence*, and *Journal of Research on Adolescence*. She is also actively engaged in bringing the research findings from these studies into the public policy sphere.

MARTIN RUCK is an Associate Professor of Urban Education and Developmental Psychology at the Graduate Center of the City University of New York. His work examines the overall process of cognitive socialization—at the intersection of race, ethnicity and class—in terms of children's and adolescents' thinking about human rights, educational opportunity and social justice. Currently, he is investigating how children's perceptions of social exclusion and discrimination are influenced by their social experiences and interpretations of rights and justice. His research on the topic of children's understanding of rights has appeared in *Child Development, Journal of Adolescence, Journal of Applied Social Psychology, Journal of Early Adolescence*, and *Journal of Research on Adolescence*. He has recently extended his work on young people's perceptions of their rights to the UK and South Africa.

Journal of Social Issues, Vol. 64, No. 4, 2008, pp. 771–790

Adolescents' Perceptions of Rights as Reflected in Their Views of Citizenship

Lonnie R. Sherrod*

Fordham University

The UN Convention on the Rights of Children (CRC), ratified by the majority of the countries of the world, is an international document that recognizes children and adolescents as worthy of citizenship and human rights. The CRC also attempts to provide a balance between children's nurturance (care and protection) and self-determination (participation) rights. Although there has been social cognitive research on children's understanding of rights, there has been little research examining adolescents' views of the specific rights they would expect to receive through citizenship. In addition, few studies have examined young people's views of the responsibilities inherent in citizenship. This article investigates adolescents' views of the rights and responsibilities of citizenship. Three hundred four adolescents, aged 13–18 years, were asked to rate the importance of various rights and responsibilities of citizenship. Findings indicated that adolescents' responses regarding rights reduced to two components, one related to entitlements (nurturance component of the CRC) and the other freedoms (self-determination/participation component of the CRC). Responsibilities consist of civic-oriented ones and polity-oriented responsibilities. Both components of rights (entitlements and freedoms) correlated significantly with civic-oriented forms of responsibilities; neither form of rights related to polity-oriented responsibilities. The two components of rights also related to the individual variables of age, parental education, ethnicity, and aspects of political self-concept. These results demonstrate the importance of research on the development of citizenship and also have implications for implementation of the CRC.

The defining characteristic of the U.N. Convention on the Rights of Children (CRC) is its provision of rights for children and adolescents. While a complex document, a simple way of describing its articulation of rights is in terms of

---

*Correspondence concerning this article should be addressed to Lonnie R. Sherrod, Society for Research in Child Development, 2950 S. State St., #401, Ann Arbor, MI 48104 [e-mail: sherrod@srcd.org].

771

nurturance (e.g., health care and protection) and participation or self-determination (e.g., freedoms and rights to consent). To some extent, this difference relates to a tension between protection and autonomy (Roche, 1997).

"Children's rights" is a relatively new idea. Attitudes to children have, in fact, undergone considerable change across the past century and a half; in the late 1800s, children came to be valued as "emotionally priceless" instead of being economic assets as they were during industrialization. Reflecting this new view of children, child labor laws, and juvenile justice laws were passed at this time (Zelizer, 1985). These laws recognized that children need protection and might therefore be considered one early example of the recognition of nurturance rights for children. Self-determination or participatory rights have only recently been recognized for children, and the CRC makes an important contribution in giving children rights of participation. Most people would agree that children need protection but giving them autonomy is a newer idea (Roche, 1997), still not endorsed by many. Nonetheless, it represents a logical evolution in our attitudes to young people. Children are valued not just through our emotional investment in them as creatures needing protection, but also through their contributions to the family and to society.

Prior to the CRC, children did not enjoy many rights. However, in most countries individuals acquire particular rights as they grow into adulthood and begin to participate as citizens—rights that are similar to those provided by the CRC. Citizenship involves rights relating both to nurturance and to participation. Children are likely to be aware of citizenship and of the fact that, as adults, they will acquire rights of citizenship and have the opportunity to participate. There are even vehicles such as student government that give children an opportunity to act as citizens. In extending rights to children and adolescents, one concern is if young people understand their rights well enough to take advantage of them in a mature way.

Children may be less aware of the CRC than they are of citizenship, and most countries that have adopted the CRC have not attended to a need to socialize children into the opportunities offered by CRC. This article examines adolescents' views of the rights they expect to acquire as citizens. Understanding the development of children's and youth's views of the rights of citizenship may help us to implement more fully and effectively the UN Convention on the Rights of Children.

The Development of Children's Understanding of Rights

There is a good history of research examining the development of children's understanding of rights generally. Much of this research is based in a Piagetian or cognitive developmental framework because it has been one of the major paradigms guiding research on children's cognitive and social cognitive development. Hence, research describes children's understanding of rights to follow a stage-like progression from egocentric to abstract modes of thinking. Initially, children in the preoperational stage of cognitive development see rights as privileges or the rewards one enjoys. By early adolescence when formal operational thought is acquired, children see rights in terms of abstract universal principles. A similar developmental progression is seen in children's ideas about friendship and in their moral reasoning (Kohlberg, 1984; Melton, 1983; Selman, 1980).

Recent research has provided a more detailed description of children's understanding of rights by examining their views of specific types of rights such as freedom of speech. Hence, this research is more directly relevant to this study. For example, young adolescents tend to see civil liberties such as freedom of speech as abstract. Because abstract thought is a developmental achievement of adolescence, adolescence may represent the age at which children begin to attend and appreciate various rights and civil liberties, such as freedom of speech (Helwig, 1995). Other research has shown that young children see nurturance rights as more important than self-determination ones, but by midadolescence they see the two types of rights as more equal (Ruck, Abramovitch, & Keating, 1998). These authors suggest that youth see nurturance rights in the context of family and social relationships whereas self-determination rights relate to their understanding of moral rules and the larger sociolegal context. Adolescents' judgments about freedoms of speech and religion have also been found to vary across the social contexts of family, school, and society (Helwig, 1997). The specific rights examined in this research such as freedom of speech and nurturance rights are rights of citizenship. Hence children's responses regarding the rights of citizenship should agree with these results.

Research on the Development of Citizenship

There has been much less research examining the development of children's and adolescents' views of the rights specific to citizenship. Research generally on the development of citizenship has, however, slowly continued to grow because of Putnam's (2000) argument that the United States faces a crisis in regard to low levels of civic engagement. The definition of citizenship is somewhat controversial, but research indicates that citizenship is viewed to involve both political participation and civic involvement (Flanagan & Faaison, 2001; Flanagan & Sherrod, 1998; Sherrod, Flanagan, & Youniss, 2002; Walzer, 1990). For example, research on teens' views of citizenship responsibilities shows that duties are seen to consist of both civic-oriented ones and polity-oriented ones (Bogard & Sherrod, 2004, 2008). This distinction is important because children and adolescents have more opportunity to participate civically than they do politically. In fact young people are often required to do community service, but they cannot vote until they obtain adult status (Bogard & Sherrod, 2004).

Acquisition of certain rights is one hallmark of citizenship. For example, as a citizen of most countries, certain freedoms are protected such as freedom of speech and freedom of religion. However, citizenship usually also comes with certain entitlements; public education is one example of an entitlement in the United States. This distinction follows rather closely the CRC differentiation of nurturance (entitlements) and self-determination or participation rights (freedoms). One interesting question is whether young people's views of the rights expected to be acquired as an adult citizen show these two dimensions of nurturance/entitlements and participation/freedoms? That is the first question addressed by this study and the first hypothesis is that views of citizenship rights will show these two components.

Citizenship involves responsibilities as well as rights. One enjoys certain rights of citizenship many of which relate to nurturance or protection, and in exchange one is expected to participate as a citizen by voting and volunteering. Just as there has been little research examining children's and adolescent's views of the rights of citizenship, so too there has been almost no research examining adolescents' views of responsibilities. One exception is the study previously mentioned which found that teens consider citizenship responsibilities to consist of two components: Polity-oriented responsibilities such as voting and expressing patriotism and civically oriented ones consisting of helping one's community and showing tolerance of others' differences (Bogard & Sherrod, 2004, 2008).

This distinction of political and civic responsibilities, like entitlements and freedoms, also relates to that of nurturance versus participation. Nurturance rights might be viewed to relate more to civic or community participation; it is through one's involvement in family, school or community that nurturance is ultimately achieved (Helwig, 1997; Ruck et al., 1998). Self-determination, on the other hand, as participation certainly relates to political involvement. However, civic involvement such as community service might also be viewed to represent self-determination or participation, particularly for children too young to participate as citizens. In addition, previous research has shown that young children typically consider nurturance rights as more important than participation (Ruck et al., 1998).

The central focus of this article is on adolescents' understanding of the rights of citizenship. However, one would hope that views of rights and of responsibilities relate to each other. One enjoys certain rights such as freedom of speech, but it is expected that one will also participate, by voting or volunteering, for example. Do adolescents see rights and responsibilities as relevant to each other? The second question addressed in this article is how young people's views of rights relate to their views of responsibilities. The second hypothesis is that the components of which rights are seen to consist will relate to the components seen in responsibilities, with both relating to the distinction between nurturance and participation.

Citizenship in Diverse Youth

Because participation as a citizen involves the individual in the larger sociopolitical sphere, any attention to citizenship must attend to variables that index the individual's place in this larger context. Bronfenbrenner's landmark social ecological theory has led developmental psychologists to pay increasing attention to cultural and other macrolevel influences on development (Bronfenbrenner & Morris, 1998). There are proximal influences on the development of citizenship, such as parental political influences and school climate (Flanagan & Tucker, 1999; Jennings & Niemi, 1974). However, citizenship generally resides in the outer circles of influences in the form of social norms and sociopolitical context. As a result, one might expect sociocultural context to have an important influence on the development of citizenship, especially on adolescents' understanding of what is involved in citizenship.

Variables of diversity such as gender, social class, and ethnicity may influence children's and adolescents' understanding of rights (Helwig, Arnold, Tan, & Boyd, 2003), especially because the rights one enjoys may vary across these variables. To date there has been little research examining possible differences in children or adolescents' understanding of rights by individual demographic variables (Ruck & Peterson-Badali, 2006). One exception is a study reporting that U.S. adolescents' views of the responsibilities of citizenship vary by gender, parental education, ethnicity, and immigrant status (Bogard & Sherrod, 2004, 2008). The third question addressed by this study is how adolescents' views of the rights of citizenship vary across individual dimensions. Finally, the third hypothesis is that different youth will emphasize different aspects of rights, reflecting the influence of sociocultural context on the development of citizenship.

Young people's development into citizenship is an important but understudied topic for research. We must understand the development of citizenship, with its inherent rights and responsibilities, in order to know how as a society we may promote its development. We must also understand children's and adolescents' views of rights in order to understand how they may benefit from the CRC and what we must do to ensure that they benefit fully. The study of attitudes toward citizenship provides one opportunity for gaining such understanding and knowledge. Hopefully this article contributes both to our understanding of the development of rights of citizenship as well as to children's potential for benefiting from the CRC.

To summarize, this study examines adolescents' views of the rights of citizenship, predicting that they will consist of components relating to freedoms and entitlements. We also predict that these views of rights will relate to previously studied views of responsibilities. Finally, it is expected that adolescents' views will differ across variables such as gender and ethnicity.

Methods

Participants

This study was part of a larger project designed to explore civic attitudes and behaviors among diverse youth. Students from four high schools in the Northeast of the United States were recruited for participation in the study between 2000 and 2002. Because the goal of the larger study was to explore attitudes and behaviors among diverse youth, two high schools were selected for their high proportion of non-European-American students, a selective academically oriented school for accelerated students and the other a low performing public school, and two schools were selected for their high percentages of European-American youth, a school in an affluent suburb and an all-boys prep school. Because schools in this urban area tend to be segregated by race, it was necessary to sample different schools in order to obtain a diverse sample.

Participants were 302 adolescents between the ages of 13 and 18 years old ($M = 15.5$, $SD = 1.4$ for girls; $M = 16.36$, $SD = 1.5$ for boys). Thirty-six percent of the participants were female, 64% male. The sample represented a range of ethnic backgrounds. Of the students who participated, 39% self-identified as European American, 16% Hispanic, 8% African American, 23% Asian, 2% American Indian, 2% Middle Eastern, 4% Multiracial, and 5% selected Other but did not indicate an ethnicity. Fifty-eight percent of the sample were first or second generation immigrants. First-generation immigrants were defined as participants themselves born in another country (16% of sample); second-generation immigrants were defined as participants born in the United States to parents who were born in another country (42%). Within the sample, 33% of youth reported their parents did not have a college degree, 27% of subjects' parents had obtained a bachelor's degree, and 38% had a postgraduate degree. A majority of students reported that their grades were in the A–B range (32.5% and 44.2%, respectively) while the remainder reported grades in the C (17.8%), D (4.8%), or failing range (.7%).

Measures

Attitudes and other variables were assessed using a measure based on prior work by Sherrod (2003), Conover and Searing (2000), Youniss and Yates (1997), and Flanagan and Sherrod (1998). The survey was designed to assess students' overall political orientation. It included 23 self-report items assessing gender, ethnicity, parental education, religion, political affiliation, and so forth. Table 1

Table 1. Percentages of Students Answering Yes or No to Questions about Political Life

Measure	% Yes	% No
Have political party affiliation	40.9	59.1
Political views formed yet	40.7	59.3
Are your political views similar to your parents	25.9[a]	24.6[b]
Participate in school government	21.2	78.8
Have had a civics class	44.6	54.4
Consider yourself a citizen	94.6	5.4
Have participated in political events	27.9	71.8
Have you done community service	74.2	25.8

Note. [a]Percentage reporting that their views are not at all identical to their parents.
[b]Percentage reporting that their views are identical to parents; 49.5% offered a neutral response.

Table 2. Factor Structure for Ranking of Importance of Citizenship Rights

Items	Factor 1	Factor 2	Mean	SD	Alpha
Entitlements					
To get health care	.853		3.63	.73	.79
To have housing	.789		3.46	.86	
To have privacy	.660		3.50	.82	
To be free of racial discrimination	.510		3.49	1.03	
To get an education	.484		3.85	.47	
To government help	.435		3.08	1.01	
Freedoms					
To join any group		.685	3.27	.95	.76
To demonstrate		.593	3.28	.94	
To vote		.555	3.75	.72	
Freedom of speech		.554	3.45	.73	
To be homosexual		.551	2.87	1.45	
Freedom of religion		.521	3.67	.67	
To work at any job		.458	3.43	.85	
Eigenvalue (% variance)	5.1(39%)	1.5(12%)			

Note. Extraction method: Maximum likelihood.
Rotation method: Varimax with Kaiser normalization.
Converged in 3 iterations.

presents the means and standard deviations for rankings and frequencies for yes/no questions relating to political orientation. Participants were also asked to rate on a 5-point Likert-type scale how important a particular right or responsibility was to citizenship, from 1 (*not at all important*) to 5 (*very important*). There were 13 items relating to attitudes about rights. The means and standard deviations for these rankings are presented in Table 2.

Procedure

Participants were recruited in their classrooms and provided parental consent forms to take home for signature. Adolescents' assent forms were distributed and signed by those students who returned parental consent forms. Surveys were administered classroom style.

Teachers distributed the surveys and either read each item aloud or let the students fill out the surveys individually. In the school for accelerated students it was not necessary to read the survey aloud; in the low performing school, the teachers thought it wise to read the items aloud.

Analyses

First frequency analyses were run on all variables (presented in Table 1). Factor analyses using maximum likelihood extraction and varimax rotation were used to ask if attitudes toward rights consisted of more than one component. Exploratory analyses were first run. Variables that did not load on any component were deleted, and the requested number of factors reduced to the number that contained at least three items. Generally, eigenvalues above 1.0 and loadings above .40 were accepted. Thereafter, correlations were used to examine relationships between the factors of citizenship attitudes and other variables such as parental education. Analysis of variance's (ANOVAs) were used to examine differences in attitudes toward citizenship rights across categorical variables such as ethnicity and immigrant status.

Results

To test the first hypothesis, a factor analysis using maximum likelihood extraction with varimax rotation was conducted on respondents' ranking of the importance of various rights of citizenship. As predicted two clear components emerged: (a) Seven items constituted ENTITLEMENTS, yielding an eigenvalue = 5.01 accounting for 39% of the variance (examples include "to get health care, to be free of racial discrimination"); (b) Six items represented FREEDOMS, yielding an eigenvalue = 1.53 accounting for 12% of the variance (examples include "to vote, to be homosexual"). The two subscales correlated ($r = .56$) indicating overlapping but distinct constructs. Internal consistencies for the subscales were good (alpha for ENTITLEMENTS = .79; for FREEDOMS alpha = .76). Factor scores or sums of rankings for all items on a factor were used in subsequent analyses. The attitudes toward citizenship rights items are listed along with factor loadings in Table 2.

The second hypothesis asked how views of rights would relate to views of responsibilities. Using factor scores from the analysis described above and from

Table 3. Intercorrelations between Rights and Responsibilities

Rights	1	2	3	4
Entitlements	1			
Freedoms	.12*	1		
Responsibilities				
Civic-Oriented	.32**	.38**	1	
Polity-Oriented	.04	−−.07	.05	1

Note. *$p < .05$ (2-tailed).
**$p < .01$ (2-tailed).

the factor analysis reported in Bogard and Sherrod (2004, 2008), simple Pearson bivariate correlations were calculated. Civic-oriented responsibilities related to both entitlements ($r = .40$) and freedoms ($r = .45$). Polity-oriented responsibilities related to neither. However, polity-oriented responsibilities related to reports of being patriotic ($r = .65, p < .001$). These correlations are presented in Table 3.

The third hypothesis asked what individual variables would relate to views of citizenship rights. Correlations were examined between factor scores for rights and other individual variables including age, gender, immigrant status, and parental education. Other variables including activities, grade point average (GPA), political affiliation, participation in political events, and sense of citizenship were included to examine how other variables might compare to the demographic variables in their relationship to views of rights. These correlations are presented in Table 4. Because the number of significant correlations was small and the significant correlations relatively small in size, regression analyses were not run.

One-way ANOVAs were used to examine differences in the two factors of citizenship rights across gender, ethnicity, immigrant status, and political party affiliation. In order to make these analyses more interpretable they were run both using factor scores and using the sum of the rankings across the items that constituted the factor. Although significance levels varied somewhat across the two analyses, results did not. Analyses using summed rankings are reported in Tables 6 and 7; means and standard deviations are reported in Table 5. There was a significant gender difference for freedoms with females ranking freedoms as more important than males ($F = 3.9, p < .05$); this result is of course consistent with the significant correlation. There was a significant difference on freedoms ($F = 2.5, p < .05$) between different ethnic groups, with European Americans and Asians offering higher rankings than other groups. There were no differences by immigrant status. Both entitlements and freedoms showed differences by political party ($F = 5.2$ for entitlements and $F = 7.0$ for freedoms, $p < .006$ and $p < .001$, respectively). Students self-reporting as Democrats or Other affiliation showed higher rankings for both compared to Republicans.

Table 4. Intercorrelations between Rights and Iindividual Variables

	1	2	3	4	5	6	7	8	9	10	11	12	13	14	15
Age	1														
Sex/gender	−.247**	1													
Were your parents born in another country	−.235**	.092	1												
Parents level of education	.039	−.020	−.263**	1											
What are your grades	−.236**	.121*	.019	.234**	1										
Do you identify yourself with a political party	.082	.063	−.129*	.146*	.079	1									
Do you believe your political opinions are firmly established	.143*	−.163**	−.175**	.108	−.023	.219**	1								
Are your political views similar to your parents	.022	.063	.051	−.015	.044	−.101	−.057	1							

Do you participate in school government	−.075	.103	−.042	.055	.197**	.147*	−.043	−.013	1						
Do you participate in community service	.208**	−.065	−.099	.146*	.237**	.084	.010	.102	1						
Do you participate in political events or support causes	.044	.018	−.251**	.204**	.067	.186**	.246**	.118*	.215**	.112	1				
Do you consider yourself a citizen	.028	−.074	−.046	−.048	−.096	.015	.043	.060	−.020	.029	−.019	1			
Have you ever had a course in civics	.469**	−.091	−.124*	−.136*	−.191**	.138*	.148*	.066	.001	.094	.188**	.068	1		
Entitlement rights	−.141*	.089	.097	.022	.052	.001	−.050	−.012	.038	−.029	.095	−.086	−.073	1	
Freedoms rights	.006	.116*	−.009	.174**	.148*	.155**	−.019	.058	.062	−.014	.176**	−.120*	−.028	.562**	1

Note. $*$ $p < 0.05$ level (2-tailed). $**$ $p < 0.01$ level (2-tailed).

Table 5. Means and Standard Deviations for Rights[a] by Individual Variables

	Entitlements		Freedoms	
	Mean	SD	Mean	SD
Gender				
Male	20.78	3.73	23.45	4.30
Female	21.45	3.34	24.47	3.94
Political party affiliation				
Democrat	21.59	3.25	25.11	3.66
Republican	18.87	4.66	21.95	3.81
Other	20.40	4.98	26.17	2.23
Ethnicity[b]				
Caucasian	20.12	3.80	23.91	3.91
Hispanic	19.84	3.47	21.46	5.06
African American	19.04	3.36	22.19	4.19
Asian	20.96	3.08	23.03	3.76
Mixed	18.46	4.36	21.26	4.42
Other	19.23	3.69	18.98	2.95
Immigrant status				
Yes	21.33	3.42	23.79	4.01
No	20.61	3.91	23.87	4.54

Note. [a]Means calculated using sums of rankings for all items on a factor.
[b]Because of small numbers, American Indian and Mid Eastern were omitted from the analyses of ethnicity.

Discussion

This article examines adolescents' views of the rights of citizenship. The reported study examined three hypotheses: Views of rights would consist of components relating to nurturance and to self-determination; views of rights would relate to views of responsibilities; and views of rights would vary across individual demographic variables. All three hypotheses were supported at least in part. Results are discussed in terms of the balance between different types of rights—nurturance and self-determination, the developing capacity of the adolescent for citizenship in terms of his/her understanding of it, and how growth into citizenship may promote the best interests of the child.

The Balance between Nurturance and Self-Determination Rights

As predicted, rights were seen to consist of two major components. The first was entitlements or the things one should obtain as a result of being a citizen. These are fully analogous to the CRC's focus on nurturance rights. The other component

Table 6. Analysis of Variance of Freedoms Rights and Gender, Political Party Affiliation, Immigrant Status, and Ethnicity

Gender Source of variance	SS	df	MS	F	p
Between groups	68.48	1	68.48	3.92	.05
Within groups	4993.49	286	17.46		
Total	5061.97	287			
Political party affiliation					
Between groups	185.59	2	92.80	7.02	.001
Within groups	1, 520.69	115	13.22		
Total	1, 706.28	117			
Immigrant status					
Between groups	.43	1	.43	.02	.88
Within groups	4, 994.65	278			
Total	4, 995.07	279			
Ethnicity					
Between groups	343.50	8	42.94	2.54	.01
Within groups	4, 718.47	279	16.91		
Total	5, 061.97	287			

was freedoms such as freedom of speech and freedom to vote. Freedoms represent participation or self-determination as described by the CRC. Hence adolescents' views of the importance of the rights they will receive as adult citizens supports the CRC's articulation of the rights it would offer children and adolescents.

In a democracy we typically emphasize the freedoms of citizenship; the United States was founded to provide particular freedoms. Entitlements resulting from citizenship have entered more recently as the federal government has grown. However, in this sample, entitlements accounted for far more of the variance in responses than freedoms so were seen as equally important to freedoms, if not more so. Interestingly, age correlated inversely with entitlements indicating that this concern for what you get from government decreases with age. Past social cognitive research shows that nurturance and self-determination rights come to be seen as equally important in midadolescence (Ruck et al., 1998). These results generally support this finding. It also is consistent with viewing nurturance rights as related to protection and participation to autonomy (Roche, 1997).

Both of these results imply that views of citizenship continue to grow as young people begin to practice their citizenship. Hence, we may need to differentiate competency for understanding from performance, a distinction often found in research on cognitive development (Flavell, Miller, & Miller, 1993). Research on the implementation of the UN CRC should explore the degree to which children

Table 7. Analysis of Variance of Entitlements Rights and Gender, Political Party Affiliation, Ethnicity, Immigrant Status, and Ethnicity

Gender Source of variance	SS	df	MS	F	p
Between groups	30.42	1	30.42	2.35	.13
Within groups	3, 798.42	294	12.92		
Total	3, 828.83	295			
Political party affiliation					
Between groups	138.30	2	69.15	5.29	.006
Within groups	1, 554.63	119	13.06		
Total	1, 692.93	121			
Immigrant status					
Between groups	35.37	1	35.37	2.69	.10
Within groups	3, 743.20	285	13.13		
Total	3, 778.58	286			
Ethnicity					
Between groups	105.75	8	13.22	1.02	.42
Within groups	3, 723.08	287	12.97		
Total	3, 828.83	295			

differentiate nurturance from participation rights as outlined in the convention and whether acquisition of these new rights affects their views of citizenship rights.

The Developing Capacity of the Child for Citizenship

The second question addressed by this study examined the maturity of adolescents' views of citizenship. One aspect of maturity is whether attitudes to rights relate to views of responsibilities. Interestingly, and contrary to our hypothesis both entitlements and freedoms related to civic-oriented responsibilities; but neither related to polity-oriented responsibilities. This may indicate that these adolescents view citizenship more in terms of civic responsibilities and see both types of rights as related to civic duties but not to political ones. Citizenship may be an area where participation is required for a full understanding; adolescents may understand rights and responsibilities in an abstract sense but it is only by practicing them through citizenship that a mature view of citizenship emerges. High school students can participate civically through, for example, community service so that it may be that they see citizenship at this age in terms of behaviors possible for them. Many teens participate in community service so that they have had an opportunity to exercise civic-oriented responsibilities and to see how they relate to rights. Because they have yet to have the opportunity to participate fully as a citizen through such activities as voting, it may be that they have yet to see how political participation relates to rights. It would be interesting to examine if and how the relationship between rights and responsibilities changes with age. Research is currently examining how the exercise of civic engagement relates to self-determination and identity development (Lerner, 2004). More research is needed, however, which examines how adolescents incorporate their sense of self politically into their overall identity, and in turn, how political identity then drives behavior. It may be that adolescents' lack of political involvement limits their sense of self in regard to politics so that they have yet to incorporate views of their rights as citizens into their polity-oriented views of participation. Repeating this study longitudinally or with an older sample could serve to address this issue.

This finding that views of rights and responsibilities are related has implications for the implementation of the UN Convention. As new rights are offered to children and teens, one must also ask what new responsibilities should accompany these rights. In the same way that children and youth should be privy to a core set of basic human rights, they also need to be given more serious and substantial responsibilities if they are to thrive (Lerner, 2004; Zeldin, Camino, & Calvert, 2003). To some extent responsibilities represent the active side of citizenship. The CRC should address the responsibilities that could or should go along with any new rights children are accorded. Offering rights without considering the associated responsibilities represents a limited view of the child as an active participant in their development and community.

Previous social cognitive developmental research has documented a progression from concrete to formal views of rights (Melton, 1983; Ruck et al., 1998) so that by adolescence, as they enter citizenship, most individuals have a relatively mature view of rights. This study illustrates that age relates to adolescents' appreciation of freedoms versus entitlements. Age was the only individual variable to relate to views of rights and it correlated inversely with entitlements; that is, older youth saw entitlements as less important than younger ones. A long history of research on social cognitive development indicates that younger children are concrete; they choose friends and understand rights generally, for example, on the basis of things they can obtain rather than psychological qualities (Ruck et al., 1998; Selman, 1980). Entitlements are more concrete than freedoms; they are closer to rewards. Entitlements, which could be seen as the more concrete idea, become less important with age, which is a healthy development in terms of the growth of citizenship.

Adolescents' views of specific rights are also relevant to development. It is, for example, interesting to note that in this study several of the entitlements viewed to be important to citizenship are not currently entitlements of citizenship in this country. Health care, the highest loading item on this factor, is a good example. Unlike entitlements most freedoms are realized through citizenship in the United

States. However, one item was freedom to be gay or lesbian, and although there are currently no laws prohibiting same-sex sexuality in the United States, gay and lesbian people may face discrimination if they are open about their sexuality, and they do not enjoy all the rights of citizenship such as marriage. Similarly, to be free from racial discrimination was seen to be one entitlement. Many would argue that this ideal is also not yet realized in this country. As teens grow into citizenship, they should come to realize the situation—that health care is not an entitlement or that freedom to be gay does not come without cost. The issue for research on the development of citizenship is whether the realization that not all freedoms and entitlements automatically come with citizenship brings cynicism and a tendency to turn off to political involvement or an increased activist type involvement to improve the status quo.

In summary, this study demonstrates that the mature view of rights found in previous social cognitive development research extends to adolescents views of the rights, as well as the responsibilities, of citizenship. Hence adolescents who are poised on the verge of exercising their citizenship are cognitively prepared in regard to their views of what adult citizenship will entail. However, their views are not fully mature, and it may be that actual participation as citizens is necessary for growth into fully mature views. This has implications for implementation of the CRC. Not only should we assess children's and adolescents' capacity for understanding the rights being offered, but we may also need to give children experience with their new rights.

The Best Interests of the Child

Article 12 of the CRC states that "Parties should assure to the child who is capable of forming his/her own views the right to express those views in all matters affecting the child, the views of the child being given due weight in accordance with the age and maturity of the child." The CRC is constructed to promote the best interests of the child by protecting their rights. Similarly, helping children to grow into adults who can benefit from the rights offered by their citizenship also promotes their best interests. In both cases, it is important that equity and fairness be represented in our efforts.

The final question addressed by this study examined the background characteristics of adolescents that relate to their views of the importance of different rights of citizenship. Previous research had found that numerous background variables related to attitudes to both civic and political responsibilities: age, gender, socioeconomic status , ethnicity, immigration status, and connectedness to family (Bogard & Sherrod, 2004, 2008). In this study several variables related to freedoms: sex/gender, parental educational, GPA, and identification with a political party positively related to freedoms. Considering oneself a citizen related inversely to freedoms. As previously discussed, age was the only variable that related to entitlements. It is of course somewhat risky to interpret such correlations because this small number could result from chance. However, interpretations are immediately suggested by past research.

Gender, parental education, and GPA also relate to freedoms. To some extent these variables hang together. Girls have higher GPAs on average and teens with educated parents do better in school. The result indicates that more educated parents are more likely to promote a view of the importance of freedoms, which has been found in past research (Flanagan & Tucker, 1991); furthermore, higher education is associated with more affluence so that entitlements are likely to be less important because these families can obtain needed resources without the help of government (Jankowski, 1999).

Differences were also found in rankings of freedoms across ethnic group with European Americans and Asians ranking freedoms more highly than did other groups. Because parental education and ethnicity are related, it is impossible to determine which of these two variables is more important. However, either social class or ethnicity seems to relate to views of citizenship rights. This result is in the predicted direction such that disadvantaged adolescents viewed freedoms as less important than adolescents from more advantaged circumstances.

It is of course not at all surprising that political party affiliation relates to views of both sets of rights; party affiliation is based on one's views. Participants who viewed themselves as Democrats see both freedoms and entitlements as more important to citizenship rights than do youth who identified as Republicans or other. Polity-oriented and civic-oriented responsibilities did not appear to differ across political affiliation. It may simply be that youth who see themselves as democrats think more about rights, but both parties have similar views on duties.

The fact that background factors such as school activities, community involvement in the form of service, and immigrant status relate to responsibilities (Bogard & Sherrod, 2004, 2008) but not to rights may indicate that socialization is more important to participation than to perceptions of the benefits of citizenship. Rights are the benefits we enjoy as citizens of a democracy. The rights one obtains results in large part from the nature of the society in which one lives (Flanagan et al., 1998). Responsibilities, however, relate more to voluntary participation. No duties are actually required of citizens.

Variables such as gender, ethnicity and social class, or parental education have profound effects on socialization into all adult behaviors including citizenship. We must recognize the multiple pathways through which children and adolescents grow into citizenship, and insure that each developmental path provides equal access to the rights and responsibilities of citizenship. Offering children rights through the CRC before they partake of those offered through citizenship may offer guidance for the promotion of citizenship, but it is equally important that the rights offered be provided in a fair and equitable fashion. The goal of the CRC is to provide fair treatment to youth by making rights available to them; similar fair treatment across individual differences is also needed in distribution of these rights and in socialization into their benefits.

Limitations of the Study and Research Directions

There are several limitations to this study. First the data are cross-sectional; longitudinal studies are one clear direction for research. Also the data are all self-report; in future research, we need to be more creative about how to obtain similar information from youth about citizenship. The sample is drawn from four separate schools in order to address the main goals of the overall study; as a result school is confounded with certain variables such as academic orientation. The questions of this study might be more effectively addressed with a more representative sample from a single school. Finally, certain variables such as parental education, ethnicity, and immigrant status were confounded making examination of their separate contributions impossible; it may be challenging to do so, but future research should strive to examine the separate contributions of these variables. Future research should also be connected to implementation of the CRC. Such implementation is not automatically a benefit for children unless the CRC is implemented in a way that works for children of different ages, social classes, and ethnicities. Because the CRC remains to be ratified by the United States, such work will need to occur internationally and should employ a cross-national comparative approach.

In Conclusion

To some extent the UN CRC offers international citizenship. It ensures that children worldwide have certain unalienable rights and receive equally fair treatment by the societies in which they live. Hence, children and teens' perceptions of the rights offered by the Convention should not differ very much from their perception of the rights they receive as citizens of a country. It would be interesting to ask about children's current perceptions of the rights being offered by the CRC to see if they are viewed to consist of freedoms and entitlements and/or contain any other dimensions. Children and teens' perceptions of the benefits offered by the Convention will determine the extent to which they are able to take advantage of their new rights and benefit from them.

References

Bogard, K., & Sherrod, L. (2004). *Allegiances and civic engagement in diverse youth.* Paper presented at International Society for the Study of Behavior Development. Ghent, Belgium, July 11–14.

Bogard, K., & Sherrod, L. (2008). Allegiances and civic engagement in diverse youth. *Journal of Ethnicity and Culture,* in press.

Bronfenbrenner, U., & Morris, P. (1998). The ecology of developmental processes. In W. Damon (Gen. Ed.) & R. M. Lerner (Vol. Ed.), *Handbook of child psychology: Theoretical models of human development* (Vol. 1, pp. 993–1028). New York: Wiley.

Conover, P. J., & Searing, D. D. (2000). The democratic purposes of education: Apolitical socialization perspective. In L. M. McDonnell, P. M. Timpane, & R. Benjamin (Eds.), *Rediscovering the democratic purposes of education* (pp. 91–124). Lawrence KS: University of Kansas Press.

Flanagan, C., Bowes, J., Jonsson, B.. Csapo, B., & Sheblanova, E. (1998). Ties that bind: Correlates of male and female adolescents' civic commitments in seven countries. *Journal of Social Issues, 54*, 457–476.

Flanagan, C., & Faaison, N. (2001). Youth civic development: Implications of research for social policy and programs. *Social Policy Reports,* no. 1.

Flanagan, C., & Sherrod, L. (1998). Political development: Youth growing up in a global community. *Journal of Social Issues, 54*(3), 447–456.

Flanagan, C., & Tucker, C. (1999). Adolescents' explanations for political issues: Concordance with their views of self and society. *Developmental Psychology, 35*, 1198–1209.

Flavell, J. H., Miller, P. H., & Miller, S. A. (1993). *Cognitive development* (3rd ed.). Englewood Cliffs, NJ: Prentice Hall.

Helwig, C. C. (1995). Adolescents' and young adults' conceptions of civil liberties: Freedom of speech and freedom of religion. *Child Development, 66*, 152–166.

Helwig, C. C. (1997). The role of agent and social context in judgments of freedom of speech and religion. *Child Development, 68*(3), 484–495.

Helwig, C. C., Arnold, M. L., Tan, D., & Boyd, D. (2003). Chinese adolescents' reasoning about democratic and authority-based decision-making in peer, family, and school contexts. *Child Development, 74*(3), 783–800.

Jankowski, M. (2002). Minority youth and civic engagement: The impact of group relations. *Applied Developmental Science, 6*(4), 237–245.

Jennings, M., & Niemi, R. (1974). *The political character of adolescence.* Princeton, NJ: Princeton University Press.

Kohlberg, L. (1984). *Essays on moral development, Volume 2: The psychology of moral development.* San Francisco: Harper & Row.

Lerner, R. M. (2004). *Liberty: Thriving and civic engagement among America's youth.* Thousand Oaks, CA: Sage Publications.

Melton, G. B. (1983). *Child advocacy: Psychological issues and interventions.* New York: Plenum Press.

Putnam, R. (2000). *Bowling alone: The collapse and revival of American community.* New York: Simon & Schuster.

Roche, J. (1997). Children's rights: Participation and dialogue. In J. Roche & S. Tucker (Eds.), *Youth in society: Contemporary theory, policy, and practice* (pp. 42–51). Thousand Oaks, CA: Sage Publications.

Ruck, M. D., Abramovitch, R., & Keating, D. (1998). Children's and adolescents' understanding of rights: Balancing nurturance and self determination. *Child Development, 64*(2), 404–417.

Ruck, M. D., & Peterson-Badali, M. (2006). Youth perceptions of rights. In L. Sherrod, C. Flanagan, R. Kassimir, & A. Syvertsen (Eds.), *Youth activism: An international encyclopedia* (Vol. II, pp. 532–539). Westport, CT: Greenwood Press.

Selman, R. (1980). *The growth of interpersonal understanding.* New York: Academic Press.

Sherrod, L. R. (2003). Promoting the development of citizenship in diverse youth. *PS: Political Science and Politics,* April, 287–292.

Sherrod, L., Flanagan, C., & Youniss, J. (2002). Dimensions of citizenship and opportunities for youth development: The what, why, when, where and who of citizenship development. *Applied Developmental Science, 6*(4), 264–272.

Walzer, M. (1990). What does it mean to be an "American"? *Social Research, 57*(3), 591–614.

Youniss, J., & Yates, M. (1997). What we know about engendering civic identity. *American Behavioral Scientist, 40*, 620–631.

Zeldin, S., Camino, L., & Calvert, M. (2003). Toward an understanding of youth in community governance: Policy priorities and research directions. *Social Policy Report, 17*(3).

Zelizer, V. A. (1985). *Pricing the priceless child: The changing social value of children.* New York: Basic Books.

LONNIE R. SHERROD received his PhD in Psychology from Yale University in 1978, an MA in Biology from University of Rochester (1976), and a BA from Duke University (1972). He is currently Executive Director of the Society for Research in Child Development and Professor of Psychology in Fordham University's Applied Developmental Psychology Program (ADP). He edits *The Social Policy Reports,* is a member and Chair of APA's Committee on Children, Youth and Families, on SRCD's Publications Committee, and a member of the NAS/IOM Committee on Adolescent Health Services. He has been Vice President (2005) of the Federation of Behavioral, Psychological and Cognitive Sciences, has been chair of the Committee on Child Development, Public Policy, and Public Information of the Society for Research in Child Development, has been on the Executive Council of Division 7 of the American Psychological Association (APA), and has served on the Program Committee for the ACYF biennial Conference on Head Start Research. He is a Fellow in both the American Psychological Association and American Psychological Society. He has serves on the editorial boards of numerous journals, including *Developmental Psychology, Journal of Research on Adolescence*, and *Applied Developmental Science*. His area of research is Youth Political Development, and he has coedited special issues of the *Journal of Research on Social Issues* (1998) and *Applied Developmental Science* (2002) on the topic.

Journal of Social Issues, Vol. 64, No. 4, 2008, pp. 791–813

Schooling, Sexuality, and Rights: An Investigation of Heterosexual Students' Social Cognition Regarding Sexual Orientation and the Rights of Gay and Lesbian Peers in School

Stacey S. Horn,* Laura A. Szalacha, and Karen Drill

University of Illinois at Chicago

Within the United States, protecting the rights of lesbian, gay, bisexual, and trans-gender (LGBT) students in school elicits much controversy and debate. On one side is the argument that all students should be able to receive an education free from discrimination, harassment, and harm. On the other side is the argument that by protecting LGBT students' rights, schools are infringing on the rights of others to their individual beliefs about homosexuality. To investigate these competing arguments, we surveyed high school-aged heterosexual adolescents (N = 1,076) regarding their beliefs and attitudes about sexual orientation and the rights of gay and lesbian peers. Results suggest that adolescents differentiate between their in-dividual beliefs about homosexuality and the rights of others to be safe in school. Further, the results provide additional support for the idea that attitudes and beliefs about sexual orientation and the rights of gay and lesbian peers are multi-faceted and draw from multiple domains of social knowledge. The implications of these findings will be discussed in relation to the rights of LGBT students and the

*Correspondence concerning this article should be addressed to Stacey S. Horn, MC 147, University of Illinois at Chicago, 1040 W. Harrison St., Chicago, IL 60607 [e-mail: sshorn@uic.edu].

The research reported in this article was supported in part by grants to the first author from the Wayne F. Placek Fund of the American Psychological Foundation and a Violence Prevention for Vulnerable Youth Grant from the Substance Abuse and Mental Health Services Administration. The authors wish to thank Larry Nucci, Shannon Sullivan, and Lee Gregory for invaluable feedback and assistance with the project, as well as Courtney Gollant, Jennifer Chin, Jason Lobdell, Melanie D'Andrelli, Chrisna Perry, and Anna Kurtz for assistance with data collection, data entry, and data management.

obligations that schools have to create safe and supportive learning environments for all students regardless of sexual orientation or gender identity.

In 2002, George W. Bush signed into the legislation The No Child Left Behind Act. One of the major premises of the act is:

> the promotion of school safety, such that students and school personnel are free from violent and disruptive acts, including sexual harassment and abuse, and victimization associated with prejudice and intolerance, on school premises, going to and from school, and at school sponsored activities through the creation and maintenance of a school environment that...fosters individual responsibility and respect for the rights of others. (No Child Left Behind Act [NCLBA], 2001)

Unfortunately, this has not been the case for many students. For those students who identify themselves as or are perceived by others as lesbian, gay, bisexual, or transgender (LGBT), school is a place where harassment and victimization are everyday occurrences. It is a place where they are subjected to prejudice and intolerance not only from their peers, but also from their teachers, counselors, school administrators, and other adults—the very people whose role it is to ensure that the learning environment is safe and supportive (Gay, Lesbian, Straight Education Network, 2005; Rivers & D'Augelli, 2001; Russell, Franz, & Driscoll, 2001).

Despite the fact that the United States is only one of the two countries that have not ratified the Convention on the Rights of the Child (CRC) (see Daiute and Ruck & Horn, both this issue for further information), the abuses perpetrated against LGBT students in school clearly violate a number of rights identified in the Convention, specifically rights to safety (Article 19), health (Article 24), freedom of expression (Articles 12 and 13), education (Article 28), as well as the right to be free from discrimination (Article 2). A report by the Human Rights Watch, an organization devoted to investigating and documenting human rights violations around the world, exposed the failure of U.S. school officials and the federal and state governments to fulfill their "obligation to ensure that all youth enjoy their right to education in an environment where they are protected from discrimination, harassment, and violence" (Bochenek & Brown, 2001, p. 5). The report documents case after case in which school officials turned a blind eye, and in some cases, participated in serious human rights abuses of gay, lesbian, bisexual, or transgender students that clearly violates the CRC and the No Child Left Behind Act. Despite the strong language in both the CRC and the No Child Left Behind Act regarding safety, tolerance for differences, and the right to be free from discrimination and harassment, very little is being done at the school, state, or federal level to ensure that all students can exercise their right to an education free from harassment and violence. Even though we can document the rights violations of LGBT youth in schools across the United States (Russell et al., 2001) and have clear evidence of the negative developmental outcomes for students subjected to this kind of abuse (D'Augelli, 1998), the situation is complex. The complexity stems from the multiple ways individuals understand the purpose of education and the role schools have in fostering youth development, particularly around issues of sex and sexuality.

One of the defining purposes of public education in the United States has been to prepare youth for their future roles as productive and contributing citizens in a democratic society (Dewey, 1916/1944; Levesque, 2000). To that end, one of the goals of schooling is to socialize youth to the norms, values, and traditions of adult membership in society. The role that schools should play in socializing adolescents into their mature roles as sexually responsible adults, however, is complicated due to the various beliefs and assumptions about sex and sexuality that people hold in the United States. As such, adolescent sexualities, particularly issues of same-sex sexuality, have become one of the defining issues in the "culture wars" between traditional/conservative and progressive/liberal viewpoints in the United States. As a result, schools have become one arena where this conflict is played out (Levesque, 2000).

One of the main arguments is that by protecting the rights of LGBT students through antiharassment policies and practices, schools promote homosexuality as acceptable. Schools, then, infringe on students' and parents' rights to believe otherwise and to raise their children according to these beliefs, which are often based on religious or cultural ideologies (Horn, 2007; Nairn & Smith, 2003). According to this argument, adolescents are passive recipients of the societal or institutional messages presented to them and, as such, should be "protected" from information that is deemed harmful or inappropriate (Levesque, this issue). It could be the case, however, that adolescents are capable of coordinating and making sense of conflicting and competing cultural messages. If so, they are able to maintain the belief that homosexuality is wrong while still believing that students have the right to be free from harassment and discrimination. The purpose of this study was to explore these issues by investigating the relationships between adolescents' beliefs about homosexuality and their judgments regarding safety rights of gay and lesbian youth.

The Multifaceted Nature of Sexual Prejudice

Sexuality, on the one hand, is an inherent part of what it means to be human and, for most, is an integral part of one's individual identity (Brooks-Gunn & Graber, 1999). As such, sexuality is defined as something that is an individual right, under the jurisdiction of the person and not subject to societal control or regulation. On the other hand, for various reasons throughout history, individuals' sexuality, and particularly their sexual behavior, has been subjected to societal control and regulation. Furthermore, beliefs about sex and sexuality and how individuals come to understand their own and others' sexuality are often influenced by the societal conventions and norms that have developed to regulate and control the expression or manifestation of sexuality. There is a tension, then, between viewing sexuality as an individual right or personal issue and viewing sexuality (or some parts of sexuality) as a public and societal issue under social control through cultural norms and societal conventions.

When addressing children and adolescents' rights related to sexuality, the inherent tension between individual and societal control comes to the fore (Levesque, 2000). Interestingly, this tension is apparent in the CRC in that the only article dealing with sexuality is related to the need to protect young people from sexual abuse and exploitation (Article 34). While these protections are critical, the CRC does not address young peoples' self-determinative rights to sexuality. Thus, the Convention frames issues related to sexuality as inherently dangerous and from which young people should be protected. Even though most individuals reach their biological adult reproductive status in adolescence, many adults assume that adolescents are not yet ready to handle the risks and responsibilities that go along with this status. To protect them from harm adults regulate adolescents' self-determinative rights regarding sexual identity and sexual behavior. The socialization of adolescent sexuality, then, is viewed as a societal responsibility rather than solely an issue of self-determination or biological maturation.

The multifaceted nature of sexuality also appears to effect issues related to sexual prejudice (i.e., prejudice based on sexual orientation). Research on this topic (the majority of which is conducted with adults) provides evidence that sexual prejudice is related to a host of demographic, psychological, and social factors such as gender, education, geographic region, and attitudes toward gender roles (Altemeyer, 2003; Haddock & Zanna, 1998; Haslam & Levy, 2006; Haslam, Rothschild, & Ernst, 2000; Hegarty & Pratto, 2001; Herek, 1994, 2000; Kite & Whitley, 1998).

More recent studies of sexual prejudice have moved beyond simply documenting the prevalence and correlates of sexual prejudice to investigating the structure and functions of individuals' beliefs and attitudes about and behaviors toward gay, lesbian, bisexual, and transgender people (Haddock & Zanna, 1998; Haslam & Levy, 2006; Hegarty & Pratto, 2001; Kite & Whitley, 1998; Van de Ven, 1994; Van de Ven, Bornholt, & Bailey, 1996). Researchers have argued that utilizing a single attitudinal measure masks the multifaceted nature of this complex phenomenon (Hegarty & Pratto, 2001; Van de Ven, 1994). Further, this research provides evidence that individuals' beliefs, attitudes, and behaviors toward gay and lesbian people are independent but related dimensions of sexual prejudice (Haddock & Zanna, 1998; Haslam & Levy, 2006; Hegarty & Pratto, 2001; Van de Ven, 1994; Van de Ven et al., 1996).

Adolescent sexuality and beliefs about sexual prejudice are multifaceted issues that involve different dimensions of social knowledge. This multidimensionality is related to how schools negotiate tensions around protecting the rights of lesbian and gay youth. On one hand, schools have an obligation to protect their students from physical victimization and harm regardless of their sexual orientation. On the other hand is the competing argument that schools must respect individuals' rights to their own religious, cultural, or ideological belief systems and in doing so have an obligation to protect young people from information, behaviors, or individuals perceived as unnatural or dangerous (such as gays and lesbians). In a study regarding perceptions of the rights of lesbian and gay youth in New Zealand schools, Nairn and Smith (2003) found that some students framed the safety argument to "argue for their rights to be safe from l/g/b students" (p. 134).

One way to begin to understand these questions and tensions surrounding the rights and treatment of LGBT students in schools is to investigate how adolescents apply different dimensions of their social knowledge to questions of sexuality and the rights of gay and lesbian people. Is it the case, for example, that adolescents can distinguish between upholding the rights of gay and lesbian peers and their own rights to believe what they want about homosexuality?

Social Cognitive Domain Theory and Reasoning about Sexuality and Sexual Prejudice

Social cognitive domain theory, as a theoretical paradigm, is inherently suited to studying reasoning and judgments regarding multifaceted and complex social issues such as sexuality and sexual prejudice, as well as individual and contextual variation in judgments about these issues (Smetana, 2006; Turiel, Hildebrandt, & Wainryb, 1991; Turiel, Killen, & Helwig, 1987). The central premise of social cognitive domain theory is that evaluative social judgments are multifaceted and draw from several conceptual domains rather than a single structure of sociomoral reasoning (Nucci, 2001; Turiel, 1983, 2006). Within domain theory, concepts of morality (issues of human welfare, rights, and fairness) are distinguished from concepts of social conventions, which are the consensually determined standards of conduct particular to a given social group that promote group functioning and group identity. While morality and convention deal with aspects of interpersonal regulation, a third domain of personal issues refers to actions that comprise the private aspects of one's life (e.g., contents of a diary) and matters of preference and choice (e.g., friends, music, hairstyle) rather than right or wrong (Horn & Nucci, 2006; Nucci, 2001). A final element included within the domain theory account of social reasoning is the role informational/factual assumptions play in generating social judgments (Turiel et al., 1991; Wainryb, 1991). That is, unlike prototypical moral judgments in which the judgments are predicated upon information regarding the effects that actions have upon the welfare of others, other situations involve the use of culturally mediated information (e.g., concepts of the afterlife) as the basis for an individual's judgments of right and wrong. In the case of homosexuality, for example, individuals' judgments about whether or not homosexuality is right or wrong are going to be based on their concepts regarding homosexuality as a natural or normal expression of human sexuality that may be informed, in part, through individuals' adherence to particular religious or cultural ideologies (Turiel et al., 1991).

Research on older adolescents' and young adults' reasoning about homosexuality provides evidence that conceptions of sexuality, and in particular, homosexuality, involve conventions and social norms, concerns with personal choice, as well as issues of individual rights and fairness (Horn, 2006a, 2007, 2008; Horn & Nucci, 2003; Turiel et al., 1991). Additionally, in a series of studies investigating adolescents' beliefs about homosexuality, as well as their judgments about the rights of others based on the sexual orientation and gender identity, Horn (2006a, 2006b, 2007, 2008) found evidence of differentiation in adolescents' judgments about the acceptability of homosexuality and their judgments regarding the rights of others. For example, Horn (2007) provided evidence that adolescents' beliefs about the acceptability of homosexuality are distinct from their judgments regarding the rights of gay and lesbian peers. In fact, many adolescents who judged homosexuality as completely wrong also judged the mistreatment of gay and lesbian peers as wrong. Additionally, Horn (2006a) found age-related differences in adolescents' and young adults' judgments regarding the mistreatment of lesbian and gay peers (e.g., younger adolescents were less likely to endorse mistreatment as wrong), but did not find age-related differences in adolescents' and young adults' judgments about the acceptability of homosexuality. These studies suggest that young peoples' beliefs about homosexuality may be conceptually distinct from their judgments regarding the treatment of lesbian and gay peers. This finding suggests that endorsing gay and lesbian students' rights to protection does not necessarily lead to endorsing a particular set of beliefs about the acceptability of homosexuality. Further, Horn (2007) argued that these two types of judgments may draw upon different domains of social knowledge.

In this study, we investigated not only adolescents' judgments regarding the acceptability of homosexuality and the rights of others based on sexual identity, but also the types of reasoning that adolescents used in justifying both of these judgments. Further, we investigated the factors that predict adolescents' judgments regarding exclusion and teasing. Based on social cognitive domain theory and the research presented above, we hypothesized that adolescents' beliefs about the acceptability of homosexuality would be correlated with their judgments regarding the treatment of others based on their sexual identity, but not predictive of these judgments. Moreover, we hypothesized that adolescents' social and moral reasoning would be more strongly predictive of their exclusion and teasing judgments than their beliefs about homosexuality (is it acceptable or not?).

Table 1. Justification Response Categories for Why It Is All Right or Wrong to Exclude or Tease

Justification Category	M (SD)	Response
Fairness/welfare	1.8 (1.43)	"It is unfair/hurtful to him."
Human equality	1.5 (1.31)	"We should treat others as we wish to be treated."
Religious human equality	.18 (.46)	"God teaches us that we should treat others as we wish to be treated ourselves."
Affirms norms	.23 (.57)	"He dresses or acts the way a guy in our society should."
Negates norms	.21 (.55)	"She doesn't dress or act the way a girl in our society should."
God's law	.22 (.59)	"He is going against God's law or the laws of my religion."
Personal choice	1.3 (1.66)	"Who you hang out with is a matter of personal choice."
Unnatural	.23 (.73)	"She is being unnatural/disgusting."
Hit on	.23 (.54)	"He might hit on them/be attracted to them."
Need to belong	.78 (.96)	"People might think they are gay if they don't."

Note. Means are summed proportions across four scenarios. Scores could range from 0 to 4.

Method

Participants

One thousand seventy-six adolescents (females, $n = 648$; males, $n = 428$) attending two different schools in the Midwest participated in the study (M age = 15.8, $SD = 1.03$). Students were from either a larger suburban high school located outside of a large midwestern city or from an urban college preparatory high school located within the downtown area of a large midwestern city. Slightly fewer than a third of the sample was European American (30.2%), 28.5% were Asian Americans, 17.8% were Latino/a, and 12.7% were African Americans. While the sample does not necessarily reflect the demographics of the United States, it is representative of the schools at which the data were collected, with one school having a large Asian/Pacific Islander population. Almost half of the sample was in 9th grade (48.5%) with approximately 20% in the 10th and 11th grades and 9.0% in 12th grade. Finally, of those who reported their religious affiliation, almost half of the sample were Catholic (46.2%) and 33.2% identified with other Christian denominations.

Only those students receiving parental consent and providing individual assent were surveyed. Parental consent was determined using parent notification letters and passive consent. The overall response rate for the survey distribution was 97%. The survey results for 17 of the students were excluded from analyses because they identified as other than heterosexual.

Procedure

At the suburban school, participants completed the survey in required freshman advisory or 10th-grade health class, or in 11th- and 12th-grade elective foreign language classes. At the urban school, participants completed the survey in their required homeroom course. The questionnaire took approximately 45 minutes. Participants received no compensation.

Measures

Exclusion and teasing judgments. Using hypothetical scenarios, participants were asked to evaluate whether or not they thought it was right or wrong for individuals to exclude or tease a lesbian or gay male target. For example, "George is a gay male high school student. He plays on the school baseball team. He is a 'B' student. He dresses and acts like most of the other guys at school. To all outward appearances, he seems just like any other male at the school." Judgments were assessed on a 5-point Likert-type scale (1 = *completely wrong*; 3 = *neither right nor wrong*; 5 = *completely all right*). Participants' judgments were averaged across the four hypothetical scenarios. Participants responded to scenarios regarding either gay male or lesbian targets and this was counterbalanced with participant gender such that half of the female and male participants responded to each version or the questionnaire.

Justifications. In order to assess participants reasoning, for each scenario we also asked students to choose, from a set of 10 responses, the reasons that best reflected their opinion for why they thought the action (exclusion or teasing) was right or wrong. For example, "It is unfair/hurtful to him." The responses were developed from pilot interviews and informed by social cognitive domain theory (Turiel, 1983; Turiel et al., 1991), and prior work on sexual prejudice (Herek, 1994; see Table 1). Students could choose more than one response. Scores were calculated as the summed proportion of a students' response that fell into each category.

Evaluative judgment about homosexuality. To measure students' attitudes regarding homosexuality, they were asked "Do you think homosexuality is all

Table 2. Adolescents' Beliefs Regarding Why Homosexuality Is Wrong or All Right

Factor	Mean (*SD*)	Justification Responses
Biological	.14 (.16)	People are born gay or lesbian; being gay or lesbian is not a matter of choice, you are who you are.
Individual rights	.49 (.35)	Whether or not someone else is gay or lesbian is no one else's business; people should be allowed to love whomever they wish; people who are old enough should be allowed to have consensual sex with whomever they wish; gay and lesbian people are also God's children; gay and lesbian people are just like anyone else; people have the right to be whoever they want.
Religious convention	.19 (.27)	Against God's law; goes against scripture; goes against the beliefs of my religion.
Negative stereotypes	.02 (.09)	Gay and lesbian people are more likely than others to engage in sexual abuse or rape; gay and lesbian people caused AIDS to exist.
Natural order/norms	.14 (.23)	It is unnatural; it is disgusting; it goes against the norms of society.

Note. Means are averaged proportions of responses that fell into each factor.

right or wrong?" Responses were given on a 5-point Likert-type scale response (1 = *completely wrong*, 3 = *neither right nor wrong*, 5 = *completely all right*).

Beliefs about homosexuality. We also asked participants to provide their reasons for why they judged homosexuality as wrong or right. After rendering their judgment, students chose from a list of 18 reasons the statements that best reflected their beliefs regarding why they thought it was wrong or not wrong to be gay or lesbian. The reasons given for this question were developed from pilot work and informed by social cognitive domain theory, as well as available research on sexual prejudice and stereotypes. Students could choose more than one response and their belief scores were calculated based on the proportion of their response that fell into each category. Principal components analyses indicated five categories of belief: biological, individual rights, informational assumptions, negative stereotypes, and religious convention (see Table 2).

Data Analysis

After examining the variable distributions, bivariate correlations, and differences, we fit a series of nested multiple regression models to the data predicting participants' exclusion and teasing judgments. We began with the control variables (gender, grade in school, and school) and then added the five belief categories. We then retained the controls and those beliefs that were significant predictors and added the 10 justifications for participants' exclusion or teasing judgments.

Finally, retaining the significant justifications, we added the students' evaluative judgment of homosexuality rating. As there were significant differences in the students' judgments regarding exclusion and teasing by gender of the target (lesbian or gay), we fit the regression models separately for each version.

Results

Overall Means for Exclusion and Teasing Judgments and Justification; Evaluative Judgments and Beliefs about Homosexuality

On average, students judged excluding to be close to neither right nor wrong ($M = 2.44$, $SD = 1.0$) and teasing to be somewhat wrong ($M = 1.83$, $SD = .96$). There were no significant differences between the stories with gay male or lesbian targets. Girls were significantly more likely to judge exclusion as wrong ($M = 2.3$, $SD = .97$) than were boys ($M = 2.7$, $SD = 1.0$, $t = 5.8$, $p < .001$) and significantly more likely to judge teasing as wrong than males ($M = 1.6$, $SD = .84$ and $M = 2.3$, $SD = 1.0$, respectively, $t = 9.4$, $p < .001$) There were significant differences by grade for both exclusion, $F(3, 1,068) = 3.7$, $p < .01$, and teasing, $F(3, 1,065) = 3.5$, $p < .01$, judgments such that 9th graders were significantly more likely to judge exclusion as acceptable than students from any other grade and judged teasing as more acceptable than 11th or 12th graders. There were no differences in exclusion or teasing judgments based on race/ethnicity or religion.

Justifications. The predominant justifications for participants' judgments regarding exclusion and teasing, for both lesbian and gay targets, were fairness ($M = 1.80$, $SD = 1.44$), human equality ($M = 1.55$, $SD = 1.32$), and personal choice ($M = 1.32$, $SD = 1.66$). These three predominant justifications were endorsed across gender, race/ethnicity, grade, and religion (See Table 1).

Evaluative judgment. On average, the students reported that being lesbian or gay was neither right nor wrong ($M = 3.0$, $SD = 1.42$), but the distribution was trimodal with 20% responding that it was completely wrong, 33% that it was neither wrong nor right, and 25% that it was completely right.

Girls judged being lesbian or gay as significantly more acceptable than boys (Girls, $M = 3.2$, $SD = 1.4$; boys, $M = 2.7$, $SD = 1.4$; $t = 5.6$, $p < .001$). In addition to gender, there were significant differences in evaluative judgment based on grade, $F(3, 1,063) = 5.6$, $p < .001$, race/ethnicity, $F(4, 1,046) = 6.9$, $p < .001$, and religion, $F(4, 737) = 11.4$, $p < .001$. Ninth graders were significantly more negative regarding the acceptability of homosexuality ($M = 2.82$) than all other grades (10th $M = 3.15$, $SD = 1.43$; 11th, $M = 3.23$, $SD = 1.38$; 12th, $M = 3.04$, $SD = 1.49$) African-American students rated being lesbian or gay as ($M = 2.60$) significantly more wrong than did European-American students ($M = 3.15$)

and both rated homosexuality as significantly more wrong than did Latino/a students ($M = 3.33$). Baptists reported the most negative evaluative judgment ($M = 2.18$) significantly lower than Catholics, who reported the most positive evaluative judgment ($M = 3.24$), significantly more positive than all other groups.

Beliefs. The strongest belief category for judgments about homosexuality was that of individual rights that was chosen almost half of the time ($M = .49, SD = .35$), followed by religious convention that was chosen approximately 20% of the time ($M = .19, SD = .35$). There were significant differences in the adolescents' beliefs about the acceptability of homosexuality by gender, grade, race/ethnicity, and religion. Approximately half of girls' responses fell into the individual rights (.53) category (vs. .43 for boys, $t = 5.4, p < .001$) with a much smaller proportion endorsing biological beliefs (.15) (vs. .12 for boys, $t = 2.1, p < .05$). In addition, boys endorsed informational assumptions more frequently than did girls (.19 vs. .11 for girls, $t = 5.9, p < .001$). There were significant differences for every belief by grade, race/ethnicity, and religion. Nonetheless, the predominant belief across race/ethnicity categories was individual rights, ranging from .42 to .58 and for grade, ranging from .46 to .53. Individual rights was the predominant belief endorsed by students from all religions, ranging from .42 to .54, with the exception of the Baptists, who endorsed religious convention the most, .44.

Correlations among Judgments about Homosexuality, Exclusion, and Teasing, and Beliefs about Homosexuality

Students' evaluative judgment about homosexuality was mildly negatively correlated with their judgments about exclusion ($r = -.34, p < .001$) and teasing ($r = -.37, p < .001$). While indicating correspondence among the three judgments (higher scores in judging homosexuality to be right were associated with lower scores in choosing to exclude or tease), these correlations serve to distinguish the three judgments as fundamentally different from each other.

Students' evaluative judgment about homosexuality was strongly correlated with various beliefs. Beliefs rooted in individual rights ($r = .71, p < .001$) and in biology ($r = .43, p < .001$) were positively related to evaluating homosexuality as acceptable, while those rooted in religious convention ($r = -.62, p < .001$), informational assumptions ($r = -.54, p < .001$), and negative stereotypes ($r = -.21, p < .001$) were related to evaluating homosexuality as wrong.

Predictors of Exclusion and Teasing Judgments

Exclusion: lesbian version. As presented in Model 1, Table 3, the only significant predictors of the exclusion judgments of lesbians were four justifications. Those students who justified their decisions in terms of needing to belong

Table 3. Final Regression Models Examining Teasing and Exclusion of Lesbian and Gay Targets ($N = 1,070$)

	Exclusion		Teasing	
	Lesbian Model 1 $\hat{\beta}$ (SE)	Gay Model 2 $\hat{\beta}$ (SE)	Lesbian Model 3 $\hat{\beta}$ (SE)	Gay Model 4 $\hat{\beta}$ (SE)
Controls				
School		−.132(.100)**		−.078(.072)*
Gender (female)		−.096(.101)*	−.144(.063)***	−.120(.070)***
Grade (9th)		.128(.130)**		
Beliefs				
Biological		−.105(.340)*		−.107(.258)**
Individual rights				−.232(.171)***
Informational assumptions				
Religious convention				−.248 (.204)***
Negative stereotypes				
Justifications				
Against God's law			.140(.059)***	
Affirms norms			.169(.047)***	
Negates norms			.082(.085)*	
Hit on			.074(.078)*	
Need to belong	−.168(.055)**	−.108(.058)*		−.169(.042)***
Personal choice	.269(.035)***	.331(.032)***	.196(.024)***	.136(.025)**
Religious human equality			.120(.084)***	.128(.073)***
Human equality	−.196(.043)***		−.103(.029)*	−.122(.031)**
Fairness	−.203(.035)***	−.118(.038)*	−.137(.024)***	−.232(.030)***
Unnatural		.124(.060)*	.108(.054)**	
Evaluative judgment			−.146(.033)**	
R^2	.39	.41	.46	.45

Note. $* p < .05$; $** p < .01$; $*** p < .001$.

($\beta = -.168, p < .01$), human equality ($\beta = -.196, p < .001$), and fairness ($\beta = -.203, p < .001$), judged excluding lesbians as wrong. Those students judging exclusion as more acceptable justified their decisions on the basis of personal choice ($\beta = .269, p < .001$). The final model explained 39% of the variation in judgments regarding the exclusion of lesbian targets ($f^2 = .64$).

Exclusion: gay male version.   In Model 2, school ($\beta = -.096, p < .05$) and gender ($\beta = -.132, p < .01$) were significant predictors judging exclusion of gay males to be wrong, and grade in school ($\beta = .128, p < .01$) indicated that higher grade (e.g., junior, senior) was a significant predictor of judging exclusion as less wrong. Only one belief category—biological belief ($\beta = -.105, p < .05$) was a significant predictor of exclusion judgments. The significant justifications were the need to belong ($\beta = -.108, p < .05$), personal choice ($\beta = .331, p < .001$), fairness ($\beta = -.118, p < .05$), and unnatural ($\beta = -.105, p < .05$). Once again, students' evaluative judgment of homosexuality was not a significant predictor of exclusion. Those students who justified their decisions in terms of needing to belong ($\beta = -.108, p < .05$), and fairness ($\beta = -.118, p < .05$), reported excluding gay males as wrong. Those students judging exclusion as more acceptable justified their decisions on the basis of personal choice ($\beta = .331, p < .001$), and that homosexuality was unnatural ($\beta = .124, p < .01$). The final model explained 41% of the variation in judgments regarding the exclusion gay male targets ($f^2 = .70$).

A comparison of the final models predicting exclusion for lesbians and gays highlights both the moral reasoning underlying actions rather than beliefs regarding homosexuality and the importance of context with regard to gay males: while neither gender, grade nor school were predictors of excluding lesbians, all three remain significant predictors for gay targets. The strongest predictor of exclusion, for both lesbians and gays, was the notion of personal choice ($\beta = .269, p < .001$, and $\beta = .331, p < .001$, respectively).

Teasing: lesbian version.   The models predicting teasing paralleled those predicting exclusion. Model 3, predicting judgments regarding the acceptability of teasing of lesbians, explained 46% of the variation ($f^2 = .85$). There were significant differences in judgments regarding the teasing of lesbian targets by gender ($\beta = -.144, p < .001$), such that girls were less likely to tease, but there were no significant differences by school or grade. There were no significant predictors of teasing by belief category, but all of the justifications, save the need to belong, were significant. Those judging teasing as wrong justified their judgments by making appeals to human equality ($\beta = .103, p < .05$) and unfairness ($\beta = -.137, p < .01$). Those judging teasing as less wrong justified their judgments with the following reasons: against God's law ($\beta = .140, p < .01$), affirms norms ($\beta = .169, p < .001$), negates norms

($\beta = .082, p < .05$), being hit on ($\beta = .074, p < .05$), personal choice ($\beta = .196$, $p < .001$), religious human equality ($\beta = .120, p < .001$), and unnatural ($\beta = .108, p < .01$).

Teasing: gay male version. Similarly, the models predicting judgments regarding teasing gay male targets echoed earlier analyses in many ways. In Model 4, the gender of the participant was significant ($\beta = -.120, p < .001$) as was school ($\beta = .135, p < .05$), indicating that both girls and participants from the urban school were more likely to judge teasing as wrong. Additionally, three beliefs—biological, individual rights, and religious convention—predicted participants judging teasing as wrong ($\beta = -107, p < .001$; $\beta = -.232, p < .001$; and $\beta = -258, p < .001$, respectively). Of the 10 justifications, three were significant factors in judging teasing the gay male target as wrong: the need to belong ($\beta = -.169, p < .001$), human equality ($\beta = -.122, p < .01$), and unfairness ($\beta = -.232, p < .001$). Those justifications that predicted judging teasing to be less wrong were: personal choice ($\beta = .136, p < .01$) and religious human equality ($\beta = .128, p < .001$). Notably, students' evaluative judgment of homosexuality was not a significant predictor. The final model predicting judgments about teasing gay targets explained 45% of the variance ($f^2 = .82$).

A comparison of the final models predicting teasing emphasizes the differences based on the targets. For the lesbian targets, along with the eight justifications, only gender and evaluative judgment were significant. For the gay targets, gender, school, three beliefs, and five justifications remained significant, while evaluative judgment was not. The strongest predictors of teasing were found in predicting the teasing of gays; religious convention ($\beta = -.248, p < .001$) and fairness ($\beta = -.232, p < .001$).

It is important to note that the estimated effect sizes from all four models ($f^2 = .64$ to .85) are fairly large and the somewhat large sample size ($N = 1,070$) lends greater certainty to these estimates (estimates themselves are not influenced by sample size).

Discussion

The results of this study provide evidence that adolescents' social reasoning regarding issues related to sexual orientation and the rights of gay and lesbian peers is multifaceted and contributes to our understanding of issues related to sexual orientation and the rights of lesbian and gay students in school in three important ways. First, this study provides evidence that adolescents' social reasoning about lesbians and gay males is different and differentially impacts their judgments regarding safety rights. Second, issues related to religious convention and social norms, while related to adolescents' evaluative judgments regarding homosexuality, were less important in relation to adolescents' judgments regarding the safety rights of lesbian and gay peers. Finally, adolescents' social cognition regarding sexual orientation is multidimensional. Judgments about the acceptability of homosexuality were related to, but not predictive of, judgments regarding safety rights of lesbian and gay peers.

Differences in Social Cognition Related to Lesbians and Gay Males

The results of this study suggest that adolescents think differently about lesbian and gay male peers. Social context variables (gender, grade, school), as well as holding the belief that homosexuality was biological or innate, more consistently predicted judgments regarding the safety rights of gay male targets than lesbian ones. This finding is in keeping with research indicating that, individuals hold more prejudicial attitudes toward gay males than lesbians, stigma associated with gay male sexuality is much stronger than stigma associated with lesbian sexuality, and in many countries same-sex behavior between men is outlawed and males are persecuted for this behavior (Herek, 1994, 1998; Nairn & Smith, 2003). Based on the results of this study, it also appears that adolescents' judgments regarding the fair treatment of gay males may be more susceptible to contextual factors and other beliefs than judgments regarding lesbians.

Holding the belief that same-sex sexuality was biological or innate predicted adolescents' judgments regarding exclusion and teasing of gay males as wrong, but not judgments regarding excluding or teasing lesbian targets. These results are interesting in light of research suggesting that holding the belief that sexual orientation is biological or innate is related to more tolerant attitudes toward gay and lesbian people in general (Hegarty & Pratto, 2001) and extend this research by suggesting that beliefs about the origins of homosexuality may be particularly related to attitudes toward gay men. Homophobic bullying (bullying someone by calling them a "fag" or gay) is very prevalent among adolescent boys (Pascoe, 2007; Poteat, 2007). This study provides some evidence to suggest that this may be due to the types of social reasoning that boys bring to bear on their interpersonal or intergroup contact with gay male peers. The stigma associated with gay male sexuality may interfere with boys constructing the negative treatment of gay male peers as wrong or unfair, while increasing the likelihood that they will legitimize this treatment using other forms of social knowledge (such as conventional or personal reasoning).

Additionally, attitudes toward gay males may be influenced more by the pervasive heterosexist messages regarding the construction of masculinity in our culture and the rigid linking of masculinity with heterosexuality (Horn, 2007; Kimmel & Mahler, 2003; Mandel & Shakeshaft, 2000; Nairn & Smith, 2003). Unfortunately, most research on issues of sexual prejudice does not separate attitudes about sexual orientation from attitudes regarding gender conformity (for an exception, see

Horn, 2006b) making it difficult to understand how gender, gender conformity, and sexual orientation impact attitudes and beliefs about homosexuality and the fair treatment of persons.

The Relationship between Religious Beliefs and Social Cognition Regarding Sexual Orientation

The results of this study also present a complex picture regarding the relationships among religion, religious beliefs, and knowledge, and adolescents' judgments about homosexuality and the rights of gay and lesbian peers. This is particularly important given that religion and religious beliefs regarding homosexuality have been central factors in the debate regarding the rights of lesbian and gay students in schools. In fact, it is often argued that schools who protect lesbian and gay students from harm are infringing on freedom of religion in terms of the rights of individuals to hold opposing religious beliefs—rights that are also expressed in the CRC.

In this study, while adolescents used knowledge about religious conventions and rules somewhat frequently regarding their judgments for why homosexuality was wrong, this type of knowledge was used infrequently in justifying judgments regarding the safety rights of lesbian and gay peers. Most notably, when religious knowledge or beliefs were used in justifying judgments about exclusion and teasing, the pattern of results was not simple or straightforward. Interestingly, conventional religious beliefs regarding the acceptability of homosexuality (against God's law, against the rule of my religion) predicted adolescents judging teasing as wrong. In contrast to this, justifications regarding religious human equality (God teaches us that you should treat others as you wish to be treated) predicted more accepting judgments regarding teasing. These results are counterintuitive regarding the relationship between religious beliefs and attitudes toward the rights of lesbian and gay people and warrant further investigation. Additionally, in bivariate analyses, religious denomination was related to differences in adolescents' judgments and beliefs about homosexuality. In the multivariate analyses, however, religion was no longer significantly related to overall differences in adolescents' judgments regarding the safety rights of lesbian and gay peers. Thus, it appears that young people do understand the difference between their rights to believe what they want and the right to act on those beliefs in ways that are discriminatory or hurtful. This distinction is also made in Article 14, Section 3 of the CRC, "Freedom to manifest one's religion or beliefs may be subject only to such limitations as are necessary by law and are necessary to protect public safety, order, health or morals, or the fundamental rights and freedoms of others" (p. 3).

Previous research on attitudes toward lesbian and gay people provides some evidence that religion and religious beliefs are related to higher levels of sexual prejudice (Herek, 1994, 1998) and suggest a direct and linear relationship between endorsing religion and holding negative stereotypes and attitudes toward homosexuality. The results presented above suggest that these relationships may in fact be multidimensional rather than linear. Religion and religious beliefs are associated with some dimensions of adolescents' attitudes about sexual orientation, such as their beliefs about the acceptability of homosexuality, but not related to other dimensions, such as judgments about rights to safety and protection from harm (Horn, 2007; Turiel et al., 1991). These results underscore, once again, that schools can work to protect gay and lesbian young people from harm without impinging on individual student's, teacher's, or familie's rights to hold particular religious or social beliefs.

The Multifaceted Nature of Social Cognition Related to Sexual Orientation

Finally, the data provide evidence that adolescents bring their understandings of individual rights and fairness to bear on both their judgments regarding the acceptability of homosexuality, as well as their judgments about issues of safety rights based on sexual orientation. Importantly, in predicting adolescents' judgments about the treatment of others, adolescents' reasoning about fairness and personal choice were consistently significant predictors regardless of type of treatment (exclusion, teasing) or type of target (lesbian, gay male), whereas adolescents' judgments about the acceptability of homosexuality was only a significant predictor regarding judgments about teasing a lesbian target. This finding supports the hypothesis that these are distinct types of knowledge that adolescents hold. Similar to research conducted by Wainryb and colleagues (Wainryb, Shaw, & Maianu, 1998) on children and adolescents' reasoning about dissenting beliefs and practices, as well as work by Flanagan, Stout, and Gallay (this issue), the results of this study suggest that adolescents make distinctions among different kinds of beliefs and coordinate their understanding of fairness and discrimination with their personal beliefs or values.

The results of this study have important implications for understanding issues of sexual prejudice, as well as how we study issues of the rights of gay and lesbian people. Our data suggest that sexual prejudice is a multidimensional issue and that different dimensions of sexual prejudice are related to different types of social knowledge that develop out of different types of social interactions or social experiences (Haslam & Levy, 2006; Hegarty & Pratto, 2001; Horn, 2007, 2008; Van de Ven et al., 1996). In relation to the rights of lesbian and gay students in school then, these data support the idea that protecting lesbian and gay students' rights to safety and to be free from discrimination and harm does not infringe on the rights of other students to hold particular beliefs about homosexuality. This distinction may become more complicated regarding other rights of lesbian and gay students, even those expressed in the CRC (e.g., rights to assemble [Article 15], rights to information [Article 13]). Individuals may be more comfortable extending rights to protection than they are extending rights to self-determination and participation to their lesbian and gay peers.

Interestingly, adolescents utilized both moral reasoning (fairness, human equality) and personal choice reasoning frequently in justifying their judgments about exclusion and teasing, thus providing support for the idea that adolescents' reasoning about intergroup interactions (particularly exclusion) is multifaceted (Horn, 2003, 2006a; Killen & Stangor, 2001; Killen, Margie, & Sinno, 2005) and extends this research to include reasoning about intergroup interactions including gay and lesbian peers. More important, adolescents' judgments about intergroup interactions were related to the specific types of social knowledge that they brought to bear on those judgments. Moral reasoning (fairness, need to belong, human equality) consistently predicted judging exclusion or teasing as wrong, while personal choice and conventional reasoning (e.g., social norms) predicted judging exclusion and teasing as more legitimate. These results provide support for Horn's (2005, 2007) hypothesis that adolescents may view exclusion and teasing as legitimate ways to regulate their environment in certain contexts.

These results have important educational implications in that they suggest that messages students receive in the school environment from teachers, administrators, and other students regarding the legitimacy of intergroup behaviors (such as exclusion and teasing) that may be harmful or discriminatory are critical to how young people construct an understanding of the fair treatment and rights of individuals. In fact, recent research by Horn and Szalacha (2008) suggested that school practices are related to adolescents' judgments regarding the rights of gay and lesbian peers. Interestingly, they did not find strong evidence that school practices were related to adolescents' beliefs about homosexuality. In contrast to previous arguments, schools can uphold the rights of lesbian and gay youth to be protected from harm while also upholding the rights of others to hold certain beliefs about homosexuality.

Implications for Understanding the Rights of Gay and Lesbian Youth in School

Our data provide compelling evidence that protecting lesbian and gay students from discrimination and harassment through safe schools practices does not promote homosexuality and force other students to believe that homosexuality is acceptable. Beliefs about homosexuality are distinct from beliefs about the rights of others to safety and to be free from discrimination and harassment. Additionally, school practices that ensure the rights of lesbian and gay students may be understood as a matter of ensuring all young peoples' rights to protection from "violent and disruptive acts, including sexual harassment and abuse, and victimization associated with prejudice and intolerance" (NCLBA, 2001), and upholding numerous articles of the CRC.

The results also provide support for the argument that adolescents should be viewed and treated as active participants in their own development and underscore their ability to coordinate multiple and varied perspectives in making decisions in their everyday lives. Adolescents' recognize that personal value systems regarding homosexuality are distinct from issues of how to treat other persons. This distinction is critical in providing evidence that by engaging in practices that protect students from harassment and discrimination related to sexual orientation and gender identity, schools are not endorsing a particular set of beliefs regarding the acceptability of one type of sexual orientation over another.

While these results are particularly interesting in relation to lesbian and gay students' rights to protection, they tell us less about how adolescents think about gay and lesbian peers' rights to self-expression in school settings. It could be the case that when schools begin to engage in activities that support the exploration of same-sex sexualities and the positive development of gay and lesbian youth, heterosexual youth may perceive that as impinging on their rights to their individual belief system. Research on children and adolescents' protection and self-determination rights suggest that rights to self-determination are less straightforward and are contingent upon perceptions of the "developing capacities of the child" and what is viewed as "in the best interest of the child" Interestingly, however, research with adolescents suggests that they are more likely to endorse young people's rights to self-determination, in general, than are adults or children (Ruck, Abramowitz, & Keating, 1998). Further research investigating adolescents' beliefs regarding lesbian and gay students' rights to both protection and self-determination, as well as research comparing adolescents' and adults' beliefs regarding these issues, is necessary to more fully understand the tension and conflict surrounding the schools' role in ensuring the rights of lesbian and gay students in school.

Conclusions

Adolescents' social cognition related to sexual orientation is complex and multidimensional, and schools provide a context where students' rights to protection and self-determination play out. Adolescents utilize and coordinate social knowledge from different domains in understanding their social worlds and making decisions about their social interactions (Smetana, 2006; Turiel, 2002, 2006). They are not simply passive recipients of the messages presented to them in their social environments, but rather continually actively construct their own understandings about the world out of multiple and diverse experiences and interactions (Moshman, 1999; Smetana, 2006; Turiel, 2006).

In pluralistic and diverse societies, the role of public education should not be to endorse a particular set of conventional or religious norms or beliefs, but rather to provide students with the skills and resources they need to negotiate the increasingly diverse and global world and to respect and affirm every individual's right to freedom from harm, intolerance, and bigotry. Students are, indeed, coming to their own conclusions about fairness and rights regarding sexuality. This does not imply, however, that schools can forego their obligation to protect students from harassment and harm. Rather, school staff needs to actively cultivate a safe climate that both protect students from undue social, emotional, and physical harm while still providing a space where adolescents are able to develop a healthy sexual identity. Schools in a pluralistic country, such as the United States, have a moral obligation to protect all students from harassment and discrimination regardless of their identities. At the same time, schools need to protect students' rights to construct their own beliefs about social issues and the world around them. The role of public education should be to ensure the right of all students to an education free from harassment, persecution, discrimination, and violence, regardless of religious background, national origin, race, ethnicity, culture, gender, *and* sexual orientation and gender expression.

References

Altemeyer, B. (2003). Why do religious fundamentalists tend to be prejudiced? *International Journal for the Psychology of Religion, 13*, 17–28.

Bochenek, M., & Brown, A. (2001). *Hatred in the hallways: Violence and discrimination against lesbian, gay, bisexual, and transgender students in U.S. schools.* New York: Human Rights Watch.

Brooks-Gunn, J., & Graber, J. A. (1999). What's sex got to do with it? The development of sexual identities in adolescence. In R. Contrada & R. Ashmore (Eds.), *Self, social identity, and physical health: Interdisciplinary explorations* (pp. 155–183). New York: Oxford University Press.

D'Augelli, A. (1998). Developmental implications of victimization of lesbian, gay and bisexual youths. In Herek, G. (Ed.), *Stigma and sexual orientation: Understanding prejudice against lesbians, gay men, and bisexuals* (pp. 187–210). Thousand Oaks, CA: Sage.

Dewey, J. (1944). *Democracy and education.* New York: Macmillan Press (Original work published 1916).

Gay, Lesbian, Straight, Education Network. (2005). *National school climate survey.* New York: Author.

Haddock, G., & Zanna, M. P. (1998). Authoritarianism, values, and the favorability and structure of anti-gay attitudes. In G. Herek (Ed.), *Stigma and sexual orientation: Understanding prejudice against lesbians, gay men, and bisexuals* (pp. 82–107). Thousand Oaks, CA: Sage.

Haslam, N., & Levy, S. R. (2006). Essentialist beliefs about homosexuality: Structure and implications for prejudice. *Personality and Social Psychology Bulletin, 32*, 471–485.

Haslam, N., Rothschild, L., & Ernst, D. (2000). Essentialist beliefs about social categories. *British Journal of Social Psychology, 39*, 113–127.

Hegarty, P., & Pratto, F. (2001). Sexual orientation beliefs: The relationship to anti-gay attitudes and biological determinist arguments. *Journal of Homosexuality, 41*, 121–135.

Herek, G. (1994). Assessing heterosexuals' attitudes toward lesbians and gay men: A review of empirical research with the ATLG scale. In B. Greene & G. Herek (Eds.), *Lesbian and gay psychology: Theory, research and clinical applications* (pp. 206–228). Thousand Oaks, CA: Sage.

Herek, G. M. (1998). *Stigma and sexual orientation: Understanding prejudice against lesbians, gay men, and bisexuals.* Thousand Oaks, CA: Sage.

Herek, G. M. (2000). Sexual prejudice. *Current Directions in Psychological Science, 9*, 19–22.

Horn, S. S. (2003). Adolescents' reasoning about exclusion from social groups. *Developmental Psychology, 39*, 71–84.

Horn, S. S. (2005). Adolescents' peer interactions: Conflict and coordination between personal expression, social norms, and moral reasoning. In L. Nucci (Ed.), *Conflict, contradiction and contrarian elements in moral development and education* (pp. 113–128). New York: Erlbaum.

Horn, S. S. (2006a). Age-related differences in heterosexual adolescents' and young adults' beliefs and attitudes about homosexuality and the treatment of gay and lesbian peers in school. *Cognitive Development, 21*, 420–440.

Horn, S. S. (2006b). Adolescents' acceptance of same-sex peers based on sexual orientation and gender expression. *Journal of Youth and Adolescence, 36*, 363–371.

Horn, S. S. (2007). Leaving lesbian, gay, bisexual, and transgender students behind: Schooling, sexuality, and rights. In J. Smetana, C. Wainryb, & E. Turiel (Eds.), *Social development, social inequalities & social justice* (pp. 131–153). Mahwah, NJ: Erlbaum.

Horn, S. S. (2008). The multifaceted nature of sexual prejudice: What we can learn from studying how adolescents reason about sexual orientation and sexual prejudice. In S. Levy & M. Killen (Eds.), *Intergroup relations: An integrative developmental and social psychological perspective* (pp. 398–437). Oxford: Oxford University Press.

Horn, S. S., & Nucci, L. P. (2003). The multidimensionality of adolescents' beliefs about and attitudes toward gay and lesbian peers in school. *Equity and Excellence in Education, 36*, 1–12.

Horn, S. S., & Nucci, L. P. (2006). Harassment of gay and lesbian youth and school violence in America: An analysis and directions for intervention. In C. Daiute, L. P. Nucci, Z. Beykont, & C. Higson-Smith (Eds.), *International perspectives on youth conflict and development* (pp. 139–155). Oxford, UK: Oxford University Press.

Horn, S. S., & Szalacha, L. A. (2008). *School differences in heterosexual students' attitudes about homosexuality and harassment based on sexual orientation.* Manuscript submitted for publication.

Killen, M., Margie, N. G., & Sinno, S. (2005). Morality in the context of intergroup relationships. In M Killen & J. Smetana (Eds.), *Handbook for moral development* (pp. 155–183). Hillsdale, NJ: Erlbaum.

Killen, M., & Stangor, C. (2001). Social reasoning about inclusion and exclusion in gender and race peer group contexts. *Child Development, 72*, 174–186.

Kimmel, M., & Mahler, M. (2003). Adolescent masculinity, homophobia, and violence: Random school shootings, 1982–2001. *American Behavioral Scientist, 46*, 1439–1458.

Kite, M. E., & Whitley, B. E. (1998). Do heterosexual women and men differ in their attitudes toward homosexuality? A conceptual and methodological analysis. In G. Herek (Ed.), *Stigma and sexual orientation: Understanding prejudice against lesbians, gay men, and bisexuals* (pp. 39–61). Thousand Oaks, CA: Sage.

Levesque, R. J. R. (2000). *Adolescents, sex and the law: Preparing adolescents for responsible citizenship.* Washington, DC: American Psychological Association.

Mandel, L., & Shakeshaft, C. (2000). Heterosexism in middle schools. In N. Lesko (Ed.), *Masculinities at school* (pp. 75–103). Thousand Oaks, CA: Sage.

Moshman, D. (1999). *Adolescent psychological development.* Mahwah, NJ: Erlbaum.

Nairn, K., & Smith, A. (2003). Taking students seriously: Their rights to be safe at school. *Gender and Education, 15*, 133–149.

No Child Left Behind Act of 2001, 2001. 115 U.S.C. Article 1425 (2001).

Nucci, L. (2001). *Education in the moral domain.* Cambridge, UK: Cambridge University Press.

Pascoe, C. J. (2007). *Dude you're a fag: Adolescent masculinity and the fag discourse.* Berkeley: University of California Press.

Poteat, V. P. (2007). Peer group socialization of homophobic attitudes and behavior during adolescence. *Child Development, 78*, 1830–1842.

Rivers, I., & D'Augelli, A. (2001). The victimization of lesbian, gay, and bisexual youths. In A. D'Augelli & C. Patterson (Eds.), *Lesbian, gay, and bisexual identities and youth* (pp. 199–223). New York: Oxford University Press.

Ruck, M. D., Abramovitch, R., & Keating, D. P. (1998). Children's and adolescents' understanding of rights: Balancing nurturance and self-determination. *Child Development, 64*, 404–417.

Russell, S. T., Franz, B. T., & Driscoll, A. K. (2001). Same-sex romantic attraction and experiences of violence in adolescence. *American Journal of Public Health, 91*, 903–906.

Smetana, J. G. (2006). Social-cognitive domain theory: Consistencies and variations in children's moral and social judgments. In M. Killen & J. Smetana (Eds.), *Handbook of moral development* (pp. 119–154). Mahwah, NJ: Erlbaum.

Turiel, E. (1983). *The development of social knowledge: Morality and convention*. Cambridge, UK: Cambridge University Press.

Turiel, E. (2002). *The culture of morality*. Cambridge, UK: Cambridge University Press.

Turiel, E. (2006). The development of morality. In W. Damon (Series Ed.) & N. Eisenberg (Vol. Ed.), *Handbook of child psychology: Volume 3. Social, emotional, and personality development* (6th ed., pp. 789–857). New York: Wiley.

Turiel, E., Hildebrandt, C., & Wainryb, C. (1991). Judging social issues: Difficulties, inconsistencies, and consistencies. *Monographs of the Society for Research in Child Development, 56* (Serial No. 224).

Turiel, E., Killen, M., & Helwig, C. (1987). Morality: Its structure, functions, and vagaries. In J. Kagan & S. Lamb (Eds.), *The emergence of morality in young children* (pp. 155–243). Chicago: University of Chicago Press.

Van de Ven, P. (1994). Comparisons among homophobic reactions of undergraduates, high school students, and young offenders. *Journal of Sex Research, 31*, 117–124.

Van de Ven, P., Bornholt, L., & Bailey, M. (1996). Measuring cognitive, affective and behavioral components of homophobic reaction. *Archives of Sexual Behavior, 25*, 155–179.

Wainryb, C. (1991). Understanding differences in moral judgments: The role of informational assumptions. *Child Development, 62*, 840–851.

Wainryb, C., Shaw, L. A., & Maianu, C. (1998). Tolerance and intolerance: Children's and adolescents' judgments of dissenting beliefs, speech, persons, and conduct. *Child Development, 69*, 1541–1555.

STACEY S. HORN is an Associate Professor of Educational and Developmental Psychology in the Department of Educational Psychology at University of Illinois at Chicago. She received her PhD from the University of Maryland at College Park in Human Development. Dr. Horn is interested in the development of moral and social reasoning, peer groups and intergroup relations, stereotypes, prejudice, and discrimination related to sexual orientation and gender identity. Her applied work investigates the relationships among institutional structures and adolescents' social and moral reasoning, specifically related to peer interactions, as well as developmental approaches to service-learning and diversity education. Stacey is on the Editorial Board for the *Journal of Youth and Adolescence*, the *Journal of Gay and Lesbian Youth*, and serves on the governing board of the Jean Piaget Society and on the Research Advisory board of the National Gay, Lesbian, and Straight Education Network. Further, she is Chair of the Governing Board for the Illinois Safe Schools Alliance. Her research has been published in journals such as *Developmental Psychology*, the *International Journal of Behavior and Development*, *Cognitive Development,* and the *Journal of Youth and Adolescence*.

LAURA A. SZALACHA was trained in human development and psychology as well as research methodologies, earning her doctorate from the Graduate School of Education at Harvard University in 2001. She is presently a Research Assistant Professor at the College of Nursing at the University of Illinois at Chicago where she teaches quantitative methods and serves as a methodologist for the Center for

Research Facilitation. As a developmental psychologist, her work has a concentrated focus on adolescent development, particularly marginalized groups, such as LGBT youth and children from immigrant families in schools. In addition, she is presently studying the relationships of sexual identity and childhood sexual abuse among adult lesbians.

KAREN L. DRILL (MA, Northwestern University, 1999) is a doctoral student in the Department of Educational Psychology at the University of Illinois at Chicago (UIC). Her research interests include moral development, adolescent development, gender, and social and emotional learning. Additionally, she teaches a variety of courses for current and future educators at UIC. Prior to enrolling at UIC, she worked as a program coordinator for Northwestern University's Center for Talent Development where she oversaw a rigorous academic program for gifted youth.

Journal of Social Issues, Vol. 64, No. 4, 2008, pp. 815–834

It's My Body and None of Your Business: Developmental Changes in Adolescents' Perceptions of Rights Concerning Health

Constance A. Flanagan*

Penn State University

Michael Stout

Missouri State University

Leslie S. Gallay

Penn State University

We examined developmental changes in adolescents' perceptions of an individual's right to engage in risky behaviors that could pose harm to health. The views of 563 early, 506 middle, and 467 late adolescents concerning the degree to which individuals have a right to engage in smoking, drinking, and drug use (private health beliefs) or whether the government has a right to impose constraints on individuals (public health beliefs) were surveyed over 3 years. Endorsements of individual rights increased between early and middle adolescence and remained stable into late adolescence. Endorsements of public health beliefs showed a curvilinear trend with middle adolescents less likely than early or late adolescents to endorse the government's right to constrain individual choices. Regardless of age, endorsements of public health were positively and individual rights were negatively related to an adolescent's belief that s/he had a right to intervene in a friend's risky choices.

---

*Correspondence concerning this article should be addressed to Connie Flanagan, The Pennsylvania State University, 201 Ferguson Building, University Park, PA 16802-2601 [e-mail: cflanagan@psu.edu].

This project was supported by Grant RO1 DA 13434-01 from the NIDA to Constance Flanagan and Leslie Gallay. The authors thank the students, teachers, and administrators in the participating school districts for their cooperation in this study.*

Health risk behaviors are one of the major foci of research in the field of adolescent behavior. The dominant paradigm is a rational choice model, that is, if provided with the facts about the potential harm of experimentation with alcohol, tobacco, or other substances, an adolescent will make decisions that are in his or her own best interest. The underlying assumption is that health and risk are choices that individuals make with the potential harm of such choices a burden they bear (Guttman & Ressler, 2001; Leichter, 2003; Minkler, 1999).

This paradigm leaves underexplored two important questions relevant to adolescents and health. The first is how adolescents conceive of the rights and responsibilities associated with health and risk. The second is whether they think the risky health choices of others (family members, friends, etc.) are matters that should concern them or whether these are private matters and that individuals have no right to interfere in the choices that others make. Our article takes up these two questions by looking at developmental patterns in early-, middle-, and late-adolescents' conceptions of rights associated with health risks and their beliefs about whether individuals have a "right" to intervene in a friend's risk taking.

The social representation (Moscovici, 1988) of health as a private choice may be a peculiarly American one. In contrast to the United States, in many countries health is viewed as a public good. There also is a shared understanding that health is a fundamental human right and thus all individuals can make legitimate claims on the state to provide for their health care needs (Haigh, 2002). An example is provided in Article 24 of the United Nations Convention on the Rights of the Child (CRC) that holds that the state has a responsibility to insure the provision of children's rights to health care (providing access and informing their and their parents' choices).

Developmental research on children's and adolescents' conceptions of rights has drawn from the CRC's framing of child rights and thus has included both self-determination and care and protection from harm in the definition of child rights (Cherney & Shing, this issue; Peterson-Badali & Ruck, this issue; Peterson-Badali, Ruck, & Ridley, 2003). This framing of rights implies relationships between parties (parents/caretakers and children or states and citizens) and the expectations and mutual obligations that bind them. In our program of work, we have employed the metaphor of a "social contract" and the concept of "social responsibility" to elucidate the "ties that bind" persons and polities. The concept of a "social contract" draws from political theory and posits that individuals choose to give up certain rights to the government in an exchange for both social order and the guarantee of their liberties.

In this article, we examine how adolescents of different ages conceive of the rights of individuals to experiment with substances (alcohol, tobacco, or other drugs [ATOD]) and how they conceive of the government's right, in the interests of the broader public good, to make and enforce laws that constrain individual rights. Adolescents are the age group most likely to experiment and take health risks. Yet we know almost nothing about how they conceive of the rights and responsibilities associated with risks to health. Should individuals have the right to take risks that could pose harm? If so, do adolescents defend that right based on the belief that it is only the individual who is harmed by the act? Or does society have a right to constrain individuals from taking risks?

The literature on adolescents' conceptions of rights concerning health risks is rather slim. However, there is relevant work on adolescents' social judgments, some of which focuses on their perspectives on personal rights and laws concering drug use. In their study of 9th to 12th graders, Nucci, Guerra, and Lee (1991) found that age-related changes in sociomoral reasoning and perspective taking had no bearing on adolescents' beliefs that an individual's drug use was a moral matter that could affect others. Adolescents in this study went so far as to say that an individual could ignore laws regulating substance use if s/he were the only one harmed by such use. Finally, Nucci et al. (1991) found that youth who used drugs considered this choice a personal matter and discounted any harm either to the self or to others. Others have pointed to the relationship between the perceived harmfulness of a substance and the defense of an individual's "right" to use it. For example, adolescents consider caffeine and nicotine use as personal choices but cocaine and crack use as moral matters that transcend an individual's personal choice (Killen, Leviton, & Cahill, 1991). Logically, if a youth perceived a substance as harmful, she or he should be more likely to endorse the state's role in restricting its use in the interests of protecting the public good.

The lack of age differences in the Nucci et al. study is rather puzzling in light of the large literature on the increase in sociocognitive competencies during the adolescent years. Based on that literature, one would expect that older adolescents should be more capable of appreciating the implications to others and to society of an individual's decisions and behaviors (Eisenberg & Sheffield Morris, 2004). According to domain theory, when we make judgments, we distinguish moral matters of human welfare from social conventions (Turiel, 1983) and further distinguish conventional from personal and private matters (Nucci, 1996). Between early and middle adolescence there is an increasing awareness of social conventions as constituent elements that regulate the social system (Horn, 2005; Nucci, 2006). Coincident with this developmental shift are basic changes in the ways in which adolescents draw distinctions between convention and personal/private prerogatives, matters that become sites of conflict with their parents and also bases for asserting their own autonomy (Smetana, 2002).

Between early and late adolescence, issues of self-determination and the rights of individuals to decide on matters that concern them increases (Smetana, 2002). Self-determination and privacy are rights that adolescents seek for themselves but also ones they defend for people in general. Older adolescents appear to be more willing than their younger peers to endorse individual rights even when the exercise of those rights implies exclusion or unfair treatment of people (Helwig, 1995). However, it is in middle adolescence when the personal prerogative to exclude others is most strongly endorsed (Horn, 2003) as a legitimate form of social regulation, a necessary convention for maintaining the social system. Perhaps it is because middle adolescents are wrangling with the conventions of the system and trying to make sense of social norms, that endorsements of personal prerogatives and the rights of individuals peak at this time (Horn, 2005). Compared to children and early adolescents (Killen, Lee-Kim, McGlothlin, & Strangor, 2002) and to late adolescents (Horn, 2003), middle adolescents are more likely to defend an individual's prerogative to exclude others based on their lack of conformity to social norms or how well they would fit in with a group.

Research on children's and adolescents' concepts of rights also points to an increase in commitments to self-determination between early and middle adolescence. Ruck and his colleagues found that children and early adolescents endorsed children's right to care and nurturance and adults' responsibility to provide it. Middle adolescents endorsed the right to care but were more likely than their younger peers to also endorse a child's right to self-determination (Ruck, Abramovitch, & Keating, 1998). Compared to early adolescents as well as to their own mothers, those in the middle adolescent years are more likely to insist on an individual's right to self-determination (Ruck et al., 1998; Ruck, Peterson-Badali, & Day, 2002). Finally, with respect to risky behavior, the commitment to an individual's "right" to choose to harm himself or herself appears to peak in middle adolescence (Berkowitz, Guerra, & Nucci, 1991; Killen et al., 1991).

Whereas endorsements of individual rights peak at middle adolescence, perceptions of the harm associated with risky activities declines at this age. Cauffman, Steinberg, and Woolard (2002) asked 11- to 24-year-olds to evaluate the danger and potential harmfulness of a range of risky activities such as riding with a drunk driver or having unprotected sex. While 11- to 13-year-olds rated these activities as risky, scary, dangerous, and more harmful than beneficial, 14- to 24-year-olds were less likely to say they were harmful or dangerous. In our own research on whether adolescents would intervene to discourage their friends' use of alcohol, tobacco, or other drugs, we found declines between early and middle adolescence in intentions to intervene and increases in deciding to ignore the friend's behavior (Flanagan, Gallay, & Elek, 2005). In summary, compared to early adolescents, middle adolescents are more committed to the rights of individuals to self-determination and privacy yet are less likely to perceive risky behaviors as harmful and less willing to discourage friends' ATOD use.

But what about endorsements of public responsibility for others? Would we expect developmental changes in beliefs about society's or the government's right to constrain individuals from choices that might pose harm to themselves or to others? Sociocentric understanding, differentiation of the social world, and the capacity to conceive of abstract categories increases between early and late adolescence (Eisenberg & Sheffield Morris, 2004; Keating, 2004). Thus, older adolescents should have a more sophisticated understanding of the purpose of laws and social institutions such as the government in protecting the public. Similarly, by late adolescence, there should be an increased awareness of the secondary harm to others of individual acts such as passive smoking and the costs to society of an individual's health risk choices. Late adolescents are more capable than younger adolescents of differentiating personal experience from abstract categories (e.g., laws, government) (Dalbert & Sally, 2004; Flanagan & Stout, 2008), and they are less likely to rely on stereotypes or social conventions as the bases for their judgments (Horn, 2003, 2005).

In light of these age-related changes, we expect that early adolescents will conceive of individual rights to decide about health (privacy beliefs) as the opposing pole to the society or government's rights to constrain individual behaviors (public health beliefs). In contrast, we expect that, as adolescents get older, these two sets of beliefs will be differentiated, orthogonal to one another: endorsing one will not be inversely related to endorsing the other. We contend that endorsing the rights of individuals to make their own health behavior choices and the right of society to constrain individuals from engaging in health related risks are *not* two ends of the same continuum. By late adolescence, youth have developed a coordinated understanding of the conventions of their social system (Nucci, 2006). Thus, by this time there should be an appreciation *both* of an individual's right to privacy and self-determination *and* of the responsibility of the state to make laws that protect the welfare of the public.

Gender and Perceptions of Rights and Responsibilities

There is a large literature documenting gender differences in social relationships and the manifestation of social responsibility. Females tend to feel more responsible for peers and guilty about neglecting those responsibilities (Eisenberg & Sheffield Morris, 2004; Williams & Bybee, 1994). Gender differences also have been found in early adolescents' responses to hypothetical dilemmas of friendship. In response to interpersonal conflicts, females are more likely to say they would accommodate whereas males are more likely to choose to stand up for their rights. If a hypothetical friend had a problem, females are more likely to say they would offer support whereas males say they would avoid or blame the friend (Rose & Asher, 1999). With respect to social exclusion, there is consistent evidence that, during both childhood and adolescence, females are more averse to excluding others than are their male peers (Killen et al., 2002; Killen & Stangor, 2001). Although there is mixed evidence for gender differences in perceptions of rights (for a review, see Peterson-Badali & Ruck, this issue), Day, Peterson-Badali, and Ruck (2006) found that females, especially 10th graders, are more likely than their male peers to endorse nurturance rights. And in our own studies of adolescents' intentions to intervene in friends' risk taking, adolescent girls are more likely to endorse various strategies to help their friends avoid harm whereas boys are more inclined to say they would ignore their friends' behaviors (Flanagan et al., 2005).

Hypotheses

In light of the relevant body of work, we formulated the following hypotheses. First, we expected to find an increase between early and late adolescence in endorsements of individual rights concerning health decisions. Given the preponderance of evidence of an increase in endorsements of self-determination rights between early and middle adolescence, we expected that the steepest increase would occur between these ages. Second, with respect to endorsements of public responsibility for health, we hypothesized a curvilinear relationship with middle adolescents less likely than early and late adolescents to endorse this belief. Third, we expected that, regardless of age, females would be more likely than their male peers to endorse public responsibility for health and males would be more likely to endorse an individual's right to take risks. Finally, we expected that young people's attitudes about individual rights and public responsibility for health would be related to their feeling that they have a right to intervene in the health risk behaviors of their friends. Endorsements of public responsibility should be positively related to the perception that one has a right to intervene whereas endorsements of individual rights should be inversely related to the perception of this right.

Methods

Sample

This analysis utilized data from the Social Responsibility and Prevention Project, a 3-year, longitudinal study designed specifically to assess those factors that influence the willingness of young people to intervene to dissuade peers from risky behaviors. We surveyed students from 5th through 12th grades in seven rural, suburban, and small-urban school districts in the northeastern United States. Surveys were conducted each spring from 2002 to 2004.

Active parental consent was obtained for all the participants and resulted in a participation rate of 51%. Demographically, participating youth reflected the school districts from which we recruited with approximately 80% from European-American backgrounds, 10% from African-American, and 7% from Latino-American backgrounds. Based on parents' reports, 20% of participating families had incomes below $30,000, 25% between $30,001 and $50,000, 45% between $50,001 and $100,000, and 10% had incomes above $100,000. Fifty-four percent of the participants were females. Students also were categorized into three age groups: early (12–13), middle (14–15), and late (16 and older) adolescents, based on their age in Wave 2 of the study.

Procedures

Surveys were administered during the second semester of each school year with approximately 1 year between waves. We surveyed 2,768 students during the first year, with 1,411 (5th, 8th, and 10th graders) eligible for the panel study. In Wave 2 we refreshed the sample with additional 6th through 12th graders from the participating schools. No new 5th graders entered the study after the first year and no additional participants were added during the third year. This resulted in 2,644 students surveyed in the second and 1,933 in the third year of the study with 839 participants at all three waves. Cross-sectional analyses take advantage of the full sample available each year and SEM analyses are based on the longitudinal sample.

Measures

All measures are based on a set of Likert-type items (1 = *strongly disagree* to 5 = *strongly agree* or 1 = *not at all important* to 5 = *very important*). A complete set of scales, items, and factor loadings is presented in Table 1.

Health rights.   Six items tapped beliefs about rights concerning health. Both exploratory and confirmatory factor analyses were performed on these items that resulted in two factors. Three items formed the "Health as an Individual Right" scale (It's my body, I can do what I want with it; If I want to smoke or drink, it's my choice; and People have a right to smoke, they are only hurting themselves) and three items formed the "Public Health" belief scale (If something is bad for your health, the government should tell you to avoid it; The government should make laws to protect society against drunk driving; and Smokers need to be responsible, not smoke when little kids are around). Both scales had adequate measures of internal consistency: Cronbach's alpha of .78 for "individual right" and .71 for "public health."[1]

No right to intervene.   Adolescents' assessment of their right to intervene in the risk behaviors of friends was measured with items developed for the Social Responsibility and Prevention project. The main dependent variable in this study is adolescents' belief that intervening in a friend's risky behaviors is "none of my

---

[1]Note that the public health items were added at Waves 2 and 3 and the individual rights items were included at all three waves.

Table 1. Descriptive Statistics of Variables for Full Sample and Three Adolescent Groups

Variables (Factor Loadings)	Full Sample (N = 1,365)		Early Adolescent (n = 474)		Middle Adolescent (n = 457)		Late Adolescent (n = 434)	
	M	SD	M	SD	M	SD	M	SD
No right to intervene (time 2)								
Drunkenness—none of my business (.84)	2.02	1.06	1.99	1.06	2.05	1.09	2.03	1.02
Smoking—none of my business (.79)	2.53	1.21	2.31	1.21	2.58	1.24	2.73	1.13
Drugs—none of my business (.90)	2.07	1.09	1.98	1.09	2.12	1.11	2.12	1.07
Party—none of my business (.83)	2.19	1.04	2.13	1.09	2.24	1.06	2.20	.97
Public health (time 1)								
Not smoke when kids around (.56)	4.27	1.02	4.36	1.05	4.24	1.03	3.52	1.07
Bad for health government intervene (.80)	3.54	1.17	3.51	1.27	3.60	1.14	4.21	.97
Drunk driving government intervene (.60)	4.17	1.00	4.39	.94	4.12	1.00	3.97	1.00
Individual Right (time 1)								
My body I can do what I want with it (.79)	3.16	1.32	2.88	1.41	3.28	1.28	3.26	1.25
Smoking or drinking is my choice (.60)	3.12	1.40	2.60	1.34	3.28	1.39	3.57	1.27
People have a right to smoke (.59)	3.24	1.32	3.20	1.39	3.25	1.30	3.36	1.12

business," that is, an individual has no right to intervene in his or her friend's tobacco, alcohol, or drug use. It was based on responses to four vignettes in which a hypothetical friend would either be smoking cigarettes, drinking alcohol, using drugs, or where a group of friends were planning to go to a drinking party. Respondents were asked to rate how likely it was that they would ignore the behavior or say nothing because it was none of their business.

Data Analysis Plan

To understand developmental patterns, we took advantage of both the cross-sectional and longitudinal data. First, we tested for age and gender differences in health beliefs. Next, we used repeated measures analysis of variance over the three (or two, for the Public Health questions) waves of the study to compare trends for the three age groups. Finally, we used structural equation models (SEM) to test the relationships over time between prior health beliefs (at Wave 2) and subsequent endorsements that individuals have no right to intervene in the risky behavior of friends (at Wave 3). We tested measurement and structural invariance in the models for the three groups as well as mean-level differences between groups.

Results

Health Rights Beliefs

Figure 1 displays the percentage of adolescents at each age who agreed or strongly agreed with the individual rights or public health scales.[2] Several trends are noteworthy. First, endorsements of individual rights were higher for older compared to younger adolescents, F (7, 2,459) = 24.4, $p < .001$: Thirteen percent of 11-year versus 38% of 18-year-olds endorsed such rights. Second, we found marginal support for our hypothesis of a curvilinear relationship between age and endorsement of public health beliefs F (7, 2,505) = 3.26, $p = .002$. Sixty-three percent of 11-year-olds, 51% of 14- to 15-year-olds, and 60% of 17- to 18-year-olds endorsed this belief. Notably, at every age, adolescents were more likely to endorse public health than individual rights beliefs.

As predicted, there were significant gender differences with boys more likely than girls to endorse health rights beliefs, F (1, 2,443) = 11.9, $p = .001$ at Wave 1 and F (1, 2,535) = 5.59, $p = .018$ at Wave 2. At Wave 3 there were no gender differences F (1, 1,857) = .432, $p = .515$. As predicted, for the public health beliefs, the opposite pattern was found: girls were more likely than boys

---

[2]For consistency, respondents' ages in this figure are based on ages reported at Wave 1.

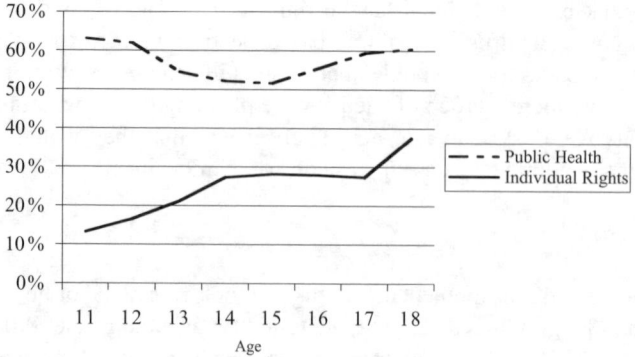

Fig. 1. Health beliefs by age: public health and individual rights.

to endorse these beliefs, F (1, 2,532) = 49.6, $p < .001$, F (1, 1,857) = 31.1, $p < .001$ at Waves 2 and 3, respectively.

Developmental Trends

To test for developmental trends, we split the sample into early-, middle-, and late-adolescent groups and ran repeated measures analysis of variance with health beliefs as the repeated measure and gender and parental education entered as covariates.

Figure 2 displays patterns for the three age groups for "Individual Rights" beliefs. Early adolescents have the lowest means at each wave whereas middle adolescents are more likely to endorse individual rights at each wave. Only at Wave 1 were late adolescents more likely than middle adolescents to endorse individual rights.

There were no interactions of time with age group on adolescents' endorsements of health as a private right. However, there was a significant between-group effect for age group, F (2,726) = 14.92, $p < .0001$. *Post hoc* tests revealed that early adolescents ($M = 2.84$) were less likely than middle ($M = 3.14$) and late adolescents ($M = 3.16$) to endorse these beliefs.

There was a significant difference between groups F (2,749) = 9.38, $p < .0001$ and an interaction of age group with time ($p < .05$) on adolescents' endorsement of public health beliefs. Consistent with our hypotheses and illustrated in Figure 3, middle adolescents ($M = 3.73$) were the least likely to endorse public health beliefs with late adolescents ($M = 3.92$) as likely as early adolescents ($M = 3.93$) to endorse such beliefs. In addition, whereas the public health beliefs of middle and late adolescents were stable over the last two waves of the study, early adolescents' endorsements of these beliefs declined between Waves 2 and 3.

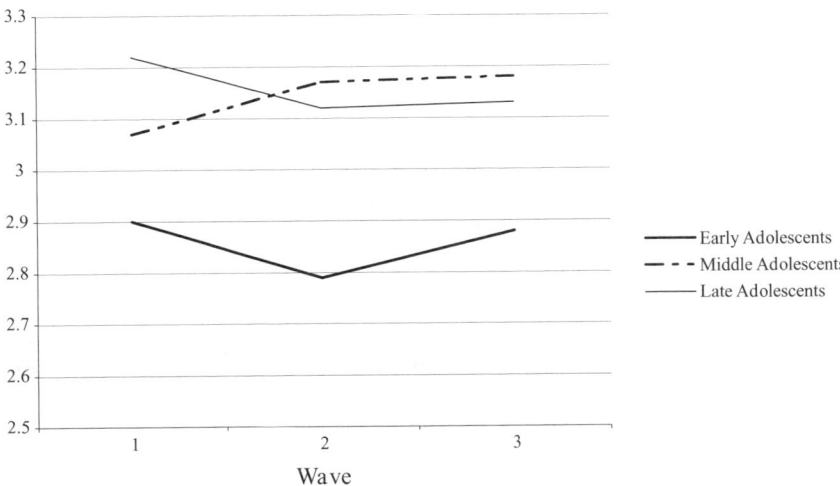

Fig. 2. Belief in health as an individual right by wave.

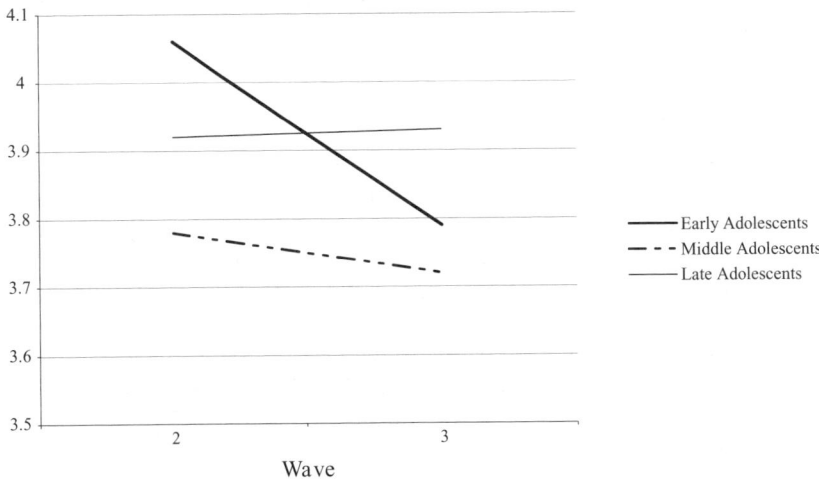

Fig. 3. Belief in health as a public responsibility by wave.

No Right to Intervene

Our conceptual model hypothesizes that adolescents' beliefs about health rights affect their assumptions about the right to intervene if friends are using drugs, drinking alcohol, or smoking: negatively related to individual rights and positively related to public health beliefs. We also expected that girls would be more likely than boys to feel they had a right to intervene. To determine whether there were developmental differences in how these processes operate, we utilized a multiple group modeling approach with early ($n = 562$), middle ($n = 506$), and late adolescents ($n = 467$) as the groups. For the construct items, the percentage of cases classified as missing ranged from 1.1% to 5.1%. Rather than deleting cases with missing data, we analyzed the data using full information maximum likelihood estimation (Eliason, 1993).

Analytic Strategy

The data analyses involved several steps. First, we used confirmatory factor analyses to show that our measurement models were an appropriate fit for the overall sample. Second, we divided the sample into three age groups and estimated a multiple group measurement model that had latent variable factor loadings constrained to be equal. Third, we estimated multiple group SEM where gender, public health beliefs at Time 1, and individual rights beliefs at Time 1 were regressed on endorsement of the right to intervene at Time 2. Our final model was a multiple-group SEM with factor loadings constrained to be equal and the parameter estimates of the path coefficients estimated freely across groups.

Measurement Model

Figure 4 shows the multiple group measurement model for the latent variables: right to intervene (t2), public health beliefs (t1), and individual rights beliefs (t1). We assessed model fit using the comparative fit index (CFI) and the root mean square error of approximation (RMSEA). Based on these measures, our multigroup measurement model fit the data well (CFI = .98, RMSEA = .04) (Bentler, 1990; Browne & Cudeck, 1993). For this model, we also conducted χ^2 difference tests and determined that there was factorial invariance for the item loadings across groups. The results suggested that a model with all factor loadings constrained to be equal across groups adequately fit the data ($\chi^2 = 187.325$, $df = 106$). The χ^2 difference ($\chi^2 = 24.21$, $df = 12$) between our unconstrained and constrained models was not significant, indicating that the model with constrained factor loadings was a good fit for the data.

Table 2 reports the correlations of the latent variables for the overall sample ($\chi^2 = 80.161$, $df = 32$, CFI = .987, RMSEA = .031) and for the three adolescent groups with correlations marked to correspond with Figure 4. For the overall sample, individual rights beliefs and no right to intervene had a moderate, positive correlation. Public health beliefs and no right to intervene were negatively related. Overall, public health and individual rights beliefs had a weak, negative correlation. All correlations, except for public health beliefs with individual rights beliefs

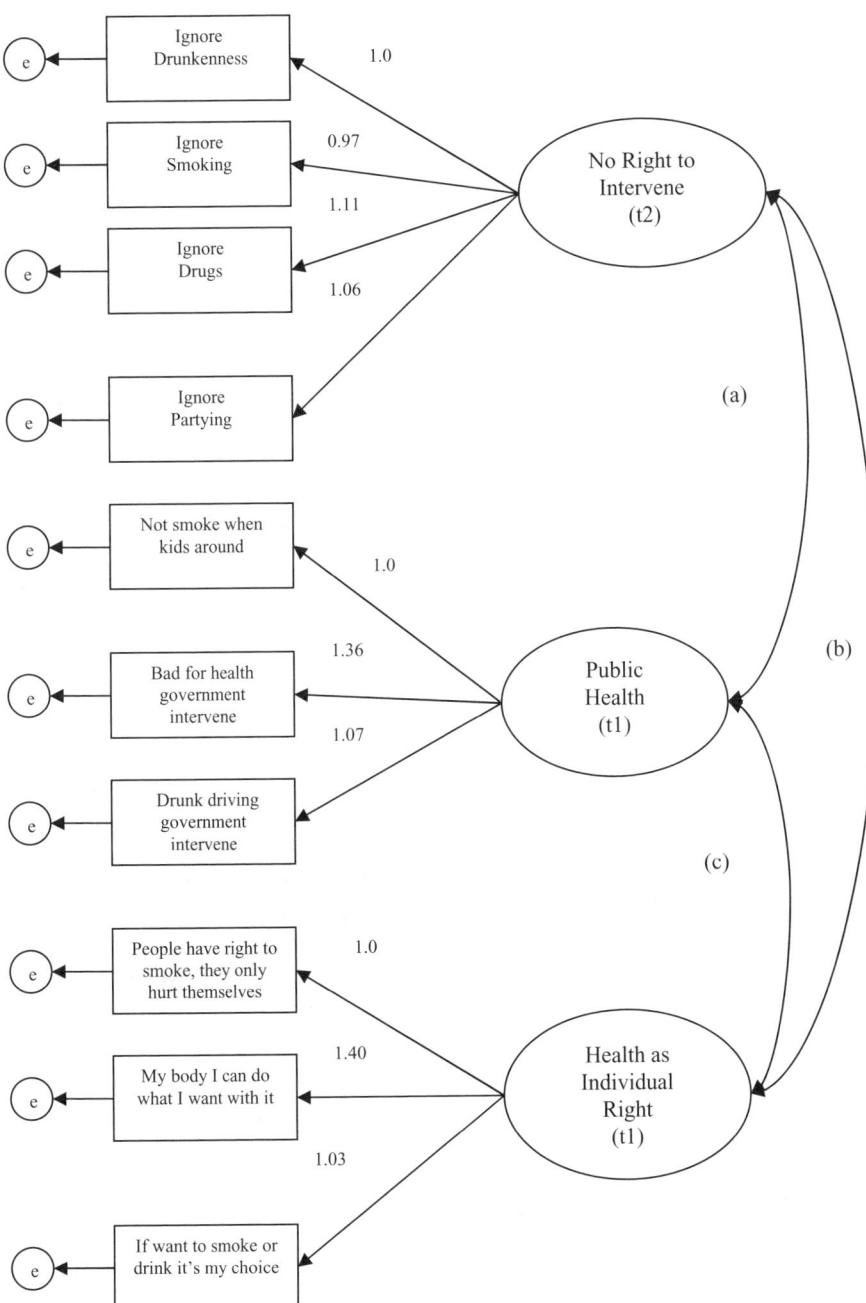

Fig. 4. Multiple group measurement model with equality constraints on factor loadings.

Table 2. Correlations of Latent Variables for Full Sample and Three Adolescent Groups

Correlation	Full Sample (N = 1,534)	Early Adolescent (n = 561)	Middle Adolescent (n = 506)	Late Adolescent (n = 467)
(a) Ignore: None of my business (t2) with public health (t1)	−.29***	−.25***	−.35***	−.22**
(b) Ignore: None of my business (t2) with individual right (t1)	.24***	.18**	.27***	.23***
(c) Public health (t1) with individual right (t1)	−.09*	−.25***	.02	.07

Note. *p < .0; **p < .01; ***p < .001.

for the middle- and late-adolescent groups, were in the expected directions, and were statistically significant.

The bivariate associations show several interesting age patterns. For instance, for middle adolescents there are stronger associations between both the individual right and public health constructs and endorsing "no right to intervene" when compared to the results for the early or late adolescents. This suggests that, for middle adolescents, there is a stronger relationship between beliefs about health rights and behavioral norms concerning the right to intervene in friends' behavior and supports contentions that, at this age, they are trying to fit in and to make sense of social conventions (Horn, 2003; Nucci, 2006). Among early adolescents, there is a negative relationship between individual rights and public health beliefs but among middle and late adolescents, these beliefs are uncorrelated. This suggests that, for early adolescents, beliefs in individual rights and public health are polar opposites whereas for middle and late adolescents they are not. The fact that endorsements of individual rights and public health beliefs are not polar opposites for the middle and late adolescents points to the increasing sophistication of their social representation of health.

Structural Equation Model

Table 3 displays the results of the structural equation models for the overall and multiple group samples. In these models public health beliefs, individual rights beliefs, and gender are each regressed on right to intervene. Table 3 presents the unstandardized and standardized path coefficients for the overall and multiple group SEMs. Unstandardized coefficients reflect differences across age groups, while standardized coefficients report the magnitude of effects within groups.

Table 3. Path Coefficients for SEMs of Adolescent Intervention Rights Beliefs

	No Right to Intervene in a Friend's ATOD Use							
	Full Sample (N = 1,533)		Early Adolescent (N = 560)		Middle Adolescent (N = 506)		Late Adolescent (N = 467)	
	Coefficient	Standardized Coefficient	Coefficient	Standardized Coefficient	Coefficient	Standardized Coefficient	Coefficient	Standardized Coefficient
Public health	−.342***	−.254	−.309***	−.209	−.437***	−.335	−.308***	−.221
(t1)	(.050)		(.097)		(.080)		(.092)	
Individual right	.067***	.209	.096	.093	.292***	.279	.249***	.240
(t1)	(.029)		(.065)		(.057)		(.060)	
Female	−.173***	−.217	−.118	−.141	.000	.000	−.211**	−.289
	(.045)		(.079)		(.019)		(.073)	
R^2	.138		.069		.216		.123	

Note. Model fit for the overall sample SEM: $\chi^2 = 80.161$; $df = 32$; CFI = .987; RMSEA = .031.
Model fit for the multiple-group SEM: $\chi^2 = 227.455$; $df = 130$; CFI = .975; RMSEA = .038.
Standard errors in parentheses. ATOD = alcohol, tobacco, and drug. *$p < .05$; **$p < .01$; ***$p < .001$.

The *unstandardized coefficients* in Table 3 reveal several differences across adolescent age groups. First, the coefficient for individual rights beliefs increases between early and middle adolescence and then declines slightly for late adolescents. Whereas for early adolescents, beliefs in individual rights have little impact on intentions to intervene, for middle and late adolescents, beliefs that health risks are an individual's decision are significantly associated with their perceptions that they have no right to intervene in their friends' risk taking. We can infer that, to the extent that they endorse an individual's right to take risks, they would be unlikely to act if a friend were taking risks. Second, the coefficient for public health beliefs is higher for middle adolescents than for early or late adolescents. This suggests that endorsements of public health are more strongly associated with the belief in a right to intervene in friends' risk taking in middle than in early or late adolescence. Table 3 also shows that gender was related to late adolescents' concepts of their right to intervene with females more likely than males to endorse this right. However, there were no gender differences in early or middle adolescents' convictions of their right to intervene in friends' risky behaviors.

The *standardized* path coefficients reported in Table 3 provide information on the magnitude of the effects of adolescent public health beliefs, individual rights beliefs, and gender on their convictions regarding the right to intervene. For early adolescents, only the coefficient for public health beliefs is a significant predictor of perceptions of the right to intervene. Neither belief in health as an individual right nor gender have a significant impact on early adolescents' convictions that they have a right to intervene in the behavior of others.

Among middle adolescents, both individual rights and public health beliefs are significant predictors of the conviction that one has a right to intervene in friends' risk taking. The direct effects of the exogenous variables indicate that public health beliefs are a stronger predictor than are beliefs in individuals' rights. For late adolescents, the differences in the magnitude of the effects of the independent variables on the conviction that one has a right to intervene are small. All three of the independent variables (gender, public health, and individual rights) are equally important for understanding late adolescents' convictions regarding their right to intervene. Furthermore, as the discussion of bivariate relationships pointed out, older adolescents no longer hold public health and individual rights beliefs as polar opposites, pointing to a maturational pattern, that is, both beliefs can exist within the same individual.

Our model explains 7% of the variance in early adolescents' convictions about their right to intervene, 22% of middle adolescents' convictions, and 12% of late adolescents' convictions. In each case, public health beliefs are the most significant predictor of adolescents' convictions that they have a right to intervene in the risk behaviors of friends. In short, young people who endorse society's right to curb individuals from risky choices that could impact others' health and well-being also believe they have a right (or obligation) to intervene in the risky behaviors of their friends.

Discussion

In this study, we revealed developmental differences in adolescents' representation of health and the rights associated with risky behaviors that might compromise health. Between early and late adolescence, there is an increase in the defense of an individual's right to engage in risks that might compromise health. At the same time, there appears to be a curvilinear relationship between age and an appreciation of the implications to the public's health of an individual's risky choices: Early and late adolescents are more likely than are middle adolescents to endorse the right of society to curb or penalize individuals for making risky choices. Taken together, these results point to developmental changes in the social representation of health and the rights associated with risky choices. By late adolescence there is a sophisticated conceptualization of health: A commitment to an individual's right to experiment with substances is tempered by a recognition of the need for laws enacted by government that constrain individuals' rights in the interest of a larger public good. The results are consistent with age trends in social judgments, social exclusion, and endorsements of individual rights: What we might refer to as an ardent commitment to personal rights as a basis for making decisions and regulating social interactions appears to peak in middle adolescence (Horn, 2003; Killen et al., 2002; Ruck et al., 1998).

Besides age, there were gender differences in beliefs about rights associated with health risks. Females were less likely than males to endorse individual rights and more likely to endorse public health, although these gender differences disappeared as adolescents grew older. This is consistent with literature on friendship in which females are more likely to offer support to a friend in need (Rose & Asher, 1999). It also supports gender differences in adolescents' perceptions of rights with females more likely than their male peers to endorse nurturance rights (Day et al., 2006; Peterson-Badali & Ruck, this issue). Finally, this result is consistent with the fact that female adolescents are more likely than their male peers to consider social exclusion a moral matter rather than a social convention (Horn, 2003).

The results also show that health beliefs have an impact on adolescents' conviction that they do or do not have a right to intervene in a friend's risk taking. For middle adolescents in particular, both public and private health beliefs accounted for a significant percentage of the variance in youths' convictions. Our models did not explain as large a proportion of the variance in early and late adolescents' convictions about intervening in friends' risky choices. Future research should consider other factors that may affect youths' convictions about dissuading friends from ATOD use.

We want to draw attention to the relatively high level of espousal of public health beliefs and comparatively low level of adherence to individual rights. Although this gap in attitudes is smaller among older respondents, it is noteworthy that, in a society where the dominant social representation of health is that it is a private rather than a public good, adolescents do appreciate the state's role in constraining individual choices in the interests of public health. These results are consistent with other work showing that both young people and their mothers are more likely to endorse nurturance than self-determination rights (Day et al., 2006; Ruck et al., 2002). The fact that we measured public health beliefs in a relatively narrow way is a limitation of our study. Additional items tapping youths' beliefs about the responsibilities of the state to its children and of health as a human right would have provided a more detailed picture of how adolescents conceive of health and the rights and responsibilities associated with it.

The results of this program of work are relevant for health promotion and risk prevention efforts with young people. Individual responsibility and informed decision making are the standards of most prevention programs but the emphasis is typically on individuals making those decisions on their own. Based on the results of this study, interventions could emphasize: (a) that there are both private and public dimensions of health, (b) that individual behaviors including risky choices have implications for others' well-being, and (c) that dissuading friends from behaviors that might compromise their health is a responsibility friends owe one another.

References

Bentler, P. M. (1990). Comparative fit indices in structural models. *Psychological Bulletin, 107*(2), 238–246.

Berkowitz, M. W., Guerra, N., & Nucci, L. (1991). Sociomoral development and drug and alcohol abuse. In W. M. Kurtines & J. L. Gewirtz (Eds.), *Handbook of moral behavior and development, Vol. 3: Application* (pp. 35–53). Hillsdale, NJ: Erlbaum.

Browne, M. W., & Cudeck, R. (1993). Alternative ways of assessing model fit. In K. A. Bollen & J. S. Long (Eds.), *Testing structural equation models* (pp. 136–162). Newbury Park, CA: Sage.

Day, D. M., Peterson-Badali, M., & Ruck, M. D. (2006). The relationship between maternal attitudes and young people's attitudes toward children's rights. *Journal of Adolescence, 29*, 193–207.

Eisenberg, N., & Sheffield Morris, A. (2004). Moral cognition and pro social responding in adolescence. In R. M. Lerner & L. Steinberg (Eds.), *Handbook of adolescent psychology* (pp. 155–188). New York: Wiley.

Eliason, S. R. (1993). *Maximum likelihood estimation: Logic and practice*. Newbury Park, CA: Sage.

Flanagan, C., Gallay, L., & Elek, E. (2005). Friends don't let friends ... or do they? Developmental and gender differences in intervening in friends' ATOD use. *Journal of Drug Education, 34*(4), 351–371.

Flanagan, C. A., & Stout, M. (2008). *Developmental origins of social trust: Patterns over two years for early, middle, and late adolescents*. Manuscript under review.

Guttman, N., & Ressler, W. H. (2001). On being responsible: Ethical issues in appeals to personal responsibility in health campaigns. *Journal of Health Communications, 6*, 117–136.

Haigh, F. (2002). Human rights approach to health. *Croatian Medical Journal, 43*(2), 166–169.

Helwig, C. C. (1995). Adolescents' and young adults' conceptions of civil liberties: Freedom of speech and religion. *Child Development, 66*, 152–166.

Horn, S. (2003). Adolescents' reasoning about exclusion from social groups. *Developmental Psychology, 39*(1), 71–84.

Horn, S. S. (2005). Adolescents' peer interactions: Conflict and coordination among personal expression, social norms, and moral reasoning. In L. Nucci (Ed.), *Conflict, contradiction, and contrarian elements in moral development and education* (pp. 113–128). Mahwah, NJ: Erlbaum.

Keating, D. P. (2004). Cognitive and brain development. In R. M. Lerner & L. Steinberg (Eds.), *Handbook of adolescent psychology* (pp. 45–84). New York: Wiley.

Killen, M., Lee-Kim, J., McGlothlin, H., & Stangor, C. (2002). How children and adolescents evaluate gender and racial exclusion. *Monographs for the Society for Research in Child Development.* Serial No. 271, Vol. 67, No. 4. Oxford, UK: Blackwell Publishers.

Killen, M., Leviton, M., & Cahill, J. (1991). Adolescent reasoning about drug use. *Journal of Adolescent Research, 6*, 336–356.

Killen, M., & Stangor, C. (2001). Social reasoning about inclusion and exclusion in gender and race peer group contexts. *Child Development, 72*, 174–186.

Leichter, H. M. (2003). "Evil habits" and "personal choices": Assigning responsibility for health in the 20th century. *Milbank Quarterly, 81*(4), 603–626.

Minkler, M. (1999). Personal responsibility for health? A review of the arguments and the evidence at the century's end. *Health Education and Behavior, 26*(1), 121–140.

Nucci, L. P. (1996). Morality and the personal sphere of action. In E. Reed, E. Turiel, & T. Brown (Eds.), *Values and knowledge* (pp. 41–60). Hillsdale, NJ: Erlbaum.

Nucci, L. P. (2006). Education for moral development. In M. Killen & J. Smetana (Eds.), *Handbook of moral development* (pp. 657–681). Mahwah, NJ: Erlbaum.

Nucci, L., Guerra, N., & Lee, J. (1991). Adolescent judgments of the personal, prudential, and normative aspects of drug usage. *Developmental Psychology, 27*, 841–848.

Peterson-Badali, M., Ruck, M. D., & Ridley, E. (2003). College students' attitudes toward children's nurturance and self-determination rights. *Journal of Applied Social Psychology, 33*(4), 730–755.

Rose, A. J., & Asher, S. R. (1999). Children's goals and strategies in response to conflicts within a friendship. *Developmental Psychology, 35*, 69–79.

Ruck, M. D., Abramovitch, R., & Keating, D. P. (1998). Children's and adolescents' understanding of rights: Balancing nurturance and self-determination. *Child Development, 64*, 404–417.

Ruck, M. D., Peterson-Badali, M., & Day, D. M. (2002). Adolescents' and parents' understanding of children's rights in the home. *Journal of Research on Adolescence, 12*, 373–398.

Smetana, J. G. (2002). Culture, autonomy, and personal jurisdiction in adolescent-parent relationships. In H. Reese & R. Kail (Eds.), *Advances in child development and behavior* (Vol. 29, pp. 51–87). New York: Academic Press.

Turiel, E. (1983). *The development of social knowledge: Morality and convention.* Cambridge: Cambridge University Press.

Williams, C., & Bybee, J. (1994). What do children feel guilty about? Developmental and gender differences. *Developmental Psychology, 30*(5), 617–623.

CONNIE FLANAGAN is a Developmental Psychologist and Professor of Youth Civic Development at Penn State University where she co-directs the intercollege minor in Civic and Community Engagement. Her program of research concerns young people's theories about the "social contract," that is, their views of the rights and responsibilities that bind members of society together, and the factors in families, schools, and communities that promote civic values and competencies in young people. She is a William T. Grant Scholar, a member of the MacArthur Network on Transitions to Adulthood, a SPSSI fellow, and a Spencer fellow.

MICHAEL STOUT is a sociologist and Assistant Professor in the Department of Sociology, Anthropology, and Criminology at Missouri State University. He received his PhD from The Pennsylvania State University in 2008. His research interests include understanding the relationship between social capital and civic engagement throughout the life course. His current research investigates the relative importance of trust, networks, and voluntary associations as resources that encourage civic engagement.

LESLIE GALLAY has a Masters in Political Science and PhD in Health Planning. He is a Research Scientist at Penn State University where he manages the Social Responsibility and Prevention Project. His work focuses on the social ecology of health and his current research interests include the relationship between social capital and health. He has conducted studies of the social determinants of health risk with different age groups within the United States and internationally.

Journal of Social Issues, Vol. 64, No. 4, 2008, pp. 835–856

Children's Nurturance and Self-Determination Rights: A Cross-Cultural Perspective

Isabelle D. Cherney* and Yee L. Shing

Creighton University and Max Planck Institute for Human Development, Berlin

Increasing awareness of children's developmental needs and rights has led to a global move toward giving children and adolescents a greater degree of autonomy in the decisions affecting their own lives. This article presents two studies examining the role of culture and religion in 12-year-old children's perceptions of their rights across three cultures. The first study showed that U.S. and Swiss children advocated for more self-determination rights than Chinese-Malaysian children; U.S. and Chinese-Malaysian children advocated for more nurturance rights than Swiss children. Within the Chinese-Malaysian sample, Buddhist children were more likely to advocate for self-determination rights as compared to Christian children. Using a revised Children's Rights Interview (rCRI), the second study showed that on average U.S. and Chinese-Malaysian children were more likely to advocate for self-determination rights than nurturance rights. However, there were no significant differences between the two cultural groups in terms of the overall responses. The results of the studies are discussed in terms of the cultural orientation and constructivist frameworks.

Children are often described as the world's most valuable resource. Unfortunately, they continue to be neglected, abused, and exploited (Glotzer, 2005). Due to their subordinate status in society, children are very often unable to assert their own rights. These rights are largely defined and controlled by the adult population. However, increasing awareness of children's developmental needs and rights has led to a global move toward giving children and adolescents a greater degree of autonomy in the decisions affecting their own lives and development (see Ruck &

---

*Correspondence concerning this article should be addressed to Isabelle D. Cherney, Creighton University, Department of Psychology, Omaha, NE 68178 [e-mail: cherneyi@creighton.edu].

We wish to thank Leah Skovran, Adam Greteman, Brittany Travers, Judith Flichtbeil, Joshua Berg, and Nicole Neff for their help with data collection. We are grateful to the staff of the participating schools and the children for sharing their valuable time and insights with us. Preliminary data were presented at the 2003 Meeting of the Society for Research in Child Development in Tampa, Florida, and the 2005 Midwestern Psychological Association in Chicago, Illinois.

Horn, this issue). The U.N. Convention on the Rights of the Child (CRC) (United Nations General Assembly, 1989) serves to improve the quality of children's lives by providing guidelines in defining and implementing children's rights. As Limber and Flekkoy (1995) contended, the Convention's articles should be viewed within the context of three overarching themes, namely that the primary consideration in any action should be in the "the best interests of the child" (Article 3), that states will provide children with rights "in a manner consistent with [their] evolving capacities" (Article 5), and that children's dignity be respected (Preamble).

One can anticipate that basic cultural differences affect how the very meaning of the term *children's rights* is understood. Understanding these types of differences would facilitate the success with which the CRC (1989) could be effectively used to guide children's policies in different countries. A major detraction for the convention is the debate over whether the rights are universal or culturally bound (Murphy-Berman, Levesque, & Berman, 1996). In addition to a potential cultural bias in the drafting of the convention, there is also disagreement over the basic definition and parameters of childhood. This disagreement demonstrates major cultural differences that are likely to hinder the implementation of children's rights, and it raises the question of whether an international governing body can adequately legislate such rights on an international level. It is therefore essential to examine which rights are culturally bound, which rights, if any, are universal, and ultimately, how the definition of a child influences the impact of this convention.

Research on children's rights is relatively sparse. In one of the earliest studies, Rogers and Wrightsman (1978) drew a distinction between nurturance rights and self-determination rights. The nurturance orientation stresses society's obligations to make decisions "in the best interests of children," to protect them from harm, and to mold their development. The determination of what is considered good or desirable *for* a child is made by the child's authority figures. It is essentially a paternalistic (or parentalistic) view. On the other hand, the self-determination orientation stresses the importance of allowing children to exercise control over various facets of their own lives, even when those decisions might conflict with the views of adults charged with the children's care. Self-determination rights are characterized by giving the child developmentally appropriate freedom in their own development.

Melton (1980, 1983) was one of the first researchers to provide an account of the development of children's reasoning about their rights. He developed the Children's Rights Interview (CRI), which contains 12 vignettes to assess when and under what circumstances children would assert a right. The vignettes involved conflict-laden situations in which the child might assert a right. His findings showed that the development of reasoning about children's rights is dependent on age and socioeconomic status (SES). He reported that high-SES children and 1st, 3rd, 5th, and 7th graders asserted more positive attitudes toward their rights approximately 2 years before the same-aged low-SES children. Consideration of

Melton's work suggests, despite some possible confounding between SES and cognitive level, socioeconomic and developmental explanations for differences in same-aged children's conceptions of their rights. Although Melton (1980) did not explicitly distinguish between nurturance and self-determination rights, his framework can best be applied to self-determination rights. It does not, however, fully capture the development of reasoning surrounding nurturance rights (see Ruck, Abramovitch, & Keating, 1998).

Cultural Orientations and Their Consequences on Children's Rights

A fundamental question in cross-cultural research and research on children's rights is the extent to which the conception of autonomy or the emphasis on individual freedom and self-determination is culturally dependent or universal. Particular goals related to autonomy may, at the same time, vary by developmental periods (Ryan & La Guardia, 2000). As children develop skills and abilities related to psychological needs for self-expression and competence, they actively pursue areas of autonomy that are being afforded by different cultural environments. These conceptions of personal autonomy and individual freedom presumably vary across cultures and environments, with limitations set by societal controls and individuals' opposing claims for personal jurisdiction.

Some researchers contend that conceptions of the self vary between individualistic and collectivistic cultures (Kim, 1990; Markus & Kitayama, 1991; Shweder, Mahapatra, & Miller, 1987; Triandis, 1989). For example, in individualistic societies, the self is regarded as separate from the social order, leading to a morality of autonomy and emphasis on individual rights. In contrast, in collectivistic societies, the self is interdependent, defined by the unique social roles that individuals occupy in the family and society. If different cultures encourage varying amounts of autonomy during childhood, then, according to a cultural explanation, individualistic cultures such as those of North America, and to a lesser extent, those of Western Europe would place a primary value on the autonomy of the individual member, whether adult or child. On the other hand, cultures that are more collectivistic, such as Asian and African societies, lead individuals to conform to the existing social roles, and to uphold the hierarchy to maintain social harmony (Shweder & Sullivan, 1993). This view would place higher priority on the nurturance and protection of children. Therefore, as different cultures encourage varying amount of autonomy during childhood, cultural variability should affect children's perceptions of their rights. One way to examine such differences is to assess cultural differences in countries embracing varying degrees of individualistic and collectivistic orientations.

In relation to the orientations of children's rights, individualism implies that judgment and reasoning of human rights are oriented toward and based on the individual rather than the social context or situation, and the protection of the individual rights tends to be emphasized. Thus, individualism is in line with self-determination rights. On the other hand, collectivism implies that judgment and reasoning are bound with mutual obligations of individuals within the social context. The care and well-being of those in need, such as children, is guarded by the adults. Furthermore, nurturance and compliance are encouraged, and fulfillment of one's duty to the group rather than the expression of one's personal rights tend to be rewarded (Helwig, Arnold, Tan, & Boyd, 2003; Hofstede, 2001). Therefore, collectivism is in line with nurturance rights. Similarly, cultural psychology (Shweder & Sullivan, 1993; Triandis, 1989) would predict that children from collectivistic cultures (e.g., Malaysia from Southeast Asia) would be less likely to endorse self-determination rights than those from individualistic cultures (e.g., United States).

Despite the useful dichotomous conceptualization of cross-cultural differences, Cherney and Perry (1996) postulated that the differentiation of social and moral concepts become increasingly complex throughout development. Similarly, the constructivist perspective of social development proposed by Turiel and colleagues (Neff & Helwig, 2002; Nucci, 2001; Turiel, 1998) rejected the idea of global stage approaches toward reasoning (e.g., Kohlberg, 1969; Piaget, 1970). This *social cognitive domain approach* postulates that children construct multiple forms of social understanding through their encounters with different types of social experiences (see Ruck & Horn, this issue). In other words, children develop understandings that simultaneously include concerns with justice, fairness, and rights, as well as social–conventional conceptions based on authority, tradition, and social rules. Thus, individuals give priority to different concerns depending on a variety of factors, such as salient situations and the way different types of conflicting concerns are interpreted at different points in development (Helwig, 2006b; Neff & Helwig, 2002). The active stance of individuals in relation to their social environment results in both shared and nonshared aspects of culture.

Religious Background and Influences on Perceptions of Rights

It is important to consider how cultural practices are evaluated by individuals, and to account for the role of diverse concepts that individuals bring to bear in interpreting and evaluating their social reality. One such concept and a potentially important variable that has not received much empirical attention in previous studies is religion. Parents play an important role in instructing their children about religious tenets and practices. It is their responsibility and right to direct and educate their child in a way that promotes their religion (or lack of religion). The Catholic Church can be considered a rather paternalistic religion because it has a distinctly stratified hierarchy (Sampson, 2000). Thus, Catholics would be expected to embrace nurturance rights in that what is good or desirable is determined for the child. While there are differences in beliefs and values among

Christian denominations, there are also differences between Western-based and non-Western-based religions. Ben-Arieh, Khoury-Kassabri, and Haj-Yahia (2006) found differences between Israeli Jewish youth and Muslim Palestinian youth. Regardless of the country of residence, Jewish youth and adults generally reported more positive attitudes toward children's rights than did the Palestinian groups. These findings demonstrate that judgments and reasoning may vary by religion regardless of the country of origin. An important question that arises is the extent to which the patterns found in this research extend to other—especially non-Western—religious and cultural contexts. Chinese family life and religion, for example, is often portrayed as a fixed hierarchy, with elders held in high esteem and obedience (Pye, 1992). How do these differences affect adolescents' view of children's rights? Thus, similar to the individualistic and collectivist orientations, Christians' and Buddhists' precepts may differ in important ways influencing children's perceptions of their rights.

The Current Studies

These studies examined children's perception of their own rights using samples of children from a collectivistic culture (Chinese-Malaysian), an individualistic culture (United States), and for the first study, a Western European culture (Switzerland). Specifically, children of moderate-SES Chinese-Malaysian ethnic background living in Kuala Lumpur, Malaysia and U.S. children of moderate SES were interviewed using a slightly modified version of the Children's Rights Interview (CRI) in the first study and the revised version (rCRI) in the second study (see list of vignettes in Table 1).

Twelve-year-old adolescents were chosen as the participants of these studies because the balance between nurturance and self-determination is of particular interest at this age. While nurturance is still necessary, children's quest for autonomy is increasing as a developmental task. As Melton's (1980) findings suggested, 12-year-old children are capable of making judgments that are based more on criteria of fairness and competence to exercise self-determination than on what authority figures actually allow children to do. At that age, children's views have shifted toward positive attitudes about children's self-determination rights and children are therefore more apt to make informed decisions about issues that may or may not affect their lives.

Malaysia is a multicultural country in Southeast Asia. In 2000, 65.1% of the Malaysian population was Malay, 26% Chinese, and 7.7% Indian (Department of Statistics Malaysia, 2001). In terms of religious practice, Islam is the most widely professed religion (60.4%, mostly practiced by Malay ethnic group). Malaysia, being a multireligious nation, also has a fair share of other religions such as Buddhism (19.2%), Christianity (9.1%), Hinduism (6.3%), and Confucianism/Taoism/other traditional Chinese religion (2.6%).

Table 1. Revised Children's Rights Interview Vignettes (rCRI; Cherney, 2003) Used in Studies 1 and 2 According to U.N. Convention Rights and Article

Types of Rights (United Nation Convention Rights and Article in Parenthesis)	Wording of Vignettes
	Self-determination vignettes
Right to be heard in custody dispute (*Participation right; Art. 12*)	1. Mary's parents are getting a divorce. Her mother wants Mary to live with her, but her father wants Mary to live with him.
Right to due process (*Participation right; Art. 12*)	2. Jim saw how a boy jumped over a neighbor's fence and how the angry neighbor hit the child repeatedly with a stick.
Expressing opinion in school newspaper (*Participation right; Art. 12 & 13*):	3. Mark wrote a story for the school newspaper. In his story he said that he didn't like the school rules. The principal told him that he couldn't print his story.
Voting (*Participation right; Art. 16*)	4. Lucy would like to vote for a political leader. Her parents told her that she was too young to vote.
Keeping a secret diary (*Participation right; Art. 16*)	5. Betty kept a diary, and she said that nobody else could read it, not even her parents.
Due process (*Participation right; Art. 12*)	6. Larry got into a fight at school. The teacher said that he would have to do extra homework for school. Larry said, "Wait! You have to hear my side of the story first."
Right to health care (*Right to health care; Art. 24 & 25*)	7. John wanted to go to a doctor to talk about some things that were bothering him, but his parents would not let him.
Right to choose own religion (*Participation right; Art. 15*)	8. Becky doesn't want to practice her parents' religion. She wants to try some other religions or maybe have no religion at all.
	Nurturance vignettes
Right to refuse vaccination (*Right to health care, Art. 24 & 25*)	9. Joan went to the doctor and he told her that she should take a vaccination. Joan said that she would not take one.
Protection from movie content (*Participation right; Art. 16*)	10. David wanted to watch a movie on television, but his parents did not think it was a good movie for him to watch.
Protection from child labor (*Protection right; Art. 32*)	11. Linda wanted to work in Mr. Smith's grocery store. Mr. Smith said that she was not old enough to have a job.
Parental oversight (*Participation right; Art. 15*):	12. Debbie wanted to go and visit her friends, but her parents would not let her because they didn't like her friends.
Providing food and clothing (*Protection right; Art. 12 & 13*)	13. Carrie's parents decided that she should have to pay for her own food and clothing. Carrie thinks that her parents should pay.
Parental assistance with peer-related conflict (*Participation right; Art. 12 & 13*)	14. Kelly had an argument with her best friend and was very upset. She wanted to talk to her parents about it but they were too busy.
Child protection (*Development right; Preamble*)	15. Terry's parents are never there when he gets home from school. Terry doesn't like being left home alone.
Parental assistance with homework (*Development right; Preamble*)	16. Randy was having trouble with his math homework. He needed his parents to help him with it. But his parents said that he had to do it himself.

According to the 2006 U.S. Census Bureau (census.org) estimates, 80.1% of the U.S. population is of Caucasian, 14.8% is of Hispanic or Latino origin, 12.4% is of African-American origin, and 4.4% is of Asian origin. Most citizens adhere to Christianity (78.5%), with roughly 52% Protestant, 24.5% Catholic, and 2% Mormon. Fifteen percent of the U.S. population has no religious affiliation. Switzerland is ranked in between Malaysia and the United States in terms of individualism (Hofstede, 2001) and can thus serve as a reasonably good comparison. Switzerland, like Malaysia and the United States, is a multicultural country. Forty-two percent of the population is Catholic and 35% is Protestant. Over 4% of the population considers Islam as their religion (swissworld.org).

Based on historical factors, and similar to Chinese society that is described as collectivistic (e.g., Helwig et al., 2003; Triandis, 1989), it seems plausible that the Chinese-Malaysian society holds a collectivist orientation, and thus a more nurturance orientation toward children's rights than children from the United States who would be expected to hold an individualistic orientation. Switzerland's political, economic, educational, and cultural complexities as well as its rich traditional history suggest that both nurturance and self-determination rights might be equally important in the decision-making process. However, such simple categorization may not be sufficient in capturing the complexity of the cultural context. For example, Lau (1992) found no distinct pattern of collectivistic value preference among the Chinese samples (from China, Hong Kong, and Singapore). Rather, Chinese from different regions differentially showed individualist and collectivist concerns as they develop complex and heterogeneous social orientations that are influenced by the multifaceted social world. Thus, rather than a strong proposition from cultural psychology (Shweder & Sullivan, 1993; Triandis, 1989) perhaps the constructivist model should be considered (Neff & Helwig, 2002). Therefore, in the case of Chinese-Malaysian, it is likely that the recent rapid social and economic changes have resulted in a transformation of conceptions of human rights and a more autonomous children's rights regime within the society.

Study 1

The first study was designed to extend Cherney and Perry's (1996) study with a sample of Chinese-Malaysian and U.S. children using a slightly modified version of Melton's (1980) CRI. For comparison purposes, we contrasted their answers with those of the Swiss children who participated in their original study (Cherney & Perry, 1996). It was hypothesized that based on the cultural perspective, Chinese-Malaysian children would be more likely to advocate for nurturance rights than Swiss and U.S. children. Conversely, U.S. children would be more likely to advocate for self-determination rights than Swiss and Chinese-Malaysian children, with the Swiss sample falling between the two other samples. Following a constructivist model (Neff & Helwig, 2002), we also hypothesized that, regardless of the cultural background, children would not advocate indiscriminately for either nurturance or self-determination rights. Rather, they would take into account the social, cultural, and economic context in which they were raised. In addition, because of the paternalistic aspect of Christianity, Christian children were hypothesized to advocate for more nurturance rights and children's rights in general than Buddhist children.

Method

Participants

The total sample consisted of 100 children (44 boys and 56 girls) between the ages of 11 and 13 ($M = 12.11$, $SD = .36$). Twenty children came from the capital of Malaysia (Kuala Lumpur) and 18 children from the midwestern United States. Their interviews were added to the existing 62 interviews of Swiss children interviewed in Geneva. In the sample, 14% of the participants were Buddhists, 21% were of Protestant denominations, 32% Catholic, and 33% did not claim any religion. All Buddhists came from Malaysia, 19% of the Protestants were from Malaysia, 5% from the United States, and 76% from Switzerland. Forty-one percent of the Catholic sample came from the United States and 59% from Switzerland. Finally, 6% of the Malaysian, 12% of the U.S., and 82% of the Swiss sample did not associate with any religion. The Chinese-Malaysian and U.S. children came from predominantly low- to middle-SES backgrounds attending public schools, and the Swiss sample from a middle- to high-SES background with most of the children attending private school. The children were given flyers of the study and consent forms to bring home to their parents. Those who returned their signed parental consent form were invited for the interview.

Materials

The first part of the CRI (Melton, 1980) questionnaire asked four preliminary questions about rights in general (e.g., definition of children's right, etc.), and the second part consisted of 12 conflict-laden vignettes (see Table 1; Vignette 1–12 were included in Study 1). Each vignette was followed by questions designed to elicit whether the participant thinks that the child or the authority/adults in the story situation should be the one to make the final decision. After the participant selected a response, she or he was asked to provide a rationale for her or his selection and at what age she or he thought that the decision of the particular right should be accorded to the child (see Table 1 for examples). The situations involved rights to information, to due process, to expression of opinion, to make medical treatment decisions, to work, and to privacy. Because several vignettes in the original version involved situations that could not be applied appropriately to the international samples, we adapted some of the stories and added questions to elicit more detailed responses from the U.S. and Chinese-Malaysian children. For example, Melton's (1980) CRI included a question asking children to decide whether a child should receive medical treatment when the parents cannot pay. We chose to omit this question because it is not relevant in countries where children have access to free medical care or where all children are insured through the government (e.g., Switzerland). After each question, the child was asked to tell the experimenter why and at what age a child could make such a decision. In total, there were eight items relating to self-determination rights (Vignettes 1–8) and four items relating to nurturance rights (Vignettes 9–12). The vignettes were categorized by matching to the definitions of rights made by the U.N. Convention's articles. Specifically, most of the nurturance vignettes adhered to the developmental and protection rights of children with parental involvement, whereas most of the self-determination vignettes adhered to the participation rights, in which the child attempts to reach out for some form of autonomy. Because the Swiss sample had been collected previously using slightly adapted CRI questions, 8 of the 12 original questions applied to all three cultural samples and 4 applied to the U.S. and Chinese-Malaysian samples only (Vignettes 2, 8, 10, and 12).

Trained raters who were blind as to the individuals' identity and the hypotheses coded each transcript. Responses to the vignettes were scored on a 3-point scale, indicating the degree to which the participant advocated for the child in the story as the decisionmaker. A score of +1 indicated that the participant advocated for the choice or decision to be made by the child in the vignette. Responses where the participant did not advocate for the child to make the decision in the vignette were coded as −1. Therefore, for vignettes involving self-determination rights, more positive scores denote more support for self-determination rights because the child in the story is advocated for making the decision. On the other hand, for vignettes involving nurturance rights, more negative scores denote more support for nurturance rights because the adult/authority involved, instead of the child, is advocated for making the decision. Finally, responses where the participant did not advocate for or against ("it depends") the choice or opinion of the child or had no opinion were coded as zero. Interrater reliability was based on 20% of the vignettes ($\kappa = .98$). The individual scores in Part 2 were summed across items and proportionalized. Self-determination and nurturance rights were also summed and proportionalized separately. Thus, the proportional scores ranged from −1.00 to +1.00.

Procedure

The questionnaire and consent forms were translated from English into Chinese for the Malaysian sample and into German and French for the Swiss sample. The questionnaires were translated back into English by another translator to assess the accuracy of the translation. After obtaining the parents' consent and children's assent, each child participated in a personal interview in his or her preferred language at their local school conducted by one of the three trained experimenters. The order of presentation of vignettes was counterbalanced. The conversations were tape recorded. All verbatim responses were later translated into English and transcribed. Children were debriefed at the end of the interview, which lasted approximately 20 minutes.

Results

Part 1: Rights in General. Twenty-two percent of the children defined a right as "something you are allowed to do" and 10% as "being able to do something you want." Twelve percent did not know how to define a right. The remaining children defined a right as a privilege, an entitlement, or mentioned a specific right (e.g., freedom of speech). A majority of the children (76%) said that everyone has rights, and 24% mentioned that mostly adults, parents, or elders have rights. Seventy-four percent believed that children have rights and 80% that children should have rights. In terms of cultural differences, the Swiss children tended to be more hesitant in their answers. Only 66.1% of the Swiss children thought that children have rights as compared to 90% of the Chinese-Malaysian children and 83.3% of the U.S. children. Similarly, 72.6% of Swiss children thought that everyone should have rights compared to 80% of the Chinese-Malaysian children and 83.3% of the U.S. children. Only 77.4% of the Swiss children thought that children should have rights (80% of the Chinese-Malaysian and 88.9% of the U.S. children), and 17.7% said that children should only have some rights (compared to 10% of the Chinese-Malaysian children and 5.6% of the U.S. children). Buddhist children were the most likely to say that children have rights (92.9%), followed by Catholics (75%) and Christians (71.4%). Children without a religious affiliation were the least likely to believe that children have rights (66.7%).

Part 2: Responses to Vignettes. We first performed a repeated measures analysis of variance (ANOVA) on the eight responses to vignettes that were common among the three countries with country as the between-subject variable. The results of the omnibus ANOVA showed significant main effects of country, $F(2, 97) = 4.99$, $p = .009$, $\eta^2 = .09$, responses to vignettes, $F(7, 91) = 54.82$, $p < .001$, $\eta^2 = .81$, as well as a significant interaction between responses to vignettes and country, $F(14, 182) = 2.08$, $p = .015$, $\eta^2 = .14$. As can be seen in Figure 1, Chinese-Malaysian, U.S., and Swiss children answered differently to certain items. Simple effects adjusted for type I error revealed that the responses of the three samples differed significantly only on three of the vignettes, $F(2, 97) = 3.45$, $p = .017$. First, Chinese-Malaysian ($M = -.60$) and Swiss ($M = -.35$) children did not think that children should be allowed to vote, whereas U.S. children favored the right to vote ($M = .22$), $F(2, 97) = 4.82$, $p = .017$, $\eta^2 = .09$. Second, Swiss children ($M = .27$) advocated for the right to work, whereas U.S. ($M = -.33$) and Chinese-Malaysian ($M = -.20$) children did not think that children should be

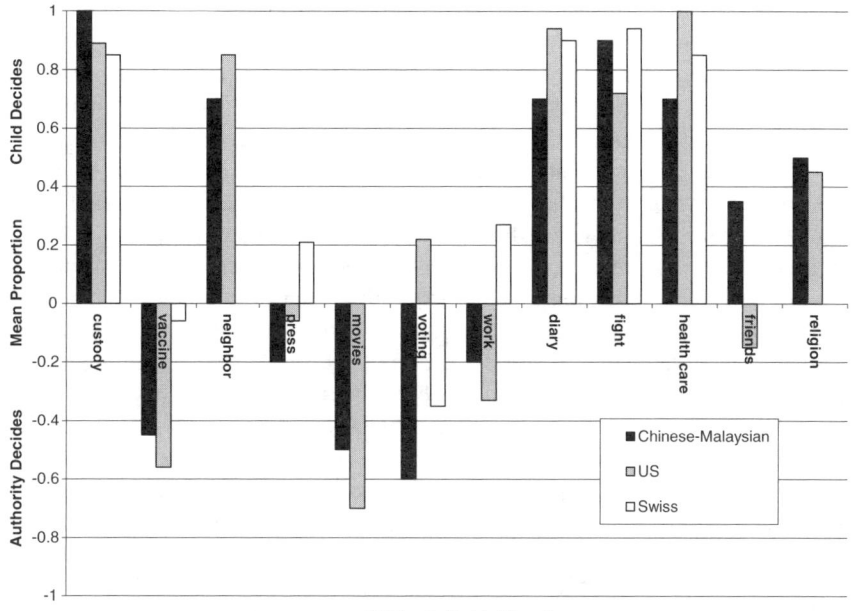

Fig. 1. Chinese-Malaysian, U.S., and Swiss children's responses to the CRI vignettes (Study 1).
Note. Figure includes answers to all 12 CRI vignettes for the Chinese-Malaysian and U.S. children. Scores from 0 to +1 signify that the child decides; Scores from 0 to −1 signify that the parent/authority decides.

permitted to work, $F(2, 97) = 3.48, p = .021, \eta^2 = .08$. Third, Chinese-Malaysian children ($M = -.45$) and U.S. children ($M = -.55$) were less likely to advocate for the right to refuse a vaccine than the Swiss sample ($M = -.06$), $F(2, 97) = 2.80, p = .05, \eta^2 = .07$.

Although the two main effects may be subsumed by the interaction, it is important to note that, on average, Swiss children were significantly more likely to advocate for the child in the eight vignettes to make the decision ($M = .45, SD = .76$) than the Chinese-Malaysian children ($M = .23, SD = .26$). The U.S. children ($M = .35, SD = .45$) did not differ from the Swiss or Chinese-Malaysian children (Tukey's HSD, $p < .05$). These findings are not necessarily consistent with the cultural hypothesis that individualistic societies would advocate for more rights than collectivistic societies. It is noteworthy that the U.S. children's responses did not differ significantly from the two samples, and that children in all three cultures advocated for rights (means are all positive).

Furthermore, on average, children favored the right to choose where to live after their parents' divorce ($M = .92$), to keep their diary secret ($M = .85$), to be heard in case of a dispute ($M = .85$), and to have access to a physician ($M = .85$). They did not advocate for the right to refuse a vaccination ($M = -.36$) but were neutral regarding the right to publish the school newspaper ($M = -.02$), to vote ($M = -.24$), or to work ($M = -.09$). These findings reveal that children did not advocate indiscriminately for autonomy. Qualitative responses revealed that participants reasoned that children would be too inexperienced to handle a cash register or that child labor was dangerous. Many also mentioned that children should not have the right to vote because they would be unduly swayed by political figures. Children from each country agreed that children should be consulted in case of parental divorce, they should not divulge their private thoughts, and that they should be allowed to talk to a physician without parental consent. U.S. and Chinese-Malaysian children also agreed that they should receive due process in disciplinary hearings, and be able to freely choose their religion. They also agreed that children should not be allowed complete autonomy in choosing movies. Helwig et al., (2003) found a similar trend in Chinese and Canadian adolescents.

We also performed one-way ANOVAs on the mean proportion scores for self-determination and nurturance rights, separately. The results showed significant differences among the samples for self-determination rights, $F(2, 97) = 3.06$, $p = .05$, $\eta^2 = .06$ and nurturance rights, $F(2, 97) = 6.57$, $p = .002$, $\eta^2 = .12$. Consistent with a cultural explanation, on average, U.S. ($M = .62$, $SD = .20$) and Swiss ($M = .57$, $SD = .29$) children tended to advocate for more self-determination rights than Chinese-Malaysian children ($M = .42$, $SD = .28$). The first two did not differ significantly from one another (Tukey's HSD). At the same time, U.S. children ($M = -.44$, $SD = .54$) were significantly more likely to want their parents or the authority involved to make decisions about nurturance rights (lower scores) than Swiss children ($M = .10$, $SD = .70$). The Chinese-Malaysian children ($M = -.33$, $SD = .61$) were significantly more likely to prefer adults or the authority making decisions about nurturance rights than Swiss children, but they did not differ from the U.S. children (Tukey's HSD, $p < .05$). These findings are not entirely consistent with the cultural hypothesis, suggesting that children in a collectivistic culture are more likely to endorse nurturance rights than children in individualistic countries. Although the Chinese-Malaysian children advocated for nurturance rights, so did the U.S. children. Interestingly, the Swiss children were rather neutral regarding advocating for nurturance rights.

We also wanted to examine the influence of religion within each country and across the three countries. Separate one-way ANOVAs on the total, nurturance, and self-determination proportion scores for each country showed significant main effects for self-determination rights $F(1, 18) = 4.85$, $p = .041$ and total rights $F(1, 18) = 5.48$, $p = .031$ for the Chinese-Malaysian sample. Buddhist children ($M = .50$, $SD = .28$) were more likely to advocate for self-determination rights than Christian children ($M = .22$, $SD = .17$). Overall, Buddhist children ($M = .31$, $SD = .23$) advocated more for the child in the vignettes to make the decision than Christian children ($M = .04$, $SD = .24$). To examine religious influence across the countries, and because of the relative lack of power, rather than using religious groups and countries as two between-subject variables within the same set of analyses, we performed an analysis of covariance (ANCOVA) on the total, nurturance, and self-determination rights proportion scores with the religious groups as between-subject variable and country as the covariate. There were no significant effects. These findings, however, may be due to a lack of experimental power. A power analysis revealed that with a doubling of the sample size, there may be a main effect (assuming a medium effect size) for nurturance rights and total rights, with Buddhist children advocating for more nurturance rights as compared to Christian children, and children with no religious affiliation. However, this conjecture needs to be corroborated with further empirical evidence.

Finally, we performed independent t-tests (adjusted with an alpha level of $p = .01$ to control for type 1 errors) on the age at which children from the U.S. and Chinese-Malaysian samples believed that the child in the vignette would be ready to make the decisions described. The U.S. children differed significantly from the Chinese-Malaysian children on five questions, advocating for self-determination rights earlier. On average, the two samples differed in the following rights: right to due process (U.S.: $M = 10.73$, $SD = 2.89$; Chinese-Malaysians: $M = 13.89$, $SD = 4.40$), the right to vote (U.S.: $M = 15.87$, $SD = 2.98$; Chinese-Malaysians: $M = 18.73$, $SD = 2.84$), the right to see a physician (U.S.: $M = 11.59$, $SD = 2.31$; Chinese-Malaysians: $M = 14.72$, $SD = 4.25$), and the right to choose one's own religion (U.S.: $M = 12.07$, $SD = 1.92$; Chinese-Malaysian: $M = 15.00$, $SD = 3.48$). The Chinese-Malaysian children advocated for the right to be heard in a dispute earlier ($M = 8.84$, $SD = 2.67$) than the U.S. children ($M = 11.45$, $SD = 1.83$). In general, U.S. children advocated for many of the rights earlier than Chinese-Malaysian children. These differences could be due to the historical factor that Chinese and Asian social and moral thinking is dominated by Confucianism (Pye, 1992). An adherence to the maintenance of existing hierarchical social structures, and the virtue of *filial piety*, may lead to Chinese adolescents to advocate for rights later than U.S. adolescents (also see Ruck et al., 1998).

It is important to note that this study relied on semistructured interviews using hypothetical vignettes that were generated by adults and we did not systematically investigate children's qualitative answers, although we examined them to interpret some of the findings. While a semistructured interview format allows detection of the reasoning used by the child, it also increases the possibility of experimenter effects. In addition, the Swiss sample was interviewed 10 years prior to the two other samples. Children currently living in Switzerland may think about rights differently than those interviewed a decade earlier. It is also unclear how old the participants thought the hypothetical child in the story may have been. It was reasonable to assume that participants identified with a same-aged child, but we do not have evidence to validate this assumption other than anecdotal evidence that children referred to themselves when explaining their reasoning. Future studies should not only examine children's qualitative responses, but they should also address the developmental, social, religious, and economic factors related to children's conceptions of rights. Mixed methodologies within culturally diverse cohorts should be utilized (see Peterson-Badali & Ruck, this issue). Also, extension of a study to a wider age range and to a longitudinal design will be desirable for charting out the developmental ordering of children's perception of their own rights.

Study 2

The vignettes utilized in the first study were based on Melton's original CRI (Melton, 1980), which involved situations that were not always easily applicable to the cultures examined in the present studies. Study 1 showed that the modification and adaptation made on the questionnaire yielded interpretable and encouraging outcomes for the investigation of children's perception of their own rights across the different cultural and religious samples in our study. However, the questionnaire did not adequately address several important rights addressed by the UN CRC (1989). In addition, it did not have the same number of self-determination and nurturance rights, and we wanted to draw participants of similar SES background more effectively in this second study. Thus, as a follow-up study and replication of Study 1, we designed a new inventory, the revised CRI (rCRI) (see Cherney & Shing, 2003) that was administered to a new sample of 12-year-old children from Malaysia and the United States.

Method

Participants

A total of 65 children (40 boys, 25 girls) between the ages of 11 and 13 ($M =$ 12.01, $SD = 1.26$) were interviewed. Thirty-six were from Malaysia and 29 from a midwestern town in the United States. Forty-five percent of the participants were Buddhists, 32% were of Protestant denominations, 14% Catholics, and 8% did not claim any religion. Of the Chinese-Malaysian sample, 83% were Buddhists, 14% were Protestants, and 3% indicated no religious affiliation. The U.S. sample consisted of 55% Protestants, 31% Catholics, and 14% with no religious denomination. The children were recruited from local public and private schools and came from similar middle-SES backgrounds (mean family income was comparable across the two samples). They were given pencils as a token of appreciation for their participation at the end of the session.

Materials

Table 1 illustrates parts of the revised CRI (rCRI) that were included in Study 2. A full version of the rCRI can be found in Cherney and Shing (2003). From the CRC, we included the right for protection from physical, and psychological abuse (Article 19), the right to grow up in a family environment (Preamble), and the right to an adequate standard of living (Article 27). In total, in Study 2 there were 6 items relating to self-determination rights (Vignettes 1, 2, 3, 4, 6, and 7) and 6 items relating to nurturance rights (Vignettes 11–16).

As in Study 1, a score of +1 indicated that the participant advocated for the choice or decision to be made by the child in the vignette. Responses where the participant did not advocate for the child to make the decision in the vignette were coded as −1, and responses where the participant did not advocate for or against a right were coded as 0. For nurturance rights, the scores were reversed scored wherever appropriate as the advocacy of a nurturance right could be based on the child's advocacy for the particular right (e.g., a secure environment, support from parents), and also protection of the child from something harmful (e.g., refusing vaccination or seeing bad friends). Trained raters who were blind as to the individuals' identity and the hypotheses coded each transcript. Interrater reliability was based on 20% of the vignettes ($\kappa = .97$). The individual scores in Part 2 were summed across items and proportionalized. Self-determination and nurturance rights were also summed and proportionalized separately. Thus, the proportional scores ranged from −1.00 to +1.00.

Procedure

Similar to the first study, the questionnaire and consent forms were translated into Chinese for the Malaysian sample and translated back into English to assess their accuracy. The personal interviews were tape recorded, and all verbatim responses were later translated into English and transcribed. Children were debriefed at the end of each interview that lasted about 30 minutes.

Results

Part 1: Rights in General. Thirty-five percent of all children did not know what a right was (58.3% of the Chinese-Malaysian children). Sixteen percent said that a right "is something you can do." Other children described a right in terms of privileges (6%), decision making (3%), legal entitlements (15%), or specific rights (25%). Seventy-one percent of the children believed that everyone has rights (44.4% of the Chinese-Malaysian children as compared to 75% of the U.S. children), 6% did not know, and 23% believed that only adults (elders, parents, presidents) have rights. A majority of children believed that children have rights (76.4%) and that children should have rights (80.6%). Taken together, these findings are quite similar to the findings of Study 1. It is noteworthy that only 48% of Buddhist children were able to provide a definition of a right, compared to 79% of the Christian children. Similarly, only 44.8% of Buddhist children believed that children should have rights, compared to 75% of the Christian children and 100% of the children without a religious denomination. Even though all denominations believed that children should have rights, this belief was more likely to be embraced by Christians than Buddhist children.

Part 2: Responses to Vignettes. An omnibus repeated measures multivariate analysis of variance (MANOVA) on the vignettes and type of right (self-determination vs. nurturance rights) with country as the between-subject variable showed a main effect for the vignettes, $F(5, 52) = 8.89, p < .001, \eta^2 = .46$, a main effect for type of right, $F(1, 56) = 11.04, p = .002, \eta^2 = .17$, and a highly significant interaction between vignettes and type of right, $F(5, 52) = 25.62, p < .001, \eta^2 = .71$. There was, however, no significant interaction involving country. In other words, there were no cross-cultural differences.

Similar to the first study, children discriminated between those rights that they thought children should have and those that they thought children should not have. They clearly differentiated between self-determination and nurturance rights, advocating for more self-determination rights ($M = .42, SD = .05$) than nurturance rights ($M = .22, SD = .05$). On average, the children in our sample did not advocate for a child's right to work ($M = -.48, SD = .88$), the right to vote ($M = -.15, SD = .98$), nor the right to express one's opinion in the school paper ($M = -.16, SD = .98$). These results partially replicated those of Study 1, although the children in the first study were more neutral about these rights. U.S. and Malaysian children agreed that children should be allowed to express their custody preference following a divorce ($M = .83, SD = .53$), should have the right to due process ($M = .52, SD = .69$), should have the right to make medical decisions ($M = .38, SD = .93$), should be allowed to choose their own friends ($M = .21, SD = .95$), should receive the help from their parents in various situations ($M = -.40, SD = .86$), and that parents should provide food and clothing ($M = -.71, SD = .59$). These findings are consistent with a constructivist hypothesis. Taken together, these findings converge with the findings of the previous study, indicating that there are many similarities in the perception of the children from the United States and Malaysia concerning their own rights.

A repeated measures ANCOVA was also conducted on the total, nurturance, and self-determination rights proportion scores with the religious groups (Buddhists, Protestants, and Catholics) as the between-subject factor and the two countries as the covariate. There were no significant differences among the religious groups. To assess within-country differences, we performed separate one-way ANOVAs on the religious groups. There were no significant differences among answers of Buddhist, Christian, and children reporting no religious affiliation.

The rCRI also included questions regarding the age at which participants thought the children described in the vignettes should be granted the various rights. Independent t-tests between the U.S. and Malaysian samples showed that, on average, U.S. children ($M = 12.35$, $SD = 2.78$) and Malaysian children ($M = 14.33$ $SD = 3.41$) responded similarly, $t(22) = -1.55$, ns. The exceptions were that U.S. participants suggested that children should have the right to due process ($M = 9.9$, $SD = 5.47$; $t(26) = 2.52$, $p = .018$) the right to vote ($M = 15.87$, $SD = 2.98$; $t(40) = 3.03$, $p = .004$), and the right to work ($M = 15.08$, $SD = 3.49$; $t(35) = 3.06$, $p = .004$) at significantly earlier ages than the Chinese-Malaysian children ($M = 18.00$, $SD = 0.00$; $M = 18.73$, $SD = 2.84$; $M = 18.61$, $SD = 3.06$, respectively).

Similar to the first study, it is important to note the methodological limitations of using semistructured vignettes and a small sample size. In Study 1, samples of different SES were compared, possibly confounding the results. With that in mind, we attempted to recruit children from similar SES in the second study. The results showed few differences across the two studies, suggesting that difference in SES may not be a confounding factor in our findings. However, we acknowledge that it is difficult to ascertain how closely we were able to match children on SES.

General Discussion

The purpose of these two studies was to compare 12-year-old children's attitudes toward their rights from three cultures: Malaysia, Switzerland, and United States, and to replicate Cherney and Perry's (1996) findings using a different instrument. The first study revealed a substantial degree of cross-national and cross-cultural commonality in reasoning about rights. It also showed that, consistent with a cultural explanation (e.g., Markus & Kitayama, 1991), the children's responses to some of the vignettes were different among the cultures. In general, U.S. and Swiss children advocated for significantly more self-determination rights than Chinese-Malaysian children. U.S. and Chinese-Malaysian children were more likely to want adults to make decisions about nurturance rights than Swiss children who remained neutral about nurturance rights. However, there is also a considerable amount of variability in children's responses in addition to the general pattern. Similar to Ruck and colleagues (1998), we found that individual rights were endorsed at different levels, suggesting that children reason differently depending on specific kinds of rights. In general, children favored the right to choose where to live after their parents' divorce, to keep their diary secret, to be heard in case of a dispute, and to have access to a physician. However, they did not advocate for the right to refuse a vaccination, to publish the school newspaper, to vote, or to work. The evidence suggests that conceptions of personal autonomy, and rights are not tied to Western cultural traditions but also appear in Asian society that is often characterized as collectivist and oriented to obedience and the maintenance of hierarchy and traditions (Helwig, 2006b).

Interestingly, the results also revealed differences among religious groups within Malaysia. Buddhist children were more likely to advocate for self-determination rights as compared to Christian children. De Bary and Weiming (1998) have argued that fundamental Confucian values of human dignity, self-cultivation, and justice, as important tenants of Buddhism, may be compatible with modern notions of human rights and individual autonomy. The finding may be explained by the differing levels of paternalism (Cherney, Greteman, & Travers, in press) in the different religions. A generally Western philosophy, paternalism suggests that there is a hierarchy of power, in which those with authority (e.g., religious hierarchies) can limit the personal freedoms of those without authority in order to obtain the betterment of the society as a whole (Worsfold, 1974). On a continuum of paternalism, the Christian Church may be considered a rather paternalistic religion because it has a more distinctly stratified hierarchy than the Buddhist religion (Sampson, 2000).

The second study introduced the rCRI. It was designed to include additional rights that are adapted to the cultural backgrounds and to interview children from similar SES backgrounds. The omnibus analysis did not show any cross-cultural differences. Rather, consistent with a constructivist explanation and replicating the first study, the second study showed that children differentiated between children's rights, advocating proportionally for more self-determination rights than nurturance rights. They also did not indiscriminately advocate for just any self-determination rights but carefully examined which rights they thought they could handle. There were no differences among religious groups across the two cultures. This may, in part be due to a lack of power. There were only seven Catholics who took part in the interviews. Taken together, the longer interview in the second study and covering wider ranges of rights resulted in even fewer differences between the samples.

Children's conceptions of rights develop and change with age. As children develop abilities related to self-expression and competence, they will claim areas of autonomy related to the exercise of these abilities (Helwig, 2006a). We asked the participants to tell us at what age children would perceive the hypothetical child in each vignette to assert the right. A clear pattern emerged between U.S. and Chinese-Malaysian children. With the exception of the right to be heard in case of a dispute, U.S. children advocated for having rights at an earlier age than Chinese-Malaysian children. Generally, U.S. children advocated for rights between the ages of almost 11 (right to due process) and 12 (choose own religious creed and the right to see a physician) to about 17 (parents to pay for food and clothing), whereas the Chinese-Malaysian children advocated for children having these rights almost 3 years later than those of the U.S. children. U.S. children were more likely to advocate for self-determination rights earlier than Chinese-Malaysian children.

Ruck and colleagues (1998) found that the age appropriateness of rights was dependent, in part, on the degree to which participants at various ages supported the story character's requests for rights. Older children (12- to 16-year olds) were more likely to be aware of the universal nature of various rights, whereas younger children (8- to 12-year-olds) viewed their entitlement to certain rights as related to their age.

In general, the results suggest that the global dichotomous orientation (individualism or collectivism; nurturance or self-determination) does not fully capture children's perceptions of their rights. The cultural transmission of social and moral reasoning of individuals through participation in cultural, political, religious, social, and economic practices suggests cultural and social differences in conceptions of children's rights. Findings from these studies suggest that culture, and to a lesser extent, religion, play an important role. In addition, our findings also suggest that the diverse social contexts and situations are important in affecting how children perceive their own rights. A constructivist (e.g., Neff & Helwig, 2002) approach to social reasoning proposes that children and adults interpret their experiences and reflect upon them, accepting and rejecting some social norms. Although in the first study, the U.S. and Swiss children tended to advocate for self-determination rights or autonomy more frequently than the Chinese-Malaysian children, a significant proportion of Chinese-Malaysian children also advocated for many self-determination rights. In fact, there were no significant differences between the U.S. and Chinese-Malaysian children in the second study, and in the first study, all children advocated for rights (positive means). To better understand the children's reasoning and decision-making process, we examined the responses given to certain questions in more details. In their reasoning, children mentioned concepts of fairness, autonomy, and democratic decision making. In contrast, support for adult authority was justified by their superior competence, wisdom, and existing laws. In many respects, proximal variables such as social contexts and situations may possess more explanatory power than global indicators such as culture in explaining differences in people's behavior.

Overall, these results provide little support for an individualist–collectivist difference in terms of how children perceive their rights. We suggest that future cross-cultural research should explore alternatives to the perhaps oversimplistic individualistic and collectivistic classifications. Furthermore, as Matsumoto (1999) suggested, future research on international perspectives of children's rights should measure more than one group within a particular nation. For example, children from different subcultures in a single nation should be compared to assess the within-nation differences and how those differences relate to the differences of similar groups in multiple nations. In order for the U.N. Convention on the Rights of the Child (U.N. General Assembly, 1989), written and agreed to by numerous nations, to produce changed behavior and conditions and improvements in the lives of children, much work lies ahead. Perhaps, criteria for making judgments about progress and change could be done by adapting the targets for progress drawn along the lines set by the Convention, but adapted to the particular nation's cultural traditions, economic circumstances, and children's social circumstances.

References

Ben-Arieh, A., Khoury-Kassabri, M., & Haj-Yahia, M. M. (2006). Generational, ethnic, and national differences in attitudes toward the rights of children in Israel and Palestine. *American Journal of Orthopsychiatry, 76*(3), 381–388.

Cherney, I. D. (2003). *The revised Children's Rights Interview.* Unpublished manuscript.

Cherney, I. D., Greteman, A. J., & Travers, B. G. (in press). A cross-cultural view of adults' perceptions of children's rights. *Social Justice Research.*

Cherney, I., & Perry, N. W. (1996). Children's attitudes toward their rights - An international perspective. In E. Verhellen (Ed.), *Monitoring children's rights* (pp. 241–250). The Hague, The Netherlands: Kluwer Law International.

Cherney, I. D., & Shing, L. Y. (2003, April). *Children's attitudes toward their rights: A cross-cultural perspective.* Poster presented at the biennial meeting of the Society for Research in Child Development, Tampa, FL.

De Bary, W. T., & Weiming, T. (1998). *Confucianism and human rights.* New York: Columbia University Press.

Department of Statistics Malaysia. (2001). *Population distribution and basic demographic characteristics report: Population and housing census 2000.* Retrieved January 26, 2007, from http://www.statistics.gov.my/english/frameset_census.php?file=pressdemo

Glotzer, R. (2005). Abandoned children. *Journal of Comparative Families Studies, 36,* 158–159.

Helwig, C. C. (2006a). The development of personal autonomy throughout cultures. *Cognitive Development, 21,* 458–473.

Helwig, C. C. (2006b). Rights, civil liberties, and democracy across cultures. In M. Killen & J. G. Smetana (Eds.), *Handbook of moral development,* (pp. 185–210). Mahwah, NJ: Erlbaum.

Helwig, C. C., Arnold, M. L., Tan, D., & Boyd, D. (2003). Chinese adolescents' reasoning about democratic and authority-based decision making in peer, family, and school contexts. *Child Development, 74,* 783–800.

Hofstede, G. (2001). *Culture's consequences: Comparing values, behaviors, institutions, and organizations across nations* (2nd ed.). Thousand Oaks, CA: Sage.

Kim, U. (1990). Indigenous psychology: Science and application. In R. Brislin (Ed.), *Applied cross-cultural psychology* (pp. 142–158). Newbury Park, CA: Sage.

Kohlberg, L. (1969). Stage and sequence: The cognitive-developmental approach to socialization. In D. A. Goslin (Ed.), *Handbook of socialization theory and research* (pp. 347–480). Chicago: Rand McNally.

Lau, S. (1992). Collectivism's individualism: Value preference, personal control, and the desire for freedom among Chinese in Mainland China, Hong Kong, and Singapore. *Personality and Individual Differences, 13,* 361–366.

Limber, S. P., & Flekkoy, M. G. (1995). The U.N. Convention of the Rights of the Child: Its relevance for social scientists. *Social Policy Report, Society for Research in Child Development, IX*(2), 1–15.

Markus, H. R., & Kitayama, S. (1991). Culture and the self: Implications for cognition, emotion, and motivation. *Psychological Review, 98,* 224–253.

Matsumoto, D. (1999). Culture and self: An empirical assessment of Markus and Kitayama's theory of independent and interdependent self-construals. *Asian Journal of Social Psychology, 2,* 289–310.

Melton, G. B. (1980). Children's concepts of their rights. *Journal of Clinical Child Psychology, 9,* 186–190.

Melton, G. B. (1983). *Child advocacy: Psychological issues and interventions.* New York: Plenum.

Murphy-Berman, V., Levesque, H. L., & Berman, J. J. (1996). U. N. Convention of the Rights of the Child: A cross-cultural view. *American Psychologist, 51*, 1234–1238.

Neff, K. D., & Helwig, C. C. (2002). A constructivist approach to understanding the development of reasoning about rights and authority within cultural contexts. *Cognitive Development, 17*, 1429–1450.

Nucci, L. P. (2001). *Education in the moral domain*. Cambridge, UK: Cambridge University Press.

Piaget, J. (1970). Piaget's theory. In P. Mussen (Ed.), *Carmichael's manual of child psychology* (pp. 703–732). New York: Wiley.

Pye, I. W. (1992). *The spirit of Chinese politics*. Cambridge, MA: Harvard University Press.

Rogers, C. M., & Wrightsman, L. S. (1978). Attitudes towards children's rights: Nurturance or self determination? *Journal of Social Issues, 34*(2), 59–68.

Ruck, M. D., Abramovitch, R., & Keating, D. P. (1998). Children's and adolescents' understanding of rights: Balancing nurturance and self-determination. *Child Development, 64*, 404–417.

Ryan, R. M., & La Guardia, J. G. (2000). What is being optimized over development? A self-determination theory perspective on basic psychological needs across the life span. In S. H. Qualls & N. Abeles (Eds.), *Psychology and the aging revolution* (pp. 145–172). Washington, DC: APA Books.

Sampson, E. E. (2000). Reinterpreting individualism and collectivism: Their religious roots and mono-logic versus dialogic person-other relationship. *American Psychologist, 55*, 1425–1432.

Shweder, R. A., Mahapatra, M., & Miller, J. G. (1987). Culture and moral development. In J. Kagan & S. Lamb (Eds.), *The emergence of morality in young children* (pp. 1–83). Chicago: University of Chicago Press.

Shweder, R. A., & Sullivan, M. A. (1993). Cultural psychology: Who needs it? *Annual Review of Psychology, 44*, 497–523.

Swissworld.org. Retrieved May, 19, 2007, from http://www.swissworld.org/eng/culture/swissworld.html?siteSect=604&sid=4046094&rubricId=14040.

Triandis, H. C. (1989). The self and social behavior in differing cultural contexts. *Psychological Review, 96*, 506–520.

Turiel, E. (1998). The development of morality. In W. Damon (Series Ed.) & N. Eisenberg (Vol. Ed.), *Handbook of child psychology: Vol. 3 Social, emotional, and personality development* (5th ed., pp. 863–932). New York: Wiley.

United Nations General Assembly, (1989, November). *Adoption of a convention on the rights of the child* (U.N. Doc. A/Res/44/25). New York: United Nations.

Worsfold, V. (1974). A philosophical justification for children's rights. *Harvard Educational Review, 44*, 142–157.

ISABELLE D. CHERNEY is an Associate Professor of Psychology at Creighton University in Omaha, Nebraska. She is the Carnegie Foundation 2007 Nebraska Teacher of the Year. Her research examines factors affecting the development of reasoning, memory, and cognitive gender differences in children and adults. In particular, she has investigated the role of culture in children's and adults' perceptions of children's nurturance and self-determination rights. She is currently studying how parents' values influence their children's conceptions of rights, and how gender, age, and moral development affect adults' reasoning about children's competence to make their own decisions. Her work has been published in E. Verhellen's *Monitoring Children's Rights* (Martinus Nijhoff Publishers), *Social Justice Research, Infant and Child Development, Sex Roles, Educational Psychology, Journal of Experimental Child Psychology, Enfance,* and *Perceptual and Motor Skills.*

YEE LEE SHING is a Postdoctoral Research Fellow of the Center for Lifespan Psychology at the Max Planck Institute for Human Development in Berlin, Germany. She received her PhD from the Humboldt University, Berlin, in January 2008. In her dissertation project, she examined the associative and strategic components of episodic memory from childhood to old age. Her research interests include changes and plasticity of basic cognitive mechanics and intellectual functioning across the life span.

Journal of Social Issues, Vol. 64, No. 4, 2008, pp. 857–880

How Adolescents in 27 Countries Understand, Support, and Practice Human Rights

Judith Torney-Purta* and Britt Wilkenfeld
University of Maryland

Carolyn Barber
University of Missouri, Kansas City

An understanding of human rights among young people forms a foundation for future support and practice of rights. We have used data from 88,000 14-year-olds surveyed in the 1999 International Association for the Evaluation of Educational Achievement (IEA) Civic Education Study to examine country differences in students' knowledge pertaining to human rights compared with other forms of civic knowledge, and in students' attitudes toward promoting and practicing human rights. A hierarchical linear modeling (HLM) analysis examines student-level predictors (e.g., gender and school experiences) and country-level predictors (e.g., history of democracy) of rights-related knowledge and attitudes. Countries with governments that pay more attention to human rights in intergovernmental discourse (i.e., dialogue between nations and international governing bodies) have students who perform better on human rights knowledge items. Students' experiences of democracy at school and with international issues have a positive association with their knowledge of human rights. Significant gender differences also exist. Looking at rights-related attitudes, students with more knowledge of human rights, more frequent engagement with international topics, and more open class and school climates held stronger norms supporting social movement citizenship, had more positive attitudes toward immigrants' rights, and were more politically efficacious. Implications are drawn for psychologists and educators

---

*Correspondence concerning this article should be addressed to Judith Torney-Purta, Department of Human Development, 3304 Benjamin Building, University of Maryland 20742 [e-mail: jtpurta@umd.edu].

The authors are grateful to Felisa Tibbitts for assistance in conducting the review of research and to David Suarez for providing data about countries' emphasis on human rights used in the analysis.

who wish to play a role in increasing adolescents' understanding, support, and practice of human rights.

Knowledge and understanding of human rights and the international systems that protect them form a foundation for educational and social policies that strengthen support for rights in the next generation. Four issues are especially important when examining students' knowledge and awareness of human rights in general and of children's rights in particular.

First, the understanding of international human rights is related to the comprehension of the United Nations as the source of international treaties on human rights. Second, in U.N. documents there has been increasing emphasis on young people's participation rights, including their beliefs about the social and political systems of their own countries and their willingness to allow members of groups that experience discrimination to exercise their rights to participate (Melton, 2005). A third issue is the potential effectiveness of citizenship education in schools when it includes explicit attention to human rights, especially participation rights (Torney-Purta, 2002). Fourth, because adults' attitudes toward the role of the United Nations in promoting international human rights vary among nations, the political contexts of governments' attention to these issues should be considered. For example, a country in which human rights violations recently occurred presents a different context for young people to learn vigilance about human rights than a country in which civil and political rights are long established. A newly established democratic government may take every opportunity to associate itself with international human rights protections to strengthen its democratization. In countries where everyday violations of rights are not prominent features of the recent past, adults may be more concerned about whether international human rights treaties conflict with national interests (McFarland & Mathews, 2005). The post-Communist countries, Chile, and Portugal fall into the former category, while the United States and some Western democracies fall into the latter category.

The International Association for the Evaluation of Educational Achievement (IEA) Civic Education Study, which collected tests and surveys in 1999 from nationally representative samples of 14-year-olds in 27 countries,[1] includes data examining adolescents' understanding and practice of human rights. The following research questions guided this analysis:

First, how do students in different countries perform when they answer knowledge questions related to international human rights and children's rights compared with knowledge questions related to domestic political rights?

---

[1] Countries participating in the IEA Civic Education Study and included in the current analysis are Australia, Belgium (French), Bulgaria, Chile, Colombia, Cyprus, Czech Republic, Denmark, England, Estonia, Finland, Germany, Greece, Hungary, Italy, Latvia, Lithuania, Norway, Poland, Portugal, Romania, Russia, Slovak Republic, Slovenia, Sweden, Switzerland, and the United States. Hong Kong (SAR) participated in the study, but country-level statistics are unavailable because of its change in status in 2000, and it has not been included in this analysis.

Second, how are students in different countries arrayed on three attitude scales related to international human rights: attitudes toward citizens' involvement in activities promoting social justice and human rights, attitudes toward rights for immigrants, and a sense of political efficacy?

Third, what factors at the country and student levels predict differences in knowledge between and within countries? We are interested in students' knowledge of human rights topics, which is either more or less than would be expected on the basis of their general knowledge of civic topics. Personal characteristics (gender and school experiences) are important, along with country characteristics, such as the history of democracy and the extent to which a country's government refers to human rights when participating in intergovernmental dialogues.

Fourth, what factors at the country and student levels predict attitudes related to human rights? Characteristics similar to those mentioned for the third research question are examined.

There is little research specifically relating to these issues in the countries participating in the IEA Civic Education Study. Therefore, our review of literature will be relatively brief, first considering concern for human rights in a historical perspective then summarizing a few studies on human rights education in general. The review by Peterson-Badali and Ruck in this issue provides additional information about distinctions between types of children's rights.

Human Rights and Education

Over the past several decades, there has been speculation and some empirical research about how young people understand the international system and human rights. When the first IEA Civic Education Study was conducted in the 1970s, with 14-year-olds in seven European countries and in the United States, an analysis compared students' national knowledge and attitudes to their international knowledge and attitudes (Torney, 1977). Few country differences emerged in perceptions of the United Nations, but there were considerable differences on other items. In countries such as the Netherlands, adolescents were more internationally aware than in countries such as the United States. In the Educational Testing Service's survey of global awareness in 1976, only half of U.S. college students knew that the United Nations promulgated the Universal Declaration of Human Rights and more than three quarters of the freshmen overestimated the number of human rights treaties that the United States had ratified (Klein & Ager, cited in Torney-Purta, 1982).

Prevalence of human rights education. Ways to address human rights in educational programs have become of interest as the worldwide human rights movement has grown in the ensuing decades. During the 1990s, the number of formal democracies in the world increased from 76 to 117 (United Nations Educational, Scientific and Cultural Organization, 2005). This third wave of democracy was associated with events such as the ending of apartheid in South Africa and the disintegration of the Soviet Union. One might expect an upswing in attention to human rights and education, especially in these new democracies.

A recent study indicated that the number of organizations dedicated to human rights education quadrupled between 1980 and 1995 (Ramirez, Suarez, & Meyer, 2006; Suarez & Ramirez, 2007). Many of these organizations provide curriculum-related materials about human rights, and in collaboration with educational authorities, human rights topics have been introduced into the national curricula in many countries (Tibbitts, 1996).

Another index of growing attention to human rights in international discourse is found in a study that examined countries' reports to the International Bureau of Education (IBE) and the United Nations High Commissioner for Human Rights (UNHCHR) (Ramirez et al., 2006). The researchers counted the number of times the term *human rights* was mentioned in official documents submitted by countries to the IBE. The score on this indicator was .82 for Eastern Europe and the former Soviet Union, .70 for countries in Sub-Saharan Africa, .64 for countries in Latin American and the Caribbean, and .11 for Western European and North American countries (Ramirez et al., 2006). Table 1 shows these data for each of the countries in the IEA study and includes a summary indicator based on participation in the U.N. Decade for Human Rights Education[2] and on the IBE ratings (with a range of 0 to 3). This is our indicator of how much a country's government focuses on human rights in education-related intergovernmental discourse.

There are several notable trends. First, the countries in the IEA study that received the highest score of 3 on the indicator are all post-Communist or Latin American countries, and a majority of the countries that received a 2 on the indicator are also in these regions. Countries whose governments participate actively in intergovernmental discourse about international human rights tend to be relatively new democracies with recent experiences of authoritarian rule. Landman (2005) noted that leaders of new democracies are wary because of their government's past treatment of citizens and are uncertain about the future. They accept international treaties without reservations and welcome participation in international human rights efforts. In fact, the older democracies, such as Australia, England, Switzerland, and the United States, have scores of 1 or 0 on this indicator of governmental emphasis on human rights. In the United States, human rights topics are often framed in a domestic rather than an international context.

To look at another indicator, Freedom House Incorporated (2006) reported annual ratings of the political rights and civil liberties accorded to citizens. These ratings show that the countries now stressing human rights in their educational

---

[2]The U.N. Decade for Human Rights Education (1995–2004) was proclaimed by the U.N. General Assembly to encourage nations to develop national action plans to incorporate topics such as democracy, humanitarian law, and human rights into their education systems.

Table 1. Indicators of National Commitments to Human Rights and Democracy

Country	U.N. Decade Participation	International Bureau of Education 1993	International Bureau of Education 1998[a]	Indicator: Government Focus on Human Rights[b]	Indicator: Freedom House Rating[c]	Indicator: Duration of Democracy[d]
Australia	1	0	0	1	5.0	2
Belgium (French)	0	1	1	2	4.5	3
Bulgaria	0	0	0	0	3.5	0
Chile	1	1	0	2	4.0	0
Colombia	1	1	1	3	2.0	2
Cyprus	1	0	0	1	5.0	1
Czech Republic	1	1	0	2	4.5	0
Denmark	1	0	0	1	5.0	3
England	1	0	0	1	4.5	3
Estonia	0	1	0	1	4.5	0
Finland	1	0	0	1	5.0	2
Germany	1	1	0	2	4.5	2
Greece	1	0	0	1	4.0	1
Hungary	1	0	0	1	4.5	0
Italy	1	0	0	1	4.5	2
Latvia	1	1	1	3	4.5	0
Lithuania	1	1	1	3	4.5	0
Norway	1	0	0	1	5.0	3
Poland	1	1	0	2	4.5	0
Portugal	1	0	0	1	5.0	1
Romania	1	1	1	3	4.0	0

(Continued)

(Continued)

Country	U.N. Decade Participation	International Bureau of Education 1993	International Bureau of Education 1998[a]	Indicator: Government Focus on Human Rights[b]	Indicator: Freedom House Rating[c]	Indicator: Duration of Democracy[d]
Russia	0	1	1	2	1.5	0
Slovak Republic	1	1	1	3	4.5	0
Slovenia	0	1	1	2	4.5	0
Sweden	1	1	0	2	5.0	3
Switzerland	1	0	0	1	5.0	3
United States	0	0	0	0	5.0	3

[a]Missing IBE data were imputed from proximal years (e.g., missing 1993 data imputed from 1998 and 2001, missing 1998 data imputed from 1993 and 2001).

[b]Government focus on human rights computed by summing the score for U.N. Decade, IBE 1993, and IBE 1998 (range is 0 to 3). Information about participation in U.N. Decade on Human Rights and mention of human rights in documents submitted to IBE obtained from D. F. Suarez, personal communication, October 2, 2006, from data used in Ramirez and Suarez (2005).

[c]Freedom House rating is a composite score of political rights and civil liberties ratings found in Freedom House (2006). Reverse coded such that 1 = *least free* and 5 = *most free*.

[d]Duration of democracy coded from Polity IV database variable called Durability of Democracy into categories: 0–19 years coded 0; 20–39 years coded 1; 40–59 years coded 2; 60 years or more coded 3.

documents include many where freedom has been threatened in recent decades and where democracy is relatively newly established (see right-hand columns of Table 1). At the country level, the indicators in our analysis will include government emphasis on human rights (based on data provided by D. F. Suarez, personal communication, October 2, 2006), the Freedom House rating (Freedom House, 2006), and the duration of democracy indicator from a political science database, Polity IV (Center for International Development and Conflict Management [CIDCM], 2003). This is the number of years since the nation's last regime transition. Because the countries in the IEA data set are all democracies, this corresponds to the number of years since the last transition to democratic government. Number of years was recoded into four categories to produce the duration of democracy variable found in Table 1. In addition to political indicators at the country level, understanding what human rights education entails is also central to explaining our results, especially those dealing with participation rights (Roberts, 2003).

The nature and effects of human rights education.   Human rights education is increasingly recognized as a special and important feature of citizenship education (Howe & Covell, 2005). That a country allows electoral participation as well as political activism and social movement participation on the part of citizens is a prerequisite of strong civic or human rights education. In many countries, global social responsibility, justice, and social action are also part of the discourse in human rights education (Tibbitts, 2002).

Evaluation data gathered in empirical studies indicate that children's rights education is an effective part of social education when it can be linked to issues of injustice (Decoene & De Cock, 1996). Children who learn about the Convention on the Rights of the Child (CRC), and about children's rights in general, are more likely to respect the rights of adults and other children, especially minority children according to Canadian studies (Covell & Howe, 1999). In these efforts the pupils themselves were involved in the design of the instructional activities, and attention was paid to the participatory climate of the classroom (Howe & Covell, 2005).

One program in a U.S. classroom used case studies of human rights abuses and simulation activities to elicit an empathetic response in students. An evaluation confirmed the intended impact for many participants. However, only a few students indicated interest in taking social or political action. The researchers concluded that empathy was an internal response rather than a response that extended into social action (Gaudelli & Fernekes, 2004). One qualitative study examined the implementation of human rights education in social studies (Wade, 1994).

Educational influences are important, but there are other correlates of students' awareness of human rights in general as well as of children's rights to nurturance and participation. Several studies have taken a developmental perspective. Older and more affluent children think about children's rights in abstract terms, often based on moral considerations. Younger children display more ego-centric reasoning in which rights are defined in terms of what one can do (Limber, Kask, Heidmets, Kaufman, & Melton, 1999; Melton, 1980; Peterson-Badali & Ruck, this issue; Torney-Purta, 1982).

Gender differences in human rights attitudes have been found. A German study found that females demonstrated higher personal engagement with human rights concepts (Müller, 2002), which may be related to findings that female young adults are more supportive of children's rights pertaining to nurturance, such as care and protection (Peterson-Badali, Ruck, & Ridley, 2003). However, this study found no gender differences in assessments of children's rights to self-determination. Other sources report that females are more likely than males to subscribe to attitudes concerned with social justice and to relate their concerns to social action (Atkeson & Rapoport, 2003; Haste & Hogan, 2006; Hess & Torney, 1967/2005; Sotelo, 1999).

In summary, many would argue that successful human rights education in-volves acquiring knowledge of rights and responsibilities, forms of injustice, the history of movements to fight inequality, and international treaties on human rights (Amnesty International, 1996). There is also agreement that programs should be adapted to the cognitive levels of students. Attitudes associated with human rights education include accepting differences, respecting the rights of others (especially members of less powerful groups), and taking responsibility to defend the rights of others (Bernath, Holland, & Martin, 1999; Claude, 1998). Several studies have found more than one dimension of attitudes toward human rights (Crowson, 2004; Doise, Spini, & Clemence, 1999; McFarland & Mathews, 2005). These studies also noted that adults who support human rights in principle may not actually take action when faced with human rights problems.

This brief review suggests first that our analysis should examine both knowl-edge of and attitudes toward human rights and second that gender, educational status of the home, exposure to international issues, and experiences of democracy (in the classroom and in the school as a whole) should be examined. By using the IEA Civic Education Study, a large-scale international survey focusing on 14-year-olds' knowledge and attitudes, we can explore how these factors influence students' understanding and attitudes in support of human rights.

The Current Analysis

Background of the IEA Civic Education Study

The IEA Civic Education Study was a rigorous international study of civic knowledge and attitudes. After a 5-year period of preparation (including national case studies and consensus building among researchers from national centers in the IEA network), test and survey data on civic knowledge, concepts, and attitudes were collected from nationally representative samples of 14-year-olds in 28 countries. The sample across all countries totals nearly 90,000 adolescents.

The countries in the IEA Civic Education Study included the United States (and 2 other English-speaking countries), 2 Latin American countries, 4 Nordic countries, 11 post-Communist countries, and 7 other European countries. One Asian country, Hong Kong, also collected data but was not analyzed here because national statistics were not available. All nations who were members of IEA in the mid-1990s were invited to participate.

Social scientists developed reliable scales of knowledge and attitudes (including 20 scales based on item response theory [IRT]; see Husfeldt, Barber, & Torney-Purta, 2005; Schulz & Sibberns, 2004). Basic analysis was reported in Torney-Purta, Lehmann, Oswald, and Schulz (2001) and follow-up articles have addressed the role of schooling (Torney-Purta, 2002), how democratic practices at school influence students' political attitudes (Torney-Purta & Barber, 2005), the knowledge and attitudes of Latino students in the United States (Torney-Purta, Barber, & Wilkenfeld, 2007), and the attitudinal clusters that exist among U.S. adolescents (Torney-Purta, Barber, Wilkenfeld, & Homana, 2008).

Analytic Techniques

This article takes a new direction in examining these data. In the first section of the analysis we will examine individual items from IEA's test data that are related to institutions and human rights. First, we describe students' performance on the three knowledge items dealing with rights in the context of international institutions. Students were asked to identify the purpose of the United Nations and to identify the rights contained in the Universal Declaration of Human Rights and the Convention on the Rights of the Child (CRC) (see item descriptions in Torney-Purta et al., 2001). The CRC item emphasized the right of children to nurturance, while the other questions dealt with human rights more generally. For comparison we also look at three knowledge items that deal with citizens' rights to participate in their own countries (e.g., what specifically constitutes a political right) and three knowledge items dealing with domestic political institutions not directly connected with rights (e.g., the purpose or function of the national legislature) to show that different countries have diverse patterns of knowledge on these subgroups of items. All of the knowledge questions are multiple-choice with four options.

In the second section of the analysis, we examine country differences in young people's views about self-determination expressed in attitudes of perceived political efficacy (especially in comprehending and discussing politics), attitudes toward the importance of social justice-related participation for citizenship, and attitudes toward immigrants' rights to participate. All attitude questions were answered with Likert-type scales that comprise four points (from *strongly agree* to *strongly disagree*). The individual items were scaled using IRT methods and the resulting IRT scales have international means of 10 (standard deviations of 2). Classical reliability indices are high across countries for these scales.

In the third section, we systematically relate 14-year-olds' knowledge of international rights to aspects of the national and international contexts in which they are growing up and their school experiences employing a series of multilevel models using hierarchical linear modeling (HLM: Raudenbush, Bryk, Cheong, & Congdon, 2004). Each of the multilevel models took into account that the students were nested within schools, and the schools were nested within countries.[3] In the fourth section are three more HLM analyses for three attitude scales.

Results

Patterns of Response to Knowledge Items Relating to Human Rights

Our first research question is cross-nationally descriptive, giving a picture of strengths and weaknesses in understanding of international and domestic approaches to rights. The percentages of students giving correct answers to three sets of items (domestic institutions, domestic protection of human rights, and international protections of human rights) are found in Table 2. One group of countries performed above the international mean on all three item composites: Cyprus, Finland, Greece, Poland, and the Slovak Republic. These countries also scored above the international mean on the knowledge test as a whole (Torney-Purta et al., 2001).

Students in another group of countries including the United States scored near the international mean on the two composites of items dealing with rights (Table 2). The relative performance of students in the United States was lower on these item composites dealing with rights and on the CRC item than on the knowledge test as a whole, where they were significantly above the international mean (Torney-Purta et al., 2001). Recall that the United States was among the countries with little emphasis on human rights in intergovernmental discourse (Table 1). Countries such as Denmark, Hungary, and Norway scored above or near the international mean on domestic institutions and rights, but relatively low on the items assessing understanding of international rights. These countries do not focus on human rights in their intergovernmental discourse.

In contrast, in some countries students scored moderately well on knowledge of both domestic and international human rights, but showed less understanding of

---

[3]HLM allows for student-level outcomes to be predicted by variables at each level of data (country and student). It also allows for the effects of predictors at each level to be estimated more accurately by taking into account the fact that students within a school are more similar than students between schools, and similarly with schools within countries.

Table 2. Percentage of Students with Correct Answers on Questions Pertaining to Domestic Institutions, Domestic Rights, and International Rights

Country	Domestic Institutions Composite[a]	Domestic Rights Composite[b]	International Rights Composite[c]	Convention on the Rights of the Child Single Item[d]
Australia	68	80+	79	80
Belgium (French)	55−	72	77	79
Bulgaria	50−	80+	76	68−
Chile	50−	53−	74−	88+
Colombia	49−	59−	71−	77
Cyprus	75+	83+	91+	89+
Czech Republic	73+	82+	81	75
Denmark	75+	73	73−	59−
England	63−	76	78	77
Estonia	70	74	76	76
Finland	76+	85+	87+	77
Germany	71	73	78	72−
Greece	78+	84+	87+	84+
Hungary	75+	88+	73−	55−
Italy	79+	78	87+	88+
Latvia	60−	72	74−	70−
Lithuania	59−	77	77	79
Norway	80+	77	75−	73−
Poland	81+	87+	86+	77
Portugal	64−	67−	84+	91+
Romania	65−	75	77	80
Russia	70	81+	82	74
Slovak Republic	81+	87+	89+	84+
Slovenia	70	83+	84+	74
Sweden	71	68−	71−	80
Switzerland	65−	69−	82	79
United States	74+	76	79	78
International	69	75	79	77

Note. + and −indicate whether the country mean is above or below the international mean percent correct by more than 3 percentage points; no sign indicates that the percentage is within 3 percentage points of the international mean percent correct.

[a]Domestic institutions is the average of three items pertaining to domestic laws, legislatures, and constitutions.

[b]Domestic rights is the average of three items pertaining to the role of citizens, political rights, and threats to democracy.

[c]International rights is the average of three items pertaining to the United Nations, Convention on the Rights of the Child, and the Universal Declaration of Human Rights.

[d]The exact wording and correct response of this single item pertaining to the Convention on the Rights of the Child, which also appears in the international rights composite, is not publicly released by IEA.

domestic institutions. These countries included Lithuania, Romania, and Slovenia, which are post-Communist nations where governments emphasize human rights in their intergovernmental discourse. Democratic domestic institutions are recent, and related concepts may not yet be covered in civic education.

Chile and Colombia scored low on all three types of knowledge items. These countries also had the lowest scores on the test overall (Torney-Purta et al., 2001). However, in Chile, 88% of the students correctly answered the item on the CRC.

Portugal was unique in a positive way. Students performed very well on the international human rights composite of items, and 91% correctly answered the item about the CRC. Although Portugal's government reported a moderate level of discourse on human rights in IBE documents, children's rights are part of the curriculum and a children's rights day is celebrated (I. Menenzes, personal communication).

Patterns of Response on Attitudes Relating to Human Rights

Our second research question is also descriptive, with a focus on attitudes. Table 3 contains the means for the 27 countries on three scales relating to norms stressing the importance of belonging to human rights or other social justice-oriented groups for adult citizens (norms of social movement citizenship), willingness to grant rights to disenfranchised groups (positive attitudes toward immigrants' rights), and participation rights (internal political efficacy).[4]

Positive human rights attitudes (above the international mean on all three scales) characterized Chile, Colombia, Cyprus, Greece, and the United States. Scores below the international mean on all three scales were found in Denmark, England, Estonia, Slovenia, and Switzerland. Other countries showed a mixed pattern, with low levels of political efficacy likely to be found in the Nordic countries. Portugal is of interest considering the high knowledge of human rights previously noted. On the attitudinal scales, Portuguese students had high scores on norms of social movement citizenship and very positive attitudes toward immigrants' rights. However, their internal political efficacy scores were below the international mean.

The profiles described here and in the previous sections describe young people's understanding and support for human rights. A more systematic approach is required to separate factors of importance that are related to these outcomes across countries.

---

[4]The first two outcomes are IRT scales created as part of the initial analysis of IEA Civic Education Study data (see Schulz & Sibberns, 2004). The third outcome is an additional IRT scale created during follow-up analyses conducted by Civic Education Study researchers (see Husfeldt et al., 2005). The emphasis in the Internal Political Efficacy scale is on a sense of competence and efficacy in understanding political issues and participating in political discourse.

Table 3. Country Means for Three Attitude Scales Relating to Human Rights

Country	Norms of Social Movement Citizenship	Positive Attitude toward Immigrants' Rights	Internal Political Efficacy
Australia	9.3−	10.0	9.9
Belgium (French)	9.1−	10.0	9.8
Bulgaria	10.0	9.7−	10.3+
Chile	10.5+	10.4+	10.4+
Colombia	11.3+	10.8+	10.8+
Cyprus	11.0+	10.9+	11.0+
Czech Republic	9.7−	10.0	9.5−
Denmark	9.5−	9.6−	9.3−
England	9.2−	9.7−	9.4−
Estonia	9.2−	9.7−	9.9−
Finland	8.9−	9.8	9.3−
Germany	9.9	9.2−	9.9
Greece	11.4+	10.6+	10.6+
Hungary	9.9	9.5−	9.9−
Italy	10.2+	9.8−	9.9
Latvia	9.5−	9.5−	10.1
Lithuania	10.6+	9.6−	10.0
Norway	10.2+	10.3+	9.5−
Poland	10.1	10.6+	10.2
Portugal	10.6+	10.3+	9.8−
Romania	10.7+	10.2	10.6+
Russia	9.9	9.8	10.4+
Slovak Republic	10.4+	9.8−	10.5+
Slovenia	9.6−	9.4−	9.8−
Sweden	9.8−	10.7+	9.3−
Switzerland	9.6−	9.4−	9.5−
United States	10.3+	10.3+	10.3+
International	10.0	10.0	10.0

Note. + and − indicate whether the country mean is significantly above or below the international mean. Norms of social movement citizenship, positive attitude toward immigrants' rights (Torney-Purta, Lehmann, Oswald, & Schulz, 2001), and internal political efficacy (Husfeldt, Barber, & Torney-Purta, 2005) are IRT scales.

Relation of Student and Country Characteristics to Rights-Related Knowledge and Attitudes

To answer the third research question, we examine the characteristics of students and countries that predict whether students responded correctly to each of the three items relating explicitly to international topics from the Civic Education Study's test of knowledge. In particular, we are interested in what predicts a correct response to each international item *over and above* content knowledge, as measured by the students' score on the 25-item test of civic content knowledge. In other words, are there factors other than general civic content knowledge that predict whether students correctly respond to these three particular items? This analytic technique was inspired by the use of logistic regression analysis to test for differential item functioning in single-level models (e.g., Swaminathan & Rogers, 1990).

Because this analysis explores predictors of a dichotomous outcome (i.e., a correct or incorrect response to each question), we used a binomial hierarchical generalized linear model (HGLM: Raudenbush et al., 2004). In essence, HGLM is a multilevel logistic regression analysis using predictors at more than one level (in this case, students and countries) to predict the likelihood of responding correctly to an item. HGLM analyzes the log-likelihood of having a correct answer to the item; for easier interpretation, these log-likelihood (or logit) coefficients can be transformed to changes in odds, or the chance that students will get an item correct. This analysis allows us to say that certain characteristics of students or the countries where they live change their odds of getting an answer correct, expressed as a percentage of the overall odds. For example, saying that females have 50% greater odds of getting an answer correct means that a female is 1.5 times as likely to get the answer correct as a male student, holding other characteristics constant. This "odds ratio" would be 1.5.

In each analysis, both student- and country-level predictors were considered. Student-level predictors came from items and scales in the IEA Civic Education Study's student-level data. We were interested in how students' experience in schools (discussion of international issues with teachers, openness of classroom climate for discussion, and confidence in the value of school participation), their overall civic content knowledge score, their attention to international topics in the newspaper, and their gender and home resource background (measured by number of books in the home) relate to their knowledge of and engagement with human rights issues. The scales assessing openness of classroom climate for discussion and assessing confidence in the value of school participation are IRT scales that are set to have an international mean of 10 and standard deviation of 2. Items related to discussion of international issues with teachers and attention to international topics in the newspaper are 4-category scales, with 1 indicating that the student "*never*" participates in the activity and 4 indicating that the student "*often*" participates in the activity. In addition, for the analysis of students' attitudes, we also included as predictors the three international knowledge items examined as part of the analysis described in the previous section, each coded as right or wrong.

At the country level, we considered the extent to which governments focused on human rights, using the country-level measures described previously and found in Table 1 (government focus on human rights) and also Freedom House ratings, and the duration of democracy index.[5] Only the government's focus on human rights in intergovernmental dialogue and Freedom House ratings were considered in the analysis of international human rights items (because duration of democracy did not significantly predict performance in initial analysis). Only Freedom House ratings and duration of democracy indices were considered in analyses of the attitudinal scales because human rights focus was not a significant predictor of attitudes.

Predictors of student responses to three international rights knowledge items. Table 4 summarizes the results of the HGLM (multilevel logistic regression) analysis for three individual items relating to international organizations or human rights instruments. Looking first at the item on the purpose of the Declaration of Human Rights, students in countries with *less* political freedom were more likely to respond to this item correctly, even after taking into account students' overall civic content knowledge and the other predictors in the model. Looking within countries, there was a significant gender effect. After controlling for content knowledge and other predictors, females had 13% greater odds than males of responding correctly to this item (for an odds ratio of 1.13, as reported in Table 4).

A similar gender effect that favored females was also found when analyzing responses to the item on the CRC. Compared to males, females had 65% greater odds of responding to this question correctly, regardless of their level of civic content knowledge (odds ratio = 1.65). In addition, students who were more confident in the value of participating in their schools and those who read more international news were also more likely to respond correctly to this item. Looking at the country level, students were more likely to respond correctly to the CRC item if they lived in countries in which the national government focused on human rights issues in intergovernmental dialogue.

Students who discussed international politics with teachers and who read about international news in the newspaper were more likely to respond correctly to the question about the purpose of the United Nations regardless of their overall level of content knowledge. Males were more likely to correctly identify the purpose of the United Nations (in contrast to the previously discussed items about rights). Females had only 85% of the odds that males did of responding correctly to this item (odds ratio = .85). Living in a country with a high score on the Freedom House index also was related to a correct answer on this item.

In summary, after taking into account students' general civic content knowledge, we found that characteristics of the countries in which they reside and characteristics of their individual engagement in school and discussing or reading about international issues predicted how students responded to specific knowledge

---

[5]In the multilevel analyses, we use the original coding of the durability of democracy index (number of years) available from CIDCM (2003) not the recoding into 4 categories.

Table 4. Individual- and Country-Level Predictors of Correctly Answering International Rights Items

	Purpose of the Declaration of Human Rights		Purpose of the Convention on the Rights of the Child		Purpose of the United Nations	
	b (SE)	Odds Ratio	b (SE)	Odds Ratio	b (SE)	Odds Ratio
Constant	1.95 (.14)	7.04	1.60 (.14)	4.94	2.59 (.09)	13.35
Country level						
Freedom index	−.20+ (.11)	.81	n.s.	n.s.	.22+ (1.12)	1.24
Government focus on rights	n.s.	n.s.	.16+ (.08)	1.17	n.s.	n.s.
Individual level						
Discuss international issues with teacher	n.s.	n.s.	n.s.	n.s.	.03* (.01)	1.03
Read international news in paper	n.s.	n.s.	.03* (.01)	1.03	.05** (.02)	1.05
Confidence in school participation	n.s.	n.s.	.02** (.01)	1.02	n.s.	n.s.
Openness of classroom climate	n.s.	n.s.	n.s.	n.s.	n.s.	n.s.
Books in home	n.s.	n.s.	n.s.	n.s.	n.s.	n.s.
Female	.13** (.03)	1.13	.50** (.04)	1.65	−.17** (.04)	.85

Note. Analysis controls for students' overall content knowledge (as measured by IRT score).
+ $p < .10$; * $p < .05$; ** $p < .01$.

items relating to international rights issues. Response patterns to the two human rights items differed from the item about the United Nations as an institution. Specifically, females were more likely to respond correctly to items pertaining to human rights documents, while males were more likely to respond correctly to the question about the United Nations. At the country level the children's rights item was more likely to be correctly answered in countries where the government focused on human rights in its intergovernmental dialogue (which are the post-Communist or postdictatorship countries). In a similar vein, countries where the observance of human rights is less consistent (those with low Freedom House scores) were more likely to correctly answer the question about the Universal Declaration of Human Rights. In contrast, the general item about the United Nations was more likely to be correctly answered in countries with high Freedom House ratings.

Predictors of student responses on three rights-related attitude scales.   In the second set of multilevel analyses, we considered how responses to each of the three specific knowledge items predict students' engagement in and attitudes toward human rights. We examined the three civic attitudinal outcomes described in Table 3: norms of social movement citizenship, positive attitudes toward immigrants' rights, and internal political efficacy. Because this analysis examined continuous not dichotomous outcomes, regular HLM modeling techniques were appropriate. Each outcome had an international mean of 10 and a standard deviation of 2.

Table 5 summarizes the results from multilevel (HLM) analysis of students' attitudes (coefficients can be interpreted as unstandardized *b* coefficients). A comparison of this analysis to the parallel analysis of knowledge items in Table 4 shows that student-level predictors were much stronger for attitudes than for knowledge. Looking first at students' norms of social movement citizenship and positive attitudes toward immigrants' rights, we found no relationship between the country-level predictors and the average student attitudes in that country. However, students who lived in more recently established democracies expressed more political efficacy than students in older democracies. Students also felt more efficacious in countries where there was *less* overall political freedom, according to Freedom House ratings. Recall that the items in the political efficacy scale relate to understanding and discussing political issues.

At the student level we found a number of characteristics that predicted attitudes toward rights. While no significant gender difference existed for norms of social movement citizenship, females had more positive attitudes toward immigrants' rights. In contrast, males expressed higher levels of efficacy in discussing political institutions and issues (perhaps a precondition for exercising participation rights). Home background related to only one attitude scale (controlling for other variables). Students from more advantaged homes had higher political efficacy.

Table 5. Individual- and Country-Level Predictors of Rights-Related Attitudes

	Norms of Social Movement Citizenship	Positive Attitude toward Immigrants' Rights	Internal Political Efficacy
Constant	10.04 (.10)	10.00 (.07)	9.99 (.07)
Country level			
Freedom index	n.s.	n.s.	−.23* (.11)
Duration of democracy	n.s.	n.s.	−.01* (.00)
Individual level			
Civil content knowledge	.003* (.00)	.01** (.00)	.01** (.00)
Item: Declaration of Human Rights	.12** (.03)	.07** (.03)	−.11** (.03)
Item: Convention on the Rights of the Child	.12** (.02)	.06** (.02)	−.11** (.03)
Item: Purpose of the U.N.	.07* (.03)	n.s.	−.19** (.03)
Discuss international issues with teacher	.04** (.01)	−.02** (.01)	.25** (.02)
Read international news in paper	.11** (.01)	.14** (.02)	.38** (.02)
Confidence in school participation	.19** (.01)	.25** (.01)	.05** (.01)
Openness of classroom climate	.07** (.01)	.09** (.01)	.04** (.01)
Books in home	n.s.	n.s.	.08** (.01)
Female	n.s.	.44** (.05)	−.64** (.05)

Note. Coefficients are unstandardized b coefficients.
*$p < .05$; **$p < .01$.

Overall civic content knowledge related positively to students' norms of social movement citizenship, to their attitudes toward immigrants' rights, and to their internal political efficacy. There were additional significant effects for responding correctly to individual items about international topics over and above the effects of the general content knowledge measure. Knowing the purpose of the Declaration of Human Rights and the purpose of the CRC significantly predicted more positive views of social movement activities as important for citizenship and more positive attitudes toward the rights of immigrants. Knowing the purpose of the United Nations had an additional significant and positive effect on the students' views of social movement citizenship (but not on attitudes toward immigrants' rights). While overall content knowledge significantly predicted political efficacy, responding correctly to individual international knowledge items *negatively* related to this outcome. This may be because the items on the efficacy scale refer primarily to competence in discussion participation, and students are likely to be discussing national politics and not human rights declarations or the United Nations.

Students' experiences in school related to the three attitudinal scales in similar ways. Students who often read about international topics in the newspaper, who perceived that their classroom climate was open to discussion, and who felt confident in the value of students' participation in their schools had stronger norms favoring social movement citizenship, more positive immigrants' rights attitudes, and a higher sense of political efficacy. Discussion with teachers about international topics was associated with a stronger view of social movement citizenship as important and with higher efficacy but was also associated with more *negative* attitudes toward immigrants' rights. It may be that when teachers discuss immigration as an international issue they emphasize its problematic aspects.

Discussion

The picture of young people's understanding, support, and practice of human rights from this international empirical analysis is an interesting one. The country's context for recognizing human rights makes a difference, particularly in the extent to which adolescents know about what is contained in the CRC. The condition of civil and political rights in a country also makes a difference, particularly in the extent to which adolescents in that country are likely to know about the Universal Declaration of Human Rights and about the United Nations.

Females across countries express lower levels of political efficacy than males, but they are more likely to support the rights of immigrants, and know about U.N. instruments covering human rights. Conversely, males across countries express higher levels of efficacy for political participation and know more about the United Nations as an institution than females. This helps to clarify some previous research on smaller samples, where gender differences favoring females in support for nurturance rights have been reported but where the picture for self-determination or participation rights has been mixed. Furthermore, this analysis of IEA data shows that students with more knowledge of human rights issues have more positive attitudes toward social justice organizations and the rights of immigrants.

There is strong corroboration that for all students the everyday experience of democracy is important in shaping attitudes. In other words, being in a classroom where students are free to discuss opinions and in a school where students feel that they can participate in a productive way are both positive for young people's human rights support. Students who read international news are more likely to be knowledgeable and to have positive attitudes about human rights even after taking other factors into account. All of these findings are based on surveys, but they could be further explored with interviews (see Richardson, 2006, for examples).

The process of formulating useful policy recommendations based on empirical analysis begins with a delineation of the nature and dimensions of the problem to be addressed. We believe that there are three dimensions to the problem faced by psychologists, other social scientists, and educators who wish to contribute to increasing understanding and action to defend human rights among young people. First, many social scientists do not sufficiently consider important aspects of context in the promotion of human rights. Second, they often lack an in-depth understanding of the development of young people's attitudes and the role of classroom processes in fostering respect for human rights among students (including the policy innovations necessary to increase attention to democratic practices or international issues in schools). Third, researchers advocating for change often use fragmentary studies of limited samples that are unconvincing to policymakers. We will look at these in turn, examining how the analysis in this article might help interested researchers and practitioners to become more effective human rights advocates and contributors to research-based policy.

Many psychologists and educators are unaware of the extent to which differences in national context affect learning about human rights in different countries, and could benefit from the perspective of other disciplines that have a more explicit focus on national and international political contexts. The results in the United States and several European countries point to the importance of the foreign policy of governments in the area of international human rights and children's rights as it may influence the implementation of civic and human rights education programs. It is striking that the policy climate itself (operationalized as a government's emphasis on human rights in its intergovernmental dialogue) has at least a modest relation to the extent to which young people in that country know what is included in the CRC. Furthermore, factors related to the implementation of guarantees of human rights for adults in the country (indexed by the Freedom House index) and how long a country has been a democracy both relate to young people's knowledge and attitudes. The country-level effects are modest, but they are maintained even after controls for several other relevant factors are considered.

Another way of framing this same issue was recently voiced by Huston (2005) in a policy brief issued by the Society for Research in Child Development. She noted that in many parts of Europe, "the U.N. Convention on the Rights of the Child is used to frame child policies that need no justification beyond the goal of promoting human rights" (p. 16). In contrast, references to "international human rights" tend to make policymakers in countries such as the United States suspicious rather than supportive.

Future analysis of the IEA data set, and further studies by psychologists, should explore other aspects of national political context. Interdisciplinary collaborations with political scientists, sociologists, or specialists in international law would be valuable. These collaborations have the potential to enrich our understanding of how national and international contexts shape the individual citizen's experience and how to make effective policy interventions. In other words, we should take further steps to understand how distal factors, such as the actions taken by governments, are translated into proximal experiences that are influential for students. This may include encouragement to include international topics in curricula, to give just one example.

Many psychologists and educators recognize that the experience of self-determination and democracy at school matters for the human rights attitudes of individual students. This analysis of IEA data corroborates that students who have the most exposure to the practice of democratic ideals in their classrooms and schools are the most likely to hold positive human rights attitudes. Creating an open and respectful climate for discussion in the classroom and giving individual students a voice in their schools should be encouraged in the practice of teachers and administrators by relevant policy initiatives and training. When psychologists in collaboration with sociologists of education and education policy researchers have considered these processes in depth, they will be in a better position to assist in the complex process of changing practices to enhance students' participatory rights in their schools.

Social scientists often conduct research with small groups to describe the nature of the gap between subscribing to ideals and actually engaging in relevant behavior. In our broader analysis, the extent to which individuals support human rights and action for social justice in principle, but not in action, is illustrated by differences in the factors predicting attitudes toward social justice activities for citizens and support for immigrant rights and those predicting a sense of political efficacy. For example, females are more likely to support rights in principle and to value membership in rights-oriented organizations, but they are less likely to feel competent to engage in the political system by discussing politics or exercising their rights to participate. These are among the issues that can be investigated using existing databases in order to provide evidence to bring to the attention of policymakers. The analysis in this article shows the advantages of being able to examine human rights education issues at both the individual and country level and allows us to investigate aspects of national context that vary in a large cross-national data set. The IEA study also collected data from teachers and principals in the schools that these students attended, and there are many possibilities for further investigations of human rights attitudes by adding the school level to our models (Barber, 2006). It is clear that schools and other societal institutions can build a strong foundation for the development of understanding, support, and practice of human rights by supporting democratic practices at school and by encouraging students to become informed about international issues. Psychologists, educators, and social scientists have a distinct and important role to play in this process.

References

Amnesty International. (1996). *First steps: A manual for starting human rights education*. London: Author.

Atkeson, L. R., & Rapoport, R. B. (2003). The more things change the more they stay the same: Examining gender differences in political attitude expression, 1952–2000. *Public Opinion Quarterly, 67*, 495–521.

Barber, C. (2006, November). *Teachers' classroom practices in relation to students' civic engagement in three countries*. Paper presented at the Second IEA International Research Conference, Brookings Institution, Washington, DC.

Bernath, T., Holland, T., & Martin, P. (1999). How can human rights education contribute to international peace-building? *Current Issues in Comparative Education, 2,* 14–22.

Center for International Development and Conflict Management. (2003). *Polity IV database.* Retrieved July 1, 2003, from http://www.cidcm.umd.edu/polity.

Claude, R. P. (1998). Human rights education: Its day has come. *American Society of International Law Human Rights Interest Group Newsletter, 8*(2), 13–23.

Covell, K., & Howe, R. B. (1999). The impact of children's rights education: A Canadian study. *International Journal of Children's Rights, 7,* 171–183.

Crowson, H. M. (2004). Human rights attitudes: Dimensionality and psychological correlates. *Ethics & Behavior, 14,* 235–253.

Decoene, J., & DeCock, R. (1996). The children's rights project in the primary school "De Vrijdagmarkt" in Bruges. In E. Verhellen (Ed.), *Monitoring children's rights* (pp. 627–636). The Hague: Kluwer Law International.

Doise, W., Spina, D, & Clemence, A. (1999). Human rights studied as social representations in a cross-national context. *European Journal of Social Psychology, 29,* 1–29.

Freedom House Incorporated. (2006). *Freedom in the World comparative rankings.* Retrieved September 11, 2006, from http://www.freedomhouse.org.

Gaudelli, W., & Fernekes, W. R. (2004). Teaching about global human rights for global citizenship. *Social Studies, 95,* 14–22.

Haste, H., & Hogan, A. (2006). Beyond conventional civic participation, beyond the moral-political divide. *Journal of Moral Education, 35,* 473–495.

Hess, R. D., & Torney, J. V. (2005). *The development of political attitudes in children* (2nd ed.). New Brunswick, NJ: AldineTransaction. (Original work published 1967)

Howe, R. B., & Covell, K. (2005). *Empowering children: Children's rights education as a pathway to citizenship.* Toronto, Canada: University of Toronto Press.

Husfeldt, V., Barber, C., & Torney-Purta, J. (2005). *Students' social attitudes and expected political participation: New scales in the enhanced database of the IEA Civic Education Study.* College Park, MD: Civic Education Data and Researcher Services.

Huston, A. (2005). *Connecting the science of children development to public policy* (Social Policy Report, Vol. 19). Ann Arbor, MI: Society for Research in Child Development.

Landman, T. (2005). *Protecting human rights: A comparative study.* Washington, DC: Georgetown University Press.

Limber, S., Kask, V., Heidmets, M., Kaufman, N., & Melton, G. (1999). Estonian children's perceptions of rights: Implications for societies in transition. *International Journal of Children's Rights, 7,* 365–383.

McFarland, S., & Mathews, M. (2005). Who cares about human rights? *Political Psychology, 26,* 365–385.

Melton, G. B. (1980). Children's concepts of their rights. *Journal of Clinical Child Psychology, 9,* 186–190.

Melton, G. B. (2005). Treating children like people: A framework for research and advocacy. *Journal of Clinical Child and Adolescent Psychology, 34,* 646–657.

Müller, L. (2002). *Human rights education at school and in postsecondary institutions.* (Occasional Paper #6, Working Group on Human Rights, University of Trier). Trier, Germany: Arbeitsgemeinschaft Menschenrechte. (Unpublished English translation.)

Peterson-Badali, M., Ruck, M. D., & Ridley, E. (2003). College students' attitudes toward children's nurturance and self-determination rights. *Journal of Applied Social Psychology, 33,* 730–755.

Ramirez, F. O., Suarez, D., & Meyer, J. W. (2006). The worldwide rise of human rights education: 1950–2005. In A. Benavot & C. Braslavsky (Eds.), *The changing contexts of primary and secondary education: Comparative studies of the school curriculum* (pp. 36–52). Hong Kong: CERC.

Raudenbush, S. W., Bryk, A. S., Cheong, Y. F., & Congdon, R. (2004). *HLM 6: Hierarchical Linear and Nonlinear Modeling.* Lincolnwood, IL: Scientific Software International.

Richardson, W. (2006). Combining cognitive interviews and social science surveys. In K. Barton (Ed.), *Research methods in social studies education* (pp. 159–182). Greenwich, CT: Information Age Press.

Roberts, H. (2003). Children's participation in policy matters. In C. Hallett & A. Prout (Eds.), *Hearing the voices of children* (pp. 26–37). London: RoutledgeFalmer.

Schulz, W., & Sibberns, H. (2004). *IEA Civic Education Study technical report*. Amsterdam: International Association for the Evaluation of Educational Achievement.

Sotelo, M. J. (1999). Gender differences in political tolerance among adolescents. *Journal of Gender Studies, 8*, 211–217.

Suarez, D., & Ramirez, F. (2007). Human rights and citizenship: The emergence of human rights education. In C. Torres (Ed.), *Critique and utopia: New developments in the sociology of education* (pp. 43–64). Lanham, MD: Rowman and Littlefield.

Swaminathan, H., & Rogers, H.J. (1990). Detecting differential item functioning using logistic regression procedures. *Journal of Educational Measurement, 27*, 361–370.

Tibbitts, F. (1996). On human dignity: A renewed call for human rights education. *Social Education, 60*, 428–431.

Tibbitts, F. (2002). Understanding what we do: Emerging models of human rights education. *International Review of Education, 48*, 159–171.

Torney, J. (1977). The international attitudes and knowledge of adolescents in nine countries: The IEA Civic Education Survey. *International Journal of Political Education, 1*, 3–20.

Torney-Purta, J. (1982). Socialization and human rights research: Implications for teachers. In M. Branson & J. Torney-Purta (Eds.), *International human rights, society and the schools* (pp. 35–47). Washington, DC: National Council for the Social Studies.

Torney-Purta, J. (2002). The school's role in developing civic engagement: A study of adolescents in twenty-eight countries. *Applied Developmental Science, 6*, 203–212.

Torney-Purta, J., & Barber, C. (2005). Democratic school participation and civic participation among European adolescents: Analysis of data from the IEA Civic Education. *Journal of Social Science Education, 4* (Special issue: The European Year of Citizenship through Education).

Torney-Purta, J., Barber, C., & Wilkenfeld, B. (2007). Latino adolescents' civic development in the United States: Research results from the IEA Civic Education Study. *Journal of Youth and Adolescence, 36*, 111–125.

Torney-Purta, J., Barber, C., Wilkenfeld, B., & Homana, G. (2008). Profiles of civic life skills among adolescents: Indicators for researchers, policymakers, and the public. *Child Indicators Research, 1*, 86–106.

Torney-Purta, J., Lehmann, R., Oswald, H., & Schulz, W. (2001). *Citizenship and education in twenty-eight countries: Civic knowledge and engagement at age fourteen*. Amsterdam: International Association for the Evaluation of Educational Achievement.

UNESCO. (2005). *Education–Human rights education*. Retrieved April 11, 2005, from http://portal.unesco.org/education/en.

Wade, R. (1994). Conceptual change in elementary social studies: A case study of fourth graders' understanding of human rights. *Theory and Research in Social Education, 22*, 74–96.

JUDITH TORNEY-PURTA is a Professor of Human Development at the University of Maryland, College Park. She received her PhD in Human Development from the University of Chicago. Her major research interests include the development of social and civic attitudes among adolescents across nations and the political engagement of college students. She received the Decade of Behavior Research Award in Democracy in 2005.

BRITT WILKENFELD is a Doctoral Candidate in Human Development at the University of Maryland, College Park, specializing in Developmental Science. Her major research interests include neighborhood and school effects on civic outcomes and positive youth development, especially among minority adolescents.

CAROLYN BARBER is an Assistant Professor of Educational Research and Psychology at the University of Missouri, Kansas City. She received her PhD in Human Development from the University of Maryland. Her major research interests include social aspects of secondary schooling, especially as related to civic and gifted education. She also has methodological interests in multilevel modeling and large-scale data set analysis.

Journal of Social Issues, Vol. 64, No. 4, 2008, pp. 881–901

Adolescents' Approach toward Children's Rights: Comparison among Christian, Jewish, and Muslim Children in Jerusalem

Mona Khoury-Kassabri* and **Asher Ben-Arieh**

The Hebrew University

With the universal ratification of the United Nations Convention on the Rights of the Child (CRC), societies have recognized children as human beings entitled to their own rights. This recognition calls for a thorough investigation of children's understanding of rights at large and their own personal rights in particular. It further calls for an examination of the role of context in forming the concept of children's rights. This study examined adolescents' (ages 12–14) approach to children's rights among three ethnic–religious groups: Arab-Christian, Arab-Muslim, and Jewish adolescents living in Jerusalem. The results indicated that Jewish adolescents had higher agreement and support for children's rights than Arab adolescents, except in the case of children's rights in governmental procedures, where Arab adolescents were in greater support. When comparing Muslim and Christian-Arab adolescents, the results show almost no significant differences. Similarly, adolescents' degree of religiosity was only partially correlated with their approach to children's rights. The findings suggest that nationality is an important factor in the formulation of adolescents' approach to children's rights.

The global recognition of children's rights as it has been expressed in the United Nations Convention on the Rights of Children (CRC) and its universal acceptance calls for a thorough investigation of children's understanding of the concept of children's rights. Critical to children's meaningful participation in a civil society, and thus their well-being, is an understanding of their rights as individuals within a family, community, and society. It is especially important to study children's own perspective of their rights (Ben-Arieh, 2005; Limber,

---

*Correspondence concerning this article should be addressed to Mona Khoury-Kassabri, Paul Baerwald School of Social Work and Social Welfare, The Hebrew University, Mount Scopus, Jerusalem, Israel 91905 [e-mail: msmona@mscc.huji.ac.il].

This article is based on a study supported by a research grant from the Warburg foundation.

Kask, Heidmets, Kaufman, & Melton, 1999; Melton & Limber, 1992) for several reasons: (a) such an understanding is fundamental to a child advocacy agenda, (b) research on the topic can illuminate situations in which children believe their rights are practically unenforceable and help to improve interventions to correct such problems, (c) studying children's own views communicates personal respect for them (CRC, 1989, Article 12), (d) such research can inform efforts to educate children about democratic values, and (e) adults rarely are skilled in identifying the matters of most concern to children.

Melton (1980) was among the first to examine children's concept of their rights. He employed Piaget's and Kohlberg's work on moral development to explain the developmental progression of children's concept of their rights in a sample of 1st, 3rd, 5th, and 7th graders from affluent and working-class backgrounds in Boston. Using open-ended questionnaires, he found that children's conception of their rights emerges in the early years of elementary school. Moreover, his study revealed that children's understanding of rights progressed through three levels or stages: at the first level, young children (i.e., first grade) conceive rights on the basis of what is allowed by authority; at the second level, rights are conceived on the basis of fairness and competence, which is found among children in third grade or older; and at the third level, older children (mostly mid to late adolescents) justify rights on the basis of abstract principles. However, he noted that the majority of the oldest children in his study (i.e., seventh graders) rarely reasoned about rights in terms of abstract principles or concepts. Melton's three-stage developmental progression in children's reasoning about rights has been confirmed in several additional studies in different cultures and countries, such as Norway (Melton & Limber, 1992), Estonia (Limber et al., 1999), and South Africa (Peens, 1997).

Contrary to Melton's finding, Helwig (1997) in a study that examined the views of 6-, 10-, 12-, and 22-year-olds, found that children's ability to think abstractly typically emerges early in middle childhood. A majority of 6- and 10-year-olds in his study affirmed freedom of speech and religion for children and adults and identified restrictions on these rights as a wrongful expression of authority by the family, the school, or the government. Thus, it seems that such ideas are usually well inculcated by age 10 (Ruck, Abramovitch, & Keating, 1998; Ruck, Keating, Abramovitch, & Koegl, 1998).

In that regard, it is interesting to note that the research literature has rarely focused on children's misconception about children rights. In the popular discourse, such misconceptions will usually be defined as understanding rights as an entitlement to get whatever I want on the one hand, or whatever the adults decide to give me on the other (Melton, 1980).

Although maturity is an important factor in children's understanding of rights, it has a stronger effect on children's reasoning about autonomy (self-determination rights) than it does on their thinking about entitlements (nurturance rights) (Ruck et al., 1998). Attitudes about the appropriateness of asserting children's rights and the importance of particular types of rights are contingent on the social and cultural context. Social class is suggested as a significant determinant of children's concepts of and attitudes toward their rights, as children from disadvantaged families are said to exhibit less-mature reasoning about rights than do children of greater privilege, who experience entitlement daily (Melton, 1980, 1983). However, little is known about the sociopolitical and cultural factors that affect children's understanding of their rights in different cultures and in different religions. This is of special interest as most of the studies to date have focused on children from Western cultures and Christian religion. Thus, studies in non-Western cultures and among other religions are critical if we are to more fully understand the special role of culture and sociopolitical context (see Cherney & Shing, this issue).

The Role of Culture and the Sociopolitical Context

Helwig and Turiel (2002) provided a thorough review of existing knowledge about children's perspective of civil liberties, autonomy, and democracy across cultures. They present ample research demonstrating that children affirm their own rights and autonomous decision making in many situations. In addition, children's judgments regarding civil liberties, autonomy, and democracy vary by both cultural context and maturational level. For example, in Western societies, even young children possess concepts of rights and civil liberties and prefer democratic social organization in a variety of social contexts, while research in non-Western settings showed that such concepts develop later in life.

Neff and Helwig (2002) examined children's reasoning about rights and authority in four cultures: China, India, Canada, and the United States. While Canada and the United States are primarily seen as oriented toward individual rights and autonomy, China and India are primarily seen as oriented toward obedience to authority. However, Neff and Helwig (2002) found that children's social reasoning, even if culturally distinct, does not necessarily follow the general cultural orientation (e.g., individualistic vs. collectivistic). Thus, additional factors (e.g. beliefs about the biological, social, or divine origins of power) are likely influencing children's reasoning about their rights. Thus, the authors suggest that research must move beyond broad cultural orientations such as individualism and collectivism to consider how specific cultural practices influence the social reasoning of autonomy and rights. They also stress that such concepts are not defined by cultural orientations that are simply "transmitted" to individuals, but rather represent shared features of social life, reasoning, and experience, all of which must be accounted for within a truly constructivist model of social cognition and development.

In a study of the allocation of authority between parents and children, Bohrnstedt, Freeman, and Smith (1981) found ethnic and religious differences in respondents' tendency toward favoring an adult or children's point of view. Anglo Americans and Asian Americans were more favorable to the child's point of view than were African Americans and Hispanic Americans; Jews and agnostics were more favorable than were Catholics and Protestants. Although their study was not specifically about attitudes toward children's rights (issues related to governmental action were not included), the authors' general thesis that "views on children's rights are rooted in more general liberal-conservative postures" (Bohrnstedt et al., 1981, p. 459) was nevertheless well supported by their findings.

As to the issue of children rights, several comparative studies suggest that the prevailing culture affects attitudes about children's rights, even among elementary school-aged children. Whereas research in several different cultures (i.e., the United States, Norway, and South Africa) suggests a shared developmental progression in children's reasoning about rights, studies of children in the United States, South Africa, Canada, and Switzerland point to some interesting cultural differences in children's attitudes toward their rights and the *saliency* of the concept of children rights (Cherney & Perry, 1996; Melton & Limber, 1992; Peens, 1997). For example, in response to the open-ended question "What rights do children have?" Norwegian children (Melton & Limber, 1992) were very likely to discuss nurturance rights (special entitlements and protections for children, such as rights to free health care, a safe home, peace, and clothing), while Estonian (Limber et al., 1999) and American children (Melton & Limber, 1992) focused on self-determination (the right to make choices, "do things," or express themselves). In a similar study of Canadian children, nurturance rights were less salient than self-determination, although not quite to the same extent as among American children (Ruck et al., 1998).

Even relatively subtle differences in sociopolitical orientation, as between American and Canadian children, are reflected in the children's emphasis on personal autonomy (Peterson-Badali, Ruck, & Ridely, 2003; Ruck et al., 1998; see also Cherney & Perry, 1996, comparing American, Canadian, and European [mostly Swiss] children). All of the studies involved societies in which Christianity was dominant, and most focused on Western cultures. Even Estonia, although a former Soviet republic, is historically Lutheran in religion (although largely Nordic secular now) and Western in political and cultural outlook, a perspective that rapidly intensified in importance in the 1990s after the Soviet occupation ended.

A few, more recent studies have ventured into non-Western cultures that are not dominated by Christianity alone. One example is Peens' (1997) study of Afrikaans, English, and Sotho-speaking children in South Africa. Peens concluded that, in general, the perception of Afrikaans, English, and Sotho-speaking children of their rights was more similar than disparate. However, two main factors appeared to contribute to the differences that were found. The first factor was respect for authority figures among Afrikaans and Sotho-speaking children; the second was the cultural meaning of the adult world, and in particular, the appropriate age for children to be taken seriously in the different groups. In other words, the respect for the elderly and the cultural meaning of adulthood played a major role in children's emerging perception of their rights.

Another recent study compared four generations (adolescents, young mothers, older mothers, and grandmothers) of Jews and Muslims living in Israel and in the Palestinian Authority (Ben-Arieh, Khoury-Kassabri, & Haj-Yahia, 2006). This study found that, for most of the items, Jewish adolescents had higher support for children's rights than Palestinian adolescents from Israel (PI) and Palestinian adolescents from the Palestinian Authority (PA). The latter two were similar in their acceptance of children's rights. However, this trend was not consistent across all types of rights examined in the study. For instance, PA adolescents were more similar to Jewish adolescents than to PI adolescents in terms of general support of the idea of children's rights. Also, the three groups were similar in their relatively low agreement with the idea of giving children rights in governmental matters (Khoury-Kassabri, Haj-Yahia, & Ben-Arieh, 2006).

Furthermore, in more traditional societies, the importance of studying children's perceptions of their rights is amplified by concomitant changes in the social order, such as the nature of parental authority (Al-Haj, 1995) and corresponding parenting styles (Haj-Yahia, Musleh, & Haj-Yahia, 2002). Such family variables influence attitudes toward children's rights (Peterson-Badali et al., 2003; Smetana, 1995; Smetana & Asquith, 1994).

Thus, the scarce literature that exists points toward an assumption that children from more Western, less-traditional, and less-authoritarian societies develop their abstract understanding of children's rights faster and tend to show more support for them. In this study, this would lead us to assume that Jewish students will be more supportive of children's rights than their Arab counterparts.

The Special Role of Religion

Research on children's participation in religious life and its developmental significance is remarkably sparse. The literature that is available on this topic is either impressionistic (e.g., Fisherman, 2002; Fowler, 1981; Hart, 2003) or based on highly skewed U.S. convenience samples (e.g., Elkind, 1971), or both. Thus, even when acknowledging the importance of religious life, social scientists are able to say little about the meaning of such experience in children's lives.

Perspectives on children's rights in particular may be influenced by religious beliefs in relation to human dignity (e.g., people as beings created in the image of God) and the nature of childhood (see the recent monographs of World Vision on children's rights and child protection at www.child-rights.org). Furthermore, religious institutions typically are distinctive from other community settings in the progressively greater participation that children are granted—for example, from children's choir members to acolyte to youth group leader to church council member—and the presence of culturally respected rites of passage.

The empirical research thus far supports the significance of religion in democratic socialization and personal identity development (Helwig, 2006), and thus supports a more careful comparative study. For example, a study conducted in the southwestern United States showed that students attending fundamentalist religious schools were relatively slow to acquire democratic values compared with their public school peers, although they ultimately did (by 12th grade)—except with regard to tolerance for nontraditional lifestyles (Godwin, Godwin, & Martinez-Ebers, 2002). Among public high school students in a Boston suburb, religiosity was linked developmentally in a longitudinal study to civic integration and avoidance of substance abuse (Kerestes, Youniss, & Metz, 2004). To sum up, research on the effects of religion on children's perception of their right is scarce and inconsistent. Further, the topic is barely studied in non-Christian societies, such as among Muslims and Jews.

As our brief introduction shows, the global interest in children's rights necessitates an examination of children's own perspectives on their rights (Helwig & Turiel, 2002). Yet there is a significant gap in our understanding of children's approach to and perceptions of their rights. In particular, there is a need to study the effect of culture, religion, and ethnicity on children's understanding of their rights. In that regard, studies among non-Western and non-Christian cultures and among less-mainstream Christian congregations are especially important. It is essential that culturally contingent concepts also be examined. For example, religion and belief in the origin of power and authority have been found to play a mediating role in the formulation of children's understanding of rights and autonomy (Helwig, 2006; Neff & Helwig, 2002). Other studies have shown that parental authority (Al-Haj, 1995) is a predictor of children's perceptions of their rights (Smetana, 1995; Smetana & Asquith, 1994) and could be a mediating variable, as could parenting styles (Haj-Yahia, 2000), which may vary across cultures and which may play a role in shaping children's conceptions of and attitudes toward their rights (Peterson-Badali et al., 2003).

This study focuses on the role of nationality and religion in the development and formulation of the concept of children rights among young adolescents (ages 12–14). Based on the literature presented above, we examine whether religiosity and one's religious background is correlated with adolescent's perceptions of children's rights. We further examine the sociopolitical context by addressing the role of nationality on young people's perceptions of their rights.

Research Goals

Our study examines, from a comparative perspective, children's understanding of their rights in differing national/cultural and religious contexts. We chose young adolescents for a variety of reasons. First, earlier research has shown that at this age they are competent and able to understand abstracts ideas such as rights and democracy (Helwig 2006; Torney-Purta, Lehmann, Oswald, & Schultz, 2001). Second, adolescence is the age at which even "secular" young people commonly experience faith-based rites of passage that are experienced usually by both religious and nonreligious youth (e.g., bar mitzvah, confirmation) and related religious instruction. Because of their obvious personal significance and cultural recognition, it is likely that such events are highly influential in children's development (Bales, 2005), but their impact has been seldom studied. Finally, on a practical level, focusing on adolescents enabled us to reach a large numbers of students from the three different religions in school settings.

Specifically, we sought answers to the following questions: Does adolescents' understanding of children's rights relate to the cultural context, nationality, religious background, and degree of religiosity?

Methodology

Our study included data collection from Jerusalem (both its eastern and western sections), including subsamples of Christian, Jewish, and Muslim children aged 12 to 14 years. The study used a structured, anonymous, self-report questionnaire filled out by the adolescents in their classrooms (in Arabic for the Arab students and in Hebrew for the Jewish students). The questionnaires were composed in Hebrew. They were then translated from Hebrew to Arabic and checked by back translation. The research team comprised Arabic and Hebrew native speakers who critically examined the translation and suggested changes based on their experience and on students' and experts' comments. A research assistant was available for any questions that arose while students filled out the questionnaire.

The Hebrew University Internal Review Board and the Israeli Ministry of Education approved the study. Before the beginning of the study school principals were sent consent forms and letters for the parents informing them of the study goals and questionnaire, giving them the possibility to refuse their child's participation. By doing so, we obtained passive consent from parents. Student assent was active and they were free to withdraw from the study at any time and for any reason. Confidentiality was ensured for all participants.

Sample

The study used a quota sampling method (where the sample is selected by dividing the population into categories or strata and selecting a predetermined number of participants from each category) in which we had two strata (Arab vs. Jewish). Within each strata we sampled the schools and their students using convenience sample method. We approached several principals of middle schools in East and West Jerusalem and asked them to participate in this study in an attempt to include participants from two national or ethnic groups (Jewish and Arabs[1]). Of the 19 schools we contacted, 11 agreed to participate. Only three students did not participate owing to parents' refusal, and a very few others chose not to participate or just did not complete the questionnaire. Overall, fewer than 5% of the students who attended the class during the time of the survey did not return a complete questionnaire. The sample was designed to include those from the Christian, Jewish, and Muslim faiths. Finally, among the Jewish subsample, we included both Orthodox and secular adolescents (ultra-Orthodox Jews were excluded). Overall, the sampling procedure yielded responses from 954 children: 580 Jewish children from five schools (317 children from two secular schools, mean ages 13.61, $SD = .63$, 49.5% females; and 263 from three religious schools, mean ages 13.60, $SD = .58$, 56.0% females), and 361 Arab children from six schools[2] (293 Muslims, mean ages 13.71, $SD = .66$, 61.9% females; and 68 Christians, mean ages 13.66, $SD = .75$, 13.6% females).

Measures

This study adapted research protocols used reliably in previous research and which included items and scales related to the following.

Children's understanding of the concept of children's rights. This scale included six items (the Appendix presents the measures and the specific items included), based on measures used by Limber and colleagues in their comparative study (Limber et al., 1999). Participants were asked to indicate to what extent they agreed that each of the six items represent "children's rights." All answers ranged on a scale from 1 (*are not at all related*) to 4 (*strongly related*). A few items measured misconceptions of rights. Factor analysis yielded three subscales of two items each: nurturance rights (alpha = .65; i.e., "To get what I need in order to live"), self-determination rights (alpha = .60; e.g., "To use self expression"), and misconception of rights (alpha = .32; e.g., "To get what I want"). The scales are based on means of the items included in them.

Children's support for rights in different contexts. This measure relied on an earlier version developed by Ben-Arieh and Haj-Yahia (Khoury-Kassabri

---

[1] All the research respondents were Israelis. However, most of the Arab adolescents (both Christian and Muslim) live in east Jerusalem where most of the population regards itself as Palestinian and sees itself as part of the Palestinian state in the occupied territories. This has resulted in the study using Jewish youth in both a national category (in contrast to their Arab-Palestinian peers) and a religious one in comparison to Muslim and Christian peers.

[2] It should be noted that Muslim and Christian children in Jerusalem study at the same schools; therefore, we refer to Arab schools that include children from both religions.

et al., 2006) and was slightly modified for this study. Participants were asked to what extent they support giving children five specific rights (the right of privacy, the rights to express opinions, the rights for due process, the rights to be heard, and the right of security). They were further asked to what extent children should be given rights within five domains (the family, the community, the educational system, the legal system, and the governmental system). Responses ranged from 1 (*do not support at all*) to 4 (*strongly support*). Factor analysis yielded two sub-scales: the personal context, which included eight items (alpha = .79), and the public/governmental context, which included two items (alpha = .30). The scales are based on means of the items included in them.

Children's understanding of violations of rights. We used a modified version of the Children's Rights Inventory (Melton, 1980, 1983). Participants were given 10 vignettes describing specific situations and were asked to indicate whether there was a violation of children's rights. Responses ranged from 1 (*no violation at all*) to 4 (*a serious violation occurred*). Factor analysis yielded three subscales (one item was deleted from these analyses because it was unrelated to any of the three factors): (a) violation by public systems, which included four items (alpha = .48; e.g., "Ron has a disability that prevents him from getting to the school by regular transportation, and the authorities did not arrange for any alternative way for him to get to school"); (b) violations by adults responsible for the child, which included three items (alpha = .10); and (c) violations resulting in direct and personal harm to the child, which included two items (alpha = .31; e.g., "Gill beat his little brother. When his mother found out, she slapped him with anger"). The scales are based on means of the items included in them. Due to the low internal reliability of the measure "violations by adults responsible for the child," it was excluded from the analyses.

Religion and religiosity. Participants were asked to indicate their religion (Muslim, Christian, or Jewish). Participants also completed one item that asked them to indicate the degree of their religiosity: 1 = *very religious*, 2 = *religious*, 3 = *conservative/ traditional*,[3] 4 = *secular*, and 5 = *atheist*. In this study this variable was recoded to three levels of religiosity: 1 = *very religious and religious*, 2 = *conservative/ traditional*, and 3 = *secular*.

Data Analysis

The study used the following analytical procedures and tests: (a) descriptive analysis (means and standard deviations) for each of the measures in this study

---

[3]In Israel, conservative/ traditional means a state of religiosity and not a Jewish congregation (as in the United States).

Table 1. Mean Scores for Children's Understanding of the Concept of Rights

	Overall N = 954	Jewish (n = 580)	Total (n = 361)	Arabs	
				Christian (n = 68)	Muslim (n = 293)
Nurturance rights	3.53 (.71)	3.56 (.67)	3.48 (.75)	3.30* (.87)	3.52 (.72)
Self-determination rights	3.53 (.71)	3.67 (.55)	3.30 (.86)	3.28 (.87)	3.30 (.86)
Misconception of rights	2.46 (.81)	2.24 (.73)	2.82 (.80)	2.64 (.83)	2.85 (.79)
Children's support for children's rights in different contexts[b]					
The personal context	3.44 (.53)	3.49 (.48)	3.35 (.60)	3.29 (.76)	3.36 (.56)
The public/ governmental context	2.65 (.80)	2.48 (.77)	2.92 (.76)	3.04 (.73)	2.89 (.77)
Children's understanding of cases of violations of children's rights[c]					
Violation by public systems	3.40 (.56)	3.43 (.51)	3.35 (.63)	3.29 (.75)	3.37 (.60)
Violations resulting in direct and personal harm to the child	3.13 (.76)	3.33 (.66)	2.82 (.81)	2.87 (.65)	2.80 (.84)

Note. [a]Answers were on a scale ranging from 1 = *not related at all*, to 4 = *strongly related*.
[b]Answers were on a scale ranging from 1 = *do not support at all*, to 4 = *strongly support*.
[c]Answers were on scale ranging from 1 = *no violation at all at all*, to 4 = *a serious violation occurred*.
*$p < .05$ (the differences between Muslim and Christian children).

(see Table 1), (b) *t*-tests were conducted to examine the differences between the two religions within the Arab sector—Muslims and Christians, (c) for the multiple analysis of variance (MANOVA), children's rights subscales (misunderstanding of rights, nurturance rights, self-determination rights, support for children rights in the personal context, support for children rights in the governmental context, violation by public systems, and violations resulting in direct and personal harm to the child) were treated as the dependent variables, and the two national groups (Jews and Arabs) and degree of religiosity were treated as independent variables main effect and interaction effects were examined.[4]

---

[4]We examined gender differences in children's rights subscales, but because there were only few significant differences, gender was not included in the analyses.

Results

We first calculated means and standard deviations for each of the measures. We also compared Jewish and Arab children. Among the Arab participants, we examined the differences between Muslims and Christians (see Table 1).

Overall, children understood the concepts of nurturance and self-determination ($M = 3.53$, $SD = .71$ for each measure) as related to and representing the general concept of children's rights. Children's misconception of their rights was lower than their understanding of the concepts of nurturance and self-determination ($M = 2.46$, $SD = .81$). We further examined the differences among the concepts of nurturance rights, self-determination rights, and misconceptions of children's rights with paired t-tests and found children to significantly support more nurturance and self-determination concepts than misconceptions of children rights (nurturance and misconception [$t = -32.66$, $df = 945$, $p < .001$]; self-determination and misconception [$t = -30.85$, $df = 945$, $p < .001$]).

Children expressed high support for their rights in the personal context ($M = 3.44$, $SD = .53$), and relatively low support for the public/governmental context ($M = 2.56$, $SD = .80$). As can be seen in the relatively high scores, participants understood both violations of children's rights when they were attributed to public/governmental systems and those violations that resulted in direct and personal harm to the child, $M = 3.40$, $SD = .56$ and $M = 3.13$, $SD = .76$, respectively.

T-tests were conducted to examine differences between Christian and Muslim adolescents. We found almost no significant differences between the two groups in terms of their understanding of what constituted children's rights. The only difference found was with respect to their reports on nurturance rights, where Christian adolescents agreed significantly less ($M = 3.30$, $SD = .87$) than Muslim ($M = 3.52$, $SD = .72$) adolescents that nurturance rights fell under the concept of children's rights ($t = 2.16$, $df = 352$, $p < .05$).

We used MANOVA to examine differences between Jewish and Arab children and level of religiosity with respect to adolescents' understanding of children's rights. In the following sections we will report main effects, *post hoc* (Bonferroni) results, and interaction effects regarding each of the children rights domain examined in our work.

Children's Understanding of the Concept of Children's Rights

National differences. Arab children agreed significantly less ($M = 3.52$, $SD = .73$) than Jewish children ($M = 3.57$, $SD = .65$) that nurturance rights fell under the concept of children's rights, $F(1, 869) = 5.47$, $p < .05$.

Jewish children scored higher ($M = 3.67$, $SD = .55$) than Arab children ($M = 3.30$, $SD = .85$) in agreeing that rights of self-determination were children's rights, $F(1, 869) = 67.43$, $p < .001$. Jewish children also showed significantly

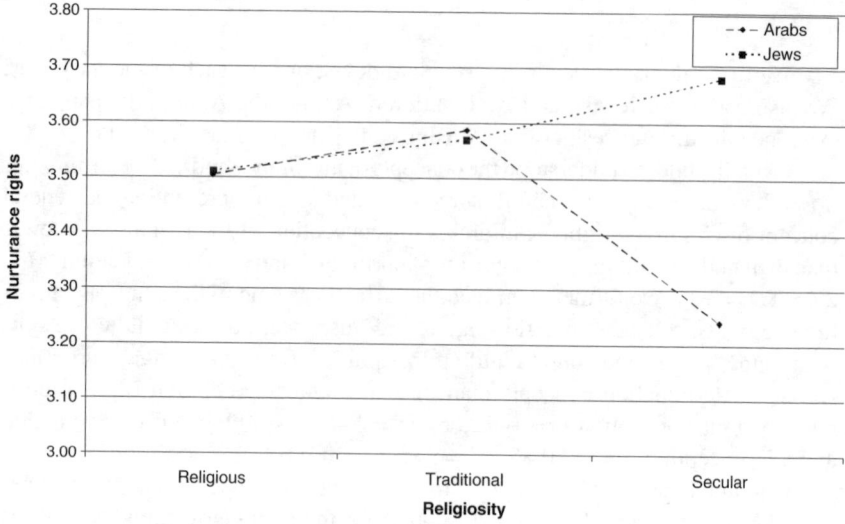

Fig. 1. Interaction between nation religiosity and nurturance rights.

less agreement ($M = 2.23$, $SD = .73$) on the items representing a misconception of children's rights ($M = 2.83$, $SD = .81$), $F(1, 869) = 81.64$, $p < .001$.

Religiosity. We found significant differences between level of religiosity and adolescents' reports on whether self-determination rights items represent children's rights $F(2, 869) = 6.67$, $p < .001$. However, *post hoc* test did not show any significant differences between any of the pairwise comparisons. The trend indicated that traditional and secular children agreed more than religious children that self-determination is part of children's rights (traditional $M = 3.58$, $SD = .69$; secular $M = 3.59$, $SD = .71$; and religious $M = 3.48$, $SD = .72$).

Interaction effects. We found that for Jewish adolescents' agreement that nurturing and self-determination rights fell under the concept of children's rights increased slightly with higher levels of religiosity. Arab children who reported their religiosity as traditional agreed more than Arab religious and secular children that self-determination and nurturance rights fell under the concept of children's rights. Results are presented in Figures 1 and 2.

Support for Children's Rights in Different Contexts

National differences. Jewish adolescents more strongly supported children's rights in the personal context ($M = 3.50$, $SD = .46$) than Arab children ($M = 3.38$,

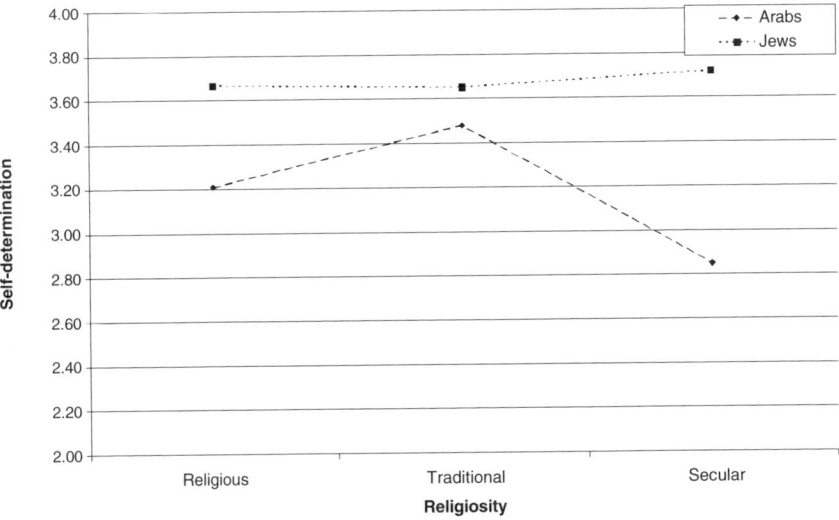

Fig. 2. Interaction between nation religiosity and self-determination rights.

$SD = .46)$, $F(1, 869) = 10.10, p < .01$. However, Arab children ($M = 2.91, SD = .76$) showed stronger support for children's rights within a governmental context than Jewish children ($M = 2.47, SD = .76$), $F(1, 869) = 30.22, p < .001$.

Religiosity. Significant differences were found in terms of level of religiosity with respect to children's rights within the personal context $F(2, 869) = 4.32$, $p < .05$. *Post hoc* test revealed that traditional and secular adolescents supported personal rights for children more than their religious counterparts (traditional $M = 3.50, SD = .52$; secular $M = 3.50, SD = .50$; and religious $M = 3.39, SD = .52$). No interaction effects were found.

Children's Understanding of Violations of Children's Rights

National differences. Significant differences were found only with respect to violations resulting in direct and personal harm to the child; more Jewish children ($M = 3.34, SD = .65$) perceived this as a violation of children's rights than Arab children ($M = 2.82, SD = .80$), $F(1, 869) = 98.69, p < .001$.

Religiosity. Significant differences were found between the three levels of religiosity and violations resulting in direct and personal harm to the child, $F(2, 869) = 3.30, p < .05$. *Post hoc* test revealed that secular children perceived this as a greater children's rights violation than religious children. No significant

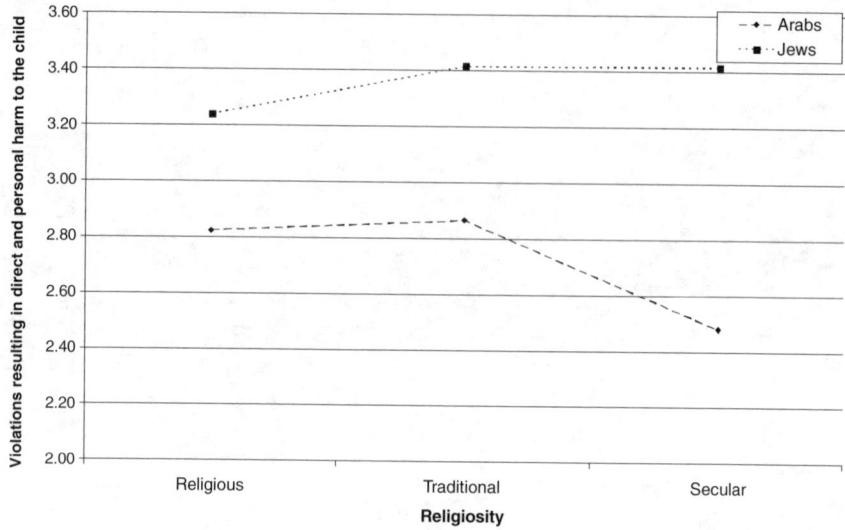

Fig. 3. Interaction between nation religiosity and violations resulting in direct and personal harm to the child.

differences were found between secular and traditional children or between religious and traditional children (secular $M = 3.27$, $SD = .72$; religious $M = 3.07$, $SD = .77$; and traditional $M = 3.18$, $SD = .73$).

Interaction effects. We found interactions only with respect to violations resulting in direct and personal harm to the child. While in the Jewish sector traditional and secular adolescents perceived this as a violation, Arab children who reported their level of religiosity as traditional perceived this item as a violation of children rights while religious and secular children showed much lower agreement. Results are presented in Figure 3.

Discussion

Understanding of Children Rights

Our findings echoed the results of earlier studies showing that young adolescents are competent and able to understand the concept of children's rights (Ben-Arieh et al., 2006; Helwig, 2006; Limber et al., 1999). In that regard, a major contribution of the study is in showing that young adolescents from non-Western cultures not dominated by Christianity support and understand the concept of children's rights. Further, we also found that children recognize rights misconceptions as well.

The fact that all of the participants in our study supported and understood the concept of children's rights does not, however, suggest there were no differences in the level of support or in support within different contexts. This leads us to the main focus of our study, the role of nationality, culture, and religion in the development of understanding of children's rights.

The Role of Culture

Although culture is a broad term and can be defined and analyzed with regard to a variety of variables, our sample consisted of two major cultural groups: Arabs and Jews. In fact, we use nationality as the differentiating variable in regard to culture. In part, this approach is similar to Peens (1997), who used three different language groups in South Africa to define her three cultures. This was also the approach used in earlier studies in Israel (Ben-Arieh et al., 2006; Khoury-Kassabri et al., 2006) on the issue of children's rights.

As in other research (Cherney & Perry, 1996; Limber et al., 1999; Melton & Limber, 1992; Peens, 1997), culture/nationality relates to most of the measures of children's understanding of their rights. These findings are also in accord with Helwig and Turiel's (2002) suggestion that different pictures of children's judgments of civil liberties, autonomy, and democracy emerge developmentally in different cultures and societies. For example, in Western societies, even young children possess concepts of rights and civil liberties and prefer democratic social organization in a variety of social contexts, while in non-Western settings, such concepts develop later in life. Similar trends are reported among Jewish and Palestinian adolescents, from Israel and the Palestinian authority with Jewish adolescents showing more support for children's rights than their Arab counterparts (Ben-Arieh et al., 2006; Khoury-Kassabri et al., 2006). This study supports these findings given that the national variable is strongly related to conceptions of rights. For most of the variables we explored in our work Jewish adolescents supported children rights more than their Arab peers, and this finding is in line with the assumption that traditionalist societies are slower to recognize children's rights (Bohrnstedt et al., 1981; Peterson-Badali et al., 2003; Helwig, 2006). In addition to the cultural explanation for the differences we found between Jews and Arabs, it might also be the case that socioeconomic differences between the two groups, where the Arab minority has fewer economic and sociopolitical resources than the Jewish population (Hareven, 2002) may have contributed to some extent to these findings. However, future research should attempt to disentangle socioeconomic status (SES) and culture in order to examine the relative contribution of each.

However, a different pattern was found in regard to cultural differences in support for children's rights in the public/governmental context (i.e., the rights within the educational system such as choosing which class to attend; and rights within the governmental system, such as the right to express political opinions and influence political processes). In this case, Arab respondents were more supportive of children's rights in the public/governmental context than Jewish children. Khoury-Kassabri et al. (2006) documented similar findings. Arab children may diverge from Jewish students in this area because they are subject to discrimination within the Israeli state; therefore, due to personal or group experience they may not perceive of their rights as irrevocable—as Jewish students tend to perceive of their personal rights (Melton, 1980, 1983). In addition, Arab children have been major players in Palestinians' struggle for independence, which may have contributed to their stronger support for children's rights in this context (Garbarino & Kostelny, 1997).

Religion and Religiosity

The Israeli context offers a unique picture of the role of religious background because both Muslim and Christian children belong to the Arab ethnic/national group and share many values such as traditional and collectivistic values, while their Jewish counterparts are usually defined by a more Western, individualistic culture. Still, in Israel, the Arab-Muslim population is usually regarded as a more traditional society than the Arab-Christians (Ben-Arieh & Haj-Yahia, 2006), and therefore should be, in theory, less attuned to children's rights (Helwig, 2006). In addition, Arab-Muslim children are commonly more disadvantaged economically than are Arab-Christian children (Ben-Arieh & Kimchai, 2008). Therefore, it is important to examine the differences among these three religion groups.

We found almost no differences between Christian and Muslim participants in their understanding of children's rights. Moreover, we found that only a few concepts of children rights were significantly correlated with degree of religiosity. Specifically, children who indicated their level of religiosity as secular or traditional supported self-determination rights, rights within the personal context, and better understood violation of children's rights when it resulted in direct and personal harm to the child than did religious children. It should be noted that these differences were not consistent within the different national groups—while this trend was true for the Jewish adolescents—among the Arab adolescents we found that secular students reported lower support for children's rights compared to religious and traditional children as we reported earlier.

Although religious beliefs conceivably could influence beliefs about rights, especially as they pertain to human dignity (e.g., people as created in the image of God), our findings do not support this presumption. However, given that the empirical research thus far supports the significance of religion in democratic socialization and personal identity development (Godwin et al., 2004; Kerestes et al., 2004), further exploration is warranted.

Conclusion

This study adds to the growing body of evidence indicating the importance of culture (and nationality) on children's understanding of their rights. As one of the few studies that have focused on non-Christian and non-Western cultures, our study provides evidence that the concept of children's rights among youth is salient across diverse cultures and nationalities. We found that religion plays a weaker role, at least within the methodological and sample constraints of our study. Further, our study failed to find a correlation between religiosity and understanding of children's rights.

Our study suffers from a number of limitations that should be considered. First, our sample is a convenience sample and not a representative one. Second, owing to the demographics of Jerusalem, even though our Christian subsample is an acceptable size, a larger sample might have been more effective in our attempt to flesh out the role of religion. Further, while we are confident with our research tools that measure the approach to or understanding of children's rights (and they are well grounded in earlier studies), still, some of our scales had only two items, which in some cases result in low internal reliability such as in misconception of rights. In addition, more work is needed in measuring religiosity among adolescents. Thus, although our results on nationality find support in past research (Ben-Arieh et al., 2006; Khoury-Kassabri et al., 2006), a definitive answer in regard to the role of nationality awaits further comparative research involving other nations. In the same vein, more work is needed to better understand the role of religion and religiosity.

Finally, future research should consider the mechanisms by which young people grow into a political culture or by which understanding of children's rights change with age. Research on this issue will be important in building a sense of collective efficacy among young people in diverse cultures and thus bringing the Convention on the Rights of the Child (1989) to life.

Our study also bears some policy implications. If indeed children's understanding of their rights is an important step in the making of a democratic society and active civilians (Sherrod, this issue), then we need to consider nationality as a prime factor in the process. In most cases, the nationality cleavage (in our case between the Jewish majority and the Arab minority) led the Arab minority to a less-progressive attitude toward the concept of children's rights but not to a negative one. Our study also showed that being a minority, such as the Arab adolescents in this case, does not necessarily interfere with the ability to develop competence to understand and support the concept of children rights. In fact, in this study for some types of children's rights, Arab minority adolescents showed greater support than did their majority peers, even though they were from a discriminated minority, which is also more conservative and socioeconomically disadvantaged group.

Thus, on the policy level it seems appropriate to invest more educational efforts in promoting the understanding and support for children's rights in all children.

References

Al-Haj, M. (1995). *Education, empowerment, and control: The case of the Arabs in Israel*. Albany: State University of New York.

Ben-Arieh, A. (2005). Where are the children? Children's role in measuring and monitoring their well-being. *Social Indicators, 74*, 573–596.

Ben-Arieh, A., & Haj-Yahia, M. M. (2006). The "geography" of child maltreatment in Israel: Findings from a national data set if cases reported to the social services. *Child Abuse and Neglect, 30*, 991–1003.

Ben-Arieh, A., Khoury-Kassabri, M., & Haj-Yahia, M. M. (2006). Generational, ethnic, and national differences in attitudes toward the rights of children in Israel and Palestine. *American Journal of Orthopsychiatry, 76*(3), 381–388.

Ben-Arieh, A., & Kimchai, M. (2008). Children's issues in Israel. In L. Limage (Ed.) & I. Epstein (Series Ed.), *Children's issues in Europe. Volume I., Encyclopedia of children's issues worldwide* (pp. 235–252). Westport, CT: Greenwood.

Bohrnstedt, G. W., Freeman, H. E., & Smith, T. (1981). Adult perspectives on children's autonomy. *Public Opinion Quarterly, 45*, 443–462.

Cherney, I., & Perry, N. (1996). Children's attitudes toward their rights: An international perspective. In E. Verhellen (Ed.), *Monitoring children's rights* (pp. 241–250). Dordrecht, the Netherlands: Martinus Nijhoff.

Convention on the Rights of the Child, G.A. Res. 44/25, U.N. GAOR Supp. 49 at 165, U.N. Doc. A/44/736 (1989).

Elkind, D. (1971). The development of religious understanding in children and adolescents. In M. P. Strommen (Ed.), *Research on religious development* (pp. 655–685). New York: Hawthorn.

Fisherman, S. (2002). Spiritual identity in Israeli religious male adolescents: Observations and educational implications. *Religious Education, 97*, 61–79.

Fowler, J. W. (1981). *Stages of faith: The psychology of human development and the quest for meaning*. New York: Harper Collins.

Garbarino, J., & Kostelny, K. (1997). What can children tell us about living in a war zone? In D. Joy (Ed.), *Children in a violent society* (pp. 32–41). New York: Guilford.

Godwin, R. K., Godwin, J. W., & Martinez-Ebers, V. (2002). Civic socialization in public and fundamentalist schools. *Social Science Quarterly, 85*, 1097–1111.

Haj-Yahia, M. (2000). Wife abuse and battering in the sociocultural context of Arab society. *Family Process, 39*, 237–255.

Haj-Yahia, M. M., Musleh, K., & Haj-Yahia, Y. M. (2002). The incidence of adolescent maltreatment in Arab society and some of its psychological effects. *Journal of Family Issues, 23*, 1032–1064.

Hareven, A. (2002). Towards the year 2030: Can a civil society shared by Jews and Arabs evolve in Israel? *International Journal of Intercultural Relations, 26*, 153–168.

Hart, T. (2003). *The secret spiritual world of children*. Makawao, HI: Inner Ocean.

Helwig, C. C. (1997). The role of agent and social control context in judgments of freedom of speech and religion. *Child Development, 68*, 484–495.

Helwig, C. C. (2006). Rights, civil liberties, and democracy across cultures. In M. Killen & J. G. Smetana (Eds.), *Handbook of moral development* (pp. 185–210). Mahwah, NJ: Erlbaum.

Helwig, C. C., & Turiel, E. (2002). Civil liberties, autonomy, and democracy - Children's perspectives. *International Journal of Law and Psychiatry, 25*, 253–270.

Kerestes, M., Youniss, J., & Metz, E. (2004). Longitudinal patterns of religious perspective and civic integration. *Applied Developmental Science, 8*, 39–46.

Khoury-Kassabri, M., Haj-Yahia, M. M., & Ben-Arieh, A. (2006). Adolescents approach toward children's rights: Comparison between Jewish and Palestinian children from Israel and the Palestinian Authority. *Children and Youth Services Review, 28*, 1060–1073.

Limber, S. P., Kask, V., Heidmets, M., Kaufman, N. H., & Melton, G. B. (1999). Estonian children's perceptions of rights: Implications for societies in transition. *International Journal of Children's Rights, 7*, 365–383.

Melton, G. B. (1980). Children's concepts of their rights. *Journal of Clinical Child Psychology, 9*, 186–190.

Melton, G. B. (1983). *Child advocacy: Psychological issues and interventions.* New York: Plenum.

Melton, G. B., & Limber, S. P. (1992). What rights mean to children: Children's own views. In M. Freeman & P. Veerman (Eds.), *Ideologies of children's rights* (pp. 167–187). Dordrecht, The Netherlands: Martinus Nijhoff.

Neff, K. D., & Helwig, C. C. (2002). A constructivist approach to understanding the development of reasoning about rights and authority within cultural contexts. *Cognitive Development, 17*, 1429–1450.

Peens, B. J. (1997). *Children's perceptions of their rights.* Unpublished doctoral dissertation, University of the Free State, Bloemfontein, South Africa.

Peterson-Badali, M., Ruck, M. E., & Ridley, E. (2003). College students' attitudes towards children's nurturance and self-determination rights. *Journal of Applied Social Psychology, 30*, 730–755.

Ruck, M. D., Abramovitch, R., & Keating, D. P. (1998). Children's and adolescents' understanding of rights: Balancing nurturance and self-determination. *Child Development, 64*, 404–417.

Ruck, M. D., Keating, D. P., Abramovitch, R., & Koegl, C. J. (1998). Adolescents' and children's knowledge about rights: Some evidence for how young people view rights in their lives. *Journal of Adolescence, 21*, 275–289.

Ruck, M. D., Peterson-Badali, M., & Day, D. M. (2002). Adolescents' and parents' understanding of children's rights in the home. *Journal of Research on Adolescence, 12*, 373–398.

Smetana, J. (1995). Parenting styles and conceptions of parental authority during adolescence. *Child Development, 66*, 299–316.

Smetana, J., & Asquith, P. (1994). Adolescents' and parents' conceptions of parental authority and personal autonomy. *Child Development, 65*, 1147–1162.

Torney-Purta, J., Lehmann, R., Oswald, H., & Schultz, W. (2001). *Citizenship and education in twenty-eight countries: Civic knowledge and engagement at age fourteen.* Amsterdam: International Association for the Evaluation of Educational Achievement (IEA).

MONA KHOURY-KASSABRI, PhD, is a lecturer at the Paul Baerwald School of Social Work and Social Welfare at the Hebrew University in Jerusalem and a member of Research Group: Mental Health and Well Being in Childhood and Adolescence.

DR. KHOURY-KASSABRI is one of the leading researchers in a series of national studies and surveys on school violence in Israel. Her work examined this issue from the student's, teacher's, and principal's point of view, and her particular focus is on student maltreatment by staff. She is also collaborating on a number of studies in Israel and Palestine on the topic of children's rights and especially its cultural and generational aspects.

ASHER BEN-ARIEH, PhD, is a Senior Lecturer at the Paul Baerwald School of Social Work and Social Welfare at the Hebrew University in Jerusalem and serves as the Associate Director of the Israel National Council for the Child. He initiated and coordinated the multinational project, "Measuring and Monitoring Children's Well-Being." He was among the founding members of the International Society for Children Indicators (ISCI) and serves as its first co-chair. He is one of the leading international experts on social indicators, particularly as they relate to child well-being, and he has published extensively on the politics of social policy and child well-being in Israel, and on child well-being indicators and its measurement.

Appendix: Items Included in Each Measure

Children's understanding of the concept of "rights"

Misconception of rights

To get what I want
To get what I am given

Nurturance rights

To get what I need in order to live
To get what I need in order to grow up and develop in a good and healthy way

Self-determination rights

To use self-expression
To have the option to protest

Children's expressing support for children's rights in different contexts

The personal context

Rights in the family
Rights in the community
Rights in legal matters
Right to security
Right to privacy
Right to express their opinion
Right to consider their opinion
Right to due process

The governmental context

Rights in the educational systems
Rights in governmental matters

Children's understanding of children's rights violations

Violation by public systems

In the school, there is a special science enrichment course. Chris is not interested in participating, but he still must pay for it.

Ron has a disability that prevents him from getting to school by regular transportation, even though the authorities did not arrange any alternative way for him.

Mika was told that, because her parents did not pay the annual payment to the school, she is not allowed to join the school trip.

Yaron's parents are getting divorced. A custody trial is occurring. Yaron asked to express his opinion in the trial. However, he was not allowed to do so.

Violations by adults responsible for the child

Jo was violent toward another student during break. To punish him, his teacher told him to stand against the wall, with his back to the class for an hour.

Martin is 12 years old. His father informed him that because of financial problems in his family, Martin will have to stay at home, once a week, and help him at the family business instead of going to school.

Sharon arranged a protest concerning student council during school break. The principal halted the protest claiming that "Protest is prohibited within school range."

Violations resulting in direct and personal harm to the child

Gill beat his little brother. When his mother found out, she slapped him in anger.

John wrote a note to his friend during the lesson. The teacher found the paper and read it to all the students in the class.

Journal of Social Issues, Vol. 64, No. 4, 2008, pp. 903–920

Beyond Balancing: Toward an Integrated Approach to Children's Rights

Gary B. Melton*

Clemson University

Discussions of children's rights often are framed in terms of balancing—balancing parents' and children's rights, balancing rights to autonomy and protection, balancing rights and responsibilities. By its nature, such a comparative inquiry pulls for relativist reasoning, but such an approach undermines the universalism that is at the root of the concept of human rights. Like the international human rights instruments that preceded it, the Convention on the Rights of the Child is based on "recognition of the inherent dignity and of the equal and inalienable rights of all members of the human family." Whether grounded in religious or secular ethical reasoning, human rights are directed toward a world in which the Golden Rule—a regime of mutual respect—serves as the guidepost for the social order. Building from that premise, recommendations are offered for social scientists' contributions to creation and preservation of such societies.

In the past generation or two, there have been remarkable changes in the recognition of children's rights. The U.S. Supreme Court first expressly acknowledged children as "persons" within the meaning of the Constitution less than a half century ago (*In re Gault*, 1967; *Tinker v. Des Moines Independent School District*, 1969). Today U.S. courts almost always recognize when minors' constitutional rights are at stake. Still, their approach to the application of those rights is often crabbed (see Levesque, 2008), typically because of an underestimate of the significance of liberty and privacy to young people (especially in the contexts of public schools and juvenile justice).

Analogously, the commitments in the past generation to meet children's rights to education and care have often been impressive. (The universal reach of free, appropriate, and minimally restrictive special education and related services to

---

*Correspondence concerning this article should be addressed to Gary B. Melton at the Institute on Family and Neighborhood Life, Clemson University, 158 Poole Agricultural Center, Clemson, SC 29634-0132 [e-mail: gmelton@clemson.edu].

children who need them is perhaps the best example. For a review, see Melton, Petrila, Poythress, & Slobogin, 2007, chap. 17; cf. Convention on the Rights of the Child, 1989, art. 23.) Nonetheless, too many children in the United States still lack the basics of health care, safety, shelter, nutrition, and so forth. Authorities in the United States have not embraced social and economic rights as a part of fundamental domestic law (*San Antonio Independent School District v. Rodriguez*, 1973) or, as a general matter, of international human rights law. Although President Carter signed the International Covenant on Economic, Social, and Cultural Rights (1966) in 1977 (a step that signifies a government's intent to work for ratification of the instrument and thus, under U.S. law, to make it part of the nation's domestic law), the Senate has never ratified that treaty. By contrast, the United States has ratified the parallel International Covenant on Civil and Political Rights (1966), a document that echoes many of the provisions in the U.S. Bill of Rights and thus is consistent with U.S. political culture.

Nonetheless, expansive articulation of social and economic rights can be found in federal and state statutory law and sometimes, as illustrated by the right to education, in state constitutional law. Further, although the solutions themselves have sometimes become threats to children's safety and well-being (see, e.g., Melton, 2005b), the fact remains that the United States often has been the originator of widely adopted reforms in policies and practices intended to ensure children's personal security. Even when the specific commitments have fallen short—as they often have (see, e.g., Melton, 2002, in regard to child protection)—of those provided in many other industrialized democracies (see, e.g., Bradbury & Jantti, 1999; Kamerman & Kahn, 1991, 1998), the difference has typically been more of magnitude than form (Melton & Sullivan, 1993).

Internationally, although momentous threats to children's safety and well-being persist in much of the world (Melton, 1993), the changes in children's status in the past generation have been even more remarkable in the world at large than the analogous developments over a somewhat longer period in the United States. Notably, as many of the contributors to this issue discuss, the nearly universal adoption of the Convention on the Rights of the Child (1989) has changed the global discourse on children's policy. This change is easily observed among academicians even in the United States, which shamefully stands alone among countries with a functioning government in having thus far declined to ratify the main body of the Convention.[1]

---

[1]Having signed the Convention on the Rights of the Child (1989), the United States is committed as a matter of international law to work toward ratification. The act of signing, which occurred during the Clinton administration, has not been renounced by President G. W. Bush. Under international law, signatories that are not yet parties to a treaty are obligated not to take actions contrary to it, but they are not bound by law to follow its dictates.

By contrast, the United States is a party to the treaty's optional protocols on children in armed conflict and on sexual exploitation and trafficking of children. Having ratified those instruments, the

The Articles in This Issue

Amid the burgeoning discussion of means of fulfilling children's rights, this issue of the *Journal of Social Issues* provides an impressive contribution to related scholarship, particularly in regard to children's own perspective on their rights. This journal issue presents a substantial expansion of such empirical research, as conducted in diverse cultures (Peterson-Badali & Ruck, this issue). Torney-Purta, Wilkenfeld, and Barber's (this issue) article breaks new ground by demonstrating that the political context, including the prevailing foreign policies, can shape young people's attitudes and beliefs about their rights. The literature is also extended by consideration of such ideas and experiences in the context of diverse cultures (Cherney & Shing, this issue; Khoury-Kassabri & Ben-Arieh, this issue; Torney-Purta, Wilkenfeld, and Barber, this issue), civil society (Sherrod, this issue), and religious life (Khoury-Kassabri & Ben-Arieh, this issue). Although some interesting differences were revealed in the exploration of young people's perspectives in a broad array of contexts, the bigger message is the general consistency of the findings in regard to the nature of adolescents' reasoning about such matters and the importance of particular rights to them.

The differences in attitudes across cultures and situations can be understood in relation to the *salience* of pertinent issues (Peterson-Badali & Ruck, this issue). For example, it would be unsurprising to find that adolescents looking toward job hunting in a tight local economy would be especially concerned with job creation and job training (see Melton, 1987a).

In that regard, adults' presumptions about the nature of *youth issues* are typically and perhaps unsurprisingly reflections of adults' perspective alone. Notably, adult "advocates" for youth often assume that issues directly related to questions of future consequences (e.g., environmental issues) are matters of special interest to young people. This categorization requires that observers overlook young people's tendency (like that of adults) to examine current issues in terms of their near-term significance to them. Although strong generational differences do appear in relation to attitudes on some political and social issues (e.g., attitudes toward the

United States, like all other functioning governments in the world, is required to report periodically to the United Nations Committee on the Rights of the Child about its compliance with the protocols. (Without an internationally recognized sovereign government, Somalia is a party to neither the Convention itself nor the related optional protocols.)

Moreover, the Convention has achieved such a wide level of adoption within the community of civilized nations that it arguably has risen to the level of customary international law. Although the U.S. Supreme Court has not ruled on this question directly, it gave weight to the Convention in holding that the Eighth Amendment to the Constitution prohibits application of the death penalty to offenders who committed capital offenses while they were juveniles [*Roper v. Simmons*, 2005; see also Convention, 1989, art. 37(a)]. However, the significance of this decision in consideration of the reach of the Convention in U.S. domestic law may be limited, because Eighth Amendment jurisprudence has long been grounded in *evolving standards of human decency*, a principle that by its nature pulls for indicia of public opinion, including international legal norms.

death penalty; see Gallup, 2002; Jones, 2002; Lyons, 2002), other demographic factors are usually stronger predictors. Hence, pollsters would undoubtedly find a much greater proportion of Republicans in the student body at Clemson University, where I am employed in South Carolina (a consistently "Red" state), than at Boston University, where I attended graduate school in Massachusetts (an equally "Blue" state).

Two of the articles in this issue present interesting, relatively novel topics in the area of adolescents' rights: Horn, Szalacha, and Dill (this issue) on rights of gay and lesbian adolescents, and Flanagan, Stout, and Gallay (this issue) on adolescents' assertion of risky behavior as matters of right. In both instances, the pertinent attitudes may not be typically associated with children's concepts of their rights,[2] but the current articles do point the way to related research that would be more clearly rights-focused.

Although the attention in this issue of the *Journal of Social Issues* to young people's attitudes toward children's rights is laudable and overdue, the contributors' concepts of children's rights reflect the continuing ambivalence in both public and academic discourse on the topic. Specifically, the need for *balancing* is a theme of the issue. Indeed, the importance of balancing was a theme of the external reviews of the manuscripts that ultimately comprised the issue. The authors variously refer to the purported needs to balance between possessors of rights (parents vs. children), between types of rights (autonomy vs. protection[3]),

---

[2]Horn, Szalacha, and Dill (this issue) examine peers' attitudes about gay and lesbian students in school. Although the context (public schools) is one that is clearly within the scope of discussions of children's rights, Horn et al. focus their research on young people's attitudes. School officials' and even voters' attitudes are undoubtedly more directly germane to questions of the nature and scope and perhaps even the assertion of gay and lesbian students' rights. Peers' attitudes become germane to policy and practice primarily as evidence of the effects of school culture (specifically, prevailing policies) on the definition and fulfillment of minority rights, not as direct determinants in themselves.

Flanagan et al.'s (this issue) work is also tangential to issues of *rights*, although it is clearly relevant to health education. Almost no one seriously contends in the contemporary era that government is unable to regulate behavior that has obvious costs to the society. Indeed, the range of mechanisms for such regulation is remarkably broad (Bonnie, 1985)—not only direct prohibition but also incentives, taxation, government speech, and indirect regulation (application of carrots and sticks to create social conditions inconsistent with risky behavior). Although the recognition of liberty inevitably carries the risk of unwise decisions (for example, foolish purchases), it does not thereby create a right to incur liabilities for the society at large. In the same vein, *conduct* (distinguished from *speech*) that creates health risks and related collective costs is not within the bounds of freedom of expression. The state may place few limits on debate about legalization of drug abuse, but that doctrine does not imply that the state lacks the ability to regulate such conduct.

In short, the assertion that risky behavior is "none of your business" does not go far. Nonetheless, there are related live issues of children's rights that do merit future examination from young people's own perspective. For example, do developmental considerations warrant *differential* regulation of behavior that threatens adolescents' health? In that regard, young people themselves may have useful insights about ways of minimizing such risk (given social norms prevailing among their peers) that would also minimally restrict liberty or invade privacy. Variations on the learner's-permit model (see, e.g., Williams, 2003) may be illustrative.

[3]Following the nomenclature in Rogers and Wrightsman's (1978) early factor analysis of attitudes toward children's rights, empirical researchers on children's rights tend to refer instead to

and between types of obligations (rights vs. responsibilities). In my judgment, these dichotomies are false. In this epilogue, I argue for an approach to children's rights that has a stronger philosophical grounding, and I offer suggestions for a corollary research agenda that would advance a rights consciousness inclusive of respectful concern for children.

Treating Children the Way That We Would Like to Be Treated

Children's Rights in Context

The seminal international human rights instrument, the Universal Declaration of Human Rights (1948), begins with the premise that "recognition of the inherent dignity and of the equal and inalienable rights of all members of the human family is the foundation of freedom, justice and peace in the world" (preamble). Toward those ends, the Declaration further proclaims (emphases added) that *"all* human beings are born free and equal in dignity and rights" (art. 1), that *"everyone* has the right to life, liberty and security of person" (art. 3), that *"everyone* has the right to recognition everywhere as a person before the law" (art. 6), and that *"all* are equal

---

self-determination (rather than *autonomy*) and *nurturance* (rather than *protection*) rights. Analyzing the attitudes prevailing among adults, Rogers and Wrightsman correctly described two broad perspectives on children's rights—popularly known as *kiddie libbers* and *child savers* (see Mnookin, 1978)—that reflect divergent views of the nature of childhood (Melton, 1983a).

As several contributors to this issue describe, cultural, political, and developmental factors affect adherence to these perspectives. Although I concur in the validity of these empirical observations, I also argue *infra* that maintenance of such a dichotomy is philosophically incoherent.

My point in this note, however, is less profound: i.e., the descriptors that Rogers and Wrightsman (1978) chose are not fully apposite. For example, freedom of expression does not by itself connote self-determination. Similarly, although expectations of privacy do entail some measure of personal control (over personal information, physical space and possessions, and one's body; Melton, 1983b), they do not necessarily entail conscious decision making, as the term *self-determination* implies. *Autonomy* better communicates the multiple dimensions of respect for personal boundaries, expression, and decisions.

Although the reference to *self-determination* rights is underinclusive, the label of *nurturance* rights is too broad. It implies that humanitarian actions by caring adults are matters of right. That something is nice to have, however, does not create an entitlement. Even demonstrable causal relation of a particular experience to an increase in children's well-being is insufficient by itself to establish a right.

The label that I am using—*protection* rights—is also not without problems, in that the term carries surplus meaning in some contexts. In particular, *child protection* is often narrowly construed to be synonymous with the right to personal security (freedom from assault). As I am using the term here, however, protection rights include not only defensive protection against assaults but also affirmative assurance of the resources—education, health care, nutrition, etc.—required to protect the opportunity to develop as a unique *personality* (see Melton, 2005a). By analogy, children have a right to protection from neglect, not just protection from abuse, regardless whether the cause is parental or societal negligence.

Thus, society has an obligation to *protect* the social and economic resources minimally necessary for children's development of personal identity. A wisely constructed social policy is apt to go further, however, *to promote* improved quality of life, economic competitiveness, and so forth.

before the law and are entitled without any discrimination to equal protection of
the law" (art. 7). Indeed, the word *everyone* appears 30 times in the 30 articles of
the Declaration.

Notice that the principles of human rights found in the Universal Declaration
do not include an age-related qualifier. Human rights were not conceived to apply
only to those people who are at least 18 or, for most purposes at the time that the
Declaration was promulgated, 21 years old.

Stunning in its scope, the Convention on the Rights of the Child (1989) is
remarkable in its sensitivity to the diverse ecology of childhood. With 54 articles,
most of which are divided into sections, the range of settings and situations that the
Convention covers is an accurate representation of childhood, whether of children
in ordinary or exceptional circumstances. Indeed, the Convention extends to "all
[government-related] actions concerning children, whether undertaken by public
or private social welfare institutions, courts of law, administrative authorities or
legislative bodies" (art. 3).

This breadth of coverage reflects the reality in modern societies that the
government is heavily involved in the lives of children in general, not only if
they are abused or neglected (arts. 19, 34, & 39), adopted (art. 21), delinquent or
accused of being delinquent (arts. 37 & 40), disabled (art. 23), ethnic minority (art.
30), trafficked (arts. 11 & 35), working (art. 32), selling or using illicit drugs (art.
33), seeking or granted asylum (art. 22), living or participating in armed conflict
(arts. 38 & 39), or separated from parents because of foster care (art. 20), their own
or parents' imprisonment (arts. 9 & 37), national borders (art. 10), or residential
treatment (art. 25). Accordingly, the Convention not only addresses assistance to
families in general (as discussed *infra*), but it also pertains directly to the settings
of everyday life: the arts and other cultural activities (art. 31), child care centers
[arts. 18(2)-18(3)], forums for public discussion (arts. 13–15), health clinics (art.
24), libraries (art. 17), mass media (art. 17), parks and recreation centers (art. 31),
places of worship (art. 14), and schools (arts. 28 & 29). Similarly, the Convention
even goes beyond recognition of a right to social security (art. 26) to assert "the
right of every child to a standard of living adequate for the child's physical, mental,
spiritual, moral and social development" [art. 27(1)].

The drafters of the Convention showed striking concern not only about *what*
children are owed but also *how* those obligations are fulfilled (see, e.g., art. 29, on
the goals of education). For example, children with disabilities are guaranteed "a
full and decent life, in conditions which ensure dignity, promote self-reliance, and
facilitate the child's active participation in the community" (art. 23). Analogously,
the Convention not only recognizes a panoply of specific due-process rights for
children accused of violating the law [art. 40(2)], but it also recognizes juvenile
respondents' right "to be treated in a manner consistent with the promotion of
the child's sense of dignity and worth, which reinforces the child's respect for the
human rights and fundamental freedoms of others and which takes into account

the child's age and the desirability of promoting the child's reintegration and the child's assuming a constructive role in society" [art. 40(2)].

In general, the Convention depicts children as *participants* in the settings of which they are a part (see generally Flekkøy & Kaufman, 1997; Melton, 2006; Smith, 2007). Any child "who is capable of forming his or her own views" has a right to be heard (art. 12; see also arts. 13–15 & 17). This standard is a very low one. Indeed, it is tautological in some circumstances, because children who express their views are *ipso facto* capable of doing so.

The drafters' principal goal was the preparation of children "to live an individual life *in society...*in the spirit of peace, dignity, tolerance, freedom, equality and solidarity" (preamble, emphasis added). Recognizing that the family is "the fundamental group of society and the natural environment for the growth and well-being of all its members and particularly children," the drafters intended for children to spend their childhood in a *"family environment,* in an atmosphere of happiness, love and happiness" (preamble, emphasis added). Without precedent for doing so, the drafters broadened the ordinary simple terminology (*family*) to *family environment,* an inspired choice of words, because it framed the relevant rights in a form that governments reasonably could fulfill (How could a government possibly ensure that every child has a family?) and that enabled protection of family and family-like relationships, regardless of the biological connection (Melton, 1996).

To add emphasis to this point, the Convention (1989) extends the obligation of states parties to respect and assist parents to, "where applicable, the members of the extended family or community as provided for by local custom" (art. 5). In effect, the Convention frames the breadth of children's rights from their own perspective—in this instance, in regard to the relationships that are so fundamental that they are critical not only to the fulfillment of children's needs, as related to their survival and development [see, e.g., arts. 6(2), 18(2), & 27(2)] but also to their establishment of a personal identity (see, e.g., arts, 7, 8, 29, & 30). In that regard, the Convention places a strong emphasis on states parties' obligations to preserve the relationships most important to children (see, e.g., arts. 5, 9, 10, 18, & 22).

In so doing, the Convention is remarkable in its "bottom-up" orientation (cf. Dahl, 1987; Nader, 1985). Not only is *family* extended to *family environment,* but the scope of children's rights is defined in terms of the requisites in the present for children's experiencing respect as persons and in the future for their continued full participation in community life.

The Content of Children's Rights

Like other human rights instruments (Melton, 1992), the Convention is focused on promotion of a sense of community in the grandest sense of that term.

It is oriented toward establishment of communities in which children *feel* that they are treated like people who count and in which their functions and opportunities in community life naturally evolve and expand (Melton, 2005a, 2005c). The expectation is that children's interactions take place in a context in which the adults in their lives, especially their parents, are also treated like people by public authorities, so that the institutions at the heart of society are strengthened as centers of community (Melton, 1996, 1999).

In this reciprocity of care, *all* of the people who are a part of children's community and the settings that constitute it (e.g., family and school), including children themselves, are worthy of notice (cf. Melton & Holaday, 2008, for detailed discussion of a community-wide child protection initiative that rests on such a premise), so that observers need not and indeed should not choose between parents and children. Protection of relationships and preservation of dignity are important to all, and recognition of one set of fundamental interests generally does not imply that others should thereby be ignored or discarded. Unsurprisingly, therefore, there is a large and long-standing body of knowledge showing that rights consciousness both reflects and stimulates a culture of caring and reciprocity. Consciousness of one's own rights is related to tolerance of expression of rights by others (see, e.g., Day, Peterson-Badali, & Ruck, 2006; Melton & Saks, 1985; Torney-Purta et al., this issue).

Indeed, the interests that are protected by children's rights vary minimally from those that are protected by adults' rights. That fact does not imply, however, that the claims that may be brought legitimately and justly are the same across the generations. For example, freedom of expression for a 10-year-old, like a 50-year-old, is derived from respect for the individual as a person, someone who should have a say (cf. Lind & Tyler, 1988, on the factors affecting perceived justice). For the 10-year-old who has little experience in community meetings, however, related education may be necessary in order to make the right to speak meaningful. Similarly, the community may need to provide special opportunities for young people to have access to the podium if freedom of expression is to be meaningful.

Analogous to the legal theory underlying the U.S. Constitution (Tremper, 1988), the overarching construct in the Convention on the Rights of the Child (1989) is protection of *dignity*, a concept that is expressly relied upon at several points [e.g., preamble; arts. 23(1), 28(2), 37(c), 39, 40(1)] and implicitly embedded throughout the instrument. Both normative (moral) and psychological in overtones (see Melton, 1992), the quest for dignity neutralizes the conflict between autonomy and protection rights. Both are necessary if one is to be or become a personality with a meaningful role in the community. As noted *supra*, freedom of expression, for example, is largely meaningless unless one has the forum, the skills, and the self-respect to articulate one's point of view.

The Obligations Associated with Children's Rights

Sen's taxonomy of criticisms. Nobel laureate Amartya Sen (2000) has articulated—and debunked—three arguments that are commonly made by skeptics about expansive human rights doctrines, including broad application of rights to children. The *legitimacy* critique refers to "the worry that human rights confound consequences of legal systems, which give people certain well-defined rights, with pre-legal principles that cannot really give one a justiciable right" (p. 227). Susceptible to the privileges accorded by the state, "human beings in nature are, in this view, no more born with human rights than they are born fully clothed; rights would have to be acquired through legislation, just as clothes are acquired through tailoring" (p. 228). Accordingly, skeptics argue, human rights have no meaning beyond that which is conferred by legislative authorities.

The *coherence* critique is an argument familiar to students of children's rights. The claim is that rights cannot be discussed without specifying who has the duty of fulfilling the rights. Unless a particular party has such a duty in a manner that results in perfect symmetry, so the argument goes, the claim of a right is empty. Further, even if the duty-holder is specified, that individual may also have just claim to rights. If so, the expected symmetry is apt still to be violated.

This is the classic form of the argument about the purportedly antithetical nature of children's rights. The societally designated protectors of children's rights are usually presumed to be their parents. In this view, recognition of rights for children is part of a zero-sum game in which parents' rights are necessarily in play and in which their successful assertion inevitably diminishes the authority of children, the state, or both.

The final critique of human rights that Sen (2000) described is also one that is familiar to proponents of children's rights. The *cultural critique* posits that human rights are not really *human* rights at all; instead, it is argued, such axioms are expressions of *Westerners'* values. The concept of human rights is said to emanate from the vision of individual persons that was the overriding idea of the Western Enlightenment. In this view, support for rights as universal attributes of children at best shows insensitivity to children, families, and communities in non-Western societies and at worst establishes expectations that undermine the very structures that are most likely to provide children with care and protection in the context of long-prevailing cultural norms.

The answers. Unsurprisingly, Sen's (2000) responses to these several criticisms in regard to human rights in general are also pertinent to understanding of children's rights in particular. The legitimacy critique is the easiest to rebut. Human rights can be conceived as potential legal rights that are grounded in fundamental moral claims. If a right is unfulfilled, it is nonetheless a right in principle.

The question is whether, as a matter of morality, the status of *person* provides an individual with just claim to a particular opportunity. As Sen (2000) noted, "The demand for legality is no more than just that—a demand—which is justified by the ethical importance of acknowledging that certain rights are appropriate entitlements of all human beings" (p. 229).

A similar rebuttal negates the coherence critique ("whether we can coherently talk about rights without specifying whose duty it is to guarantee the fulfillment of the rights"; Sen, 2000, p. 230). Statements of human rights should connote what people—in this instance, children—*should* have. In Sen's (2000) words, "The claims are addressed generally to anyone who can help, even though no particular person or agency may be charged to bring about the fulfillment of the rights involved" (p. 230). Rights language announces shared expectations about how people should be treated—in effect, a Golden Rule.

Finally, the cultural critique (whether "human" rights really are simply "Western") is based on a simplistic concept of culture in which diversity of ideas within cultural traditions is ignored. In fact, values consistent with recognition of human rights (e.g., tolerance; egalitarianism) can be found in Eastern as well as Western philosophies and religions. Indeed, a number of the articles in this issue also make this point. Moreover, people have worked to overcome oppression in all parts of the world. Further, although compliance is undeniably incomplete, the realities that rights language has been embraced by governments around the world and that democracy now has a foothold in almost every world region cannot be overlooked. Dismissal of children's rights as "Western" and therefore inapplicable in much of the world shows an unbecoming snobbery in itself. In that regard, it is telling that the ideas in the Convention on the Rights of the Child (1989) that are the most closely related to autonomy have been relatively slow to be adopted in the West as well as the East. (See Daiute's, 2008, observations about the provisions of the Convention that have been most troublesome for governments.) Indeed, review of the legislative history of the Convention (Office of the United Nations High Commissioner, 2007) shows ironically that many of the provisions that have been most commonly the source of political controversy in the United States were included at the insistence of the representative of the United States in the drafting group, typically during the Reagan administration.

Conclusions

Although the demand for balancing in matters pertaining to children's rights is strong, it is not a sensible practice. Those who would pit parents against children fail to see that respect for children implies no diminution of respect for the adults who care for them. Indeed, protection of such relationships is of mutual importance. Not only is there a shared interest in protection of family relationships from unwelcome intrusions, but there is also a joint interest in promoting respect within the family. A rights-oriented climate in "the smallest democracy at the heart of society"[4]—in effect, a setting in which the legitimacy of the rights of all family members is recognized—is likely to result in a better functioning family in which such relationships are strengthened (Tyler & Degogey, 1995).

In the same vein, neither autonomy nor protection rights are preeminent. All are important elements of treating children as people should be treated, with due consideration of both developmental and situational factors. Autonomy and protection rights are *integrated*, not *balanced*, in the effort to protect children's dignity.

Moreover, rights need not be balanced by responsibilities in one-to-one fashion. In that regard, those who believe that a declaration of children's rights should be accompanied by a declaration of responsibilities miss the point in three ways. First, the enforcement of legal rights is not the responsibility of private parties. Although parents and, in some cultures, other elder authorities are recognized by the state and by children themselves as having a special role in the lives of children, it is the government itself that bears the obligations recognized in international instruments. Analogously, assurance of the fulfillment of moral rights is a responsibility of the community at large.

Second, as already noted, rights do not exist in a zero-sum environment. Rather, sense of duty is apt to flourish in a context in which all people, including children, are shown proper respect. Thus, when children—or any disadvantaged class—are treated as members of the community, everyone's sense of worth increases. The expression of dignity *multiplies* amid the recognition and exercise of rights; there are no losers. By the same token, each fulfillment of the Golden Rule reverberates; it confirms the humanity of both receiver and giver and establishes the expectations for future interactions.

Third, a requirement that a child (or any person) accepts a responsibility before a right is conferred shows a fundamental misunderstanding of the concept. There is no entitlement if rights are contingent. Human rights have no meaning if they do not accompany the status of human being. In the same vein, a conception of children's rights that is effectively limited to good (responsible) children is empty indeed.

In determining the scope of children's rights, ultimately there are just two questions. First, *are children persons deserving of respect?* The answer to this question is unequivocally yes, whether the answer is based on law, morality, or religion.[5] Second, *what interests must be protected for a child to be (as a child) and become (as an adult) a meaningful participant in community life and,*

---

[4]"Building the smallest democracy at the heart of society" was the slogan of the International Year of the Family, as proclaimed by the United Nations, in 1994 (see Sokalski, 1993).

[5]For a religiously grounded exposition of children's rights, see World Vision (2002). Although the secular ethical theories underlying most academic commentary on children's rights are compatible with most relevant religious doctrines, religious arguments on point generally rest on the notion that

in so doing, to develop and express her or his unique personality? Note that no balancing test is embedded in this inquiry. Instead, the question demands a straightforward normative analysis (in regard to the criteria for "meaningful participation in community life") and corollary social impact analyses in regard to the effects of various policies, programs, settings, and situations in facilitating such experiences.

Questions of Politics

The Politics of Children's Rights

Of course, the latter question does have a corollary: how best to conduct the requisite social planning and then to implement the desired programs and policies in various political structures and community settings. In that regard, thoughtful discussion of the questions at hand in child policy has often been disastrously impeded by the tendency to view the core questions as primarily symbolic and to overlook their practical meaning (Melton, 1987b). More than in most policy contexts, the issues are not clarified, the interests at stake are not fully identified, and the most relevant information is neither sought nor used. Unfortunately, the reframing of such issues in terms of children's rights rarely reduces the triumph of sloganeering over reason.

Discussions of children's rights are easily co-opted. On the one hand, politicians jockey to define their side as pro-children, even when the issue is not distinctively focused on children (see Melton, 1987a, on child policies as *valence issues*). Such a strategy is intended to make thoughtful discussion impossible by making the opponent's position unthinkable. Politicians want to be cast as anti-children as much as they want to be remembered as antiflag!

On the other hand, association with children's rights is apt to result in a characterization as antiparent or antifamily, also hardly a winning position. As illustrated by the history of child mental health policy (see Melton, Spaulding, & Lyons, 1998), framing of an issue in terms of children's rights is especially likely

---

people, including children, are created in the image of God and therefore worthy of sacred respect (Melton & Anderson, 2008).

This viewpoint was expressed in a resolution of the United Methodist Church (2004):

> Human dignity is the foundation of all human rights. . . . Human dignity is the image of God in each human being. Human dignity is the sum total of all human rights. We protect human dignity with human rights. . . . It is God's gift of love for everyone. . . . As peoples and governments increase the catalogue of rights that are recognized and protected,. . . . our approximation of and striving for human dignity also increase.

In the Christian tradition, support for *children's* rights is given extra credence by Jesus' expression of special concern for "the least of these" (see Mercer, 2005). It is further amplified by the concept of the child as a gift from God (see, e.g., Episcopal Church, 1997).

to pull for symbolic debate about the relative power of various family members. This battle then distracts policymakers and the public from consideration of their unity of interests in protection of family relationships and in provision of resources to make child rearing easier.

This polarization is especially applicable to the Convention on the Rights of the Child (1989), because it is a transformative document. Consider, for example, how daily life would change if public officials (not only politicians but also teachers, recreation leaders, pediatric health workers, and social workers) took seriously the requirement at least to have a conversation with children before taking actions affecting them [art. 12(1)]. Although the values at stake flow easily from the best traditions of U.S. culture, the revolutionary nature of full recognition of children's rights in practice becomes obvious when one considers that the thought-problem just raised concerns only one section of one article among 54 in the Convention itself, a number that is expanded by the two optional protocols.

Effective Advocacy for Children's Rights in Practice

In this context, the advocate's first challenge is to avoid the definition of the topic as children's rights *per se*, while also functionally applying the concept. For example, in Strong Communities for Children, our current initiative to prevent child maltreatment in a portion of the Upstate region of South Carolina, we have so far united more than 5,000 volunteers and hundreds of organizations in an area (adult population in 2000, 97,000) known for its political and theological conservatism (Melton, in press; Melton & Holaday, 2008). Although the term *right* is not commonly used in the language of the initiative, the concept is deeply embedded in the approach. Specifically, the participating communities have pledged to ensure that *every child and every parent will know that, whenever they have reason to celebrate, worry, or grieve, someone will notice, and someone will care.* Promising to that end that *no families will be left outside*, the communities are dedicated to such watchfulness and mutual assistance in all sectors of everyday life, so that *everyone*—all children—will be kept safe.

In effect, we are committed to fulfillment of each child's rights to personal security and, to that end, to a family environment that is supported sufficiently by the community at large to ensure that the child's basic needs are met in a setting that is safe, humane, and responsive. Meeting these goals requires the attention and dedication of all sectors of the community.

These ideas have been remarkably conflict-free. Usual "turf" issues have simply not appeared, notwithstanding fundamental differences that some of the organizations have with each other on other issues. Regardless of politics, theology, ethnicity, gender, class, and age, everyone believes that children deserve an environment in which they will grow up noticed and cared for as individuals, their families will be supported through a collective expression of good will, and that in the end children will live securely in dignity. The actions that have been taken by various community groups and volunteers to fulfill their collective obligation have been stunning not only in their quantity but also in the creativity, thoughtfulness, and passionate concern that they represent.

In a sense, the local culture for consideration of—and response to—children's interests now reflects a psychological mindedness that is attuned to the everyday experience of children themselves and of the adults who care for them. This wisdom, in turn, emanates from Strong Communities' straightforward expression of its normative underpinnings—of the moral principles at stake—in a commonsense manner that comports with community values and that enables citizens in general and organizational leaders in particular to understand how they can operationalize the principles in daily life in their own corner of the world.

Questions for Research

This approach—starting with inquiries about particular requisites for children's meaningful participation in community life in a way that the personality of each can emerge in safety and dignity—dramatically contrasts with the common readiness to "balance" one part of the community against another or, for that matter, one part of children's personalities against another. Ironically, the common tendency to enter into balancing tests about the application of rights to children opens a wide door to consideration of psychological evidence (Mnookin, 1985) about matters that would be settled in a more psychologically minded analysis. A particularly gross, but by no means a singular example, was the Supreme Court's approval of the constitutionality of preventive detention of juveniles because their "undoubtedly substantial" fundamental "interest in freedom from institutional restraints . . . must be qualified by the recognition that juveniles, unlike adults, are always in some form of custody" (*Schall v. Martin, 1984*, p. 266). Uncovering the fallacy of this logic should not have required deep inquiry into conditions in juvenile detention centers or the meaning to young people of being locked up.

Elsewhere (Melton, 2005c), I have argued that a rights-oriented program of research relates not only to the topics chosen but also to the process, the analysis, and the reporting of findings. For example, analysis of data should not rest simply on comparison across groups or time:

> The ordinary goal in children's services is to do greater good—to achieve higher quality inputs or better outcomes.
> In a rights-based agenda, however, the data should be analyzed in relation to their match with minimum standards (*entitlements*) derived from a normative inquiry. In that sense, the standard is not what is best or even good for children but instead what is morally required. Therefore, the aspiration in fulfilling rights usually is not just to do more but instead to do something different. The question that the researcher must address is whether a right is being met, not how much good is being done. (Melton, 2005c, p. 651)

Analogously, the research base on young people's reasoning about rights is now sufficiently rich and sufficiently consistent that it is time to change directions to focus more directly on the strategies that are most apt, directly or indirectly, to enable children to be meaningful participants in the community.[6] For example, in discussing Strong Communities, I alluded to approaches that may increase community sensitivity to such needs and, therefore, may enhance adults' interest in children's place in the community. Similar questions can be posed about children's own experience: "Under what circumstances do children feel like people? When do they feel that they are meaningful participants in the settings of which they are a part?" (Melton, 2005c, p. 651). In designing rights-sensitive settings for children, developmental and situational research on the meaning of key constructs in the Convention (e.g., dignity; exploitation; honor; privacy) can also be useful. Administrative data systems and evaluation research may also be helpful in determining whether rights-based thresholds are crossed.

The potential for such a program of research is extraordinary:

> The vision that is embedded in our work is grand, but it is also mundane. It applies our highest aspirations to the seemingly inconsequential actions of everyday life. Communities in which children feel safe, in which they are heard, in which they and their parents are treated with respect, and in which there are strong norms of caring and mutual assistance would be fine places to live.
>
> Scholarship that systematically increased understanding of such experiences and the conditions under which they occur would be profound indeed. It would also be likely to change public discourse—to achieve a resonance between the scientific enterprise and the most sensitive stirrings of human hearts. At a time when people—especially young people— feel ever more disconnected, such a goal is a formidable challenge, but its achievement would be stunning. Such an accomplishment would require scholarship that is fueled by moral fervor, structured by careful logic, guided by psychological sensitivity, sustained by creative policy analysis, and refined by systematic empirical study in a climate of openness and common concern. (Melton, 2005c, p. 656, citation omitted)

References

Bonnie, R. J. (1985). The efficacy of law as a paternalist instrument. In G. B. Melton (Ed.), *Nebraska Symposium on Motivation: Vol. 35. The law as a behavioral instrument* (pp. 131–211). Lincoln: University of Nebraska Press.

Bradbury, B., & Jantti, M. (1999). *Child poverty across industrialized countries*. Florence, Italy: UNICEF Innocenti Research Centre.

Cherney, I. D., & Shing, Y. L. (2008). Children's nurturance and self-determination rights: A cross-cultural perspective. *Journal of Social Issues, 64*, 835–856.

Convention on the Rights of the Child, G.A. Res. 44/25, 44 U.N. GAOR Supp. 49 at 167, U.N. Doc. A/44/49 (1989), *entered into force* Sept. 2, 1990.

---

[6]This program of action research should go beyond the scope of this special issue to include elementary-school-age children. Research suggests that a child's general political orientation—in essence, the attitudes that comprise the political culture—is well-established by the end of the primary grades (Melton & Limber, 1992).

Dahl, T. S. (R. L. Craig, trans.). (1987). *Women's law: An introduction to feminist jurisprudence*. Oslo: Norwegian University Press.

Daiute, C. (2008). The rights of children, the rights of nations. *Journal of Social Issues, 64*, 701–723.

Day, D., Peterson-Badali, M., & Ruck, M. D. (2006). The relationship between maternal attitudes and adolescents' attitudes toward their rights. *Journal of Adolescence, 29*, 193–207.

Episcopal Church. (1997). *Children's charter for the church*. Retrieved July 11, 2008, from http://www.episcopalchurch.org/documents/Child_Charter_8.5x11.pdf

Flanagan, C. A., Stout, M., & Gallay, L. (2008). It's my body and none of your business: Developmental differences in adolescents' perceptions of health. *Journal of Social Issues, 64*, 815–834.

Flekkøy, M. G., & Kaufman, N. H. (1997). *The participation rights of the child: Rights and responsibilities in family and society*. London: Jessica Kingsley.

Gallup, G. H., Jr. (2002, October 29). The death penalty: American views over time. *The Gallup Poll* (Tuesday Briefing Series, Commentary).

Horn, S., Szalacha, L. A., & Dill, K. (2008). Schooling, sexuality, and rights: An investigation of heterosexual students' social cognition regarding sexual orientation and the rights of gay and lesbian peers in school. *Journal of Social Issues, 64*, 791–813.

In re Gault, 387 U.S. 1 (1967).

International Covenant on Civil and Political Rights, G.A. Res. 2200A, 21 U.N. GAOR Supp. 16 at 52, U.N. Doc. A/6316 (1966), 999 U.N.T.S. 171, *entered into force* Mar. 23, 1976.

International Covenant on Economic, Social, and Cultural Rights, G.A. res. 2200A, 21 U.N.GAOR Supp. No. 16 at 49, U.N. Doc. A/6316 (1966), 993 U.N.T.S. 3, *entered into force* Jan. 3, 1976.

Jones, J. M. (2002, August 30). The death penalty. *The Gallup Poll* (Tuesday Briefing Series, Special Report).

Kamerman, S. B., & Kahn, A. J. (Eds.). (1991). *Child care, parental leave, and the under 3s: Policy innovation in Europe*. Westport, CT: Greenwood.

Kamerman, S. B., & Kahn, A. J. (Eds.). (1998). *Family change and family policies in Great Britain, Canada, New Zealand, and the United States*. New York: Oxford University Press.

Khoury-Kassabri, M., & Ben-Arieh, A. (2008). Adolescents' approach toward rights: Comparison between Christian, Jewish, and Muslim children in Jerusalem. *Journal of Social Issues, 64*, 881–901.

Levesque, R. J. R. (2008). Regardless of frontiers: Adolescents and the human right to information. *Journal of Social Issues, 64*, 725–747.

Lind, E. A., & Tyler, T. R. (1988). *The social psychology of procedural justice*. New York: Plenum.

Lyons, L. (2002, April 2). Teen verdict: Death penalty versus life in prison. *The Gallup Poll* (Tuesday Briefing Series).

Melton, G. B. (1983a). *Child advocacy: Psychological issues and interventions*. New York: Plenum.

Melton, G. B. (1983b). Minors and privacy: Are legal and psychological concepts compatible? *Nebraska Law Review, 62*, 455–493.

Melton, G. B. (1987a). Children, politics, and morality: The ethics of child advocacy. *Journal of Clinical Child Psychology, 16*, 357–367.

Melton, G. B. (1987b). The clashing of symbols: Prelude to child and family policy. *American Psychologist, 42*, 345–354.

Melton, G. B. (1992). The law is a good thing (Psychology is, too): Human rights in psychological jurisprudence. *Law and Human Behavior, 16*, 381–398.

Melton, G. B. (1993). Is there a place for children in the new world order? *Notre Dame Journal of Law, Ethics, and Public Policy, 7*, 491–532.

Melton, G. B. (1996). The child's right to a family environment: Why children's rights and family values are compatible. *American Psychologist, 51*, 1234–1238.

Melton, G. B. (1999). Parents *and* children: Legal reform to facilitate children's participation. *American Psychologist, 54*, 935–944.

Melton, G. B. (2002). Chronic neglect of family violence: More than a decade of reports to guide U.S. policy. *Child Abuse and Neglect, 26*, 569–586.

Melton, G. B. (2005a). Building humane communities respectful of children: The significance of the Convention on the Rights of the Child. *American Psychologist, 60*, 918–926.

Melton, G. B. (2005b). Mandated reporting: A policy without reason. *Child Abuse and Neglect, 29,* 9–18.

Melton, G. B. (2005c). Treating children like people: A framework for research and advocacy. *Journal of Clinical Child and Adolescent Psychology, 34,* 646–657.

Melton, G. B. (2006). *Background for a general comment on the right to participate: Article 12 and related provisions of the Convention on the Rights of the Child* (Report to the U.N. Committee on the Rights of the Child). Clemson, SC: Clemson University, Institute on Family and Neighborhood Life.

Melton, G. B. (in press). How Strong Communities restored my faith in humanity: Children *can* live in safety. In K. A. Dodge & D. L. Coleman (Eds.), *Community based prevention of child maltreatment.* New York: Guilford.

Melton, G. B., & Anderson, D. (2008). From safe sanctuaries to strong communities: The role of communities of faith in child protection. *Family and Community Health, 31,* 173–185.

Melton, G. B., & Holaday, B. J. (Eds.). (2008). Strong communities as safe havens for children [Special issue]. *Family and Community Health, 31*(2).

Melton, G. B., & Limber, S. P. (1992). What rights mean to children: Children's own views. In M. Freeman & P. Veerman (Eds.), *Ideologies of children's rights* (pp. 167–187). Dordrecht, The Netherlands: Martinus Nijhoff.

Melton, G. B., Petrila, J., Poythress, N. G., & Slobogin, C. (2007). *Psychological evaluations for the courts: A handbook for mental health professionals and lawyers* (3rd ed.). New York: Guilford.

Melton, G. B., & Saks, M. J. (1985). The law as an instrument of socialization and social structure. In G. B. Melton (Ed.), *Nebraska Symposium on Motivation: Vol. 33. The law as a behavioral instrument* (pp. 235–277). Lincoln: University of Nebraska Press.

Melton, G. B., Spaulding, W. J., & Lyons, P. M., Jr. (1998). *No place to go: The civil commitment of minors.* Lincoln: University of Nebraska Press.

Melton, G. B., & Sullivan, M. (1993). The concept of entitlement and its incompatibility with American legal culture. In M. A. Jensen & S. G. Goffin (Eds.), *Visions of entitlement: The care and education of America's children* (pp. 47–58). Albany: SUNY Press.

Mercer, J. A. (2005). *Welcoming children: A practical theology of childhood.* Saint Louis, MO: Chalice Press.

Mnookin, R. H. (1978). Children's rights: Beyond kiddie libbers and child savers. *Journal of Clinical Child Psychology, 7,* 163–167.

Mnookin, R. H. (Ed.). (1985). *In the interest of children: Advocacy, law reform, and public policy.* San Francisco: W. H. Freeman.

Nader, L. (1985). A user theory of legal change as applied to gender. In G. B. Melton (Ed.), *The law as a behavioral instrument* (pp. 1–33). Lincoln: University of Nebraska Press.

Office of the United Nations High Commissioner for Human Rights. (2007). *Legislative history of the Convention on the Rights of the Child.* New York & Geneva, Switzerland: United Nations.

Peterson-Badali, M., & Ruck, M. D. (2008). Studying children's perspectives on self-determination and nurturance rights: Issues and challenges. *Journal of Social Issues, 64,* 749–769.

Rogers, C. M., & Wrightsman, L. S. (1978). Attitudes toward children's rights: Nurturance or self-determination? *Journal of Social Issues, 34*(2), 59–68.

Roper v. Simmons, 543 U.S. 551 (2005).

San Antonio Independent School District v. Rodriguez, 411 U.S. 1 (1973).

Schall v. Martin, 467 U.S. 253 (1984).

Sherrod, L. (2008). Adolescents' perceptions of rights as reflected in their views of citizenship. *Journal of Social Issues, 64,* 771–790.

Sen, A. (2000). *Development as freedom.* New York: Anchor Books.

Smith, A. B. (Ed.). (2007). Children as social actors [Special issue]. *International Journal of Children's Rights, 18*(1).

Sokalski, H. J. (1993). Aims of the International Year of the Family. *Development, 1993*(4), 6–10.

Tinker v. Des Moines Independent School District, 393 U.S. 503 (1969).

Torney-Purta, J., Wilkenfeld, B., & Barber, C. (2008). How adolescents in 27 countries understand, support, and practice human rights. *Journal of Social Issues, 64,* 857–880.

Tremper, C. R. (1988). Respect for the human dignity of minors: What the Constitution requires. *Syracuse Law Review, 39*, 1293–1349.

Tyler, T. R., & Degogey, P. (1995). Community, family, and the social good: The psychological dynamics of procedural justice and social identification. In G. B. Melton (Ed.), *Nebraska Symposium on Motivation: Vol. 42. The individual, the family, and social good: Personal fulfillment in times of change* (Vol. 42, pp. 53–91). Lincoln: University of Nebraska Press.

United Methodist Church. (2004). *Globalization and human rights*. Resolution adopted by the General Conference.

Universal Declaration of Human Rights, G.A. Res. 217A, U.N. Doc A/810 at 71 (1948).

Williams, A. F. (Ed.). (2003). Graduated driver licensing [Special issue]. *Journal of Safety Research, 34*(1).

World Vision. (2002). *Protecting children: A biblical perspective on children's rights*. Morovia, CA: Author.

GARY B. MELTON is Professor of Psychology and Director of the Institute on Family and Neighborhood Life at Clemson University. The author of more than 300 publications, he has received awards for his contributions to research and public service from the American Psychological Association (three times), APA Divisions 18 and 37, the American Professional Society on Abuse of Children, Prevent Child Abuse America, and the American Orthopsychiatric Association. Past president of Childwatch International, he has traveled in almost 50 countries and territories, in most cases for research, consultation, or lecturing on issues related to children's rights.

Journal of Social Issues, Vol. 64, No. 4, 2008, pp. 921–923

Introduction to Kay Deaux's Lewin Award Address

Brenda N. Major
University of California

It gives me great pleasure to introduce Kay Deaux as the winner of the 2007 Kurt Lewin Award from the Society for the Psychological Study of Social Issues (SPSSI). Named after the late Kurt Lewin, a pioneer in the science of group dynamics and a founder of the SPSSI, this award is presented annually by the Society for "outstanding contributions to the development and integration of psychological research and social action." Kay Deaux's four decades of scholarship and leadership in the field of social psychology exemplify the spirit and goals of this award. Kay has consistently brought the highest standards of theoretical sophistication and empirical rigor to bear on understanding important social issues of our time. Her work illuminates the ways in which gendered contexts and gender stereotypes shape people's self-concepts and social interactions, how people negotiate multiple and sometimes conflicting social identities, and most recently, how social psychology can contribute to understanding the individual, group, and intergroup dynamics of immigration.

Like Kurt Lewin, Kay Deaux emphasizes the importance of considering the person in a social context—a context that can include the immediate situation, the larger social structures, and the cultural beliefs and social representations that shape our world. Behavior, in her view, is ultimately shaped by the interaction of self-processes and the social context. Thus, gender differences are fluid—present in some social contexts and absent in others. Identities are dynamic, influencing and being influenced by social contexts. Most recently, Kay has brought this perspective to bear on the topic of immigration, one of the hot button issues of our time. In her book *To Be an Immigrant,* Kay articulates how macro events in society, such as social representations of immigrants and immigration policies, become represented in the individual psyches of members of society through the mediating vehicle of social interactions. She also illustrates how social interactions mediate the impact of the actions and core values of individual immigrants on the larger society. Kurt Lewin, who was himself a Polish immigrant to the United States in the 1930s, would have approved both of her perspective, and of her selection for this award in his name.

No introduction, of course, is sufficient without some background information about the recipient. Kay's sojourn as an academic began in the Midwest, where she earned her BA from Northwestern University in 1963, and her PhD from the University of Texas in 1967. Shortly thereafter she moved to Purdue University, where she flourished academically among the cornfields for 17 years before following her heart to New York, where she is currently a Distinguished Professor of Psychology and Women's Studies at the City University of New York Graduate Center. After 20 years as a New Yorker, I think it is safe to say that Kay has at last shed her Midwestern roots.

Kay showed her promise as a scholar early, winning First Prize in the Graduate Student Paper Competition from the American Association of Public Opinion Research in 1967. She went on to receive the Gordon Allport Intergroup Relations Prize from SPSSI in 1986, the Carolyn Wood Sherif Award from Division 35 of APA in 1987, the Heritage Research Award from Division 35 of APA in 1993, and the CWP Leadership Award from APA in 2001. Kay has also been a Visiting Scholar at the Russell Sage Foundation and twice a Fellow at the Center for Advanced Studies in the Behavioral Sciences.

Kay has been president of nearly every major professional society associated with social psychology in the United States. She has been president of the Midwestern Psychological Association, the Eastern Psychological Association, the Society for Personality and Social Psychology, the Society of Experimental Social Psychology, the American Psychological Society, and the Society for the Psychological Study of Social Issues. Recently, she co-organized a conference on immigration in Toronto, sponsored jointly by SPSSI and the European Association for Experimental Social Psychology.

Given this lifetime of success and honors, it is easy to forget that when Kay started in the field, she was a pioneer. Women were few and far between in the academy and the belief that they did not belong there was widespread. This social context undoubtedly shaped Kay's career and identity and contributed to her interest in how the social context influences gender differences in social behavior and gender stereotyping. Kay became an inspiring role model for numerous young women entering the field, including me. I first met Kay when I was a graduate student at Miami University of Ohio. At that time there were no women on the faculty at Miami University, and Kay came to speak as part of a two-day conference on women in psychology, organized by the female graduate students. My encounter with Kay at that conference changed my life, prompting me to transfer programs from Miami University to Purdue to study with Kay. I will be forever grateful for her wisdom, guidance, and inspiration.

BRENDA MAJOR is Professor of Psychology at the University of California, Santa Barbara. She is the author of more than 120 articles in refereed journals and edited books, and co-edited the book *The Psychology of Legitimacy*. She is the recipient of the Gordon Allport Intergroup Relations Prize from the Society for the Psychological Study of Social Issues in 1986 (with Kay Deaux) and again in 1988 (with Jennifer Crocker). She has served as President of the Society of Personality and Social Psychology and on the Executive Committees of the Society of Experimental Social Psychology and the International Society for Self and Identity. She has also served as Associate Editor of *Personality and Social Psychology Bulletin* and *Group Processes and Intergroup Relations*. Dr. Major's research centers on psychological resilience—how people cope with, adapt to, and overcome adverse life circumstances, especially those associated with stigma, prejudice and discrimination.

Journal of Social Issues, Vol. 64, No. 4, 2008, pp. 925–943

To Be an American: Immigration, Hyphenation, and Incorporation

Kay Deaux*

Graduate Center, City University of New York

Central to many immigration debates in the United States, past and present, are questions about what it means to be an American. In this article, I address three forms of this question: (a) What is an immigrant? (b) What is an American? and (c) What is a hyphenated American. Answers to these questions can vary, depending upon whether one is taking the perspective of the observer/host or of the immigrant himself or herself. Data suggest that neither unidimensionality nor simple dichotomy are appropriate frames for analyzing national identity.

As I look back at my career in social psychology, I can see that I have always been interested in social categories—as they are used by others to locate us on the social map and as we use them ourselves to relate to the collective groupings that constitute a society or a nation or a species. For many years, beginning in the early 1970s, gender was the focus of my interest. After I moved to New York City in 1987, other categories moved to the foreground for me—in particular, ethnicity, as it is expressed by the many immigrant groups who populate the city

━━━━━━━━━━

*Correspondence concerning this article should be addressed to Kay Deaux, CUNY Graduate Center, 365 Fifth Avenue, New York, NY 10016 [e-mail: kdeaux@gc.cuny.edu].

The substance of this article was first presented on August 18, 2007, at the convention of the American Psychological Association in San Francisco in conjunction with the receipt of the Kurt Lewin Memorial Award. I am grateful to Nida Bikmen, Sam Glucksberg, Sara McClelland, and Shaun Wiley for their comments on earlier versions of this article.

and who demonstrate in their daily lives the fluctuations, dynamics, and challenges of ethnic and national categories.

I introduced some of these issues in my presidential address to SPSSI (Deaux, 2006a). Here I continue that story, focusing particularly on questions of what it means to be an American and how immigrants are part of that larger discussion. As I noted in my 2006 paper, this is a topic in which Lewin himself was deeply interested, specifically with reference to immigration to Israel, both as a general phenomenon and as a personal possibility (Bargal, 1998). Had Lewin lived longer, I suspect that the psychological analysis of immigration would be much more developed than it now is.

The Immigration Debate: A Contemporary Version

In the United States today, it is virtually impossible to pick up a newspaper, turn on the radio or television news or talk show, or eavesdrop on conversations at local diners and coffee houses without encountering talk about immigration. During the 2007 legislative session of the U.S. Congress, an immigration bill was debated, defeated, reintroduced, and defeated again as the Senate and House of Representatives struggled to find some common ground in addressing the quagmire that U.S. immigration policy has become. The 2008 presidential campaigns have also struggled with the topic, often avoiding discussion because of the conflicting and frequently impassioned views that exist within as well as between the two major parties.

The voices of opposition and fear of immigration as a threat to the well-being of the United States appear to have gained the larger megaphone in current debates. The historian Samuel Huntington (2004) epitomized these voices of despair and his position is clearly marked in the title of his book: *Who are we? The challenges to America's national identity.* Within the covers of this book, fears of Latino immigration are particularly strong, as Huntington talks of a "demographic *reconquista*" of parts of the United States (2004, p. 221), "the possibility of a defacto split between a predominantly Spanish-speaking American and English-speaking America" (p. 243), and major threats to "the cultural and ... political integrity of the United States" (p. 243). Scary thoughts!

Stanley Renshon (2005) developed a similar theme in deploring what he termed *The 50% American*—and adding as a politically charged subtitle, *Immigration and national identity in an age of terror.* Renshon's focus is on issues related to dual citizenship, as it exists not only in legal status but in psychological realities; his central claim is that multiple national attachments are seriously problematic, compromising a person's loyalty and commitment and sense of patriotism to, in this case, the United States.

The immigration debates bring out a variety of concerns, both explicit and implicit, that reflect conflicting values and assumptions about concepts such as multiculturalism and diversity, nationalism and patriotism, identity and racism

(Deaux, 2006b). Here I want to address some of the key issues that arise in this area—questions concerning what it means to be an immigrant, what it means to be an American, and whether it is possible to have loyalty to more than one culture. These are questions that require us to consider both the perspective of the immigrant and the perspective of the host, positions that are not always in synchrony with one another, as my analysis will show.

In discussing these issues, I focus primarily, but not exclusively, on the United States situation. This in no way is meant to suggest that immigration is primarily a U.S. issue. Throughout the world, the movement of people from one country or continent to another is a major phenomenon of the 21st century and issues of ethnic and national identity, as well as loyalty and patriotism, are ubiquitous. Thus one could just as easily ask what it means to be a German, a citizen of France, or a Chilean. Specific historical and political events and contexts will necessarily influence the formulation of answers to these alternative questions. Yet I would argue that the general processes that I consider here have considerable relevance to other countries as well.

Immigration Debates of History

In contemporary immigration debates, we can hear a replay of many early 20th century themes. Renshon harks back to the Civil War for a parallel to what he perceives as a conflict between basic values, as he sees American culture being bombarded by the spectre of those who would recognize diversity rather than endorse "*E Pluribus Unum.*" And indeed, during that era, concerns about the ethnic composition of American society were often contested. These challenges more often took place at local and state levels than at the federal level, as Zolberg (2006) observed, because federal power was more constrained under the states-right norms that were part of the slavery compromises. That well-recognized chronicler of U.S. society, Alexis de Toqueville, who had originally seen the United States as a unified Anglo American people, worried later in his life about the consequences of incorporating both free Blacks and Europeans, the latter driven to the United States by "misfortune and misconduct" (quoted in Zolberg, 2006, p. 126). De Toqueville predicted that the increasing presence of these minority groups in the large cities of America (pointing primarily to New York and Philadelphia at that time) would cause the demise of the cities unless federal armed forces took control. Though violence and police intervention are surely part of the city history (though not necessarily related to immigration), by and large this De Toquevillian prediction seems to have rather badly missed its mark.

Debates about who should be allowed in this country and what laws should be formulated gained national momentum in the early decades of the 20th century. In the late 1800s and early 1900s, some restrictions were placed on the immigrant pool, for example, the adoption of a literacy requirement and the exclusion of certain categories of would-be immigrants, such as Asians and people with some forms of mental or physical disability (Zolberg, 2006). With the immigration bills of 1924 and 1927, however, overall quotas were imposed that sharply limited accessibility across the board.

Then as now, questions as to whether immigrants should maintain distinctive cultural patterns or whether they should melt into a single American prototype were central to the debate. And then as now, underlying and precipitating many of these debates about blending were the demographic shifts in *who* was coming to the United States. Thus the study of immigration offers material for a century-long time-series analysis. Data from the earlier periods are largely archival and anecdotal, but nonetheless informative. In current times, with a highly sophisticated repertoire of theories and methods at our disposal, we are poised as a field to make major contributions to scientific understanding and policy formulation in this critically important time in history.

Basic Psychological Questions: Conceptions, Misconceptions, and Data

This discussion is framed in terms of three basic questions—questions about social categories that are fundamental to the immigration debate. These three categorically focused questions are:

- What is an immigrant?
- What is an American?
- What is a hyphenated American?

Each of these questions is central to the contemporary rhetoric of immigration. Yet like most social categories, terms such as *immigrant* or *American* are fuzzy sets with indefinite boundaries, and their definitions can fluctuate with the position of the speaker (Deaux & Philogène, 2001). In the case of immigration, the opinions of those who are themselves members of the category of immigrant, for example, can differ sharply from the views of those who were born in the country and look on from the outside (although they too may be influenced by family histories of immigration). Further, for psychologists these questions are not resolved by simple demographic facts. Often the answers lurk below the surface in a web of unstated values and unexamined prejudices that must be explored and interpreted if we are to contribute to the policy debates. In this analysis I will at various points consider the perspectives of both immigrants and native-born residents, looking at points of convergence and discrepancy as well as variability in the meanings given to these pivotal categories.

These three questions, in turn, lay the groundwork for a further discussion, one that looks beyond the categories to outcomes, to process, and to future possibilities. One way to characterize this discussion is with another deceptively simple question: Who is a good citizen? More broadly, I want to think about how we define citizenship in a globally interdependent and mobile world; how loyalties

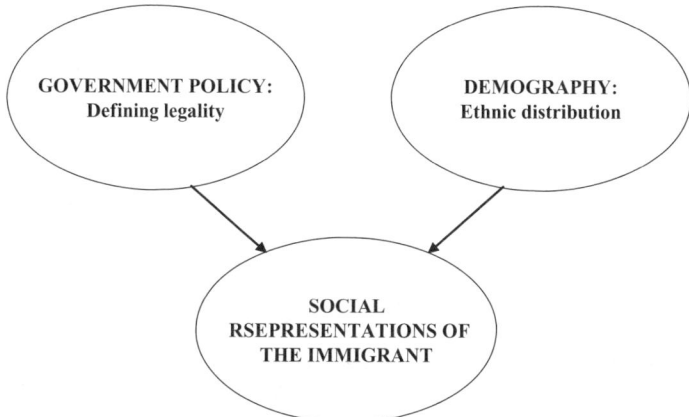

Fig. 1. Constructing the representation of immigrants.

and ties to family, culture, and country can co-exist; and what the implications of these questions are for the future—both for our societies and for the ways in which we as social scientists can contribute to the policies that define those societies.

What Is an Immigrant?

In its most basic, denotative sense, the term *immigrant* refers to someone who is born in a country other than the one in which she or he is now residing. Yet like all of the other terms that make me lose sleep some nights, when used in common discourse *immigrant* takes on a varied set of meanings and values. Such is the nature of social representations, of which immigrant and immigration surely qualify in our contemporary world.

Two of the major aspects at work in the socially constructed concept of immigrant are (a) issues of legal status and government policies that affect category definition, and (b) characteristics of immigrant groups that shape the social representation of the category. Figure 1 is similar to one that I have used previously (Deaux, 2006a, 2006b), depicting the interrelationship between policy, demography, and social representations of immigration. In using this image now, I focus first on legal status as a factor that links policy to social representations, setting parameters for whom the society considers to be a member of the category. Secondly, characteristics of immigrant groups themselves—both real and perceived—are an issue in analyzing the link between demographics and representations. Let me begin with the issue of legal status.[1]

---

[1]Local context is critically important in analyzing the influence of legal status, as each country has its unique history and policies regarding immigration. This discussion centers on the United States, although with occasional examples in other national contexts.

In the United States, the concept of illegal immigration can be traced back to the mid 1920s, when the first broad-reaching restrictions on immigration were put into place. Thus immigrants arriving before the 1920s (those ancestors often held up as the "good immigrants" in contemporary debate) were in a sense neither legal nor illegal, in terms of official laws and policy, because the category itself was not particularly salient. The country was founded on the arrival of immigrants and their right to be here was not seriously questioned. After the legislation of the mid 1920s, a concern with legal status and the exercise of deportation practices became more common (Massey, Durand, & Malone, 2002) and now, at the beginning of the 21st century, the concept is central to the political debate. Although actual numbers are difficult to verify, a reasonable estimate is that 11–12 million immigrants are currently living in the United States without appropriate legal status. This represents approximately 30% of first-generation immigrants (Passel, 2005). In contrast, survey data show that Americans generally believe that a majority of immigrants have entered the country illegally. In a 1993 survey, for example, 68% of those questioned believed that a majority of immigrants in the United States were illegal (Lapinski, Peltola, Shaw, & Yang, 1997), and I suspect that number would be higher today.

This parsing of the concept of immigrant has some interesting implications. Many people who speak out strongly against illegal immigration will at the same time claim to be highly supportive of the "legal" immigrant, often pointing to ancestors who came before immigration policy had established the clear categories.[2] In this partitioning we can see something akin to symbolic racism, in which blatant negative evaluations are disclaimed while policies that are seen as favoring the targeted group are rejected for presumably legitimate reasons.

Another facet of the representation of immigrant concerns the different meanings attached to the terms *undocumented* and *illegal*, as they are used in the United States (Deaux & Wiley, 2007). Demographically, both refer to people who have entered the country without going through official procedures—either because they entered legally on a visa but then remained in the country after the visa had expired, or because they initially circumvented the legal entry points. The two terms have quite different connotations, however, and are used by different segments of the population to convey different political sentiments. *Illegal* suggests moral censure and invokes accusations of criminality on the part of the immigrant. *Undocumented*, a term more often used by immigrant rights groups and immigrants themselves, constrains the meaning to bureaucratic procedures, making the attribution more situational than dispositional.[3] Although I have not done a content analysis, my impression is that *illegal* is the term used more often in current legislative debates, with the expected attributional connotations that we could predict.

---

[2] I thank Nida Bikmen for this observation.
[3] In France, there is a similar term, *les sans-papiers*.

A related example of how language can influence perceptions of immigrants comes from recent work by Victoria Esses and her colleagues, this in the Canadian context (Esses, Veenvliet, Hodson, & Mihic, 2008). Using material taken verbatim from an editorial in a Canadian newspaper, Esses et al. showed how the use of derogatory language (e.g., describing political refugees as queue jumpers, liars, and cheaters) stimulates emotional reactions such as lack of admiration and contempt, leading to a dehumanization of the refugee and less favorable attitudes toward the country's refugee policy. In contrast, an editorial constructed by the experimenters that omitted the derogatory terms and used more neutral situation-based descriptions of refugee status yielded significantly more favorable views of both immigrants and government policy. Language matters!

As the right side of Figure 1 suggests, demographic factors also shape the social representations that emerge in a society, particularly as those images are held by the resident population. In the case of immigration, a major factor is the ethnic distribution of the immigrant groups. In the early 20th century, it was the shift from a primarily English-speaking immigrant population to a southern and Eastern European base that flamed the immigration debates, eventually resulting in the restrictive policies of the 1920s. Similarly, much of the current debate can be seen as stemming from the dramatic geographical shift of sending countries. Immigrants from the developing countries of the world (defined as Latin America, the Caribbean, Asia, and Africa) have increased from approximately 43% when the 1965 immigration reform bill was passed to 75% now (Zolberg, 2006). It is Asians and Latin Americans who are the face of the new immigration, and for many native-born residents, this is a very different face from theirs or their ancestors. Not surprisingly, surveys and questionnaires repeatedly show differences in how different immigrant groups are evaluated, typically finding that white groups are evaluated more favorably and groups of color evaluated less favorably, though the strength of these differences and in some cases the patterns depend upon the ethnicity of the respondent (Deaux, 2006; Mizrahi, 2005). I will return to this point later.

What Is an American?

The second question addresses national identity: What does it mean to be an American (or any other nationality) and how are geographical definitions translated into psychological terms? As Reicher and Hopkins have observed, it is a "myth that there is always a single valid definition for any given identity" (2001, p. ix). Moreover, as Reicher and Hopkins argue persuasively in their account of self and nation, national identity is a dynamic project both by those who claim the identity and by those who observe the claims of others, and clear agenda are at work in both cases.

These competing claims and multiple definitions assume high profile in discussions of immigration. Both for those born in the country and for those who

Table 1. Characteristics of a "True American"

Item	Mean rating
Vote in elections	5.61
Respect America's political institutions and laws	5.29
Treat people of all races and backgrounds equally	5.28
Try to get ahead on your own effort	5.06
Feel American	4.96
Be able to speak English	4.69
Have American citizenship	4.58
Be patriotic	3.85
Defend America when it is criticized	3.71
Have lived in America most of one's life	3.37
Have been born in America	2.54
Believe in God	1.89
Be a Christian	1.56

Note. Ratings were made on a 7-point scale.
Adapted from Devos and Banaji (2005).

have made the typically arduous journey to come to the United States, potentially to take on American citizenship, being an American is imbued with meaning, with affect, and with behavioral implications.

Can we begin to explicate what those meanings and implications are? Devos and Banaji (2005) provided one starting point, from the perspective of a select group of American citizens. They offered students at Yale University a list of criteria and asked the students to rate the importance of each for being a "true American." As shown on Table 1, the most highly endorsed item was voting behavior, followed by respect for the country's political institutions/laws and equal treatment of people from all backgrounds and races. Having been born in America was rated relatively low.

These ratings represent the views of only one segment of the society—in this case, a relatively privileged, perhaps relatively liberal set of young people. Other segments of society might well show different priorities. In the Devos and Banaji data, for example, language usage—specifically, speaking English—was rated only moderately important (4.7 on a 7-point scale). Yet in the current political discourse, this attribute seems to carry much heavier weight. As a retired Navy man in Colorado told a *NYTimes* reporter:

> "Portugal is Portugal because of the Portuguese language: Spain is Spanish; France is—God knows—France is French; Germany is Germany, all because of language." (Johnson, 2007)

Holding in abeyance the fact that the United States was a country of immigrants from its inception, in contrast to the more homogeneous histories of Portugal,

Spain, Germany, and France, this line of argument suggests that not only do immigrants to the United States not speak English when they arrive in the country—an issue highlighted by Huntington (2004) in his analysis of threats to national identity—but that they are averse to learning the language and that over time, nothing changes.

Two comments are in order here, one anecdotal and the other based on more extensive empirical data. Contemporary pundits often contend that what they see as the bad traits of immigrants now are in sharp contrast to an idealized portrait of immigrants from generations back (often with reference to a hardier, more responsible immigrant stock from which they themselves are descended). Yet as Foner (2000, 2005) has so convincingly argued, then and now are often not so very different. As the anecdotal support of this argument where language is concerned, I need only to turn to memories of my own Finnish grandmother. She came to the United States at the beginning of the 20th century speaking no English, and she died in the United States 50 years later knowing very little more; her life was spent in Finnish enclaves of church and friends, resisting all initiatives to become an English-speaking American. Were the Finns of the early 1900s the Chinese and Mexicans of today?

Yet perhaps this single case is no more representative of its time than of our current times. Virtually all recent studies of immigrant language usage report a steady increase in the acquisition and practice of English over generations. Portes and Rumbaut (2001) observed that knowledge of English was nearly universal in a second-generation sample of high school students from Miami/Ft. Lauderdale and San Diego, and that preference for speaking English was extremely high as well. Similarly, López (1999) reported data from Los Angeles showing that over 90% of third-generation immigrants (both Mexican and Asian) speak English very well or speak only English. Thus, although it is certainly true that many immigrants arrive in the United States not knowing English, it is definitely not true that the majority does not want and does not learn English over time. (In our global economy, one might also want to compare these statistics to an account of how many Americans are capable of speaking a language other than English!)[4]

Less often explicit in discussions of what it means to be American, but no less relevant, I would argue, are issues of color. Like obscenity, people claim to know an American when they see one—and what they see is often color-coded. Referring again to the Devos and Banaji (2005) work, students in their study explicitly expressed beliefs that all groups of Americans are equal. At the same time, however, they showed evidence of variable standards for inclusion. Asian Americans and African Americans, although described as being born in the United States, living in the United States, and having U.S. citizenship, were judged on

---

[4]As Zolberg (2006) notes, the concerns about Mexicans on the basis of language differences echo some of the religious-based fears expressed about Irish immigration 150 years ago.

both explicit and implicit measures (but more strongly on the latter) to be less American than were whites. The strong conclusion that the authors draw from their work is that "To be American is to be White" (2005, p. 463).

Yet the Devos and Banaji (2005) data also show that perspective is important when one attempts to define the prototypical American. For White Americans, the criterion seems most clear and reflects hegemonic values, whereby to be American is to be White. The Asian Americans that Devos and Banaji included in one study appeared to adopt a similar criterion. In contrast, African American students were not willing to use color as the basis of inclusion and associated American with Black and White equally. The Devos and Banaji study did not deal specifically with impressions of immigrants, although a substantial proportion of their Asian American and a few of their African American participants were first-generation immigrants. Their results might suggest, however, that some immigrants would also use different criteria for defining who is most American. Reaffirming the words of Reicher and Hopkins (2001), there is surely not a single valid definition for national identity.

What Is a Hyphenated American?

Thus far, my argument may suggest that I am pitting two categories against each other—American versus immigrant. Such a dichotomy echoes much of the current debate, not only in the United States but in many countries of the world as well. Often in Europe, for example, the dichotomy is framed in terms of a national identity versus a Muslim identity, again with the implication that it is difficult if not impossible to have allegiance to both (Verkuyten & Yildiz, 2007). Yet while I believe that such zero-sum thinking does not accurately characterize the internal state of the immigrant, it is often characteristic of the views from outside.

Often an apparent need for simplicity drives people to demand one category or another in their attempt to position others. Multiplicity between different types of categories—for example, seeing another person as both a man and a Republican, or as an accountant and a Catholic—is somewhat easier for observers to envision than is multiplicity within a single category. Yet even in the former case, stereotypical beliefs about the required attributes of a particular category can cause discordance in the observer, as in the perceived conflicts between work and family, particularly for mothers (Biernat, Crosby, & Williams, 2004), or doubts as to whether members of certain religious groups are able to be president of the United States, raised by John F. Kennedy's candidacy 50 years ago and Mitt Romney's presidential aspirations in 2008.

The outsider's acceptance of multiple identities when two are in the same or closely related categories, as is raised in the case of ethnicity, nationality, and immigration, is more contentious. Here many take the position that an either-or decision is the only acceptable resolution. For Stanley Renshon, as a contemporary example, the "50% American" is oxymoronic and dangerous, just as it was for

Theodore Roosevelt some 100 years ago when he said, "There is no room in this country for hyphenated Americanism. . . .There is no such thing as a hyphenated American who is a good American. The only man who is a good American is the man who is an American and nothing else" (Roosevelt, October 12, 1915). Or consider the words of another U.S. president, Woodrow Wilson (as quoted by Sanchez, 2005): "Any man who carries a hyphen about with him carries a dagger that he is ready to plunge into the vitals of this Republic." These beliefs in intractable dichotomies have a long history, suggesting a pervasive aspect of human thought.

Biracial or multiple identity is not just an issue of immigration: intermarriage between native Americans and early white settlers, for example, set the stage for this issue in the United States, and the sociological interest in intermarriage across the Black–White divide, as well as among other ethnic groups, have kept the issue salient over generations. And indeed, the sociological realities of multiple lineages led the U.S. Census bureau to allow people to check multiple ethnic categories in the 2000 Census. Thus, there is some inconsistency in the discourse, between those who would require unidimensionality and those who acknowledge more fluidity.

Combinations of two ethnic strains, while troublesome to some, are not the major source of volatility and contention where immigration is concerned, although immigration is a source of mixed ethnicity in the society. Rather the concern relates to beliefs about *national* identity: what does it mean to be an American and what is expected of those who are, or who wish to be, citizens of the country? Here is where issues of patriotism and nationalism come to the fore, as flags are waved and flag pins are displayed. One cannot be loyal to two masters, it is argued by some, and any evidence of adherence to a culture of origin is assumed to mean disloyalty to the country of residence.[5]

The argument goes deeper than just the relative importance of two identity categories, however. Beyond the belief that greater importance of one means lesser importance of another lies a meaning system that often defines the two identities as incompatible. That is, from the observer's perspective what it means to be Chinese or Mexican or Dominican is sometimes seen as qualitatively different and perhaps incompatible with what it means to be American. Thus a person's allegiance to the country of origin is threatening not just because one is more important than the other, but also because one is thought to hold values that are incompatible with American standards.

Against this backdrop of assumed dichotomies and unidimensionality, we need to look very carefully at the view from inside. Particularly for those of us

---

[5]It is interesting to compare the United States to Western Europe in this regard. As Foner and Alba (2008) have cogently discussed, the key question for most Western Europeans is the perceived incompatibility between religion, and in particular Islam, and national identification. In the United States, in contrast, religious commitments and differences are more readily tolerated and not considered inconsistent with national identification.

who are interested in identity as it is subjectively experienced, it is clear that a great many people in this country embrace two or more identity categories, combining them in some form in the same living body. What is the experience of biculturalism? Do people move back and forth between sides of the hyphen, enacting a human form of teeter totter as they respond to different identity domains and influences? Or is there a more complicated pattern at work, both structurally and dynamically, for people who have the capacity to draw from more than one identity field?

A mounting body of work from a number of investigators suggests that people are creating new forms of identity that are internally complex but still coherent, and that are at the same time highly tuned to situational demands and opportunities (Wiley & Deaux, 2008). Phinney and Devich-Navarro (1997) offered an early version of this view with their discussion of two forms of integrated identities (building on Berry's earlier framework), namely blending and alternating. A classic statement of blending can be seen in this interview conducted by Wiley (2005) with a second-generation immigrant whose father is Mexican and mother is American. "For me, it's kind of like a blending...Cause I am mixed, I feel like I am half and half, like I have this part of me that is very Americanized and I have another part of me that is actually seeking the Mexican." Yet as Wiley (2005) and an increasing number of other investigators have shown (e.g., Itzigsohn, in press; Itzigsohn, Giorguli, & Vasquez, 2005; Verkuyten & DeWolf, 2002), this static choice does not really capture the dynamic nature of bicultural identities. A more accurate depiction is one that allows for the person to draw upon available resources as the situation demands or allows. By this view, identities are, as Verkuyten and DeWolf (2002) described, "interactional accomplishments that are sensitive to potential criticisms and justifications."

A statement from a second-generation Dominican immigrant interviewed by Jose Itzigsohn (in press) is illustrative: "Depends on who I am talking to, who the audience is. If my audience are Government officials, I am Latino. If I am talking to a friend, I am Dominican. If I am talking to my neighbor who happens to be Caucasian, I tell him I was born in New York City and that I am also a citizen. So it depends on who I am relating to."

A solid body of research on bicultural identity has developed in recent years, showing both the ways in which two identities may be combined (Benet-Martínez & Haritatos, 2005) and the ways in which specific situations can activate one or another identity, often termed frame switching (Hong, Morris, Chiu, & Benet-Martínez, 2000). Westernized Chinese students in Hong Kong, for example, make more situational attributions when Chinese culture is primed than when American culture is primed (Hong et al., 2000). Bicultural people of Greek descent living in the Netherlands were less positive about personal traits and more positive about family integrity and friendship when Greek, in contrast to Dutch, culture was made salient (Verkuyten & Pouliasi, 2006).

These alterations in perspective are not totally dependent on circumstances, however. Rather, as Verkuyten and Pouliasi (2006) have shown, strength of ethnic identification is a partial mediator of the relationship between cultural frame and attitudes, a finding that alerts us to the important variations among bicultural people in their ways of dealing with multiplicity. Further complexity can be anticipated if we deconstruct the concept of identification, recognizing the multiple aspects that may not always covary (Ashmore, Deaux, & McLaughlin-Volpe, 2004; Wiley & Deaux, 2008). Thus, a simple measure of strength of identification with one or another ethnic group may not be fully informative of the degree to which social networks are distinct or integrated, or the degree to which the person engages in behaviors typically associated with one group or the other. Clearly, the zone of the hyphen for the hyphenated American is a territory rich in meaning and dynamic in process, belying efforts to impose simple categorical systems.

Cultural Combinations and National Loyalties

It appears that immigrants are able to deal, either simultaneously or sequentially, with more than one category of membership. The question thus shifts from one of whether to one of how—how can multiple identities be managed? Further, taking into account the outside as well as the inside view, how can the immigrant identity be managed in such a way that it is accepted by those in the host country whose categorical perspective is less flexible? Although no single formula can be applied to the immigrant experience, two general conditions can be said to shape the experience and the resolution of multiple loyalties. One is the broad context in which the immigrant lives; the second is the specific characteristics of the group itself, vis-a-vis the dominant group.

Adopting an international perspective on context, we know that countries differ in their histories and policies with regard to immigration. Some countries, such as the United States and Canada, have their foundations in immigrant movement; for others, as is the case in many European countries, immigration is a more recent phenomenon. Research by Berry, Phinney, Sam, and Vedder (2006) found that the correlations between self-reported ethnic identity and national identity differ in these two contexts. In societies that have traditionally been a site for large-scale immigration, the association between ethnic and national identity tends to be positive or to approach zero; in contrast, the relationship is largely negative and seemingly incompatible in countries in which immigration has fewer historical roots.

Even within a single country, the conditions for combination can vary substantially. In some cities in the United States, New York City being one, the term "majority minority" is being used to describe the demography of a place in which nonwhite groups outnumber the traditional white population (Kasinitz, Mollenkopf, & Waters, 2002), a condition that now characterizes almost one third of the most populous counties in the United States and nearly one in 10 of all counties (Roberts, 2007). Accordingly, the normative position in these cities may be to consider a combination of ethnicity and Americanism as standard operating practice, consistent with the variability expressed by the Dominican immigrant quoted earlier.

A second important factor is group specific and concerns the degree to which members of a particular group are more or less accepted by the receiving society. Here experiences of discrimination and the insidious color line are key elements. I again refer to the work of Jose Itzigsohn. In his work with Dominican immigrants, Itzigsohn finds that "being American is consistently associated with the themes of rights, freedom, and opportunity." (Itzigsohn, in press). As elaborated by one of his respondents, a man who served in the U.S. army: "Being American is being proud of the freedom we have...It's just being able to do things that a lot of people can't...Here, everybody complains, but we have it so easy compared to other countries so I'm glad we have it that way, and I'm proud of that." At the same time, while expressing these patriotic views of the country in which he was born and in whose army he served, this same man identifies himself primarily as Dominican. At issue here, as it is for many immigrants from the Caribbean, Africa, and parts of Latin American, is color. Many Dominican immigrants, as a case in point, believe that most Americans see them first as black, and as a result they feel that they "can't claim Americanness because they are not white." (Itzigsohn, in press, p. 24 of chapter "Identity and Incorporation").

Portes and Rumbaut (2001) found that experiences with discrimination can strengthen an immigrant's ethnic identification. In a study of second-generation teenagers, these authors pointed to a phenomenon that they call *reactive identification*, wherein the teenagers became *more* strongly identified with the ethnic or national origin of their parents. It is notable that this shift occurs in spite of the increased facility with and use of English. Whereas language may be functionally useful, it is experiences with discrimination, the authors posit, that intensify the identification with ethnic origin.

As the Portes and Rumbaut (2001) data suggested, generation is an important part of the immigrant story, and a factor that operates in more complex ways than earlier straight-line assimilation models predicted. Here is a place where psychology has much to contribute in terms of elucidating the processes and mechanisms that underlie these more complex pathways. Generation, in this case, should not be considered only in developmental terms that might compare children to their parents or grandparents. In our own work, we are finding significant differences between groups who are equivalent in age but who differ in their immigration history, either being born in the United States to immigrant parents (second generation) or being immigrants themselves (first generation). We have observed differences in performance on academic tests in stereotype threat conditions (Deaux et al., 2007), in patterns of self-esteem (Wiley, Perkins, & Deaux, 2008), and in the endorsement of political ideology and orientations to collective action (Deaux, Reid, Martin, & Bikman, 2006). In each case, we see evidence that second-generation immigrants are responding to the context in which they live with a different set of strategies and beliefs than are those who have arrived in the country more recently. These are not differences that can be explained by historical immigration patterns or by the inherent motivation of immigrants (given that the first generation in our studies typically came as children and had limited input in the decision to migrate). Rather, they are vivid evidence of the ways in which people respond at a more immediate, micro level to the obstacles and opportunity structures that they encounter. We also find numerous differences between immigrant generations that are associated with ethnic group, particularly as those groups are characterized by color of skin. Again, these differences signal not inherent characteristics, particularly as they differ noticeably between generations, but rather they serve as markers for what we must assume are very different experiences, often involving discrimination and limitations to opportunity.

Recognizing that issues of identity and citizenship need to be understood against this background of differential experience, I'd like to turn to the more general question of multiple loyalties and the relationship between individual identity and what is termed transnationalism, that is, activities that cross the boundaries between country of residence and country of origin (see Levitt & Waters, 2002). Here the acceptability of multiple categories, from the perspective of the observer, becomes more charged with issues of national loyalty and patriotism and the question of who can be a good citizen of the country.

As discussed earlier, many people appear to hold a zero-sum belief that it is not possible to identify with or be loyal to two groups simultaneously (and even short-term sequentiality is somewhat suspect). Stanley Renshon states the position in the following way: "Consider [a model] in which sending money 'home' represents the lowest level of American community attachment" (2005, p. 9). Clearly, this statement suggests a unidimensional, bipolar model in which one must choose to be loyal to one or the other group. Samuel Huntington expresses a belief in this same model when he says that "The ultimate criterion of assimilation is the extent to which immigrants identify with the U.S. as a country . . . *and correspondingly reject* loyalty to other countries and their values and cultures" (Huntington, 2004, p. 241; emphasis added).

In both statements, the either-or position is clearly articulated and implies that transnationlism in any form would be undesirable. But do these statements have grounding in scientific fact? Does devotion to one's country of origin preclude loyalty to the nation of residence (and in many cases citizenship)? Although the evidence is still emerging, there is much to suggest that a zero-sum model does not fit the data.

Consider the following examples. A study of first-generation immigrants from Colombia, El Salvador, and the Dominican Republic found that those who have *more* exposure to U.S. society are *more* likely to engage in transnational activities such as participating in a home country association or sending money for projects in their town of origin (Itzigsohn & Giorguli-Saucedo, 2005). In another study of African Americans and Latinas in two cities on the West Coast of the United States, beliefs that one's ethnic group is valued in and of itself was associated with *more* rather than less loyalty to country (Huo & Molina, 2006). Thus, those who felt that their subgroup is more respected by the American majority were *more* likely to identify as American and were more likely to trust the American justice system than those who did not perceive that positive regard. Similar work in the Netherlands has shown that when the positive characteristics of a minority group (in this case Muslim women) are recognized, members of that group are *more* motivated to perform well in domains that are identified with the majority status group, a process that the authors call "double valuation" (Derks, van Laar, & Ellemers, 2007).

The behavioral manifestations of blended loyalties take many forms and play out in different domains. A person can send remittances to a home community of origin or can become active in group-relevant activities in the country of residence. With regard to the latter, it may well be that loyalty to both cultures is actually necessary for some forms of political action. Recent work in Germany, for example, finds that Turkish immigrants who identify both as Turkish and as German are *more* likely to be politically active in Germany, working within the system to change policies (Simon & Ruhs, 2007).

Findings, such as these, clearly argue against the more simplistic positions espoused by Renshon and Huntington, which suggest that loyalty to home country cannot co-exist with commitment to one's present locale. Yet they also point to the critical role played by the reactions of others toward one's group. Discrimination and rejection are likely to foster the kind of oppositional identity that Renshon and Huntington speak of; in contrast, acceptance of diversity and respect for the contributions of various cultures can create stronger commitments to the country in which the immigrant resides.

Being a 21st Century American

Questions about assimilation and incorporation of immigrants into the fabric of a nation have always been central to the discourse of countries whose doors have been opened to others. Indeed, assimilation theory has been the dominant model within social science investigation for nearly a century (Alba & Nee, 2003; Gordon, 1964; Park & Burgess, 1921). In varying degrees, perhaps most notably in the underappreciated multidimensional model of Milton–Gordon, these models showed some awareness of the different positions that host and immigrant can occupy. Now, with a clearer understanding of the operation of social categories and the negotiation of social identities, social psychologists stand ready to add their voices to the immigration discussions.

A central question in these current discussions is whether immigrants can maintain their values and experiences and aspirations and still be full citizens of the new country. Can cultural loyalty and newly formed patriotism co-exist? Some recent polemics would suggest that the answer to this question is no and that one model—a model that assumes common lineage and often European roots—must work for all. But the data suggest otherwise. As social psychologists, we know that situations are rarely simple, that complex person–situation interactions are likely to be the rule, and that interpersonal dynamics can change a situation from one moment to the next. By charting the terrain and revealing the variations and dynamic possibilities, we are in a position to explicate the alternative paths that a society and its individual citizens and citizens-to-be can choose, clarifying both the options and the likely consequences of different alternatives. We do this not by pointing fingers at immigrants or by building longer fences to impede their entry. Rather, we can (or at least the optimist in me always hopes we can) use our knowledge and tools to inform and enlarge what it means to be an American—and perhaps to be a citizen of the world as well.

References

Alba, R., & Nee, V. (2007). *Remaking the American mainstream: Assimilation and contemporary immigration.* Cambridge, MA: Harvard University Press.

Ashmore, R. D., Deaux, K., & McLaughlin-Volpe, T. (2004). An organizing framework for collective identity: Articulation and significance of multidimensionality. *Psychological Bulletin, 130,* 80–114.

Bargal, D. (1998). Kurt Lewin and the first attempts to establish a department of psychology at the Hebrew University. *Minerva, 36,* 49–68.

Benet-Martínez, V., & Haritatos, J. (2005). Bicultural identity integration (BII): Components and psychosocial antecedents. *Journal of Personality, 73,* 1015–1049.

Berry, J. W., Phinney, J. S., Sam, D. L., & Vedder, P. (Eds.). (2006). *Immigrant youth in cultural transition: Acculturation, identity, and adaptation across national contexts.* Mahwah, NJ: Erlbaum.

Biernat, M., Crosby, F. J., & Williams, J. C. (Eds.). (2004). The maternal wall: Research and policy perspectives on discrimination against mothers. *Journal of Social Issues, 60*(4).

Deaux, K. (2006a). A nation of immigrants: Living our legacy. *Journal of Social Issues, 62*(3), 633–651.

Deaux, K. (2006b). *To be an immigrant.* New York: Russell Sage Foundation.

Deaux, K., Bikmen, N., Gilkes, A., Ventuneac, A., Joseph, Y., Payne, Y., et al. (2007). Becoming American: Stereotype threat effects in black immigrant groups. *Social Psychology Quarterly, 70,* 384–404.

Deaux, K., & Philogène, G. (Eds.). (2001). *Representations of the social: Bridging theoretical traditions.* Oxford, UK: Blackwell.

Deaux, K., Reid, A., Martin, D., & Bikmen, N. (2006). Ideologies of diversity and inequality: Predicting collective action in groups varying in ethnicity and immigrant status. *Political Psychology, 27,* 123–146.

Deaux, K., & Wiley, S. (2007). Moving people and shifting representations: Making immigrant identities. In G. Moloney & I. Walker (Eds.), *Social representations and identity: Content, process, and power* (pp. 9–30). New York: Palgrave Macmillan.

Derks, B., van Laar, C., & Ellemers, N. (2007). The beneficial effects of social identity protection on the performance motivation of members of devalued groups. *Social Issues and Policy Review, 1*, 217–256.

Devos, T., & Banaji, M. H. (2005). American = White? *Journal of Personality and Social Psychology, 88*, 447–466.

Esses, V.M., Veenvliet, S., Hodson, G., & Mihic, L. (2008). Justice, morality, and the dehumanization of refugees. *Social Justice Research, 21*, 4–25.

Foner, N. (2000). *From Ellis Island to JFK: New York's two great waves of immigration.* New Haven, CT and New York: Yale University Press and Russell Sage Foundation.

Foner, N. (2005). *In a new land: A comparative view of immigration.* New York and London: New York University Press.

Foner, N., & Alba, R. (2008). Immigrant religion in the U.S. and Western Europe: Bridge or barrier to inclusion? *International Migration Review, 42*, 360–392.

Gordon, M. M. (1964). *Assimilation in American life.* New York: Oxford University Press.

Hong, Y., Morris, M. W., Chiu, C., & Benet-Martínez, V. (2000). Multicultural minds: A dynamic constructivist approach to culture and cognition. *American Psychologist, 55*, 709–720.

Huntington, S. P. (2004). *Who are we? The challenges to America's national identity.* New York: Simon & Schuster

Huo, Y. J., & Molina, L. E. (2006). Is pluralism a viable model of diversity? The benefits and limits of subgroup respect. *Group Processes & Intergroup Relations, 9*, 359–376.

Itzigsohn, J. (in press). *American faultlines.* New York: Russell Sage Foundation.

Itzigsohn, J., & Giorguli-Saucedo, S. (2005). Incorporation, transnationalism, and gender: Immigrant incorporation and transnational participation as gendered process. *International Migration Review, 39*, 895–920.

Itzigsohn, J., Giorguli, S., & Vasquez, O. (2005). Immigrant incorporation and racial identity: Racial self-identification among Dominican immigrants. *Ethnic and Racial Studies, 28*, 50–78.

Johnson, K. (2007, June 24). Anxiety in the land of the anti-immigration crusader. *The New York Times.*

Kasinitz, P., Mollenkopf, & Waters, M. C. (2002). Becoming American/becoming New Yorkers: Immigrant incorporation in a majority minority city. *International Migration Review, 36*, 1020–1036.

Lapinski, J. S., Peltola, P., Shaw, G., & Yang, A. (1997). Trends: Immigrants and immigration. *Public Opinion Quarterly, 61*(2), 356–383.

Levitt, P., & Waters, M. C. (2002). *The changing face of home: The transnational lives of the second generation.* New York: Russell Sage Foundation.

López, D. E. (1999). Social and linguistic aspects of assimilation today. In C. Hirschman, P. Kasinitz, & J. DeWind (Eds.), *The handbook of international migration: The American experience* (pp. 212–222). New York: Russell Sage Foundation.

Massey, D. S., Durand, J., & Malone, N. J. (2002). *Beyond smoke and mirrors: Mexican immigration in an era of economic integration.* New York: Russell Sage Foundation.

Mizrahi, K. (2005). *Americans' attitudes toward immigrants and immigration: The role of values, social identification, and attitudinal ambivalence.* Unpublished doctoral dissertation, Graduate Center of City University of New York.

Park, R. E., & Burgess, E. W. (1969). *Introduction to the science of sociology.* Chicago: University of Chicago Press. (Original work published 1921)

Passel, J. S. (2005). *Estimates of the size and characteristics of the undocumented population.* Washington, DC: Pew Hispanic Research Center.

Phinney, J. S., & Devich-Navarro, M. (1997). Variations in bicultural identification among African American and Mexican American adolescents. *Journal of Research on Adolescence, 7*, 3–32.

Portes, A., & Rumbaut, R. G. (2001). *Legacies: The story of the immigrant second generation.* Berkeley and New York: University of California Press and Russell Sage Foundation.

Reicher, S., & Hopkins, N. (2001). *Self and nation: Categorization, contestation and mobilization.* London: Sage Publications.

Renshon, S. A. (2005). *The 50% American: Immigration and national identity in an age of terror.* Washington, DC: Georgetown University Press.

Roberts, S. (2007, August 9). Minorities now form majority in one-third of most-populous counties. *The New York Times.*

Roosevelt, T. R. (1915, October 12). "Hyphenated Americanism" speech delivered to the Knights of Columbus, Carnegie Hall, NY. Available at http://home.comcast/net/ñhprman/tr.htm#top.

Sanchez, M. (2005, October 27). Demonizing dual citizens. *Washington Post.*

Simon, B., & Ruhs, D. (2007, May 31–June 2). *Identity and politicization among Turkish immigrants in Germany: The role of dual identification.* Paper presented at SPSSI/EAESP conference: International Perspectives on Immigration, Toronto, Canada.

Verkuyten, M., & DeWolf, A. (2002). Being, feeling and doing: Discourses and ethnic self-definitions among minority group members. *Culture and Psychology, 8,* 371–399.

Verkuyten, M., & Pouliasi, K. (2006). Biculturalism and group identification: The mediating role of identification in cultural frame switching. *Journal of Cross-Cultural Psychology, 37,* 312–326.

Verkuyten, M., & Yildiz, A. (2007). National (dis)identification, and ethnic and religious identity: A study among Turkish-Dutch Muslims. *Personality and Social Psychology Bulletin, 33,* 1448–1462.

Wiley, S. (2005). *"Proving yourself in both worlds": A study of bicultural identification with Mexican and Dominican immigrants.* Unpublished master's thesis, Graduate Center of the City University of New York.

Wiley, S., & Deaux, K. (2008, February 7–9). Proving yourself in both worlds: Multidimensionality and categorization in bicultural identification. Symposium presentation at Society of Personality and Social Psychology, Albuquerque, NM.

Wiley, S., Perkins, K., & Deaux, K. (2008). Through the looking glass: Ethnic and generational patterns of immigrant identity. *International Journal of Intercultural Relations, 32,* 385–398.

Zolberg, A. R. (2006). *A nation by design: Immigration policy in the fashioning of America.* New York and Cambridge, MA: Russell Sage Foundation and Harvard University Press.

KAY DEAUX is Distinguished Professor of Psychology and Women's Studies at the Graduate Center of the City University of New York and a Research Affiliate in Psychology at New York University. She served as President of the Society for the Psychological Study of Social Issues (SPSSI) in 2004–2005 and President of the Association for Psychological Science (formerly American Psychological Society) in 1997–1998. She is currently co-editing (with Rupert Brown, Vicki Esses, and Richard Lalonde) a *JSI* issue on immigration, and with Mark Snyder, she is editing a new *Handbook of Personality and Social Psychology* for Oxford University Press.

UNITED STATES POSTAL SERVICE®

Statement of Ownership, Management, and Circulation
(All Periodicals Publications Except Requester Publications)

1. Publication Title	2. Publication Number	3. Filing Date
Journal of Social Issues	0 0 1 _ 6 5 2	10/1/08

4. Issue Frequency	5. Number of Issues Published Annually	6. Annual Subscription Price
Quarterly	4	$717.00

7. Complete Mailing Address of Known Office of Publication (Not printer) (Street, city, county, state, and ZIP+4®)

Wiley Subscription Services, Inc., 111 River Street, Hoboken, NJ 07030

Contact Person
E. Schmidichen
Telephone (Include area code)
(201) 748-6346

8. Complete Mailing Address of Headquarters or General Business Office of Publisher (Not printer)

Wiley Subscription Services, Inc., 111 River Street, Hoboken, NJ 07030

9. Full Names and Complete Mailing Addresses of Publisher, Editor, and Managing Editor (Do not leave blank)

Publisher (Name and complete mailing address)

Wiley Subscription Services, Inc., 111 River Street, Hoboken, NJ 07030

Editor (Name and complete mailing address)

Rick H Hoyle, Department of Psychology, Duke University, Box 90085, Durham, NC 27708

Managing Editor (Name and complete mailing address)

None

10. Owner (Do not leave blank. If the publication is owned by a corporation, give the name and address of the corporation immediately followed by the names and addresses of all stockholders owning or holding 1 percent or more of the total amount of stock. If not owned by a corporation, give the names and addresses of the individual owners. If owned by a partnership or other unincorporated firm, give its name and address as well as those of each individual owner. If the publication is published by a nonprofit organization, give its name and address.)

Full Name	Complete Mailing Address
The Society for the Psychological Study of Social Issues	1901 Pennsylvania NW Ste 901
	Washington, DC 20006

11. Known Bondholders, Mortgagees, and Other Security Holders Owning or Holding 1 Percent or More of Total Amount of Bonds, Mortgages, or Other Securities. If none, check box ▶ ☑ None

Full Name	Complete Mailing Address

12. Tax Status (For completion by nonprofit organizations authorized to mail at nonprofit rates) (Check one)
The purpose, function, and nonprofit status of this organization and the exempt status for federal income tax purposes:
☐ Has Not Changed During Preceding 12 Months
☐ Has Changed During Preceding 12 Months (Publisher must submit explanation of change with this statement)

13. Publication Title	14. Issue Date for Circulation Data
Journal of Social Issues	September 2008

15. Extent and Nature of Circulation		Average No. Copies Each Issue During Preceding 12 Months	No. Copies of Single Issue Published Nearest to Filing Date
a. Total Number of Copies (Net press run)		4327	4330
b. Paid Circulation (By Mail and Outside the Mail)	(1) Mailed Outside-County Paid Subscriptions Stated on PS Form 3541 (Include paid distribution above nominal rate, advertiser's proof copies, and exchange copies)	2938	1784
	(2) Mailed In-County Paid Subscriptions Stated on PS Form 3541 (Include paid distribution above nominal rate, advertiser's proof copies, and exchange copies)	0	0
	(3) Paid Distribution Outside the Mails Including Sales Through Dealers and Carriers, Street Vendors, Counter Sales, and Other Paid Distribution Outside USPS®	0	0
	(4) Paid Distribution by Other Classes of Mail Through the USPS (e.g. First-Class Mail®)	0	0
c. Total Paid Distribution (Sum of 15b (1), (2),(3), and (4))		2938	1784
d. Free or Nominal Rate Distribution (By Mail and Outside the Mail)	(1) Free or Nominal Rate Outside-County Copies lincluded on PS Form 3541	388	402
	(2) Free or Nominal Rate In-County Copies Included on PS Form 3541	0	0
	(3) Free or Nominal Rate Copies Mailed at Other Classes Through the USPS (e.g. First-Class Mail)	0	0
	(4) Free or Nominal Rate Distribution Outside the Mail (Carriers or other means)	0	0
e. Total Free or Nominal Rate Distribution (Sum of 15d (1), (2), (3) and (4))		388	402
f. Total Distribution (Sum of 15c and 15e) ▶		3326	2186
g. Copies not Distributed (See Instructions to Publishers #4 (page #3)) ▶		1001	2144
h. Total (Sum of 15f and g) ▶		4327	4330
i. Percent Paid (15c divided by 15f times 100) ▶		88.34	81.61

16. Publication of Statement of Ownership

☑ If the publication is a general publication, publication of this statement is required. Will be printed
in the ___December 2008___ issue of this publication.

☐ Publication not required.

17. Signature and Title of Editor, Publisher, Business Manager, or Owner

Elizabeth Konkle, Associate Financial Manager

Date
10/1/08

I certify that all information furnished on this form is true and complete. I understand that anyone who furnishes false or misleading information on this form or who omits material or information requested on the form may be subject to criminal sanctions (including fines and imprisonment) and/or civil sanctions (including civil penalties).

PS Form **3526**, September 2006